The Deception

CW01023899

Christian Prince

My work is for whomever looking for the truth, so he may find it as I did.

"And ye shall know the truth, and the truth shall set you free"
John 8:32

CONTENTS

ACKNOWLEDGMENTS

The Deception of Allah is about the faith of Islam. The name of this book is taken from Qur'an 3:54, which says, "plus they deceived and Allah deceived and Allah is the best of deceivers." V1 exposes some of the claims of Muslims about the Qur'an and scientific miracles, but In V 2 (Qur'an And Science in Depth) of the book covers the rest of it. The book is made to be a powerful tool in your hand to prevent any kind of deception can come to you or your family. Muslims are trying to spread Islam all over USA and the rest of the world by deception, using the ignorance of the Western regarding Islam, and Arabic language. Imagine your son or daughter coming back from school and telling you "I became a Muslim". I am sure you do not want this to happen to your house and your family, and the best way to prevent it is education. This book is nothing more than masterpiece of education. Every page in this book comes with the actual text and sources with truthful translation, with no political correctness and the totalitarian mentality. "The Deception of Allah Volume I" addresses the things you need to know about Islam, basing its information on citations and quotes from accepted Islamic sources. The author shoots down one myth and misconception after another by revealing exactly what the Qur'an, Sunnah and Tafsirs (commentaries) say about each subject. The author is a native Arabic speaker. He has a degree in Islamic Law (Sharia Law) & Civil Law, which make him qualified to be a Judge in Islamic court and has intimate knowledge of the foundation Islamic texts. He uses this knowledge to address an expansive list of topics representing typical questions or myths about Islam. The coverage of each topic includes explanation and specific relevant quotes from Islamic sources. "The Deception of Allah" is a must read for anyone wanting to understand Islam and its relevance to western civilization.

Don't forget to get your copy of Qur'an And Science in Depth @Amazon.com

i

Your Notes

Allah's words

"Why do they do not understand the Qur'an? If it's not from Allah, they will find many contradictions in it?" (Qur'an 4:82)

This is an important verse that we will use as a scale to examine the Qur'an. As long as Allah himself created this rule to examine, whether it's a book of god or not, this means that Muslims have to accept the rules of Allah and his way of examination! If we find contradictions in the Qur'an, it cannot be from the real God as the verse says.
Let us see the Muslim's claims, and expose the contradictions of the Qur'an, plus show the false claims about it and its miracles.

Answering Harun Yahya

On Harun Yahya's websites (http://miraclesofthequran.com and www.harunyahya.com), Mr. Harun has made numerous claims about the Qur'an. I will show the readers how each of these claims are false, and that Mr. Harun's false claims were meant to intentionally deceive. The following are some of his claims from his website. In this book, I will also expose the real meaning of these verses of the Qur'an, with which Mr. Harun is trying to scam readers. I am going to put all his claims about sky science together, for all are connected. Before I do that, I need to give you some introduction about Islam and Muhammad.

Islam is an establishment based on Three Important Names:
1. Allah is the god and he has ninety-nine names.
2. Angel Jibreel (Gabriel), whom Muslims say is the Holy Spirit (but this claim is never made in the Qur'an).
3. Muhammad is the Prophet of Islam, he is the Seal of Allah's Prophets (of a claimed 124,000).

Islam Religion Summaries:

⋏ Allah is the god of the two worlds (mankind and jinn), but somehow, Allah forgot about the angels! It's because they are not from these two worlds!

- Allah sent 124,000 Muslim prophets (book, Tu'afat Al-'Abib 'Ala Shar'h Al-'KHatib, page 431/432).

- Muslims are the hypocrites (Qur'an Chapter 4, Verse 142).

- All of Allah's books are corrupted, except the Qur'an (Qur'an 4:46).

- Muhammad is the last prophet (Qur'an 33:40).

- Beheading non-Muslim captives (Qur'an 8:67; 47:4).

- Allah has no sons (Qur'an 4:171).

- Allah has no girlfriend (until the time of Muhammad), (Qur'an 6:101; 72:3).

- Allah has only ONE leg (a single shin) (Qur'an 68:42).

- Allah has two hands both in his right side (Allah has no left hand), (Qur'an 49:1). Note: Based on Islamic teaching, the left hand is the defiled one (e.g. used for toilet). Only Satan has and uses the defiled (left) hand (Sahih Muslim, Book 023, Hadith 5007). Allah cannot have a defiled hand; therefore, Allah's two hands must be right (undefiled) hands.

- Allah has a face (Qur'an 55:27).

- Allah does not like to have female children (Qur'an 53:21-22).

- Allah knows everything, as long as you do not ask him, and no one is allowed to ask him (Qur'an 5:101-102).

- Muslims cannot take the non-believer (non-Muslims) as friends (Qur'an 3:28; 4:139; 5:51, 57, 81).

- Satan is a friend for all non-believers (not Muslims), (Qur'an 7:27; 30).

- Non-believers are friends to each other only, but not to Muslims (Qur'an 8:73).

- Muslims cannot even take their own family as friends if they are from the non-believers (non-Muslims), (Qur'an 9:23).

- Allah sent a prophet to every nation, but still Muslims cannot name one prophet for nations such as China, India, Japan, etc. (Qur'an 10:47; 16:36, 84, 89; 23:44).

- Allah sent a prophet to every nation speaking to them in their own languages (Qur'an 14:4). I wonder what the book of Allah is in the Russian language?

- Qur'an is the holy book of the Muslims. It has two kinds of commandments: valid to practice and abrogated. Abrogated means the verses are either there or missing, but Muslims are not allowed to practice them anymore (Qur'an 2:106).

- Allah will abrogate all the satanic verses from the Qur'an (Qur'an 22:52).

- The Kaaba is nothing more than a way to know who is a Muslim, and who is not, by their direction of prayer (Qur'an 2:143).

- The dead people are not equal to living ones (Qur'an 35:22). We must then conclude that Muhammad is not equal to Jesus at all, because Jesus is alive. Muhammad is dead!

- The ones who die for the sake of Allah are alive (Qur'an 2:154).

- Allah is the best of deceivers (Qur'an 3:53; 7:99; 8:30; 10:21; 27:50).

- To Allah is all the ownership, and he is the Master of Deception (Qur'an 13:42).

- There is no guidance for the one Allah deceives (Qur'an 4:143; 6:39, 125; 7:178, 186; 13:27; 16:37, 93).

- Allah might deceive and mislead the one he has already guided (Qur'an 9:115; see Tafsir Al-Jalalayn trans. Feras Hamza, and Tafsir Ibn-Kathir, V2, page 395 {Arabic})!

- Allah will make ugly behavior look like beauty to the infidels in order to make them go further astray! (Qur'an 6, Verse 137)

- Muslim men can beat their wives (Qur'an 4:34; 38:44).

- Muslim men can marry up to four women at the same time, and have intercourse with an unlimited number of slaves outside of marriage (Qur'an 4:3).

- Muslim men can rape a married slave woman (Qur'an 4:24).

- Muslim men can rape their wives and force them into bed anytime, anywhere and in any position (Qur'an 2:223).

Who is Allah?

If we ask Muslims who Allah is, they will say that God is the Creator, the All-Knowing. Their answer is not that much different from the answers that we will get from everyone else about their god, but when it comes to Allah as god, there are a lot of problems, and we will go over them.

Before we can understand the person of Allah, we need to understand his name first. Muslims try to make us believe that Allah is the same as the God of Christianity and of Moses. They even try to convince us that *Allah* is an Aramaic word and that Jesus used it when he spoke in Aramaic. How true is this claim?

When the movie "The Passion of the Christ" came out some years ago, Muslims took clips from the movie in which Jesus spoke Aramaic saying the name of God. They then used those clips to create their own videos to prove their claim that the name *Allah*, is indeed Aramaic. The Aramaic word they were trying to

3

adopt is *Elah*, *El* not *Al* like Allah.

Here's a quick and easy study in Qur'an 4:125:

وَمَنْ أَحْسَنُ دِيناً مِمَّنْ أَسْلَمَ وَجْهَهُ لله وَهُوَ مُحْسِنٌ واتَّبَعَ مِلَّةَ إِبْرَاهِيمَ حَنِيفاً وَاتَّخَذَ اللَّهُ إِبْرَاهِيمَ خَلِيلاً

In Qur'an 4:125, there are two words for Allah, but they do not mean the same. If you don't know Arabic, you will not notice much difference between the two words except one letter, but actually their difference is much more than that.

The first one is لله (**lillah**) and the second one is اَللَّهُ (**Allah**). In Arabic, *al* means *the*, so if we take **Al** away from **Allah** and **lil** away from **lillah**, that leaves us with **lah** (god), a word that is common to both names. In fact, **lah** was the name for the moon-god, the main Egyptian god and a god being worshiped by the Arabs. In English, **lillah** translates to *to god* and *Allah* translates to *the god*.

Lil Lah = لله	Al Lah = اَللَّهُ

As you can see from the preceding illustration, although *lillah* and *Allah* are each written as one word in Arabic, *lil* and *Al* are not part of the word *lah*, itself—that is, *lillah* and *Allah* are each made up of two words. Again, lillah is *to god* and allah is *the god*.

In Arabic, *al* is always equal to "*the*" and it is attached to names which are attributed to god only. This is why all the 99 names of Allah start with *Al* or *The*. Take note however, that *The* is not part of the name. It is just a device used to indicate that the name is unique to god--only god can be given this distinction. For example, we cannot say "The Muhammad", because Muhammad is just a name for a person.

It is interesting to note the Messiah is called Al-Maseeh in the Qur'an. It means he is the only Messiah in the whole world. He is the only man in the Qur'an who has *Al* or *The* attached to his name.

Who is Lah? It's the moon god, but how Lah can be the moon god if the Quran forbidding worshiping the moon and the sun?

What Allah Says About Himself

Allah wants Sons, NOT Daughters as seen in Qur'an 53:19-22:

19 Did you see Al-Lat and Al-'Uza

20 and Manat the third one?

21 What for you the male gender ones and to Allah the females?

22 This is a really unjustified division

I've never heard of a god saying such a thing before. First, Allah says it is unfair for him to have daughters (Al-Lat, Al-'Uza, and Manat) instead of sons. Second, it is unfair that the Arabs get sons—"for you the males and for me the females"—while he gets only daughters. Now think about it. Allah is complaining that the Arabs are more blessed than he is, because they are blessed with sons, while he only gets daughters. Isn't Allah the Creator? Why doesn't he bless himself with sons? Qur'an 6:101 (Pickthal translation) explains why:

بَدِيعُ السَّمَاوَاتِ وَالْأَرْضِ ۖ أَنَّىٰ يَكُونُ لَهُ وَلَدٌ وَلَمْ تَكُن لَّهُ صَاحِبَةٌ ۖ وَخَلَقَ كُلَّ شَيْءٍ ۖ وَهُوَ بِكُلِّ شَيْءٍ سورة الأنعام

> The Originator of the heavens and the earth! How can He have a child, when there is for Him no consort, when He created all things and is aware of all things?

Qur'an 6:101 is a question about how is Allah supposed to have a son if he never had a girlfriend! Allah cannot have sons because, how can he have a son when he hath no girlfriend?

As long as this is the answer Muslims give to Christians about why Allah cannot have a son, it only shows that Allah has a very wrong idea about what Christians believe. No Christian believes that Mary, the mother of Jesus, was the girlfriend of God.

This complete misunderstanding proves to me that Allah cannot be the same as the God of Christians; not only because Allah does not know what Christians believe, but also because he thinks that he is the same as any man—that he cannot have children unless he has a woman with whom to have sex and procreate. This alone tells me that the one who created Qur'an 6:101 was speaking from the mentality of a man, not God—a man who is sure that if he does not have a woman, then he cannot have children. He tried to speak for God, but he can only speak within his limits as a man.

Who is the Holy Spirit in Islam?

Who spoke to Mary?
As I have shown you in Qur'an 6:101:

> To Him is owed the foundation of the heavens and the earth: How can? He has a son when He hath no girl friend. He created all things, and He hath top knowledge of all things.

Allah cannot have children unless he has a woman to have sex and children with, yet the Qur'an also tells us that Mary was a virgin when she became

CHRISTIAN PRINCE

pregnant with Jesus (or 'Isa, as He is called in the Qur'an).
Qur'an 3:47 tells us:

قَالَتْ رَبِّ أَنَّىٰ يَكُونُ لِي وَلَدٌ وَلَمْ يَمْسَسْنِي بَشَرٌ ۖ قَالَ كَذَٰلِكِ اللَّهُ يَخْلُقُ مَا يَشَاءُ ۚ إِذَا قَضَىٰ أَمْرًا فَإِنَّمَا يَقُولُ لَهُ كُن فَيَكُونُ
سورة آل عمران

> She (Mary) said, "My God, how I am going to have a son when no man had intercourse with me." He said, "This is how Allah creates. He says 'be' and it would be!"

Regarding this verse, Muslims will tell you that it was the Angel Gabriel, or Jibreel, who was talking to Mary. (Remember that we are not discussing the same story that is in the Bible. We're following the story in the Qur'an. Don't mix them up.) Muslims will also tell you that Mary was actually speaking with the Holy Spirit who appeared to her in the form of Angel Jibreel. What they will not tell you is that the Qur'an never named Angel Jibreel as the one who spoke to Mary.

Let's review the verse 47 carefully:

> She (Mary) said, "**My God,** how I am going to have a son when no man had intercourse with me." He said, "**This is how Allah creates**. He says 'be' and it would **be!**"

This verse presents us with another proof that the Qur'an is a man's creation. Notice the following:

- Mary called the Holy Spirit (who appeared to be a man, (see Qur'an 19:17) "My God" (قَالَتْ رَبِّ) RABY), but he told her that he is only a messenger, not God (see Qur'an 19:19).

- As long as Mary called the Holy Spirit "My God," in Qur'an 3:47 and assuming that he was Allah, why was he talking about himself in the third person—that is, why did he say, "This is how *Allah* creates," instead of, "This is how *I* create"?

- Mary made a mistake calling the Holy Spirit "My God;" or was it actually Allah? Either way, nowhere does it say in the Qur'an that the one who spoke to Mary was the Angel Jibreel (Gabriel), and nowhere in the Qur'an does it say that the angel Jibreel is the Holy Spirit.

In Qur'an 3:45 we read:

> Moreover, recall when the **angels said**: "O Mary! Lo! Allah gives thee joyful tidings of a word from him. Whose name is the Christ Jesus, son of Mary, glorious in the world and the Hereafter, and nearer unto Allah?"

Notice here it says, "angels said", but in Qur'an 19:16 one spirit became a perfect man! Therefore there is a clear mistake, because if the angel is one angel, and he is the Holy Spirit, and he is the one who brought the news, and he spoke as a singular person, then why in Qur'an 3:45 did all the angels talk? Are they all the Holy Spirit too?

➤ This would mean that the Holy Spirit is holy **spirits.** However, this contradicts another story of the announcement, which we find in Qur'an 19:16-21. See Qur'an 19:17:

فَاتَّخَذَتْ مِن دُونِهِمْ حِجَابًا فَأَرْسَلْنَا إِلَيْهَا رُوحَنَا فَتَمَثَّلَ لَهَا بَشَرًا سَوِيًّا

So she (Mary) screened herself from them. So we send to her **our spirit**, who appeared to her as a normal man.

➤ As we see, it's one spirit which became one man. Moreover, Muslims claim that the Holy Spirit is one person and it's the angel Gabriel.

➤ Most Muslims translate the word spirit into "angel." These are incorrect and false translations.

➤ Note that the Holy Spirit is called *God* by Mary, but at the same time that Holy Spirit is talking about himself as a messenger of God. The Holy Spirit says in Qur'an 19:19:

I am only a messenger from your Lord, to announce to thee the gift of a holy son.

Why even in the Qur'an can't the Holy Spirit be the Angel Gabriel? To find out we read Qur'an 16:2:

He dispatches down the angels with the Ruh (Spirit) of His Command to whom of His slaves He wills, saying, "none has the right to be worshiped but I, so protect yourself from me."

➤ Allah will send the angels with the Spirit. This means the angels cannot be the spirit.

➤ Muslims try to translate the word Ruh, الروح, as revelation, which is a lie and a shame.

➤ Muhammad Pickthal's translation shows the truth about verse 16:2:

He sendeth down the **angels with the Spirit** of His command unto whom He will of His bondmen, (saying), "Warn mankind that there is no Allah save Me, so keep your duty unto Me."

There is further evidence in Qur'an 26:192-193:

192 Verily these are scriptures from the Lord of the two Worlds (world of mankind, and Jinn).
193 With it, came <u>down with it, the Faithful spirit</u>.

⋏ Again, Allah is not saying it came down with Gabriel? It's just a word? Why didn't Allah make it clear if it's that angel?

Qur'an 70:4 reads:

The <u>angels and the spirit</u>, rise up unto him (Allah), in a Day which is identical to fifty thousand years of your years.

⋏ If the angels are the spirit, why is Allah saying that they go up to him, **angels AND the spirit?**

Qur'an 78:38 says:

In that day (Judgment day) **the Spirit and the angels** will line up in ranks, and not one of them shall talk except by Allah's order Most Gracious, and He speaks correct.

⋏ **Again, Allah is saying they will stand next to each other, in ranks, Spirit and the angels. This is proof that Muslims are quite confused. I do not blame them. If their prophet is the last to have answers, then why shall they have one?**

Why doesn't Allah say it as in the Bible, with clear words such as in Luke 1:19?

And the angel answering said unto him, I am Gabriel, that stand in the presence of God; and am sent to speak unto thee, and to shew thee these glad tidings.

It is funny that there are many verses in the Qur'an, like Qur'an 7:52, which claim that it is a very clear book.

For We had definitely sent unto them a Book, based on wisdom which We explained it to them in clear details, as a guide and a mercy to people who believe.

At the same time, the Qur'an clearly says in Verse 3:7 that the Qur'an has two parts. The first part is clear, and the other one is not only vague, but also indicates that no one except Allah knows what it means; "but no one knows the Qur'an's real meaning except Allah."

Who was Muhammad (real name, قثم, Qathem)?
When was He Born?

The following chart provides the basic data on Muhammad.

First Name (Actual)	Qathem
Last Name	Son of Dogs Ibn Kilab (this is for real, no insult)
The Family - Great-grandfather	Qusy Ibn Kilab (Qusy son of Dogs)
New Names	Muhammad & Ahmad
Actual Father	Unknown
Named Father	Abduallah
Mother	Amena
Birth	570(can not be confirmed)
Cause of death	Poisoned by a Jewish woman in the year 632
Number of Known Wives	13
Maids (Concubines)	Too many to count
(Muhammad data chart cont.)	
Sexual power	Power of 40 men (Muhammad's claim)
Special skills	Fairy tale stories

Muhammad was born in the year 570, which is four years after his named father, Abduallah, died! Some might say, "How can a child be born four (4) years after his father's death?" The answer is simple. Abduallah was called his father, but he was not.

Before Islam there was a kind of marriage, they called Zawaj Al Rahe't, which means group marriage. This is how the marriage worked: The woman sleeps with many men, seven, ten, or more. It doesn't matter really. All are called Raht or Groups. You could say it's not marriage at all. It was more of a sex practice accepted by the society. The mother then chose the father of her baby when she gave birth.

The real name of Muhammad's designated father was never Abduallah. His real name was Abd Allat, which means the slave of Allat (one of the three daughters of the pagan deity, Allah). Muslims only use the name Abduallah as his father's name, because the actual name of his father is insulting to Allah.
I could go into great details about Muhammad's childhood, but that is not the point of my book, although I will give some short references to prove this point about Muhammad's birth.

Muhammad's mother had many children, not only Muhammad. If the first and only individual man who ever had her was Muhammad's father, how does she have so many children? In the book of Imam Al Suoty the Al Kasa's Al-Kubra V1 page 132/133/134/135 Muhammad's mother said:

قالت حملت به فما حملت قط أخف منه فأريت في النوم حين حملت به أنه خرج مني نور

I was pregnant with him, and it was the easiest one of my pregnancies.

No one speaks about his brothers. How can he have brothers, since Muslims claim that Muhammad never saw his father? And his mother, she was newly married? Add to that, Muhammad's father died a few months after he married her (as Muslims claim). The only way is if his mother would have had other husbands, or at least one other.

There are many stories we can tell, but I will try not to make things complicated. In the coming Hadith, I will clearly prove that the father of Muhammad (the claimed one, Abd Allah) never did marry Muhammad's (Qathem's) mother. I am going to show the story as it is in Arabic, and translate it, for I know the Muslims will say, "No way could this be found in our books!" Not only that, but I will give a link to the biggest Islamic website for books on the net.

The Book of Al Sirah Al-Halabia (another name of the book, Insan Al-Ueoun Fe Serat Al-Ma'mun), V1 page 128:

السيرة الحلبية
وهو الكتاب المسمى
(إنسان العيون في سيرة الأمين المأمون)
علي بن برهان الدين الحلبي

وفي الإمتاع: لما مات قثم بن عبد المطلب قبل مولد رسول الله صلى الله عليه
وسلم بثلاث سنين وهو ابن تسع سنين وجد عليه وجداً شديداً، فلما ولد رسول الله

THE DECEPTION OF ALLAH

صلى الله عليه وسلم قثم سماه حتى أخبرته أمه آمنة أنها أمرت في منامها أن
تسميه محمداً، فسماه محمد

After the death of Qathem Ibn Abd-Al-Mu'taleb (Muhammad's Uncle) at the age of nine, three years before Muhammad was born, his father Abd-Al-Mu'taleb felt so sad, so when the prophet was born, he named him Qathem.

Hadith from Islamic Book website:
http://library.islamweb.net/hadith/display_hbook.php?bk_no=334&pid=156549

الطبقات الكبرى
الجزء الأول
118 حتى 4من

وحدثنا عبيد الله بن محمد بن صفوان عن أبيه وحدثنا إسحاق بن عبيد الله عن سعيد بن محمد بن جبير بن
مطعم قالوا جميعا هي قتيلة بنت نوفل أخت ورقة بن نوفل وكانت تنظر وتعتاف فمر بها عبد الله بن عبد
المطلب فدعته يستبضع منها ولزمت طرف ثوبه فأبى وقال حتى آتيك وخرج سريعا حتى دخل على آمنة بنت
وهب فوقع عليها فحملت برسول الله صلى الله عليه وسلم ثم رجع عبد الله بن عبد المطلب إلى المرأة فوجدها
تنظره فقال هل لك في الذي عرضت علي فقالت لا مررت وفي وجهك نور ساطع ثم رجعت وليس فيه ذلك
النور

The Hadith Translation (Book of Al-Tabaqat Al-Kubra, Printing 1, 1968, V1, page 95/96):

Obed Allah told us that ... it was Warqa Ibn Naofal's sister in the road looking for men. As she looked, she did not like any until she saw Abd Allah (Muhammad's father) walk by. She said to him, holding him from his clothes, "What do you think about my goods?" (Get what you need from me.) He said, "Not now. When I am back!" He went out fast and entered to Amenah Bent Wahab (Muhammad's mother) and had sex with her. On his way back, he came to meet with Warqa Ibn Naofal's sister and said to her, "You still like to sleep with me!" She said, "No! When you walked by, before you left me, I saw a shiny face, but now you have lost that shiny face." (Maybe he is tired from sex.)

We can find the same story in a book titled, Alsyrah Al-Nbwyah Le-Ibn-Hisham (Arabic), Printing 2.02 ,Volume 1, Page 292, Author: Ibn Hisham Al-'Ansaary/'Abd Allh blin Yusuf:

- لابن هشام2.02السيرة النبوية، الإصدار
المجلد الأول >> ذكر المرأة المتعرضة لنكاح عبدالله بن عبدالمطلب >> عبدالله يرفضها

قال ابن إسحاق : ثم انصرف عبدالمطلب آخذا بيد عبدالله ، فمر به - فيما يزعمون - على امرأة من بني أسد بن
فهر ، وهي أخت ورقة بن نوفل /292 1عبدالعزى بن قصي بن كلاب بن مرة بن كعب بن لؤي بن غالب (بن
بن أسد بن عبدالعزى ، وهي عند الكعبة ؛ فقالت له حين نظرت إلى وجهه : أين تذهب يا عبدالله ؟ قال : مع أبي
، قالت : لك مثل الإبل التي نحرت عنك ، وقع علي الآن ، قال : أنا مع أبي ، ولا أستطيع خلافه ، ولا فراقه

The hadith translation of the above book, Chapter about Woman Offering

Herself For Nukah (sex) to Abd-Allah Ibn Abd-Al-Mu'taleb (Muhammad's father):

> Ibn Ishaq said: "Then Abd-Al-Mu'taleb (Muhammad's Grandfather) left, and he took with him Abd-Allah, in same time they pass by a woman, she is from the family of Assad son of 'Uzaa son of 'Qusai son of Dogs (dogs was the name of Muhammad's early grandfather) son of Murah son of Ka'eb son of Lu'e son of Galeb son of Faher." She said when she saw his face: "Where are you going Abd-Allah?" He said, "With my father," then she said, "I will give you the same number of camels as was offered in the day of Sacrifice (100 camels) if you sleep with me." He said, "I cannot now, I am with my father. I cannot leave him."

Now as we study this story, it tells us that women had no control at that time. They slept with whoever they liked, and they offered themselves to any of their choice. Did you notice in the first version that Muhammad's claimed father did not say no to the deal, but he had a rendezvous with Muhammad's (Qathem's) mother? He wanted to have sex with Warqa Ibn Naofal's sister, but when he came back, she changed her mind. Why?!

This proves that the word marriage had no meaning at that time. As I said, and have proven, Muhammad's father practiced this kind of open sexual relationship. I am wondering what the relationship was between Waraqa and Muhammad from before his birth? I would not be surprised if Warqa Ibn Nofal is the real father of Muhammad. I do not think this story came to life from nothing. In those days, Arabs used to offer their sisters or daughters for their own purposes. Maybe Waraqa Ibn Naofal tried to prevent Muhammad's father from having sex with Amenah because she was a favorite of his! Perhaps he sent his sister on this mission! Had it worked, he (Muhammad's father) would have been hooked up with the sister instead of that woman.

On the same page, another story shows up.

> Fatima Bint Mur was among the most beautiful women and most noble with honor. She read books and was educated! All the young men of the Qurish tribes talked about her. The story says that she saw the light of prophet-hood in his face!
> She offered Muhammad's father to sleep with her for the payment of one hundred camels!!

فاطمة بنت مر وكانت من أجمل الناس واشبه واعفه وكانت قد قرأت الكتب وكان شباب قريش يتحدثون إليها
فرأت نور النبوة في وجه عبد الله فقال يافتى من أنت فأخبرها قالت هل لك أن تقع علي وأعطيك مائة من الإبل

How decent Muhammad's father was, to the point that women offered him money for sex! I am not talking about how good he was, as in pleasant looking. What I mean is that a man with honor would not be jumping from one woman to another, or even get paid for sex as a prostitute.

The reason I am pointing out these stories is to show you some background about the daily life of the Arab tribe of Qurish at that time. I want to make it clear, that when Muslims speak about Muhammad's family as being a noble family, it does not match the reality. Don't forget that Muhammad's parents were at the top of all of this, and they were pagans and died as such.

In the book Al-Rahi'q Ma'khtom, Page 45, his uncle Hamza was sharing the same breast feeding women (two women breastfed Hamza). Later, the same two women breast fed Muhammad. The names of the two women were Thaubia and Halima Al-Sadia.

وكان عمه حمزة بن عبد المطلب مسترضعًا في بني سعد بن بكر، فأرضعت أمه رسول الله صلى الله عليه
وسلم يومًا وهو عند أمه حليمة،فكان حمزة رضيع رسول الله صلى الله عليه وسلم من جهتين، من جهة ثويبة
ومن جهة السعدية.
صفي الرحمن المباركفوري45 الرحيق المختوم ص

Translation :

And his uncle 'Hamza was a person who was breastfed from the family of Bany Sa'ed son of Baker, and his mother (Hamza's Mother), she did breastfeed Muhammad while he was being suckled by 'Halima, therefore 'Hamza had breastfeeding, sharing from both women who suckled Muhammad.

After this short introduction to Muhammad's life, it's time to put the light on this man, so we can figure out who he is, not as a name, but as a person and a man. Muhammad had his own experience as a human. His life was not easy until he got his hand on wealth.

If you remember the first story, how the sister of Waraqa, her name was Qatilah Bint Naofal, offered herself to Abduallat (Abduallah), Muhammad's named father, so he would not have sex with Amenah. When he did anyway, she did not want Abduallat (Abduallah) anymore. If we connect this with other stories, we will find Waraqa Ibn Naofal is in every step of Muhammad's life. In the same book (Book of Al-Tabaqat Al-Kubra, Printing 1, 1968, V1, Page 95), it says that Muhammad:

تزوج عبد المطلب بن هاشم وتزوج عبد الله بن عبد المطلب في مجلس واحد فولدت هالة بنت وهيب لعبد
المطلب حمزة بن عبد المطلب فكان حمزة عم رسول الله صلى الله عليه وسلم في **النسب وأخاه من الرضاعة**
قال أخبرنا هشام بن محمد بن السائب الكلبي عن أبيه وعن أبي الفياض

الخثعمي قالا لما تزوج عبد الله بن عبد المطلب آمنة بنت وهب أقام عندها
ثلاثا وكانت تلك السنة عندهم إذا دخل الرجل على امرأته في أهلها.

Abd Al-Mu'taleb Ibn Hashem and his son Abd-Allah did marry on the same day, so

13

Halah daughter of Waheb gave birth to 'Hamza therefore 'Hamza was Muhammad's uncle and his brother by breast feeding (Muslims believe if two had been suckling from the same woman, they became brothers.), and we had been told by Ibn Ishaq that when the father of Muhammad married 'Amena (Muhammad's mother) he stayed with her three nights, and that was the tradition at that time.

Continuing on the same page, we find that the grandfather of Muhammad and his son had sex with two sisters, Amenah (Muhammad's mother) and Halah. Technically speaking, Muhammad's aunt is his grandfather's woman, or we can call her his wife. On top of that, it says that Halah gave birth to Hamza (Muhammad's uncle). This means both Muhammad and Hamza **were breastfed** by the mother of Hamza. That made Hamza, the uncle of Muhammad, his brother (by suckling the same woman's milk), but not in the same time period (year). Add to that, Muhammad's father **slept only with Muhammad's mother for three days! He even slept with her in her house!** How can she be his wife? Why didn't he, if he was married, take his wife to his house?! This means that Muhammad's mother never moved into Abdallat's (Abduallah's) house!!

In the book of Ibn Kathir, V1/255, Ibn Hisham said the battle of Al-Fajar war started and Muhammad was 14 or 15 years old.

السيرة النبوية الأبن كثير حرب الفجار 255/1
وقال ابن هشام: فلما بلغ رسول الله صلى الله عليه وسلم أربع عشرة سنة ـ أو خمس عشرة سنة

We find the same story from the book Al-Sira Al-Naboiah, by Dr. Muhammad Ahmed Mahmoud Hasabalah (this is his whole name) and Dr. Muhammad AbduAlqader Al-'Khateb. Both are professors of Islamic history and civilization in Al Azhar University (the top accepted university by Osama and Al-Zawahiri and all the Muslims).

They both say in their book that the battle of Al-Fajar started 12 years after the death of Abd-Al-Mu'taleb, the father of Hamza, and that Hamza was 22 years old at that time!!!

In the same book, both doctors agree that Muhammad, at that time, was 15 years old when the war (Al-Fajar) started! Below is the link for their book. I know Muslims will not believe this. Let us say 99% of Muslims never read books, so how would they know?

Visit this link and see for yourself: http://www.alsiraj.net/sira/html/page08.html,
حرب الفجار

If Hamza was 22 at the time of that war and Muhammad was 15, this means, according to these scholars, Hamza is <u>seven years older</u> than Muhammad! But Hamza was born in the same year Muhammad's father died! This would mean that Muhammad was born seven years after his father's death.

من كتاب السيرة النبوية بقلم الدكتورمحمد أحمد محمود حسب الله أستاذ التاريخ و الحضارة الاسلامية بجامعة الأزهر و الدكتور محمد محمد عبد القادر الخطيب أستاذ التاريخ و الحضارة الاسلامية بجامعة الأزهر
شهد حمزة حرب الفجار الثاني، وكانت بعد عام الفيل بعشرين سنة، وبعد موت أبيه عبد المطلب باثنتي عشرة سنة، ولم يكن في أيام العرب أشهر منه ولا أعظم، وتعد " حرب الفجار" أول تدريب عملي بالنسبة لحمزة ـ رضي الله عنه ـ مارس فيها التدريب العملي على استخدام السلاح وعاش في جو المعركة والحرب الحقيقية، وكان عمره آنذاك نحو اثنتين وعشرين سنة.

The book of Sira Ibn Kathir V1/263 says:

When Muhammad wanted to marry Khadija, he told his uncle about her and Hamza went to Khadija and asked for her hand for Muhammad.

ابن كثير السيرة الجزء الأول 263
فخرج معه عمه حمزة حتى دخل على خويلد بن أسد فخطبها إليه، فتزوجها عليه الصلاة والسلام.

In Arab tradition, and I know our traditions very well, you do not ask someone of your own age to go on your behalf to ask for someone's hand. It's not acceptable at all. In this case, Hamza fits in two ways to do the job: He is Muhammad's uncle and he is older.

Now we will find if we read in the book of Da'ert Al-Ma-Ma'aref Al-Islamyiah, V 29, Page 9112 (ج دائرة المعارف الإسلامية 29ص9112), that Muhammad was born in year 570 AC and the battle of 'Ohod was in year 625, as all Islamic books agree.
This means if we take the year 625 ('Ohod Battle) - 570 (his birth date) = 55 years (The age of Muhammad).

In the book of Al-Tabakat Al Kubra, V3/ 29/118,
Hamza held the flag in the attack against the children of Qanika'a (the Jewish tribe who were all killed by Muhammad) and when he died, his age was 59. Here Hamza was older than the Prophet by <u>4 years</u>.

وحمل حمزة لواء رسول الله صلى الله عليه وسلم في غزوة بني قينقاع ولم يكن الرايات يومئذ وقتل رحمه الله يوم أحد على رأس اثنين وثلاثين شهرا من الهجرة وهو يومئذ بن تسع وخمسين سنة كان أسن من رسول الله **صلى الله عليه وسلم بأربع سنين**

Again Muslims might say I am making things up. This is can be found in many Islamic books such as:

- book Sabil الكتاب : سبل الهدى والرشاد، في سيرة خير العباد، 83/11

15

Al-Huda Wa Al-Rashad, Vol. 11, Page 82-83:

إذا كان أسن من رسول الله صلى الله عليه وسلم بأربع سنين، كيف يصح أن
تكون ثويبة أرضعتهما معا، والحديث صحيح فهو مقدم على غيره إلا أن تكون أرضعتهما في
زمانين،

If 'Hamza was four years older than the messenger of Allah then how [could he] be suckled from the same woman? The answer is, the hadith is correct and has been favored above other hadiths because she did breastfeed them both in two different timing.

- Al-Mustadark Fe Al-Sahih, V3, Page 212, Hadith 4873:

حمزة بن عبد المطلب كانت له كنيتان أبو يعلي و أبو 4873] حديث رقم 212 - صفحة 3المستدرك [جزء
عمارة لابنيه يعلي و عمارة أسلم حمزة في السنة السادسة من النبوة و كان أسن من رسول الله صلى الله عليه
و سلم بأربع سنين و قتل يوم السبت في المغزى بأحد لسبع خلون من شوال سنة ثلاث من الهجرة

'Hamza's used to have two names, Abu-'Ali and 'Emarah. He became a Muslim six years after Islam started, and he was four years older than Muhammad. He was killed in battle of 'Uhod Saturday the seventh of the month of Shoual (Islamic).

- Book of Al-Tabaqat Al-Kubra, Printing 1, 1968, V3, Page 103:

" وقتل، رحمه الله، يوم أحد على رأس اثنين وثلاثين شهرا من الهجرة وهو يومئذ بن تسع وخمسين سنة، كان أسن من
" رسول الله، صلى الله عليه وسلم، بأربع سنين.

"'Hamaza may Allah have mercy on him was killed by a man his name Wahshy, he was fifty nine years old and four years older than the prophet."

What do we have from all of these stories?

If Muhammad's grandfather and his father slept with the same sisters in the same time period, and after that Muhammad's father left Amenah in the few days after, (or few months after that for the sake of argument because that will not change anything) then:

- Muhammad's grandfather and his son, Abduallah, had two sisters on the same day;
- Hamza was born in the same time period of Muhammad's father's death;
- Hamza is older than Muhammad (Muslim scholars disagree if it is by four years or perhaps seven years);
- Hamza was killed at the battle of U'hod at the age 59. Muhammad then

was 55;

- Muhammad cannot be the son of that man whom the Muslims call Abduallah as we see in Ibn Kathir's book of Al-Bidayah & Al-Nihayiah, V2, Page 316. At the end, a tribe of Banu Nader came asking for Muhammad, when he was a child, claiming that he was their child. It's so clear that he does not have a father.

) "بلغ النبي أن رجالاً من 316ص 2البداية والنهاية لابن كثير باب تزويج عبد المطلب أبنه عبد الله ج)
كندة يزعمون أنهم منه وأنه منهم ... فقال: إنا لن ننتفي من آبائنا، نحن بنو النضر بن كنانة

To cover this obvious discrepancy, Muhammad told them that a woman can be pregnant for many years. This is how his grandfather was convinced that Muhammad must be his grandson, even if his mother gave birth to him many years after Abduallah's death.

Who is Muhammad

Muhammad Is an Adopted Son

To conclude this exploration of Muhammad's ancestry, read with me Bukhari, Book 40, Hadith 563. This important Hadith shows that Muhammad was no more than a slave to the family he grew up with:

As I saw that unpleasant view, I went to the Messenger of Allah and told him the story. The Prophet came out in the companion of Zaid bin Harith, who was with him afterwards, and I too went in the company of them. The Messenger went to Hamza (Muhammad's uncle) and spoke roughly to him. Hamza looked up at the Messenger and said, "Are not you no more than the slaves of my forefathers?" The Messenger withdrew and left out. This incident occurred before the banning of drinking.
(Bukhari, Book 40, Hadith 563)

- Why would the uncle of Muhammad say such a lie, unless it's true?
- Also, why did Muhammad withdraw right after without even saying a word?
- It must have been something he knew was exactly the truth, so he couldn't fight back.
- Mostly, Muhammad was worried that if he talked more, Hamza would

say more things that he did not want to hear.

⋏ It's so clear that Muhammad was not expecting Hamza, who is supposed to be his uncle, to say that in the first place.

⋏ This all leads to one thing. Muhammad is the son of an unknown father.

⋏ When this family adopted him, they called him Qathem, after one of their sons that had passed away.

Who Told Muhammad That He Was A Prophet?

The first few words that Muhammad claimed he received from his God, by the delivery of angel Gabriel, are recorded in Qur'an 96:1. Gabriel said to Muhammad, "Read!" Muhammad said, "Read what?!" Muslims say that he said "I can't read." Sahih Al-Bukhari Book 1, Hadith 3 reads (also see Qur'an 96:1-3):

> The angel came to me and said to me, The angel said, "Iqra'a" (read). I said to him, "I cannot read." He squeezed me and he said again, "Read." I said, "I cannot read." And then he squeezed me again, and he said, "Read." I said, "I cannot read." Then he squeezed me for the third time and said, "Read by the name of your lord."

Now this story does not make sense in any way. Let us think about it together. The angel said read? Shouldn't I give you a paper or a book to read before I tell you to read something? Muslims, to cover this mistake, claim that it means to recite. However, if it means to recite, why didn't Muhammad say, "I cannot recite!?" Five year old children can recite. It must be about reading, because the Arabic word clearly means read. This shows a few things proving Islam to be false from the beginning of the story.

- If Muhammad can't read and he is illiterate, why is the angel using the wrong word of "read?!"
- If God told a man to read, and he is illiterate, shouldn't he be able to read as a miracle of God?

In order to explain this further, imagine Jesus had said to the blind man, "See". But the blind man said, "I can't see." And then Jesus said again, "See." But the blind man said once more, "I can't see!" Then Jesus said one more time, "See". Lastly, the blind man said over again, "I cannot see!!!"

This must be a joke! What's the point of him saying it three times when nothing changed? Muhammad was still not able to read!

- If it's about recite, why was the angel using the word Iqra'a, which means read?! Remember, it's not the angel who chose the word Iqra'a. It was Allah. Allah chose the wrong word to start with and that caused confusion to Muhammad!

- What is the secret of squeezing Muhammad? Did the squeezing make Muhammad understand what the angel was trying to say?! Not at all!

1. Why three times?! It's about numbers. Islam started from the beginning with a trinity of perfection! One "read" was not enough, but the third was the consummate one!

2. Every single thing in Islam is based in the number three. Saying three names of Allah before anything. Action is based on three to make perfect cleansing! Blowing the nose three times, wiping hands three times, shaking their private parts is three times...everything is three times. Why?!

3. I think there is deeper revelation in this made-up story.The fact is, Muhammad is getting his made-up story from his master, Waraqa Ibn Naofal. To understand who the one was who actually created Islam, read with me Isaiah 40:5-6:

5 *And the glory of the LORD shall be revealed, and all flesh shall see it together: for the mouth of the LORD hath spoken it.*
6 *The voice said, Cry. And he said, What shall I cry? All flesh is grass, and all the goodliness thereof is as the flower of the field:*

أشعياء40
.«وَيَتَجَلَّى مَجْدُ الرب، فَيُشَاهِدُهُ كُلُّ ذِي جَسَدٍ، لأَنَّ فَمَ الرَّبِّ قَدْ تَكَلَّمَ 5
وَعِنْدَئِذٍ قَالَ صَوْتٌ: «نَادِ بِرِسَالَةٍ». فَأَجَبْتُ: «أَيَّةُ رِسَالَةٍ؟» فَقَالَ: «كُلُّ ذِي جَسَدٍ عُشْبٌ، وَكُلُّ بَهَائِهِ كَزَهْرِ 6
الصَّحْرَاءِ

It's very clear that Muhammad is trying to be the prophet Isaiah by changing the story, but thinking that he would be giving a logical story. However, the fact is, his story proves him false. All this drama is not needed. The story shows that this false god cannot perform miracles, because if Jesus had said to Muhammad, "Read," I am sure he would have read, even if he was illiterate as the Muslims claim.

Allah's Order	Muhammad's answers	Angel's actions	Total orders to read & squeeze
Read	I cannot read	Squeezing	1
Read	I cannot read	Squeezing	1

Read	I cannot read	Squeezing	1
Result:			
After three orders to read and three squeezings, Muhammad still didn't understand what the angel was asking him to do. The angel who spoke Allah's orders was not able to make him read—or understand!			

Compare to Jesus in Action	
Said to the blind, see	He saw
To the disabled, walk	He walked
To the dead man, rise from grave	He raised

Why does Allah order Muhammad three times to read, but he's still unable to do so in this fabricated story? What is the point of it!

What Islam Is About!

I've given some useful information about Muhammad's background as a start. Now let's take a look to find out what Islam is about.

What will Muslims say is the most important thing about Islam? They will say...

The **Five Pillars of Islam** are the foundation of Muslim life:

1. Faith or belief in the Oneness of God and the finality of the prophet-hood of Muhammad.
2. Establishment of the daily prayers.
3. Paying Zakat (amount of money as charity).
4. Self-purification through fasting.
5. The pilgrimage to Mecca for those who are able.

Rather, the following are what Islam is established on as part of the total package. Not the pillars. That is absolutely false information, because Islam is based on six elements as told by Muhammad himself in the following Hadith (Sahih Al Bukhari Vol. I, p. 13):

أن أقاتل الناس ، حتى يشهدوا أن لا إله إلا الله ، وأن محمدا رسول الله ، ويقيموا الصلاة ، ويؤتوا الزكاة ، فإذا
فعلوا ذلك عصموا مني دماءهم وأموالهم إلا بحق الإسلام ، وحسابهم على الله تعالى) رواه البخاري و مسلم .

"I have been ordered by Allah to **fight to kill (do Jihad)** all the people **until they say that there is no God but Allah and that Muhammad** is **his messenger**, and that they **establish prayer** and pay Zakat **(money)**. If they **do it, their blood and their property (their Honor) are safe from me.**"

When we look at this Hadith, we learn what Muhammad and Islam wanted from all mankind. Therefore, this is the...

Islamic Constitution

1. Muhammad has the duty to fight to force people to convert, or kill them,
2. Until they convert to Islam,
3. Until they say that there is no God but Allah.
4. And that Muhammad is his messenger.
5. Then you have to pray to Allah, or Muhammad will still kill you (if you do not do the prayer, Muhammad will kill you),
6. And then, and only then, are your money and blood safe from Muhammad and his army.

Let's look at it in other ways. What if I don't accept Islam?

■ Muslims have to fight you. Muhammad is dead, but they are not, and it's the duty of every Muslim to follow their prophet and do Jihad. Qur'an 9:14 says to, "Fight them (by the sword), and Allah will penalize them by your hands, cover them with humiliation. Allah will give to you victory over them, heal the chests of worshipers."

■ Muslims have the right to kill you.

■ They have the right to enslave your women and children, and to rape them (this is the right hand possession of property).

■ They will take your money and your country.

■ They will dominate your land by Islamic government. Their greatest joy is practicing Islamic Law, beheading, stoning to death, cutting hands, and praying for the death of the infidel.

21

- These are the rules in general, but there are inside rules Muhammad established to generate great income without costing him a penny.

- Christians and Jews have to pay Jizyah to stay alive if they refuse to convert.

As always, Muslims lie to you saying that in any country you have to pay tax. Jizyah—a TAX? This is an absolute falsehood!

How can you take their (Christian) land and then make them pay you money? As an example, if America were an Islamic country, the American soldier should take Jizyah from all Iraqis, or they would have to be killed! The excuse for Jizyah, as Muslims claim, is that you pay money for protection. Protection from whom? The Muslims! It's as I said, Islam is a gang of thugs (like the mafia). If you don't become one of them, you have to pay them, or you are dead. The Qur'an tells us about Jizyah:

- ◆ Chapter 9:29 in the Qur'an says in very clear words that we have to pay it while being disgraced, humiliated and belittled. Do Muslims pay tax in America with disgrace, humiliation and belittlement?

- ◆ The word Jizyah in Arabic means punishment and penalty. Why doesn't the Muslim tax have the same name?! They pay Zakat, not Jizyah If it's taxing, then the tax is a tax! Is this a kind of discrimination penalty?! Absolutely, yes. From Ibn Kathir's interpretation of Qur'an 9:29, I would like for you to go to and read all of the following link, please; www.qtafsir.com

- ◆ You will see how ugly this belief is. It's based on oppressing other nations and humiliation to all who are not Muslims. I will quote from the Muslim translation:

> Paying Jizyah is a Sign of Kufr (Disbelief) and Disgrace.

These are not my words. You will see how Muhammad even ordered Muslims to humiliate any Christian or Jew for no crime, but only for refusing to embrace Islam. He even said (Tafsir Ibn Kathir, interpretation of Sura 9):

> Do not approach with the greeting of peace (salam) to the Jews and Christians, and if you meet any of them in a road, force them to its narrowest road. (Force them to walk in the sewerage.) ...

In old days, the sewerage was a narrow channel in the side of the road. Christian and Muslims could not share the same road at the same time. We hear the Muslims trying to fool the African-American by saying to them, "Look what the white man did to you!" When the fact is, the African American was sold to the European by the Arab Muslims in North Africa.

Beheading Non-Muslim Captives

Qur'an 8:67:

It is not Allah's wish for any prophet to have captives up to the time of he hath caused the massacre in the land. Ye desire the temptation of this world and Allah's plan for the afterlife, and Allah is all powerful and wise.

We do remember the outrage of the prison of Abu Ghraib in Baghdad and how the world became so angry, but we do not see any anger toward Muslims beheading any of their captives, that included civilians, women, doctors and children, in addition to the soldiers.

For that reason, Muhammad made it clear to kill them all, and manufactured it as always to be Allah's wish, not his as we see in Qur'an 6:44-45:

> 44 afterwards, at the same time as they ignored what we reminded them of, We opened unto them the gates of all things (like wealth) until, they delighted in that which they were given, We seized them suddenly when they are not aware, They were overwhelmed.
> 45 As a consequence of the people who did not accept Islam, they wiped out all, Praise be to Allah, Lord of the Two Worlds! (Human, Jinn.)

However, Muhammad was terribly weak when it came to money. He preferred to hold live captives, if they were rich, he could ask for a large ransom from any relatives out of his reach, whom he had not yet killed; or if they could teach his army special skills, such as reading and writing.

Qur'an 47:3-4:

> 3 This on account of those who decline Allah and follow self-conceits whilst those who believe follow the truthfulness from their Lord: Thus does Allah arrange for men their teachings by parallel.
> 4 Because of that when ye meet the non-Muslims, strike at their necks until you achieve big harm; fasten a chain firmly on them until the war lays down its responsibilities. Moreover, goodness or ransom; therefore, you are ordered, but if Allah wants, He, Allah, could certainly have vanquished them and punish them, except, He causes you to fight in order to make you kill each others.

However, those who are slain for the sake of Allah, He will not let their deeds go lost.

However, afterwards we see Allah changing his mind again. He does not like to have any captive, but wants them to be killed. On top of that, he accuses those who like to have the captive. They are not obeying Allah's orders, because their desire is to be wealthy (Allah meant Muhammad). Then why is Qur'an 47:4 telling Muslims to ask for a ransom?

Qur'an 8:67:

It is not Allah's wish for any prophet to have captives up to the time of he hath caused the massacre in the land. Ye desire the temptation of this world and Allah's plan for the afterlife, and Allah is all powerful and wise.

Note here how Allah is the same as a toy in the hands of Muhammad. If Muhammad needs money, he makes a chapter to accept ransom. When there is no money left in the hands of his enemy, he makes a chapter saying it's a sin to seek a ransom!

Definitely, he needed to be sure that no one in the future would say that he was a false prophet ever again. Taking all their money, they had no money or family to pay off the ransom! Why would he keep them alive?

During the time we read about Islam, we have to always keep in mind that Islam is a government and political party, not only a religion, based on racism and hate against everyone who is not willing to participate as a Muslim, a slave, or as one who is obedient to the system, but who is not part of it (Islam). Such a person cannot get any protection, or any political right, or social benefit beyond that if he chooses not to be Muslim. As such, he chooses to be a criminal, filthy, in the eye of Muslims, Allah and Islam.

If the Muslims Take Over America—Then What?

How the Muslims will treat you is based on who you are.

- If you are an Atheist, Hindu, Buddhist or any other religion other than the Christian or Jewish faith, all the men will be killed. If a Muslim chooses not to enslave your women and children as sex toys, then they will be killed too.
- Christians have to pay Jizyah. Added to that, they have to obey the

following orders, which are called the pact of 'Umar or 'Omar.

The Pact Of 'Omar

From the book of JalaL Al-Deen Al-Soueuty Hadith 30999, Book of Ahkam Ahel Al Zimmad (dimma) v2/661, The book of Al-Sunan Al-Kubra Hadith 19186, Book of Al Jawab ak Al-Sahih Liman Badal Deen Al-Maseeh.

والراوي عبدالرحمن بن غنم30999جلال الدين السيوطي (مسند عمر بن الخطاب) رقم الحديث

) .بنفس الراوي662 - 2/661أحكام أهل الذمة لابن القيم (

وفي كتاب : السنن الكبرى
المؤلف : أبو بكر أحمد بن الحسين بن علي البيهقي
19186بنفس الراوي ورقم الحديث

وفي كتاب : الجواب الصحيح لمن بدل دين المسيح
المؤلف : أحمد بن عبد الحليم بن تيمية الحراني أبو العباس
عبد الرحمن بن غنم : كتبتُ لعمر بن الخطاب رضي الله عنه حين صالح 3ونفس الراوي الجزء الأول ص/
نصارى الشام، وشرَط عليهم فيه

بَابٌ فِي شُرُوطِ عُمَرَ رَضِيَ اللَّهُ عَنْهُ عَلَى أَهْلِ الذِّمَّةِ) أَنْبَأَنَا جَمَاعَةٌ عَنْ ابْنِ الْمُقِيرِ عَنْ ابْنِ نَاصِرٍ ثَنَا أَبُو رَجَاءٍ)
وَأَبُو عُثْمَانَ قَالَا أَنَا ابْنُ عَبْدِ الرَّحِيمِ أَنَا أَبُو الشَّيْخِ أَنْبَأَ أَبُو يَعْلَى الْمَوْصِلِيُّ ثَنَا الرَّبِيعُ بْنُ ثَعْلَبٍ حَدَّثَنِي يَحْيَى بْنُ
عُقْبَةَ بْنِ أَبِي الْعَيْزَارِ عَنْ سُفْيَانَ النُّورِيِّ وَالرَّبِيعِ بْنِ نُوحٍ وَالسَّرِيِّ عَنْ طَلْحَةَ بْنِ مَصْرِفٍ عَنْ مَسْرُوقٍ عَنْ عَبْدِ
الرَّحْمَنِ بْنِ غَنْمٍ قَالَ : كَتَبْتُ لِعُمَرَ رَضِيَ اللَّهُ عَنْهُ حِينَ صَالَحَ نَصَارَى أَهْلِ الشَّامِ : بِسْمِ اللَّهِ الرَّحْمَنِ الرَّحِيمِ هَذَا
كِتَابٌ لِعَبْدِ اللَّهِ عُمَرَ رَضِيَ اللَّهُ عَنْهُ أَمِيرِ الْمُؤْمِنِينَ مِنْ نَصَارَى مَدِينَةِ كَذَا وَكَذَا إِنَّكُمْ لَمَّا قَدِمْتُمْ عَلَيْنَا سَأَلْنَاكُمْ الْأَمَانَ
لِأَنْفُسِنَا وَذَرَارِيِّنَا وَأَمْوَالِنَا وَأَهْلِ مِلَّتِنَا وَشَرَطْنَا لَكُمْ عَلَى أَنْفُسِنَا أَنْ لَا نُحْدِثَ فِيهَا وَلَا فِيمَا حَوْلَهَا دَيْرًا وَلَا كَنِيسَةً
وَلَا قَلَّايَةً وَلَا صَوْمَعَةَ رَاهِبٍ وَلَا نُجَدِّدَ مَا خَرِبَ مِنْهَا وَلَا نُحْيِيَ مَا كَانَ مِنْهَا فِي خُطَطِ الْمُسْلِمِينَ وَأَنْ لَا نَمْنَعَ
كَنَائِسَنَا أَنْ يَنْزِلَهَا أَحَدٌ مِنَ الْمُسْلِمِينَ فِي لَيْلٍ وَلَا نَهَارٍ وَأَنْ نُوَسِّعَ أَبْوَابَهَا لِلْمَارَّةِ وَابْنِ السَّبِيلِ وَأَنْ نُنْزِلَ مَنْ مَرَّ بِنَا
مِنَ الْمُسْلِمِينَ ثَلَاثَةَ أَيَّامٍ نُطْعِمُهُمْ وَلَا نُؤْوِيَ فِي كَنَائِسِنَا وَلَا فِي مَنَازِلِنَا جَاسُوسًا وَلَا نَكْتُمَ غِشًّا لِلْمُسْلِمِينَ وَلَا نُعَلِّمَ
أَوْلَادَنَا الْقُرْآنَ وَلَا نُظْهِرَ شِرْكًا وَلَا نَدْعُوَ إِلَيْهِ وَلَا نَمْنَعَ أَحَدًا مِنْ ذَوِي قَرَابَتِنَا الدُّخُولَ فِي الْإِسْلَامِ إِذَا أَرَادُوهُ وَأَنْ
نُوَقِّرَ الْمُسْلِمِينَ وَنَقُومَ لَهُمْ مِنْ مَجَالِسِنَا إِذَا أَرَادُوا الْجُلُوسَ وَلَا نَتَشَبَّهَ بِهِمْ فِي شَيْءٍ مِنْ لِبَاسِهِمْ فِي قَلَنْسُوَةٍ وَلَا
عِمَامَةٍ وَلَا نَعْلَيْنِ وَلَا فَرْقِ شَعْرٍ وَلَا نَتَكَلَّمَ بِكَلَامِهِمْ وَلَا نَتَكَنَّى بِكُنَاهُمْ وَلَا نَرْكَبَ السُّرُجَ وَلَا نَتَقَلَّدَ السُّيُوفَ وَلَا
نَتَّخِذَ شَيْئًا مِنَ السِّلَاحِ وَلَا نَحْمِلَهُ مَعَنَا وَلَا نَنْقُشَ عَلَى خَوَاتِيمِنَا بِالْعَرَبِيَّةِ وَلَا نَبِيعَ الْخَمْرَ وَأَنْ نَجُزَّ مَقَادِيمَ رُءُوسِنَا
وَأَنْ نَلْزَمَ دِينَنَا حَيْثُ مَا كُنَّا وَأَنْ نَشُدَّ زَنَانِيرَنَا عَلَى أَوْسَاطِنَا وَأَنْ لَا نُظْهِرَ الصَّلِيبَ عَلَى كَنَائِسِنَا وَأَنْ لَا نُظْهِرَ
صُلُبَنَا وَلَا كُتُبَنَا فِي شَيْءٍ مِنْ طُرُقِ الْمُسْلِمِينَ وَأَسْوَاقِهِمْ وَلَا نَضْرِبَ نَاقُوسًا فِي كَنَائِسِنَا إِلَّا ضَرْبًا خَفِيًّا وَلَا نَرْفَعَ
أَصْوَاتَنَا فِي كَنَائِسِنَا فِي شَيْءٍ مِنْ حَضْرَةِ الْمُسْلِمِينَ وَلَا يَخْرُجَ سَاعُونَا وَلَا بَاعُونَا وَلَا نَرْفَعَ أَصْوَاتَنَا مَعَ مَوْتَانَا
وَلَا نُظْهِرَ النِّيرَانَ مَعَهُمْ فِي شَيْءٍ مِنْ طُرُقِ حَضْرَةِ الْمُسْلِمِينَ وَلَا أَسْوَاقِهِمْ وَلَا نُجَاوِرَهُمْ بِمَوْتَانَا وَلَا نَتَّخِذَ مِنْ
الرَّقِيقِ مَنْ جَرَتْ عَلَيْهِ سِهَامُ الْمُسْلِمِينَ وَلَا نَطَّلِعَ عَلَيْهِمْ فِي مَنَازِلِهِمْ . فَلَمَّا أَتَيْتُ عُمَرَ رَضِيَ اللَّهُ عَنْهُ بِالْكِتَابِ زَادَ
فِيهِ وَلَا نَضْرِبَ أَحَدًا مِنَ الْمُسْلِمِينَ شَرَطْنَا لَكُمْ ذَلِكَ عَلَى أَنْفُسِنَا وَأَهْلِ مِلَّتِنَا وَقَبِلْنَا عَلَيْهِ الْأَمَانَ فَإِنْ نَحْنُ خَالَفْنَا
عَنْ شَيْءٍ مِمَّا شَرَطْنَاهُ لَكُمْ وَضَمِنَّا عَلَى أَنْفُسِنَا فَلَا ذِمَّةَ لَنَا ، وَقَدْ حَلَّ لَكُمْ مِنَّا مَا يَحِلُّ مِنْ أَهْلِ الْمُعَانَدَةِ وَالشِّقَاقِ

When the Muslims attacked Syria (at that time Israel, Jordan, and some of present day Iraq), they started forcing their conditions on the poor Christians. The pact of 'Omar presents, as Muslims claim, the most justice you can imagine. They all agree that what 'Omar did was an amazing justice. They even called 'Omar the Khalifa, the Just.

This is the pact that the Christians agreed to (with no choice) just to stay alive.

'Abd Al-Rahman Ibn Ghanam, I wrote this letter to the Khalifa 'Omar Ibn Al-Khattab, to the Christians of Ash-Sham (Syria). In the name of God, the most Merciful and most Graceful. This is a letter to the servant of God 'Omar, the Khalifa of the believers, from the Nassarah (Christians) of Ash-Sham (Syrian cities). You came against us and we asked for our safety and security for our people and property, and we undertook the following obligations toward you:

We agree not to build, in our cities or around them, any new Christian monasteries, or churches, Christian buildings, or monks' houses, nor shall we fix or repair, by daytime or by night time, if any of these buildings fall in ruins or are situated in the land now owned by Muslims (the Muslims now own all the country so, you are in their land).
We agree to give shelter to any Muslim who chooses to be in our houses, and we shall give free food and shelter for any Muslim who stops by for three days.

We agree not to allow any spy to have shelter in our churches or in our houses or to hide him from Muslims.

We agree not to teach the Qur'an to our children.

We agree not to manifest our religion publicly or try to convert anyone to it.

We will not prevent any of our people from converting to Islam if they wish it.

We agree to pay and show respect toward the Muslims, and we shall rise and stand from our seats when they wish to sit (if a Muslim enters a place you should stand up and give him your chair, or you will die).

We agree not to try to resemble or to look like the Muslims by dressing in their clothes, the turban, footwear, or the parting of the hair. We shall not speak as they do, nor shall we adopt their first or last names.

We shall not mount on saddles, nor shall we carry a sword, nor own or bear any kind of arms, nor carry weapons with us.

We agree not to engrave Arabic symbols on our seals.

We agree not to sell wine.

We agree to shave the front hair of our heads.

We agree to dress always in the same kind of clothes, all of us, and we shall bind the shame belt around our waists.

We agree not to display nor expose our crosses or our books. We agree not to let our buyers or sellers in the roads or markets in the presence of Muslims.

We agree to use only church bells in our churches very softly. We will not raise our voices when in funerals or in the presence of Muslims.
We agree not to show any fire on any of the roads (for lighting) of the Muslims or in their markets.

We shall not bury dead Christians near the grave of a Muslim.

We agree not to take slaves whom Muslims have chosen by or allotted to Muslims.

We agree not to build high houses exposing the houses of the Muslims.

And when I brought this letter to 'Omar, he added to it:
We shall not strike a Muslim.

We accept these conditions for ourselves and for the people, and if we disobey any of these conditions, we will pay the outcome of disobeying as people of the rebel.

The end of the Pact of 'Omar.

When Muslims read these lines, they feel the rejoicing of the old days when Muslims conquered most of Africa, most of Asia and some of Europe. The dream of every Muslim is that one day he can institute every band of the Pact of 'Omar on you, your family and your country. The day the Muslims have the power, they will not hesitate for a second to do it, because it's Allah's order and it's the easiest way of wealth. Muslims in that era, even the homeless ones, lived like kings. They got free money, housing, women, sex, and even your wife! What can you do about it? Nothing! You have to take it or die.

Even if you are a prince and a Muslim enters your house, even if he is of no social status, you have to stand and give him your chair, your bed, your food and women for three days and nights. Before the end of the three nights, a new Muslim could come! Your house will be a free pimp hotel for every Muslim.

A Muslim can beat you, but you cannot hit back. Be careful or you are breaking the treaty! You have to shave the front part of your head, as an insult, to make you look like a fool.

If a Muslim makes fun of your Bible, you have no right to answer back, or you will be accused of trying to convert a Muslim. The punishment is death.

I Know a Muslim and He Is a Very Friendly Person, And He Is My Friend!

This is something you always hear in western countries. Most of those who say it are just trying to prove me wrong!

First of all, I am talking about Islam, not Muslims. The word, Muslim, means nothing if the person doesn't practice Islam. Maybe he isn't playing the deception game as those who committed the atrocity of 9/11. They went to strip clubs and drank! Why? To deceive the FBI in case they were watching them.

You should know that the Qur'an says that Muslims are not allowed to take us as friends or protectors, as Qur'an 5:51 says:

Take not Christians and Jews as friends and protectors, they are friends to each other, and if any of you take them as friends, he is one of them an unjust to himself (which means he is out of Islam, and he will be punished by death).

See the Yousuf Ali translation of Qur'an 5:51:
O ye who believe! Take not the Jews and the Christians for your friends and protectors. They are but friends and protectors to each other, and he among you that turns to them (for friendship) is of them. Verily, Allah guides not the unjust people.

By the way, a Muslim may say to you that this is about not taking a friend from those who are at war with them! If you both were at war, why would that person take you as a friend anyway?

The fact is, yes, "do not take anyone we are in war with" includes all Christians and Jews, for Islam divides the entire earth into two parts; Land of Peace and Land of War. There are even those who try to fool the West about the so called peaceful Islam, like Sheikh Yusuf Al-Qaradawi. He said in Al-Sharq Al-Awsat newspaper in London on July 19, 2003, that "It has been determined by Islamic law that the blood and property of the people of Dar Al-Harb (house of war—any land that is not submitting to Allah), where Muslims are in war and battle, is not protected."

Now this is a man who works hard trying to give a better appearance to the West, but he did agree that all who are not in a sublimation stage to Islam have to be killed. He is basing this on his prophet's words (Sahih Al Bukhari, Book 8, Hadith 387):

> "I have been commanded to fight (fight to kill) all the people up to the time that they say: 'None should be worshiped but Allah.' And if they say so, and pray like we pray, face our Qibla (direction of the Kaaba) and butcher the same as we slaughter, then and only after that their blood and property will be protected from me..."

I think these are very clear words from Muhammad, convert or **die**. This will take us to the word Islam, and the Muslim claim that it's a word meaning peace!

Islam Means Peace?

It upsets me when some ignorant person goes on TV and gives us their rubbish saying, "Islam is peace and peaceful." Even, "Islam means peace!"

I do not need to remind you about those who lie, like President Obama and other western leaders, saying that Islam is peace. Either they are unbelievably ignorant about Islam, or they are simply liars.

First of all, Islam does not mean peace. Peace in Arabic is **Salam**. Does Islam look the same to you? أسلام and سلام

ISLAM	م	ﻻ	س	ا
SALAM		م	ﻻ	س

I	S	L	A	M	Islam
S	A	L	A	M	Peace

Islam is totally the opposite from the word peace.

Muhammad said, أسلموا تسلموا, ASLIMO TASLAMO
aslimo = convert to Islam
taslamo = you will be safe

The best verse to expalin what islam is 48:16 where the word Yu-Slmon (become a Muslim) translated correctly as Surrender, with clear threat from Muhammad if they do not surnder to him (convert to Islam) they shall face his army;

*"bedouins who lagged behind: "You shall be called to fight against a people given to great warfare, then you shall fight them, or they shall **surrender.** Then if you obey, Allah will give you a fair reward; but if you turn away as you did turn away before, He will punish you with a painful torment."*

(سورة فـ تح الـ), Al-Fath, Chapter #48, Verse #16), (Mohsin Khan translation)

And then the Arab in the previous verse convert to Islam to avoid death, they said we are believers but Muhammad knew that they never believed on him but only they became Muslims (surrender) to avoid death.

In the coming chapter, we will see how Muhammad proves that the new Muslims did not accept Islam by faith, but by the sword. He's telling them in clear words, "You cannot fool me by claiming that you converted, because you only did after you surrendered yourself to my sword." This is what Islam means exactly.

The Bedouins say: "We believe." Say: **"You believe not but you only say**, 'We have **surrendered** (in Islam),' **for Faith has not yet entered your hearts**. But if you obey Allah and His Messenger (SAW), He will not decrease anything in reward for your deeds. Verily, Allah is Oft-Forgiving, Most Merciful."

(سورة الـ حجرات), Al-Hujuraat, Chapter #49, Verse #14),(Mohsin Khan translation)

I'm not sure how good your memory is, but do you remember this Hadith (Sahih Al Bukhari Vol. I, p. 13)?

"I have been ordered by Allah to **fight to kill (do Jihad)** all the people **until they say that there is no God but Allah and that Muhammad** is **his messenger**, and that they **establish prayer** and pay Zakat **(money)**. If they **do it, their blood and their property (their Honor) are safe from me.**"

The same story can be found in Sahih Muslim, Book 1, Number 29, 30 and 32.

If Islam is peace, why was Muhammad ordered to fight until we convert? If we convert and become slaves of Muhammad, because he is the real god of Islam, not Allah, then and only then will our blood not be shed and our women will not be enslaved, raped and killed.

If a Muslim kills you, he will not be punished for it, for your blood is free. Notice, if you kill a cow in Islam, you have to pay the owner for it, but if you kill a Christian or Jew, your blood is free for Muslims, as we see in this coming hadith.

Justice in Islam

Sahih Bukhari, Book 3, Hadith 111, Sahih Bukhari, Book 52, Hadith 283 and Sahih Bukhari, Book 83, Hadith 50:

> **"The prophet said that no Muslim should be killed as punishment for the killing of a disbeliever."**

What justice Muhammad had! He was full of it! Imagine if we had a law saying that if you kill a Muslim, you don't get any punishment!

President Obama quoted in his speech, on his trip to Egypt, a portion of the verse from the Qur'an 5:32. He said:

> **"The Holy Koran teaches that whoever kills an innocent, it is as if he has killed all mankind; and whoever saves a person, it is as if he has saved all mankind. The enduring faith of over a billion people is so much bigger than the narrow hatred of a few. Islam is not part of the problem in combating violent extremism - it is an important part of promoting peace."**

The fact is, Muhammad took this verse from the Jewish Mishnah, Sanhedrin 4:5 and it is recorded in the Bible in Genesis 9:6 (New King James Version):

> 6 *Whoever sheds man's blood, By man his blood shall be shed; For in the image of God He made man.*

- ⚔ Note here the real justice. If you are Jewish and kill anyone, not only a Jew, you will be killed.
- ⚔ Later we will see that if a Muslim kills a non-Muslim, he will not be killed!

But President Obama didn't quote the first part of Qur'an 5:32, which clearly states that this verse was given as a direction to the Children of Israel. This referenced portion of the verse is only incumbent on the people of Israel. What that verse actually means is that killing is fine for those who do mischief on earth, from the Muslim perspective. Who are the ones that can be killed for doing mischief on the earth?

1. The Christians
2. The Jews
3. The Hindus
4. The Buddhists
5. The Atheist

To make it short; all non-Muslim blood is free to shed.

Muhammad was ordered to kill us all, or we convert, or we pay Jizyah. Note: The Jizyah option is only for the Christian and the Jew. Death is a must for all others as in Qur'an 9:29:

> **Combat those** who disbelieve in Allah nor the Judgment Day, nor forbid what Allah and His Messenger command to be forbidden, nor embrace the religion of truthfulness (Islam) from the People of the Book (Christian & Jewish), until they pay the Jizyah with force and surrender and feel themselves humiliated and conquered.

The word "fight" in Qur'an 9:29 is FIGHT TO KILL.

FIGHT to Kill Them	FIGHT TO KILL	KILLED	KILLING	KILL as order
(قاتلوا) as in Qur'an 9:29, Qatelo	يقاتل Youqatel	قتل QATALA	يقتل Yaqtol	قاتل Qatel

In the correct Arabic, we do not say Qatel for someone fighting with another by hitting each other. This word's meaning is fight to kill!

To prove that the mischief with words in this verse is about us, we can read again Sahih Bukhari, Book 8, Hadith 387; Sahih Bukhari,Book 52,

Hadith 196; Sahih Bukhari, Book 84, Hadith 59; Sahih Bukhari, Book 92, Hadith 388:

> "I have been ordered by Allah to <u>fight to kill (do Jihad)</u> all the people <u>until they say that there is no God but Allah and that Muhammad is his messenger</u>, and that they <u>establish prayer</u> and <u>pay Zakat</u> (money). If they do it, their blood and their property (their honor) are safe from me."

The same story can be found in (Sahih Muslim, Book 001, Number 0029 and 0030).

You can read many verses in the Qur'an like Qur'an 9:29. But to prove that this verse refers only to the killing of a Muslim when it (Qur'an 5:32) says, **"The one who killed one man is as if he killed all mankind"** and has to be punished, we simply turn to the Hadith (Sahih Bukhari Book 3, Hadith 111; Sahih Bukhari Book 52, Hadith 283; and Sahih Bukhari Book 83, Hadith 50):

> The prophet said that no Muslim should be killed as punishment for the killing of a disbeliever.

Why won't a Muslim be punished if he kills a Christian? The answer is simple. You (the Christian) are doing mischief by rejecting Islam according to Muhammad, and that makes you and your blood free. This is how Muhammad spreads Islam, as we showed you in Hadith Sahih Al Bukhari Vol. 1, Page 1.

The coming verse in the Qur'an will tell us who the one is doing mischief on earth.

From Ibn Kathir, we find the following Tafsir. Read the Muslim's translations yourself on this link: http://tafsir.com/default.asp?sid=5&tid=13723

On the other hand, read my translation: What the Muslims translate as, "...it would be, as if he killed all mankind" should be translated, **"Whoever kills a single soul that Allah has given protection from killing,** is the same, as he who kills all mankind."

Book of Tafsir Al-Qur'an, Ibn kathir, Printing 2, 1999, V3, Page 93:

> Similarly reported from Sa`eed Bin Jubaer, he revealed, "**He who authorizes himself to spill the blood of a Muslim,** is same as he who allows shedding the blood of all mankind. He who prohibits shedding the blood of single Muslim is the like of he who forbids shedding the blood of all mankind.

It's about shedding the blood, which Allah forbids to shed, and that is the **Muslim's blood only**. This is why Muhammad said (Sahih Bukhari Book 3, Hadith 111; Sahih Bukhari Book 52, Hadith 283; and Sahih Bukhari Book 83, Hadith 50):

> **"...The prophet said that no Muslim should be killed as punishment for the killing of a disbeliever...."**

If killing a single soul was not meant to refer only to the Muslims, then the punishment should be death. The verse says in clear words, death is the punishment for he who kills. However, Muhammad made it clear that this is about someone killing a Muslim. The fact is, you do not need to kill a Muslim to be killed. As I previously showed, you are an enemy of Allah if you aren't a Muslim. It's the duty of each Muslim to shed your blood, unless you convert to Islam. As we discover in the hadith (Al-Muwatta'Imam Malik Ibn Anas, Book 43, Hadith 15:8), **"Jew or Christian, his blood-money ransom is half the blood-money of a free Muslim:"**

> Yahya notified me from Malik, whom he heard that 'Omar Ibn 'Abed Al-'Aziz (Muslim Khalifa) granted a judgment that when a <u>Jew or Christian was killed, his blood-money ransom is half the blood-money of a free Muslim.</u>
>
> Malik said, "What is accomplished in our community is that a <u>Muslim shall not be killed in retaliation for the death of Christian or a Jew,</u> unless the Muslim killed him doing a treason. In such a matter, he is killed for it."

In the book of العبر في خبر من غبر, Al-'Ebar Fe Khaer Man Gaber By AL-Zahabi V1 page 175, Ibn Kathir book of Al-Bedaiah Wal Elnihayah V3, Page 318, and V 11, The Great Year Of 398:

> "The destroying of the garbage (the Muslim name given to The Church of the Holy Sepulcher) in the year 398. In that year, the Muslim ruler (Khalifa) ordered the destruction of the church of garbage (The Church of the Holy Sepulcher), and it's the church of the Christian, and allowed all the Muslims to steal from it, all the furniture and whatever was in it. The reason for that was their (Christians) claim of the Holy fire that comes from the sky from the empty grave of Jesus on the Easter day is false, and they are trying to make the naive Christian believe it, when it's made from the paint of Al-Balsan!"

During the same time, they ordered the destruction of many Christian churches in Egypt, and they started calling for the Christians to leave the land of Islam, if they didn't want to accept Islam and accept the Islamic conditions imposed on them. The Khalifa also added more to the Pact of 'Omar.

1. Every Christian has to wear a four-pound cross made of wood on his neck.

2. Every Jew has to carry on his head a bull (bovine) made of wood weighing six pounds.

3. When they go to the public bathroom they have to hang on their necks a six-pound water container and attach bells to this container.

4.   And they are forbidden from using horses.

البداية والنهاية/الجزء الحادي عشر/ثم دخلت سنة ثمان وتسعين وثلاثمائة

تخريب قمامة في هذه السنة

وفيها: أمر الحاكم بتخريب قُمامة وهي كنيسة النصارى ببيت المقدس، وأباح للعامة ما فيها من الأموال والأمتعة وغير ذلك، وكان سبب ذلك البهتان الذي يتعاطاه النصارى في يوم الفصح من النار التي يحتالون بها، وهي التي يوهمون جهلتهم أنها نزلت من السماء، وإنما هي مصنوعة بدهن البلسان في خيوط الإبريسم، والرقاع المدهونة بالكبريت وغيره، بالصنعة اللطيفة التي تروج على الطغام منهم والعوام، وهم إلى الآن يستعملونها في ذلك المكان بعينه.

وكذلك هدم في هذه السنة عدة كنائس ببلاد مصر، ونودي في النصارى: من أحب الدخول في دين الإسلام دخل ومن لا يدخل فليرجع إلى بلاد الروم آمنا، ومن أقام منهم على دينه فليلتزم بما شرط عليهم من الشروط التي زادها الحاكم على العمرية، من تعليق الصلبان على صدورهم، وأن يكون الصليب من خشب زنته أربعة أرطال، وعلى اليهود تعليق رأس العجل زنته ستة أرطال.

وفي الحمام يكون في عنق الواحد منهم قربة زنة خمس أرطال، بأجراس، وأن لا يركبوا خيلا.

A poor black slave woman had been slaughtered, with no mercy, for one crime. She insulted Muhammad. Muhammad gave his blessing to the killer, as we see in this following hadith. Book of Ibn Dawood, 'Hodood (punishment) of those who insult the prophet (Sunan Ibn Dawood Hodood, Page 129, Hadith 4361, Arabic; Book 38, Hadith 4348, English):

2.سنن أبي داود - كِتَاب الْحُدُود - ألا اشهدوا أن دمها هدر

- «بَاب الْحُكْم فِيمَن سَبَّ النَّبِيَّ صَلَّى اللَّه عَلَيْهِ وَسَلَّمَ129ص -»

حَدَّثَنَا عَبَّاد بْن مُوسَى الْخُتَّلِيُّ أَخْبَرَنَا إِسْمَعِيل بْن جَعْفَر الْمَدَنِيّ عَنْ إِسْرَائِيل عَنْ عُثْمَان الشَّحَّام عَنْ 4361 عِكْرِمَة قَالَ حَدَّثَنَا ابْن عَبَّاس أَنَّ أَعْمَى كَانَتْ لَهُ أُمُّ وَلَدٍ تَشْتُمُ النَّبِيَّ صَلَّى اللَّه عَلَيْهِ وَسَلَّمَ وَتَقَع فِيهِ فَيَنْهَاهَا فَلَا تَنْتَهِي وَيَزْجُرُهَا فَلَا تَنْزَجِر قَالَ فَلَمَّا كَانَتْ ذَات لَيْلَة جَعَلَتْ تَقَع فِي النَّبِيِّ صَلَّى اللَّه عَلَيْهِ وَسَلَّمَ وَتَشْتُمُهُ فَأَخَذَ الْمِغْوَل فَوَضَعَهُ فِي بَطْنِهَا وَاتَّكَأَ عَلَيْهَا فَقَتَلَهَا فَوَقَع بَيْن رِجْلَيْهَا طِفْلٌ فَلَطَّخَتْ مَا هُنَاكَ بِالدَّم فَلَمَّا أَصْبَح ذُكِرَ ذَلِكَ لِرَسُول اللَّه صَلَّى اللَّه عَلَيْهِ وَسَلَّمَ فَجَمَع النَّاس فَقَالَ أَنْشُدُ اللَّه رَجُلًا فَعَلَ مَا فَعَلَ لِي عَلَيْهِ حَقٌّ إِلَّا قَام فَقَامَ الْأَعْمَى يَتَخَطَّى النَّاس وَهُوَ يَتَزَلْزَل حَتَّى قَعَدَ بَيْن يَدَي النَّبِيِّ صَلَّى اللَّه عَلَيْهِ وَسَلَّمَ فَقَالَ يَا رَسُول اللَّه أَنَا صَاحِبُهَا كَانَتْ تَشْتُمُك وَتَقَع فِيك فَأَنْهَاهَا فَلَا تَنْتَهِي وَأَزْجُرُهَا فَلَا تَنْزَجِر وَلِي مِنْهَا ابْنَان مِثْل اللُّؤْلُؤَتَيْن وَكَانَتْ بِي رَفِيقَةً فَلَمَّا كَانَ الْبَارِحَة جَعَلَتْ تَشْتُمُك وَتَقَع فِيك فَأَخَذْت الْمِغْوَل فَوَضَعْتُهُ فِي بَطْنِهَا وَاتَّكَأْت عَلَيْهَا حَتَّى قَتَلْتُهَا فَقَالَ النَّبِيُّ صَلَّى اللَّه عَلَيْهِ وَسَلَّمَ أَلَا اشْهَدُوا أَنَّ دَمَهَا هَدَرٌ

The book of Ibn Dawood, 'Hodood (punishment) of those who insult the prophet (Sunan Ibn Dawood Hodood, Page 129, Hadith 4361, Arabic; Book 38, Hadith 4348 English):

Reported Abdallah Ibn 'Abbas: That a blind man had a slave-mother of one of his offspring, which used foul language at the Prophet of Allah and disrespected Him, and her owner commanded her not to do that, but she did not stop insulting the Prophet. One night she began making fun of the Prophet so, he took a stiletto, pierced her belly with it, and he put his weight on it and went through her belly, and killed her. Her child who stood between her legs, and he was wrapped with her blood. When the morning came, the Prophet was told about the incident. He gathered the people and said: "I seek by Allah the man who has done what he has done (killing the slave), and I ask him by my right on him that he should stand up." The blind man stood up trembling to the Prophet. He sat in front of the Prophet, and said: "Oh Apostle of Allah! I am her master; she used to insult you and say bad things about you. I forbade her, but she did not stop, and I rebuked her, but she did not abandon her habit. I have two sons like pearls from her, and she was my companion. Last night she began to abuse and disparage you. So I took a stiletto, put it on her belly, and I put my weight on it until it went through her until I killed her." Thereupon the Prophet said: Oh the people be witnessing, no punishment for killing her and her blood for free.

This is why Muslims in London had big signs saying, "Behead those who insult the Prophet," and "I think Islam is just about peace and justice!" Did you notice that Muhammad did not even investigate if the man was telling the truth or not? This means if you live in an Islamic land and you kill your slave, or even your wife, all you need to do to be free from any punishment is to claim that she insulted the Prophet and then you are a hero!

See this fatwa Muslim sheikh giving an answer to Muslims who are asking if this story is true (http://www.islam.tc/cgi-bin/askimam/ask.pl?q=6491&act=view).

> **Answer to Question 6491 from United Kingdom:**
> **We confirm the authenticity of this narration. The reason for which no punishment was imposed on the man who murdered the women is that she had explicitly sworn Rasulullah (Sallallaahu Alayhi Wasallam). Such a person is termed as 'Mubaah-ud-dam', i.e. if killed, there can be no claim of retaliation. (See Badhlul Majhood vol.6 pg.125). There is Ijmaa (consensus) on this ruling. and Allah Ta'ala Knows Best Moulana Muhammad ibn Moulana Haroon Abbassommar FACULTY OF SPECIALTY IN HADITH CHECKED AND APPROVED: Mufti Ebrahim Desai**

This also shows that Muhammad is more important than Allah. In Islam, if you insult Allah, you are given three days to repent or you die, but if you insult Muhammad, you are killed even if you do repent.

When they quote Qur'an 5:32 to show you that Islam IS PEACE, it's a big _FAT LIE!_

Whoever says Islam means peace, demonstrates his ignorance. What is known today as political correctness is based on "let's pretend that we do not know that

Islam is evil, and if someone says the truth, he must be Islamophobic!"

As long as we are talking about justice, let's see how Muhammad was unfair in his good justice, not only between Muslims and non-Muslims, but also between the Muslims themselves, when it comes to males and females.

Muhammad, The God

Muhammad named himself God. You might wonder what I'm talking about. Did not Muhammad say repeatedly that he was the slave of God?

We need to know that Muhammad made a jump from someone who did not have faith and did not know the scriptures to someone who became a prophet of God overnight, as we see in the following verse (Qur'an 42:52, Muhammad Pickthall):

> And thus have We inspired in thee (Muhammad) a spirit of Our command. Thou knowest not what the scripture was, nor what the faith. But We have made it a light whereby We guide whom We will of Our bondmen. And lo! thou verily dost guide unto a right path.

How can Muslims claim that Muhammad was a follower of Abraham when he did not know "what the scripture was, nor what the faith" is? This shows us that Muhammad himself was a kafir (infidel). How can an infidel who did not know what faith meant and never heard of Scripture, as revealed to us in the verse, suddenly choose to be a prophet and place himself as God?

Well, Muhammad used the name of God to make himself God. I will prove to you that Muhammad's real name is Qathem (قثم). Muhammad changed his name when he was 30 years old, and he did so at the instigation of his wife, Khadija, and her cousin. At that time, Khadija and her cousin worked out a plan to make Muhammad the ruler of all tribes in Arabia. They knew that it was easy for Muhammad to control and dictate authority over the people, if he claimed that his authority came from God—so they proclaimed to him, "By the name of God, you are God!"

Muhammad takes the place of God (Sunan Ibn Majah, book of Jihad, Hadith 2859):

سنن ابن ماجه ـ كِتَاب الْجِهَادِ ـ من أطاعني فقد أطاع الله ومن عصاني فقد عصى الله

باب طَاعَةِ الإمَامِ

حَدَّثَنَا أَبُو بَكْرِ بْنُ أَبِي شَيْبَةَ وَعَلِيُّ بْنُ مُحَمَّدٍ قَالَا حَدَّثَنَا وَكِيعٌ حَدَّثَنَا الْأَعْمَشُ عَنْ أَبِي صَالِحٍ عَنْ أَبِي 2859 هُرَيْرَةَ قَالَ قَالَ رَسُولُ اللَّهِ صَلَّى اللَّهُ عَلَيْهِ وَسَلَّمَ مَنْ أَطَاعَنِي فَقَدْ أَطَاعَ اللَّهَ وَمَنْ عَصَانِي فَقَدْ عَصَى اللَّهَ وَمَنْ أَطَاعَ الْإِمَامَ فَقَدْ أَطَاعَنِي وَمَنْ عَصَى الْإِمَامَ فَقَدْ عَصَانِي

The Prophet said whoever obeys me, he does obey Allah, and whomever disobeys me, he disobeys Allah, and whomever obeys the Imam, he obeys me and whomever disobeys the Imam he disobeys me.

Qur'an 4:80:

He who abides by the Apostle, he indeed obeys God. However, [those] whom obey him not, Allah is watching him (as a threat), We have not sent [one] to watch over them.

مَّن يُطِعِ الرَّسُولَ فَقَدْ أَطَاعَ اللَّهَ وَمَن تَوَلَّى فَمَا أَرْسَلْنَاكَ عَلَيْهِمْ حَفِيظًا
(سورة النساء)

As we see in the above verse, there is a written approval in the Qur'an for Muhammad to take the place of God. This means then that the laws of Islam have two sources: Muhammad and the Qur'an (which comes from Muhammad anyway!).

The fact is that the main sources of Islamic law are solely from the actions and speeches of Muhammad.

4. Muhammad's recitations (Qur'an).
5. Muhammad's speeches and orders (Sunnah).
6. Muhammad's actions (even the simple or silly ones, like how to pee) (Sunnah).

Clearly, Muhammad and God became one. The word of Muhammad is the word of God, and the order of Muhammad is the order of God.

Muhammad takes precedence over God (Qur'an 4:80):

Whoever obeys the Prophet, he indeed obeyed Allah; and whoever did not obey, we send not a protector over them.

It is more important to obey Muhammad than to obey God. This is why we notice that there is a huge interest on the part of God to satisfy the sexual

38

desires of Muhammad, and whatever Muhammad wished became law.

From Qathem to Muhammad

All of this was not enough for Muhammad. Something was missing and that was the title. I do not mean the title of "Prophet"—he got that already by his sword.

When he was born, he was given the name Qathem, not Muhammad. Why change his name to Muhammad, and what is that name all about? Let's look at the following biblical figures and their titles:

1. Abraham - Father of Prophet-hood.

2. Moses - One who spoke to God (Kalem Allah كليم الله).

3. Jesus - The Messiah.

So, the new man in the theater, Qathem (Muhammad), needed a new name.

The following verse explains why Muhammad chose his names and titles (Sahih Al-Bukhari, Book 56, Hadith 732):

أنا محمد وأنا أحمد ، وأنا الماحي الذي يمحو الله بي الكفر ، وأنا الحاشر الذي يُحشَرُ الناس على قدمي ، وأنا))
((العاقب الذي ليس بعده نبي)) رواه البخاري (4343) ومسلم (3268

Allah's messenger said, "I have five names: I am **Muhammad** and **Ahmad**; I am the **Eraser (Al-Mahi)**, one through whom Allah will erase Infidels (Christianity), I am the **Collector (Al-Hashir, means mankind will be gathered in front of him)**, the first to be resurrected, no one ahead of me; and I am **The Last (Al-Aqib)**, no one comes after me."

Let us take a closer look at these names:

	The Meaning of the Names/Titles	Equivalent Names of Allah
Muhammad	The All Praiseworthy	Al-Hamīd (#56)
Ahmad	The Praised One	Al-Hamīd (#56)
Eraser (Al-Mahi)	The one through whom Christianity will be erased	Al-Mahi (As Allah, in Qur'an 22:52, does "yansakh" {erase} what satan casts, Muhammad assumes the attribute for himself to erase other

39

		religions). (See Bukhari, Book 56, Hadith 732)
Collector (Al-Hashir)	The one through whom Allah will collect all humanity on Judgment Day	Al-Muhsi (#57)
The Last (Al-Aqib)	No one comes after me	Al-'Akhir (#74)

I'm not sure how you feel or think about these names, but I feel Satan's words in them. Notice that Muhammad chose "The Praised One," which, not surprisingly, is one of the 99 names of Allah. He declared himself as God, so that Muslims would follow him without question. They approve what he approved, and forbid what he forbade, even if what he said contradicts the orders of Allah in the Qur'an. The Muslims continue to follow Muhammad over Allah.

Muhammad (The All Praiseworthy) and Ahmad (The Praised One)

To verify the meaning of any verse quoted, go to: www.altafsir.com.

Qur'an 61:6, Muhammad Pickthall:

> And when Jesus son of Mary said, O Children of Israel! Lo! I am the messenger of Allah unto you, confirming that which was (revealed) before me in the Torah, and bringing good tidings of a messenger who cometh after me, whose name is the Praised One. Yet when he hath come unto them with clear proofs, they say: This is mere magic.

Throughout the Qur'an, "The Praised One" is used for Allah, except in Chapter 61:6, where Muhammad is given the privilege to share Allah's name. Muhammad is also The Praised One.

The root word is 'ham'd. The following words all come from the root word 'ham'd, and all of them mean the same, "the praised one".

'Ham'd	Praise
'Hameed	The praised one
Mu'hammad	The praised one

A'hmad	The praised one
'Hamdan	Praise

The first name, 'ham'd, is the name of Allah, exactly as we see in the following verses:

⚔ سورة البروج , Al-Burooj, Qur'an 85:8 ⚔

⚔ سورة الممتحنة , Al-Mumtahana, Qur'an 60:6 ⚔

⚔ سورة الحديد , Al-Hadid, Qur'an 7:24 ⚔

⚔ سورة الحديد , Al-Hadid, Qur'an 57:24 ⚔

⚔ سورة الشورى , Al-Shura, Qur'an 42:28 ⚔

⚔ سورة فاطر , Fater, Qur'an 35:15 ⚔

⚔ سورة لقمان , Lu'qman, Qur'an 31:26 ⚔

⚔ سورة الحج , Al-Hajj, Qur'an 22:64 ⚔

⚔ سورة الحج , Al-Hajj, Qur'an 22:24 ⚔

⚔ سورة إبراهيم , Ibrahim, Qur'an 14:1 ⚔

If Muhammad was a slave of God, why then did he hijack God's name? The answer is easy. Muhammad knew that he was a false prophet, and knew exactly what he could achieve by proclaiming himself "The Praised One." He wanted absolute obedience, absolute control, and absolute deception. By proclaiming himself as "The Praised One," he made sure that no one would dare to question him.

The Hadiths point to one conclusion; Muhammad is God (Sahih-Al-Bukhari, Book of Ablution Hadith 186):

صحيح البخاري ـ كتاب الوُضُوء ـ فتوضأ فجعل الناس يأخذون من فضل وضوئه فيتمسحون به فصلى النبي صلى الله عليه وسلم الظهر ركعتين والعصر ركعتين

قَالَ وَهُوَ الَّذِي مَجَّ رَسُولُ اللَّهِ صَلَّى اللَّهُ عَلَيْهِ وَسَلَّمَ فِي وَجْهِهِ وَهُوَ غُلَامٌ مِنْ بِئْرِهِمْ وَقَالَ عُرْوَةُ عَنْ 186 الْمِسْوَرِ وَغَيْرِهِ يُصَدِّقُ كُلَّ وَاحِدٍ مِنْهُمَا صَاحِبَهُ وَإِذَا تَوَضَّأَ النَّبِيُّ صَلَّى اللَّهُ عَلَيْهِ وَسَلَّمَ كَادُوا يَقْتَتِلُونَ عَلَى وَضُوئِهِ

The Prophet did his ablution so the people were taking the remaining of his water and spread it all over their faces... even to the point some of the prophet's companions were fighting over his leftover water.

Sahih Al-Bukhari, Book 72, Hadith 750:

I witnessed Bilal's picking the left over water that the Prophet had used for his ablution, and lots of the Muslims were seizing of that water and applying it on their face. Whoever could not get anything of it, would apply the moisture from the hand of his companion to spread it all over on his face.

Now think about it, ablution water is the wash water, and in case you don't know, this is the water Muhammad used to wash such things as his penis and testicles. So how and why did these Muslims think that the water Muhammad used to wash his private parts was holy water for blessing?

References of how Muslims used to be blessed by Muhammad:

[1] صحيح البخاري ج: 2 ص: 976. Sahih Al-Bukhari, Volume 2, Page 976. **"The prophet almost died with Muslims fighting for his ablution."**

[2] صحيح مسلم ج: 4 ص: 1812 برقم 2325. Sahih Muslim, Volume 4, Page 1812, Hadith 2325. **"Muslims getting blessed by the falling hair of the Prophet, and Khalid Ibn Al-Waleed fought and killed many men to get back his turban because he did hide in it two hairs of the prophet."**

[3] صحيح البخاري كتاب الوضوء حديث186 Sahih-Al-Bukhari, Book 4 (Ablution), Hadith 186. "...The Prophet did his ablution so the people were taking the remaining of his water and spread it all over their faces... even to the point some of the prophet's companions were fighting over his leftover water."

[4] صحيح مسلم ج 2 ص 947 برقم 1305. Sahih Muslim, Volume 2, Page 947, Hadith 1305. **"The wife of Muhammad used to collect the hair of the prophet in water, so they could drink it to be blessed by it."**

[5] سير اعلام النبلاء – ج محمد بن احمد الذهبي ص 11 212. Book of Seer Al-A'lam, Volume 11, Page 212. **"The father of Abu Hanbal said, 'My father used to have three of the prophets hairs, and he used to kiss it and drink the water he washed it by, and he asked [for it] to be kept in his grave, so he can face Allah with it.'"**

[6] رواه البخاري – ج ص2 165 . Sahih Al-Bukhari, Part 2, Page 165. **"We used to kiss his hand to be blessed with his skin."**

[7] المستدرك على الصحيحين ج: 3 ص 589 برقم 6181.Book of Al-Mustadrik in the Two Sahih, V3, Page 589, Hadith 6181. **"Used to be blessed by touching the dishes he ate from."**

[8] صحيح مسلم / كتاب اللباس والزينة (145 / 3). Sahih Muslims, Book of Al-Libas (Dress and Adornment), Part 3, Page 165. "This is the dress of the prophet he used to dress, and we did hide it for the sick ones, so they can recover by it."

صحيح مسلم - كِتَاب اللِّبَاسِ وَالزِّينَةِ - إنما يلبس هذا من لا خلاق له
«1641»ص - 2069 -»
أَسْمَاء فَخَبَّرْتُهَا فَقَالَتْ هَذِهِ جُبَّةُ رَسُولِ اللَّهِ صَلَّى اللَّهُ عَلَيْهِ وَسَلَّمَ فَأَخْرَجَتْ إِلَيَّ جُبَّةً طَيَالِسَةٍ كِسْرَوَانِيَّةً لَهَا لِبْنَةُ
دِيبَاجٍ وَفَرْجَيْهَا مَكْفُوفَيْنِ بِالدِّيبَاجِ فَقَالَتْ هَذِهِ كَانَتْ عِنْدَ عَائِشَةَ حَتَّى قُبِضَتْ فَلَمَّا قُبِضَتْ قَبَضْتُهَا وَكَانَ النَّبِيُّ
صَلَّى اللَّهُ عَلَيْهِ وَسَلَّمَ يَلْبَسُهَا فَنَحْنُ نَغْسِلُهَا لِلْمَرْضَى يُسْتَشْفَى بِهَا

The Underwear of the Prophet is a Medicine To Recover the Sick Ones

Book of Sahih Muslim, Book of Clothes, page 1641 Hadith 2069:

'Aisha came back to Asma' ('Aisha's sister) and she told her this is the under clothes of the prophet ...we do wash it so the sick ones can be recovered by it.

Muhammad's Selling Lands in Heaven

Pay for a place in Heaven with a farmland

حَدَّثَنَا خَلَفُ بْنُ خَلِيفَةَ عَنْ حُمَيْدٍ الأَعْرَجِ عَنْ عَبْدِ اللَّهِ بْنِ الْحَارِثِ عَنْ عَبْدِ اللَّهِ بْنِ مَسْعُودٍ قَالَهُ : لَمَّا نَزَلَتْ : " مَنْ
ذَا الَّذِي يُقْرِضُ اللَّهَ قَرْضًا حَسَنًا " قَالَ أَبُو الدَّحْدَاحِ : يَا رَسُولَ اللَّهِ أَوَإِنَّ اللَّهَ تَعَالَى يُرِيدُ مِنَّا الْقَرْضَ ؟ قَالَ : (نَعَمْ
يَا أَبَا الدَّحْدَاحِ) قَالَ : أَرِنِي يَدَكَ ; قَالَ فَنَاوَلَهُ ; قَالَ : فَإِنِّي أَقْرَضْتُ اللَّهَ حَائِطًا فِيهِ سِتُّمِائَةِ نَخْلَةٍ , ثُمَّ جَاءَ يَمْشِي
حَتَّى أَتَى الْحَائِطَ وَأُمُّ الدَّحْدَاحِ فِيهِ وَعِيَالِه , فَنَادَاهَا : يَا أُمَّ الدَّحْدَاحِ ; قَالَتْ : لَبَّيْكَ ; قَالَ : أُخْرُجِي , قَدْ أَقْرَضْتُ
رَبِّي عَزَّ وَجَلَّ حَائِطًا فِيهِ سِتَّمِائَةِ نَخْلَةٍ .
Taha سوره التغابن اية64 17

Qur'an 64:17 (Pickthal translation):
   If ye lend unto Allah a goodly loan, He will double it for you and will forgive you, for Allah is Responsive, Clement.

The Book of Al-Qur'tubi interprets Qur'an 64:17 as follows:

   Muhammad sold a land in Allah's heaven to a man called Abu Al-Da'hda'h for a 600-palm-tree farm. Muhammad told Abu Al-Da'hda'h that the farm was a loan to Allah, and then he granted Abu Al-Da'hda'h a place in heaven.

The same story can be found in:
Interpretation of Ibn Kathir, V8, Page 14, 2000 Printing (Arabic), Qur'an 2:245.

Interpretation of Ibn Kathir, V1, Page 663, 1999 Printing, Kingdom of Saudi تفسير

القرآن العظيم بن كثير القرشي الدمشقي

AL 'Tabarani Al-Mu'ejam Al-Kaber, V22, Page 301 الطبراني في المعجم الكبير 22/301

We always hear Muslims speak about the Catholic pope who sold to people promises for a place in heaven. Whether this is true or not, Christians know that this is a crime of deception and theft. It is against the teachings of Jesus Christ. On the other hand, Muhammad took it upon himself to exchange land for a man's place in heaven. How about the poor who cannot afford to exchange land or money for their place in heaven?

Note that Muhammad was taking the land as his own. He did not make the exchange to donate to the poor.

Muhammad Loves Money

Sahih Al-Bukhari, book 46, Hadith 711: http://sunnah.com/bukhari/49/19

> Reported by Jaber Ibn Abdullah: There was a man who promised his slave that the slave will be freed after his (the master's) death. After the slave's master died, the Prophet called the slave and sold him. The slave died in the same year he was sold.

Look how evil this act is. God knew that this slave received a promise that he would be freed after his master's death. However, Muhammad had other ideas. He sent his men to take the slave, and then he sold him to a new master. Muhammad stole the slave's freedom from him just to make money. It's so clear that Muhammad had no morals to stop his greed. He was supposed to be this ideal man that everybody should follow as a perfect example of morals.

No Money, no private talk to Muhammad

This verse show the true color of Muhammad, he is making the Muslims think its a sin if they do not pay him, and its going be a guilt which would not be forgiven by Allah unless you do not have money at all to pay!
"O ye who believe! When ye consult the Messenger in private, spend something in charity before your private consultation. That will be best for you, and most conducive to purity (of conduct). But if ye find not (the wherewithal), Allah is Oft-Forgiving, Most Merciful". (Muhammad Yusf Ali translation)

THE DECEPTION OF ALLAH

Muhammad Ordered the Murder Of a Great Believer Out Of Jealousy

Sahih, Al-Bukhari, Book of Al-Futo'h, Hadith 4599:

Reported by Anas Ibn Malik: "There was one of us, a young man with great act of worship and faith, who is humble and does good faithful work. So we mention his name to the Prophet, but he did not recognize him. Then we described him to the Prophet, but still he did not recognize him. Then we said to the Prophet, "Oh, here he is!" The the Prophet said, "His face has the look of Satan."

So the man came and said, "Peace to you all." The Prophet said to him, "Do you think of yourself as the best man in here?" He (the young man) said, "By Allah, yes, I am." Then **he left and went inside the mosque**. The Prophet said, "Who would kill this man (for me)?" Abu Bakr said, "I will." So Abu Bakr went after the young man inside the **mosque** and found him standing in prayer. Abu Bakr said to himself, "The Prophet forbids us from killing a Muslim while he is praying!"

Then the Prophet said again, "Who would kill the man?" Omar said, "I will do it, Prophet." So Omar entered the **mosque and found the man bowing down on his face in prayer.** So Omar said, "The Prophet forbids us from killing a Muslim while he is praying. I will come back (to kill him after he is finished with his prayers)." Then the Prophet said, "Who will kill the man?" Then Ali said, "I will kill him, Prophet." So Ali entered the **mosque and found the young man had gone! Then Muhammad said, "If that man was killed, no two of my nation will disagree with each other!"**

This story can also be found in Book of Jwawame' el Fawa'ed, Volume 6, Hadith 10401: http://www.al-eman.com/Islamlib/viewchp.asp?BID=272&CID=91

Let us study this story. The man Muhammad wanted to be killed did not commit any crime. All Muslims, even the leaders, agreed that this man is a great Muslim. He is a devout believer, humble, faithful, and diligent with his prayers. He accepted Muhammad as Allah's Prophet. He was such a good Muslim that other Muslims around Muhammad thought that his goodness deserved to be recognized by the Prophet, so they mentioned his name to Muhammad. When he was called to meet with the Prophet, the man greeted him with peace. After the meeting, he again left Muhammad in peace and went straight to the mosque to pray.

We would think that Muhammad would praise this man as a good example for all Muslims, but according to the story, Muhammad wanted him killed instead. Why? The answer is, he posed a threat to Muhammad's position as the ideal Muslim. In a very short time, Muslims around Muhammad noticed and praised the man's piety. They clearly held him with much respect, but Muhammad reacted differently. During the man's short meeting with the prophet, he was asked if he thought he was the best of men. The man confidently answered, "By Allah, yes, I am." Muhammad's insecurity couldn't take it. He did not want to be compared to the piety of this man, so he ordered him to be killed.

Muhammad's treatment of this pious man shows Muhammad's ugly side. He is supposed to be a prophet, but he is more satanic than holy. If he was holy, why would he order the death of a good Muslim believer, who obeyed Allah and accepted Muhammad as a prophet? Not only that, he knows that the man is in the mosque praying, but Muhammad continues to send men to kill the man. After many unsuccessful tries, the man finally ran for his life.

Original Sin

Muslims make fun of Christianity when it comes to original sin and they say it's very wrong, but the fact is, in Islam they believe in it even more than in Christianity.

We are told many times that Islam does not accept the Christian idea of *original sin*. If that is the case, how do Muslims explain the following hadith, (Bukhari, Book 77, Hadith 611)?

> Reported Abu Huraira: Allah's Messenger said: Adam and Moses debated with each other. **Moses said to Adam, "To You Adam! You are our ancestor who displeased us and fired us out of heaven."**

- ⅄ "Moses said to Adam, "To You Adam! You are our ancestor who displeased us and fired us out of heaven." *(NOTE: Muhammad apparently confused the Garden of Eden with Heaven and thought that Adam and Eve lived in Heaven in the sky, before they sinned and were cast out).*

- ⅄ Is this not exactly what original sin is about? Muslims are out of heaven (Paradise) due to Adam's sin not Muslims' sin (Sahih Muslim, Book 016, Hadith 4156):

Allah's Messenger said, "No man who is murdered unjustly, but the share of this transgression of his also descends from the first son of Adam for he was the first to establish killing."

Now you might say this has nothing to do with original sin. The fact is, it does. When Cain, the first son of Adam, killed his brother, it was his choice. If I kill today, I do it by my own choice also. In other words, I did not kill because Cain killed, but I sinned (by killing), because sin started with Cain. Cain's capacity for sin became our inheritance, or as Muhammad put it, **we *share* the sin of Cain**.

Other hadiths even show a stronger connection (Sahih Al-Bukhari, Book 55, Hadith 547):

Abu Huraira Reported: The Messenger said, "If there were no Jewish existence, meat would never spoil and if Eve did not exist, wives would never cheat on their spouses."

This is proof that even Muhammad thinks that there is an endless connection between the sin of Eve and sin of every woman. Otherwise, how can we explain the connection between what Eve did and what women do today?

- ⋏ Eve's sin is the reason for the sins of all women, according to Muhammad.
- ⋏ It looks like the words of Muhammad are trying to make us accept that sin is the same as an inherited disease.

It is explained in Qur'an 2:35-38 that Adam was given the gift of heaven, then he sinned, which caused him to be expelled from heaven. Since Adam is the one who sinned, why are the rest of us not in heaven? If there is no connection between his sin and our sin, we should be in heaven now.

Is it the fault of Adam or is it our fault? Are we out of heaven due to the sin of Adam or due to our sin? Remember that a newborn baby has no sin yet to deserve not to be born in heaven. If given the same chance as was given to Adam and Eve, he would be out of heaven if he did wrong. It is so clear that we are out of heaven because of Adam's disobedience to God.

We also see Muhammad showing his hypocrisy by blaming women today for the sin of Eve, as if it was Eve's fault alone. It is important to remember that even in the teachings of Islam, the first sin or original sin--that is, sin committed by Adam and Eve together--is connected to our life today.

Ask No Questions. Hear No Evil.

By reciting this verse and making it into a permanent law, Muhammad successfully subjugated the minds of his followers. To question Muhammad is to be against Allah (Qur'an 5:101):

101 يَا أَيُّهَا الَّذِينَ آمَنُوا لَا تَسْأَلُوا عَنْ أَشْيَاءَ إِن تُبْدَ لَكُمْ تَسُؤْكُمْ وَإِن تَسْأَلُوا عَنْهَا حِينَ يُنَزَّلُ الْقُرْآنُ تُبْدَ لَكُمْ عَفَا اللَّهُ عَنْهَا ۗ وَاللَّهُ غَفُورٌ حَلِيمٌ

Ask not questions about things that look ugly for you in the Qur'an.

Muhammad made this threat clear with a follow-up verse that condemns anyone who asks questions as a traitor, as an apostate (Qur'an 5:102):

The people before you asked the very same questions and they became infidels.

You cannot question Muhammad and the Qur'an. If you do, you will be accused of:

1. Being an apostate (out of Islam).
2. Trying to convert others out of Islam.
3. Insulting the prophet.

Questioning Muhammad and/or the Qur'an is frowned upon. To question them is the same as saying that Muhammad must be a liar.

Anyone who is found guilty of any of the accusations I mentioned above can be punished with a death sentence.

When you find yourself asking what Muhammad fears from questions, you find your answer in Qur'an 5:102. It clearly tells you that you will leave Islam when you ask questions. Why? Because (a) Muhammad has no convincing answers, (b) the Qur'an is not convincing and (c) the Qur'an is not clear and will never be clear.

Only Allah Knows

The Qur'an itself confirms that no one knows what a huge portion of it means except Allah. Only Allah knows (Qur'an 3:7, Usama Dakdok translation):

> He is who has sent down on you the book (Qur'an); some of its verses are decisive. Those are the mother of the book and the others are ambiguous. So those whose hearts deviate, so they will follow what is ambiguous of it, desiring the sedition and desiring its interpretation, and no one knows its interpretation except Allah. And those deeply rooted in knowledge say, "We believe in it, all of it from our lord."...

What we get from this verse completes what we said before in 5:101, that no one should ask questions. Qur'an 3:7 clearly tells us that Muhammad himself has no answers.

The Author of Confusion

Muhammad shot himself in the foot when he invented Qur'an 3:7. By saying that no one— NO ONE except Allah —knows the meaning of the majority of verses in the Qur'an, it means Muhammad himself has no right to interpret them. This leaves his followers with no one to turn to for real explanations.

- Since no one understands a huge portion of the **Qur'an except Allah,** then all interpretations of all the verses in that ambiguous portion are wrong.
- Since all interpretations are wrong, then all of Muhammad's and everyone else's interpretations are also wrong.
- Since all of Muhammad's and everyone else's interpretations are wrong, then what's the use of revealing all those ambiguous verses?

The only answer Allah gives us is that they can be used by "those whose hearts deviate, so they will follow what is ambiguous of it, desiring the sedition and desiring its interpretation." So, did Allah reveal those verses only to give malicious people something to use to confuse and deceive other people? Allah, in this verse, admits that his book is full of confusion, and that he is the author of confusion.

People will naturally want and try to interpret Allah's words to understand what he wants from his people, but they will fail. Allah never offered to guide anyone who wants to know and understand his words. He discourages questions. He only wants people to understand that he knows what he means, and all they need to do is believe that he spoke to them through Muhammad.

We can safely say then, that in order for you to be considered knowledgeable, all you need to do is believe blindly. Earn your knowledge by rote memorization, not by asking questions. This is how Muhammad indoctrinated Muslims into simply memorizing the Qur'an instead of studying it. He also kept them away from asking questions and reflecting on the meaning of the verses by keeping them busy with praying five times a day and constantly fighting wars for him.

Don't Ask, Memorize

One example of how Muhammad encouraged Muslims to memorize verses is when he promised that those who could recite the ninety-nine names of Allah would be granted passage to heaven (Sahih Bukhari, Book 75: Number 419; Bukhari Book 50, Hadith 894).

> Allah's Messenger revealed: Your God Allah has ninety-nine names, one hundred names minus one, and whoever learns by heart and recites them will go to Paradise...

But wait, there's more! Book of Zad Al-Ma'ad, Volume 1 Page 57-59:

إنا لله عز وجل ألف اسم وللنبي صلى الله عليه وسلم ألف اسم ، قاله أبو الخطاب بن دحية ومقصودة
1/57-59 بتصرف من زاد المعاد0الأوصاف

> Allah, all praiseworthy, has one thousand names and the prophet has one thousand names.

Notice here

Muhammad has 1000 names	Allah has 1000 names

Muhammad's intention is clear: Memorizing is much more favorable to Allah than asking questions in order to understand.

Other examples include seventy rules to follow before going to the bathroom; the same before prayer, before sex, before eating, after eating, and numerous other rules—all of these to keep Muslims busy all their lives asking silly questions about what is halal (permissible/lawful) and what is haraam

THE DECEPTION OF ALLAH

(forbidden) under Islamic law.

If you speak Arabic and watch Islamic TV shows, you will hear the funniest and silliest questions and comments like:

- Is it halal to buy Christian underwear?
- Is it halal to eat ice cream, which we know is the idea of infidels?
- I am a married Muslim woman, and I have six children with my husband. Is it halal for me to kiss him first or do I have to wait for him to start?
- When I was having sex with my wife, I drank some of her breast milk. Is she haraam to me now?!
- I am a left-handed man. Does that make Satan control me, eat with me, and sleep with me? (Sahih Muslim, Book 23, Hadith 5007):

  Allah's Messenger, may Allah pray on him, said: "Do not feed yourself with your left hand, since Satan eats with his left hand."

- I walked with one sandal the other day after losing it at the mosque, and the prophet forbids us to walk with one shoe. Am I going to hell? Note: It is forbidden that a man should eat with his

  left hand or walk with one sandal. (Sahih Muslim, Book 24, Hadith 5234).

- **Caller**: "I am a Muslim and sometimes I read books in the bathroom while I'm doing the call of nature. Can I take the Qur'an with me inside the   bathroom?
  Scholar: No, the bathroom is a dirty place, and the Qur'an is holy. You cannot do that. It's forbidden.
- **Caller**: I memorized the Qur'an since I was eight years old. What should I do then—leave my brain out when I go to the bathroom?

Review

- Muhammad could not give correct interpretations of the Qur'an, but he was given the authority of God on earth.
- If Muhammad could not understand what Allah was saying, how did he know if he was executing Allah's orders correctly?
- Muhammad provided the verses in the Qur'an, but he could not explain the majority of them.

⅄ Muhammad forbade asking questions about verses that were not clear and made Islam look bad. So, are we supposed to ask questions about verses that are clear to us? Is this a joke?

⅄ Since Muhammad himself is ignorant about the verses in the Qur'an, this probably explains why Allah said in Qur'an 62:2 that he sent an ignorant to the ignorant!

This reminds me of a verse in the Bible that proves that the Qur'an cannot be from God (1 Corinthians 14:33):

For God is not the author of confusion, but of peace, as in all churches of the saints.

Gay and Lesbian Justice in the Qur'an

Lesbian Punishment in the Qur'an.

سورة النساء , An-Nisa, Qur'an 4:15:
For those who are lesbian of your women, bring four witnesses on them, to testify against them. Then jail them in their houses until they die, and find His own ways.

If women are lesbians, the punishment is jailing them until they die. Is the punishment for gay men the same?

Punishment of Gay men in Qur'an

سورة النساء , An-Nisa, Qur'an 4:16:

If two of your men among you are guilty of homosexuality, punish them both. If they both repent, leave them alone, for Allah is accepting of repentance, Most Merciful.

What we notice in here is:

1. Gay men will not be jailed.
2. They have the chance to repent.
3. Punishment is easy for them, even if they do not repent (beating them with sandals) as we see in Ibn 'Abbas interpretation of Qur'an 4:16:

Punish both of them, with insults and beatings with sandals; but if they repent of this, leave them alone.

Gay Men	Lesbian Women
Beating with sandals	Beating is part of beating the wife in Islam (Qur'an 4:34)
They can repent	No repentance
If they repent leave them alone (no more insult)	They will be jailed until they die

Is that really a rule of a god? If Allah views this as a crime, shouldn't it be the same for a man with a man and a woman with a woman? Why is the punishment totally different; very harsh for women and so easy to men?

Some Muslims will say to you, "Oh, this verse was abrogated later." It does not matter if your god keeps changing his mind. This is not the issue. God is about justice, but this god is not fair at all.

Why did Allah abrogate this verse?
Did he find himself so wrong that he repented?

A Muslim Cannot Take Even His Own Family as Friends

If someone converts to Islam, he has no choice but to hate his own family and he cannot have them as friends as long they are from the non-believers (non-Muslims) (Qur'an 9:23):

O you who believe! Take not your fathers nor your brethren as friends or protectors if they obtain happiness in disbelief rather than believe [Islam]. Those of you who take them for friends, they should blame no one but themselves.

⋏ A Muslim cannot give you a speech that his god means the enemy, when he speaks about not taking them as friends, because it's so clear, that your father and mother, brothers, or sisters love you, even if they reject your faith.

- ⋏ Therefore, why can't they even be just friends?
- ⋏ Note here there is no condition saying if they are bad, take them not as friends. It's an order for all Muslims to practice such a thing if they have such of a case.

Does Allah Love You as a Christian?

I always hear Muslims saying that Islam does not hate Christians. They quote to you verses which have been abrogated. Abrogate means to abolish by formal or official means; annul by an authoritative act; repeal, to abrogate a law. With Islam, it's still in the Qur'an, but Muslims cannot follow it anymore.

Let's see how much Allah is in love with the Christians. Let me show you in Qur'an 5:51; Allah is saying:

> Take not Christian and Jew as friends and protectors; they are friends to each other, and if any of you take them as friends, he is one of them and unjust to himself (which means he is out of Islam and he will be punished by death).

Then this is this command in Qur'an 9:29:

> Fight those who believe not in Allah nor the Judgment Day, nor forbid what Allah and His Messenger order to be forbidden, nor accept the religion of truth (Islam), of the People of the Book (Christian and Jew), until they pay the Jizyah with willing submission, and feel themselves humiliated and subdued.

I explained how Muslims have to fight us until we either convert to Islam, or pay them monthly fees to stay alive, and that we have to pay it with humiliation, like dogs.

Allah shows his amazing love to the Christians in this next verse! I hope every Christian will remember it forever. You need clear proof that Islam hates Christians, and this is one of the best verses to prove that point, if you want to expose Islam. Qur'an 5:14:

> From those, who call **themselves Christians,** We did take a covenant, but they forgot part of scriptures that We (Allah) sent to them: therefore We **estranged them, with enmity and hatred between the one and the other**, until the Judgment day. Soon Allah will show them what it is they were doing.

وَمِنَ الَّذِينَ قَالُوا إِنَّا نَصَارَىٰ أَخَذْنَا مِيثَاقَهُمْ فَنَسُوا حَظًّا مِّمَّا ذُكِّرُوا بِهِ فَأَغْرَيْنَا بَيْنَهُمُ الْعَدَاوَةَ وَالْبَغْضَاءَ إِلَىٰ يَوْمِ الْقِيَامَةِ ۚ وَسَوْفَ يُنَبِّئُهُمُ اللَّهُ بِمَا كَانُوا يَصْنَعُونَ

In Qur'an 5:14, Allah has a plan for you as a Christian. The plan is so clear that Allah will fuel us with hate and enmity between Christians (**estranged them, with enmity and hatred).**

Let us study this plan of war; Allah's war on Christians

1. Allah will not make us hate the Muslims (Christians do not hate Muslims).
2. Allah will make us hate and fight each other as Christians! Allah has been so successful for a long time in this war, and many Christians are following the plan of Allah. We see Christians attacking each other's churches, but they will never open their lips against Islam.

What I am trying to say is that it's the plan of Satan to prevent us from uniting as Christians (Orthodox, Protestant, and Catholic). IT IS Allah's plan and he is saying it in clear words, "I will divide you and make you hate each other, so that I will make the Church of Jesus a divided kingdom."

Remember, Christ said in Matthew 12:25 (KJV):

And Jesus knew their thoughts, and said unto them, Every kingdom divided against itself is brought to desolation; and every city or house divided against itself shall not stand:

It's painful to see Christians speaking evilly against each other, but when you ask these priests or these ministers about Islam, they do not dare say one word! It's the plan of Allah, the Anti-Christ, to divide us. Whoever he helps in that direction is working for Allah. Read this verse again, carefully, and tell me if I am wrong.

Qur'an 5:14:

As for those who call themselves Christians, We did take a pledge, but they forgot a good part of scriptures that we sent to them. Therefore, We (Allah) **estranged them, with animosity and hatred** between the one and the other, until the Judgment day. And soon will Allah show them what it is they were doing.

We should be believers and followers of Christ! Not a man. Not a bishop. Not a minister. No name, but His name! Why should we follow the sinners? See Romans 3:23 (KJV):

For all have sinned, and come short of the glory of God;

Unity with Christ is the way to his kingdom. This is what Islam fears; all of us being the good fruit of Jesus the Christ. See Romans 3:28:

Therefore we conclude that a man is justified by faith without the deeds of the law.

When Jesus comes, he will not ask you the name of your church, but for the fruit. Without the good fruit, there is hypocrisy. This is why Jesus said (Matthew 7:16):

Ye shall know them by their fruits. Do men gather grapes of thorns, or figs of thistles?

Also see Galatians 5:22-23:

But the fruit of the Spirit is love, joy, peace, patience, kindness, goodness, faithfulness, gentleness, self-control; against such things there is no law.

This is how we know Islam is false and from Satan. From their fruits, not only words. Most of them are liars in word. They speak skillfully, but show me your fruit and I will tell you who you are.

What I am trying to say to all who consider themselves Christian, whether Protestant, Catholic or Orthodox, do not divide the Church of Christ, for all of us are one in Him. As you see, Allah is targeting all of us, not a named church. We make Christ sad when we are not united. Do not let leaders, for their own glory, make us and turn us to something far from what Christ wants us to be. If you adhere to the plan of Allah, are you working for him?! It's a good question, to which you know the answer. See 1 Corinthians 12:13 (KJV):

For by one Spirit are we all baptized into one body, whether we be Jews or Gentiles, whether we be bond or free; and have been all made to drink into one Spirit.

Allah and the Jews; How Much Does Allah Hate Them?

Sahih Muslim, Book 41, Hadith 6981:

Messenger of Allah said: "You will be in fighting with the Jews, and you will murder them until even a rock would say: 'Move towards here, Muslim, there is

56

a Jew, he is hiding himself behind me, come and slaughter him.'"

Sahih Muslim Book 41, Hadith 6985:

Messenger of Allah said: "The judgment hour would not come until the Muslims fight against the Jews, and the Muslims would kill them all, and if a Jew hides behind a stone or a tree and the stone or the tree would shout saying: 'Oh Muslim, there is a Jew behind me; come and kill him;' but the tree called Gharqaad would not say, for it is the tree of the Jews!"

Even the rocks (the Muslim's rocks) will report the Jewish men, women and children if they try to hide, so that the Muslims will do their duty and kill them all. And note here, there is a Jewish tree!

Islam and Israel

One of the most famous conflicts in the world today is the so-called Israeli-Palestinian conflict. For most of us, all we know is that Israel is fighting with the Arab world over the land. This is true, but it is not the whole story. Most of those who debate about the conflict talk from a political point of view, and as a result try to find political solutions. Our world leaders show their ignorance by ignoring the fact that the conflict is beyond political. In fact, there is no solution for it except war, and only war. I'm not saying that I would love for a war to break out. I am simply stating a fact. Let's look at the following hadiths.

Sahih Muslim, Book 41, Hadith 6981:

The Messenger of Allah said, "You will be in fighting with the Jews, and you will slaughter them until even a rock will say, 'Move towards here, Muslim. There is a Jew hiding himself behind me. Come and slaughter him.'"

Sahih Muslim, Book 41, Hadith 6985:

The Messenger of Allah said, "The judgment hour will not approach until the Muslims fight against the Jews and the Muslims will slaughter them all, and if a Jew hides behind a rock or a tree, the rock or tree will scream saying, 'Oh Muslim, over here is a Jew behind me. Come and kill him,' but the tree called Gharqaad will not say, seeing that it is the tree of the Jews!"

According to Muhammad, even rocks will betray all Jews—men, women, and children—who will hide behind them to make sure that no Jew will survive the slaughter. Muhammad doesn't call for mercy. He calls for complete elimination of Jews. Knowing this, how are we supposed to be convinced that Muslims are willing to look for a peaceful solution to the Israeli-Palestinian conflict? This is something that will happen, and no one has ever been able to stop it from the time of Muhammad until the Day of Judgment.

Muhammad always based his religion on hate. It's the fuel of Islam. He tried to take the side of the Jews against the Christians with the hope that the Jews would like him for it. When that did not work, he tried to make himself look like a friend to the Christians by attacking the Jews, this time hoping to win the Christians.

In Qur'an 5:82:

> You will find that the most ones who hate you are the Jewish and those who take associates with Allah, as well as the kindest people to Muslims are the ones who call themselves Christians.

(سورة المائدة , Al-Maeda, 5:82)
لَتَجِدَنَّ أَشَدَّ النَّاسِ عَدَاوَةً لِّلَّذِينَ آمَنُوا الْيَهُودَ وَالَّذِينَ أَشْرَكُوا وَلَتَجِدَنَّ أَقْرَبَهُم مَّوَدَّةً لِّلَّذِينَ آمَنُوا الَّذِينَ قَالُوا إِنَّا نَصَارَىٰ

Muhammad uses the so-called revelations from Allah to drive his political agenda. It shows how he switches sides whenever he feels like it, and Allah switches sides along with him. See Qur'an 2:62:

> Those who believe and the Jews in addition to Christians, who do good have no worry. Allah will give them their prize, and they will not have misery or sadness.

Now in Qur'an 2:62, both the Jews and the Christians are good. They will even go to heaven.

Muhammad's Stages of Taking Down his Enemy

I. Muhammad, the Man of Peace

At this stage, Muhammad was nothing. He had no power, no army, and no followers. In the first thirteen years of his prophet-hood, he only had 70 followers. He had no choice, but to remain a peaceful man.

Most of the people who became his followers later were slaves as narrated by 'Ammar bin Yasir in the following Hadith. (Sahih Al-Bukhari, Book 58, Hadith 197):

> I saw the Messenger of Allah, and accompanying him were the only ones who converted to Islam, five slaves, two women, and Abu Bakr.

Notice that his five followers were still called slaves even after they accepted Islam. Muhammad still considered his brothers in faith as his slaves.

For sure, the slaves had no choice but to convert to Islam. In the beginning, Muhammad manipulated the slaves into becoming Muslims and fighting for him by promising them freedom afterwards. This is what happened to the poor man, Bilal, who converted to Islam and fought for Muhammad, but was never granted his freedom.

II. The Hijra Stage (Immigration)

This stage is exactly what Muslims practice today.

To get ready for a big war in someone else's land, they gather themselves in that land to plan and prepare for the attack until their population is big enough to establish an army. This is what Osama bin Laden and Al-Qa'ida did when they went to Afghanistan. They immigrated there to get ready for the big attack, and when they were ready, they attacked without mercy—exactly as Muhammad did in his time. At this stage, Muslims get their income from thievery.

Through thievery, they accomplish two goals:

⚔   They collect wealth by taking other people's money, animals, and goods.

⅄   They instill terror in the hearts of the disbelievers.

Instilling terror is fundamental in Islam. It is one of the best and quickest ways to take down an enemy regardless of his size. When fear is in his heart, even an elephant will bow down to a mouse (which reminds me of Obama bowing to the king of Saudi Arabia). Muslims understand the significant change in the enemy's life when he is afraid. They know that all they need to do is to be patient and wait for the fear to spread and take hold. With fear in his heart, the enemy will never win. (As long as America is in fear, it will never win.)

Before he became the God-on-earth in Arabia, Muhammad made more than 56 attacks against merchants, 28 of those attacked were called Gazwah (caravan riders).

III. Stage of Total War; Either You Are With Me or Against Me

In this final stage, Muhammad was no longer weak. He proclaimed his agenda in more open and clear words. Anyone who did not bow down to him was killed. All who refused him, especially those who opposed him—like the Jews, were killed.

The Qur'an Identifies the Rightful Inhabitants of Israel

We always hear the same arguments from either side of the Israeli-Palestinian debate. The Muslims say the Israelis took away their land, and the Israelis say it's rightfully theirs since Biblical times. Unfortunately, the world is filled with liberal media exemplified by TV shows like Oprah's, who does not know until now where coffee comes from, or shows like Jon Stewart's, which make us laugh, but I am not sure at what. Beyond that is the YouTube propaganda. Regardless of numerous outlets for information, none of them are honest enough to discuss what is truly in the heart of the conflict.

Let us do a real study and find out who really belongs in Israel. We will not use the he-said-she-said argument. We will present facts, and our facts will show that Israel belongs to the Jews. We already know that Israel belongs to the Jews according to the Bible, but we will set aside the Bible and get our evidence from the Qur'an itself. This is the best way to shut up the liberals and Qur'an worshipers who do not dare to say that the Qur'an is wrong.

Many of you do not know that the Qur'an declares in very clear words that Israel, or Palestine as some insist on calling it, is the land of the Jews. Let us read the following passage together:

Qur'an Chapter 5

Qur'an 5:20-26 (Usama Dakdok translaton):

20 And when Moses said to his people, "O my people, remember the grace of Allah on you when he made prophets among you. And he made you kings, and he gave you what he did not give to anyone in the world.

21 "O my people enter the holy land which Allah has prescribed for you, and do not turn away your back, so you will be turned back as losers."

22 They said, "O Moses, surely in it are giant people, and surely we will not enter it until they come out of it. So if they come out of it, so surely we will enter."

23 Then said two men among the fearers, Allah was gracious above them, "Enter on them the door, so when you enter, so surely you will be victorious in Allah, so dependable, if you were believers."

24 They said, "O Moses, surely we will never enter it as long as they are in it, so go you and your lord. So engage in war, surely we are sitting down here."

25 He said, "My lord, surely I do not own anything except myself and my brother, so differentiate between us and the transgressing people."

26 He said, "So surely it (the Promised Land) is forbidden to them forty years; they will be lost on the earth. So do not grieve on the transgressing people."

Now let us study each verse:

Verse 20 - We learn that the Jews are the chosen people of God, not only in the Bible, but also in the Qur'an, as we read, He (Allah) "gave you what he did not give to anyone in the world."

Verse 21 – Allah orders the Jews to engage in war and take the land away from the inhabitants. He warns them not to turn away from war or he will punish them. "O my people enter the holy land which Allah has prescribed for you, and do not turn away your back so you will be turned back as losers."

Verse 22 – The peaceful Jews refuse to enter and engage in war, but Allah wanted war and bloodshed. They said, "O Moses, surely in it are giant people, and surely we will not enter it until they come out of it. So if they come out of it,

so surely we will enter."
Verse 23 – Of all the Jews, two of them agreed to go to war. Allah was pleased with them and promised them victory.

Verse 24 – The Jews continue to refuse to go to war. They asked Moses why his Lord loves war. They told Moses to go with his Lord, but they are staying behind. They said, "O Moses, surely we will never enter it as long as they are in it, so go you and your lord. So engage in war, surely we are sitting down here."

Verse 25 – Allah gives names and titles for the bad ones and the good ones. Read with me. "He said, 'My lord, surely I do not own anything except myself and my brother, so differentiate between us and the transgressing people.'" Here, Allah made a judgment over the Jews for refusing to go and kill for the inhabitants of the land. He called them **transgressing people.**

Verse 26 – Allah becomes angry because the Jews refuse to fight and kill the giants. He punishes them with 40 years of wandering in the desert.

Now it's time to ask some questions. The Qur'an identified the inhabitants of Palestine as giants. These cannot be the same people who are called Palestinians today, because they are short and smaller than average in body size. So, who are the Palestinians? Where did they come from? The answer is easy. They are the Muslims who entered the land with Omar Ibn El-Ka'tab in the year 717 A.D. (Read the Pact of Omar.) Yasser Arafat cannot be a descendant of the giants because he is not even five feet tall.

Why did they all choose this land and called it a "holy land" (Qur'an 5:21), when no prophet of Allah lived in it yet?

Allah, himself, declared Israel as the land prepared specifically for the Jews (Qur'an 5:21), even if it meant taking it by force from the inhabitants. Muslims today say that it is not right, it's ugly, disgusting, a crime, and not human to take Israel (Palestine) from the Palestinians. Would the Muslims dare to say that Allah's decision to have the giants killed and driven away from Israel is not right, ugly, disgusting, a crime, and inhuman?

What is unfair is for Allah to punish the Jews by wandering through the desert for 40 years as a result of their refusal to go to war against the giants. It shows that in order for the Jews to be right in the eyes of Allah, they needed to kill the giants and take the holy land. Then and only then would Allah like the Jews.

Daily Curse for the Jews and Christians

Notice that Muslims curse the Jews and Christians five times a day. Qur'an 1:7 describes both the Jews and Christians as the cursed ones:

> In the way of those whom You have bestowed Your grace, not like those they lost (Christian) or who earned Your anger (the Jews).

The Jews today are cursed by Muslims five times everyday for not killing all the giants (Palestinians?).

I asked a Muslim scholar in one of thousands of debates I have had, why it was okay for Allah back then to kill the giants. He said that the giants at that time were not Muslims, so it was the duty of the believers to kill them. In Islam, that is called justice. I call it hypocrisy.

Here are my concluding points:

- Why did Allah choose this land for the Jews? Why did he assign the land to them?
- If Allah is the true God, he would have known that giving the land to the Jews would be a big mistake, and that his choice would create a big war today. Since he was the one who assigned the land to the Jews, then the bloodshed we see there today is his own crime.
- It is so clear that Allah did not know at that time that the ones who would live in the holy land one day would be Muslims. Like I said, the giants cannot be the same people who live there today.

- Allah never mentioned the name of the Palestinians in the Qur'an. Was it because he was short of information?
- The most significant point we get from all this is that the Qur'an itself gives proof that the claim of Muslims over Israel is false. Allah clearly states that Israel belongs to the Jews.

Why Allah Turned the Jews Into Pigs and Monkeys

Qur'an 2:65:

وَلَقَدْ عَلِمْتُمُ الَّذِينَ اعْتَدَوْا مِنكُمْ فِي السَّبْتِ فَقُلْنَا لَهُمْ كُونُوا قِرَدَةً خَاسِئِينَ
(سورة البقرة , Al-Ba'qara, Qur'an 2:65)

You have been informed about those who transgressed on Saturday, so we said to them, "Be as filthy monkeys."

Qur'an 5:60:

We made from them the monkeys and the pigs.

I suppose Allah was angry with the Jews who went fishing on a Saturday, the Sabbath day, so he cursed them by turning them into pigs and monkeys. My question is, why hasn't even one Jewish man or woman during the last few thousand years been transformed into a monkey or a pig?

Note that Allah never released the Jews from the Sabbath day. Note also that the curse is still active today. Take a Jewish guy fishing with you next Saturday and bring a video camera along with you. Watch if your Jewish friend becomes a monkey or pig. If he remains a man at the end of the Sabbath day, then Allah's curse must be ineffective.

Since Allah does not want Jews to do any work on Saturdays, why does he allow Muslims to work all of Friday?

Allah transformed the Jews to monkeys and pigs for fishing on the Sabbath. Here is the story in Qur'an 7:163:

Question them regarding the village standing close by the sea. Behold! They misbehaved in the concern of the Sabbath. For on the day of their Sabbath their whale did come to them, but on the dayother than Saturday, they came not: this is how We arrange a trouble to them, on behalf of their sin.

Let us read Ibn Kathir's interpretation of Qur'an 7:163 (Ibn Kathir, 2002 Printing, Published by Dar-'Tiba, V2, Page 163):

تفسير ابن كثير
163إسماعيل بن عمر بن كثير القرشي الدمشقي المجلد الثاني ص
دار طيبة
م2002هـ / 1422سنة النشر:

ابن عباس، وقوله: {إذ يعدون في السبت} أي يعتدون فيه ويخالفون أمر الله فيه لهم بالوصاة به إذ ذاك {إذ تأتيهم حيتانهم يوم سبتهم شرعاً}، قال ابن عباس: أي ظاهرة على الماء، {ويوم لا يسبتون لا تأتيهم كذلك نبلوهم} أي نختبرهم بإظهار السمك لهم على ظهر الماء في اليوم المحرم عليهم صيده، وإخفائها عنهم في اليوم الحلال لهم صيده.

While their fish came to them floating to the top of the water on the Sabbath day, and being visible on top of the water, according to Al-Dahhak, who reported it from Ibn `Abbas Ibn Jarir who said, "Allah's statement (but on the day other than Saturday, they came not: this is how We arrange a trouble to them, on behalf of their sin) means, this is how We tested them by making the fish swim close to the surface of the water, on the day which they were prohibited to fish. And in remainder of the week, the fish would be hidden from them on the day when they were allowed to fish, (this is how We arrange a trouble to them,) so that We test them...

The double standard of Allah is shown in this story (Qur'an 2:17):

Allah hath forbidden to you dead meat, and blood, and the flesh of swine, and that on which any other name hath been invoked besides that of Allah. However, but whoever is driven to a necessity (like starving) not desiring, nor exceeding the order of Allah, no sin shall be upon him; surely, Allah is Forgiving, Merciful.

- So it's fine for a Muslim to eat pork if he has to break the law of Allah due to his hunger.
- Then why is Allah not being at all merciful toward the poor Jews, whom he caused to suffer hunger six days a week, and afterwards the fish come only on Saturday. How many weeks can the Jews fast with no food at all? Which means, it was Allah's own handiwork and crime, and subsequently he desired to punish them for having to fish on the Sabbath?

- Allah told them not to fish on Saturday, but he made the fish come only on that day!
- How will these poor men feed their family six days out of the week if Allah makes the fish disappear and he then makes them come to the top of water on Saturday only?
- Is that justice? Allah is playing with the Jews, forcing them into hunger so they will break his orders; and subsequently he exacts his punishment on them by transforming them into rats and pigs and monkeys!
- It's very clear that the one who made up this story has an evil mind, explaining to us that Allah makes us suffer only for his human type of amusement—the enjoyment of watching little children get so hungry six days a week, all just to enhance his own self-esteem.

65

Even Rats are Made from the Jews!

Sahih Al-Bukhari, Book 54, Hadith 524:

> It is reported by Abu Huraira: The Prophet said, "A clan of children of Israel was lost. No person knows what they acted. However, I do not see them except that they were cursed (by Allah) and transfigured into rats, because if you put the milk of a she-camel in front of a rat, it will not drink it, but if you put in front of it the milk of a sheep, it will drink it." I told this to Ka'eb who asked me, "Did you hear this from the Prophet?" I said, "Yes." Ka'ebe asked me the same question several times; I said to Ka'eb "Do I read the Torah? (i.e. I tell you this from the Prophet.)"

Let us study the logic of Muhammad concerning what an animal will not accept. What an animal does not accept as drink means the animal is from the same ethnic group as you. But Allah transformed them into that kind of animal as punishment for some wrong deed based on this?

We are going to use the logic of this genius discovery of Muhammad to learn another mystery:

Donkeys do not drink whiskey or alcohol, and Muslims do not drink alcohol. Therefore, donkeys used to be human Muslims and Allah turned them into donkeys?

Remember, I am not calling Muslims donkeys, absolutely not, but I am trying to be smart like Muhammad by using his logic. After all, isn't he the best example to follow?

Then I have a question about how Muhammad even came up with such an idea? Muhammad cannot stop thinking about the Jews. Even when he ordered Muslims to do things, he based his orders not on Allah's teaching or right and wrong, but on doing the opposite of the Jews, as we see in many hadith. A few examples follow.

Muhammad Creates Rules, Not by Allah's Teaching, But Just to Oppose the Jews.

Sunan Abu-Dawood, Book 2, Hadith 0652:

Reported Aws ibn 'Thabit al-Ansari: "The messenger of Allah said: 'Act differently from the Jews, on behalf of they do not pray in their sandals or their shoes.'"

Can Muhammad not tell them how to pray without remembering what the Jews do? Why should Muslims be the opposite of the Jews in all things? It gets even funnier with the coming hadith (Sunan Abu-Dawood, Book 20, Hadith 3170):

Reported by 'Ubadah Ibn Assamet: "The messenger of Allah used to stand up during the funeral until the corpse was placed in the grave. A learned Jew once passed him while he (Muhammad) was standing by a grave during a funeral, subsequently the Jew said: 'This is how we do (meaning praying standing).' The Prophet sat down and said: 'Sit down and act differently from them (the Jews).'"

- ⚰ Is this real? Muhammad always prayed in the funeral standing until a Jew said this is how we do it, and then he changed to the opposite?
- ⚰ Does that mean Muhammad was wrong all the time that he performed his prayer standing at graves?
- ⚰ Why did Muhammad not ask Allah to teach him about the right way to do prayers instead of acting like a child when "The Prophet sat down and said: 'Sit down and act differently from them'"

Another example is in Sahih Al-Bukhari. Book 56, Hadith 668:

It reported by Abu Huraira: Allah's messenger said, "The Jews and the Christians do not dye their gray hair, as a result you shall do the opposite of what they do (which means dye your gray hair and beards)."

It's so clear that Islam is deliberately made to be the opposite of what Christianity and Judaism stand for. As a result, if a Muslim comes to you and says, "We have the same god," he is trying to fool you. He knows that whatever we believe or whatever we do, his prophet in every act and teaching chose to be the opposite, not because we are wrong, but just to be the opposite of us.

Peace Agreement in Islam

I am not sure if you understand how dangerous Islam is. As you've seen, Allah hates Christians and orders the Muslims to fight them. There are about three billion humans who are Christian and have to be fought by Muslims. The choices are to pay in submission, convert or be killed. Add to that what the last hadith revealed. What we hear about Islam and Muslims from political leaders, like Obama and other western liars, is ignorance. Their foolishness is making them blind. All they care about is just pushing it away until tomorrow to see what is coming!

What is coming is ugly. The earth will be covered by blood, for Islam is a beast hungry for blood. Some might say, "What about some Islamic countries that signed a peace agreement with Israel?" Yes, it's true, but it's temporary, until the Muslims have the power to take Israel and the entire West down, as we see Allah ordered in the Qur'an. It is explained in Qur'an 47:35:

فَلَا تَهِنُوا وَتَدْعُوا إِلَى السَّلْمِ وَأَنتُمُ الأَعْلَوْنَ وَاللَّهُ مَعَكُمْ وَلَن يَتِرَكُمْ أَعْمَالَكُمْ

(سورة محمد , chapter of Muhammad, Qur'an 47:35)

> Cry not and ask not for peace as long you have the uppermost and the strength and Allah will reward you for your deeds.

It's so clear that Muslims are not allowed to go for peace, because Islam is against any kind of peace. There are conditions when Muslims can agree about peace, and Allah approves it as long as it's temporary.
If the Muslims cannot beat the Jews, it's okay to have a treaty. Muhammad did this himself with the Christians and the Jews. He did this when he was weak. If he had gone to war, he would have lost, and they would have been able to kill him easily, so Muhammad signed a peace agreement and then broke it when he became strong as we see in Qur'an 9:1:

بَرَاءَةٌ مِّنَ اللَّهِ وَرَسُولِهِ إِلَى الَّذِينَ عَاهَدتُّم مِّنَ الْمُشْرِكِينَ

(سورة التوبة , At-Taubah, 1)

> Freedom from any obligation or promise or treaty of peace from Allah and His messenger toward those of the Mushrikeen (pagans and Christians and Jews) with whom ye made a treaty.

As simple as that is, why would any country in the world trust a treaty made by Muslims? It's based on foolishness and ignorance. This is what Israel is facing now. They are being forced by the USA to do such a thing. Soon Iranian Muslims will have their nukes, which some Muslim countries already have. I guess the party of bloodshed will start in less than 25 years. It's just a matter of time when we will see the Muslim population growing fast in the West, and then they will force their rules over the world. They might even be able to use western countries' nukes to destroy Israel, and then they could nuke any country that does not accept Islam. I am saying, if they could!

I am sure that if Muslims had an army as powerful as the United States, they would make one speech saying, "You've got three days. Either you convert or you die."

This is why Muhammad sent three letters to the three kings of the three largest kingdoms around him at that time, threatening them to convert or go to war! Terror was the way for Muhammad to have victory. Read Qur'an 8:12:

إِذْ يُوحِي رَبُّكَ إِلَى الْمَلَائِكَةِ أَنِّي مَعَكُمْ فَثَبِّتُوا الَّذِينَ آمَنُوا ۚ سَأُلْقِي فِي قُلُوبِ الَّذِينَ كَفَرُوا الرُّعْبَ فَاضْرِبُوا فَوْقَ الْأَعْنَاقِ وَاضْرِبُوا مِنْهُمْ كُلَّ بَنَانٍ

(سورة الأنفال , Al-Anfal, 12)

When Allah inspires the angels that I am with you (Muslims) **I will cast terror** in the heart of the Disbelievers, so cut their neck and every finger tip of them.

This is how the Muslims made George W. Bush go to the mosque like a puppy. The same happened for all who came after, even from Hillary Clinton to Obama. Many after them will bow to Muslim kings, because they are afraid of the Islamic terror.

Maybe you do not understand what I am trying to say yet! How many movies have been made against Christ? How many books? How many lies? At the same time, who dares to speak or to make a movie against Muhammad?! Why, even in Hollywood, did they have a conference to **change the way they look at the Islamic world**, and then forced all movie makers to **make positive movies about Muslims**?

Terror is powerful! They will try to silence anyone who will speak the truth.

Can Muslims Lie in Islam?

The normal answer should be no way, right? It does not make sense that any religion would allow that! The fact is hard to believe, but it's the truth. Islam permits lying!

There are two kinds of lies in Islam:

- Lies to non-Muslims about anything. Especially about Islam (to cover up bad things).
- Lies to Muslims.

We will take a look at the first principle in Qur'an 3:28:

> The believers are not allowed to take disbelievers to be their friends in instead of the believers. Whoso does that, he hath no connection with Allah, unless (it be) that ye but guard yourselves against them, taking to as it where security. Allah warns you from himself. Unto Allah is your destiny.

This verse is often seen as the primary verse that sanctions deception towards non-Muslims. Believers (Muslims) cannot take disbelievers (infidels/non-Muslims) for friends and allies instead of believers. Whoever does this shall have no relationship left with God unless you "**guard yourselves against them,**" with some translations adding, "**taking precautions.**" This is something that all Muslims know. It's called Taqiyya, تقية (defensive deception). If we ask Muslims about lying, they will recite the same verse when answering you. They will say this is about war, as if someone is an enemy who puts a sword to your neck asking you if you are Muslim. If you say yes, he will kill you! Allah is saying you can lie to save yourself from them.

Is that true? YES and NO!

The verse gives Muslims all kinds of rights to protect themselves. Muslims have been told that <u>all non-Muslims are enemies</u>. They can lie to their enemies. This is how they always see you. As an enemy, not as you see them.

If I have a Muslim living next door to me, I am an enemy as revealed in Qur'an 5:51 (Yousuf Ali translation):

> O ye who believe! Take not the Jews and the Christians for your friends and protectors: They are but friends and protectors to each other, and he among you that turns to them (for friendship) is of them. Verily, Allah guides not the unjust people.

But, you may say, "He (my neighbor) calls me every morning saying to me, 'Good morning, my friend!'" Well, this is Taqiyya. It's a lie to survive until they have the upper hand. To prove my point, let's see the verse and the Muslims' interpretation of it. Not my interpretation. Go to the Qur'an commentary, Tafsir Ibn 'Abbas (Mokrane Guezzou translation), and read the explanation of this verse:

لاَّ يَتَّخِذِ ٱلْمُؤْمِنُونَ ٱلْكَافِرِينَ أَوْلِيَآءَ مِن دُونِ ٱلْمُؤْمِنِينَ وَمَن يَفْعَلْ ذٰلِكَ فَلَيْسَ مِنَ ٱللَّهِ فِي شَيْءٍ إِلاَّ أَن تَتَّقُواْ مِنْهُمْ تُقَاةً وَيُحَذِّرُكُمُ ٱللَّهُ نَفْسَهُ وَإِلَى ٱللَّهِ ٱلْمَصِيرُ

By taking the kafir and disbelievers as friends, he hath no connection with Allah, has no honor, mercy or safety from Allah; unless it be that ye but safeguard yourselves against them, maintain yourselves from them, taking as it were safety-measures saving yourselves from them by speaking in a kindly way towards them with, while your hearts hate this.

This verse is telling Muslims not to take the disbelievers as friends instead of the believers, for the one who will do that has no protection from Allah, unless you are taking them as friends for protection. Allah himself warns you, and to Allah are all orders.

The bottom line, as seen in the explanation, Muslims cannot be friends with non-Muslims.

Muslims Can Lie Even When Taking An Oath

Qur'an 2:225 (Muhammad Habib Shakir):

لَّا يُؤَاخِذُكُمُ اللَّهُ بِاللَّغْوِ فِي أَيْمَانِكُمْ وَلَٰكِن يُؤَاخِذُكُم بِمَا كَسَبَتْ قُلُوبُكُمْ ۗ وَاللَّهُ غَفُورٌ حَلِيمٌ
(Al-Ba'qara, 225) , سورة البقرة)

Allah does not call you to account for what is vain in your oaths, but He will call you to account for what your hearts have earned, and Allah is Forgiving, Forbearing.

Again, in Qur'an 5:89 (Muhammad Habib Shakir) we read:

(Al-Ma'eda, 89) سورة المائدة)
لَا يُؤَاخِذُكُمُ اللَّهُ بِاللَّغْوِ فِي أَيْمَانِكُمْ وَلَٰكِن يُؤَاخِذُكُم بِمَا عَقَّدتُّمُ الْأَيْمَانَ

"Allah does not call you to account for what is vain in your oaths."

These verses are saying that you can take an oath and not really mean it in your heart. Think about it. Allah is saying that you can use his name in vain and not be punished for it. Imagine each Muslim taking an oath anytime, but meaning something else in his heart. For example, failed Times Square car bomber Faisal Shahzad was asked by the judge about the oath that he took in order to become a citizen. Shahzad admitted that he "swore but I didn't mean it."

Also, this lying oath is considered an especially "blessed oath," if it is made to Christians and Jews. As clearly stated in Qur'an 3:28, Allah gives Muslims permission to lie to Christians and Jews. He also says that he loves Muslims who do so. A Muslim may claim to be your friend with his lips, but truly hates you in his heart.

Lying can also extend to the Muslim's own family. You can make an oath to your wife and not mean it. What Allah cares for is not what you say with your tongue, but what you say in your heart. Allah encourages double-crossing, or making unfaithful oaths, which in turn, creates a society of liars. How can you trust a man who is permitted by Allah to lie to you? This must be a teaching from Satan, because it is contrary to what Christ said in Matthew 5:37:

> "But let your 'Yes' be 'Yes,' and your 'No,' 'No.' For whatever is more than these is from the evil one."

He, As a Muslim, Cannot Take You as a Friend!

We did read together many verses like 3:28 and 5:51 and 60:1, which all order Muslims concerning one thing, they are not allowed to be a friend to us. However, we then might meet a Muslim who seems to be a nice person. How then can we explain this?

If there is a nice person who is Muslim by birth, is really a good man or woman and hates no one, Allah says in Qur'an 3:28 that this Muslim is not a Muslim anymore. This is why he lost the protection of Allah from the sword of Muslims.

They speak to us in a friendly way, even though their **"hearts hate this**!" This means we are friends? No war! He claims to be a friend, but by his lips, not in his heart! The interpretation of Qur'an 3:28, Tafsir Ibn 'Abbas, translated by Mokrane Guezzou, explains it this way:

> Safeguard yourselves against them, maintain yourselves from them, taking as it were safety measures saving yourselves from them by speaking in a kindly way towards them with, while your hearts hate this.

After reading all of this, am I going to ever trust a Muslim?

How can the United States Government give them jobs in airports, FBI, CIA or even to be officers in the army, such as Nidal Malik Hasan, a U.S. Army Major?

Maybe there is a Muslim, who is not practicing Islam or perhaps has never read the Qur'an. What is my guarantee that he won't one day open this book and read this verse, or many other verses that are full of hate, and will turn into a terrorist in one second? The Qur'an is the most satanic book that you can ever put your hand on. This is why my book is called, *The Great Deception*.

Repentance in Islam

Many, if not most, times in the Qur'an, we see Allah speak about repentance. The fact is, that word has a false and empty meaning in Islam for many reasons. If we look at the story of the pharaoh in the Qur'an, we find that the pharaoh repented to Allah, but he (Allah) did not accept the pharaoh's repentance. As in Qur'an 40:84-85:

فَلَمَّا رَأَوْا بَأْسَنَا قَالُوا آمَنَّا بِاللَّهِ وَحْدَهُ وَكَفَرْنَا بِمَا كُنَّا بِهِ مُشْرِكِينَ 84

فَلَمْ يَكُ يَنفَعُهُمْ إِيمَانُهُمْ لَمَّا رَأَوْا بَأْسَنَا ۖ سُنَّتَ اللَّهِ الَّتِي قَدْ خَلَتْ فِي عِبَادِهِ ۖ وَخَسِرَ هُنَالِكَ الْكَافِرُونَ 85

84 When they saw Our strength, they (pharaoh) said, "We believed in Allah only, and we rejected the partners we had before."
85 But their belief wouldn't profit on them after they saw our power of punishment. It's Allah's ways to deal with mankind for a long time and the infidel were always the losers.

As we see here, the pharaoh said the Shahada (Accepting Allah as God), but did you notice that Allah still didn't accept his conversion to Islam? Allah, even so, punished him. That reminds me of the repentance of Adam, but in that situation Allah accepted his repentance, but he still punished Adam and kicked him out of heaven! As we see in Qur'an 2:37-38:

فَتَلَقَّىٰ آدَمُ مِن رَّبِّهِ كَلِمَاتٍ فَتَابَ عَلَيْهِ ۚ إِنَّهُ هُوَ التَّوَّابُ الرَّحِيمُ 37

قُلْنَا اهْبِطُوا مِنْهَا جَمِيعًا ۖ فَإِمَّا يَأْتِيَنَّكُم مِّنِّي هُدًى فَمَن تَبِعَ هُدَايَ فَلَا خَوْفٌ عَلَيْهِمْ وَلَا هُمْ يَحْزَنُونَ 38

37 Thereafter Adam received from his words and He repented to him; truly He is the Relenting, the Merciful.
38 We said to them, "Go down from it all of you together, yet until my guidance comes to you, and whoever follows My guidance, no fear on themselves, neither shall they be sad."

1. As we see from the two stories, punishment for the pharaoh was death, but for Adam it was to get down to earth.

2. Why did Allah keep asking mankind in the Qur'an to repent when it was not going to help anyway? We read in Qur'an 5:44:

73

Verily, We did send down the Taurat (Torah) [to Musa (Moses)], therein was guidance and light, by which the Prophets, who submitted themselves to Allah's Will, judged for the Jews.

Moses in Islam

Prophets of Allah Have the Best Testicles

تفسير Tafsir Al-Jalalayn Qur'an 33:69

{ يَاأَيُّهَا الَّذِينَ آمَنُواْ لاَ تَكُونُواْ كَالَّذِينَ آذَوْاْ مُوسَىٰ فَبَرَّأَهُ اللَّهُ مِمَّا قَالُواْ وَكَانَ عِندَ اللَّهِ وَجِيهاً }

Announced by Sahih Al-Bu'kharī. كتاب الغسل , Volume 1, Book 5 (Bathing), Number 278 (www.altafsir.com)

يَا أَيُّهَا الَّذِينَ آمَنُوا لَا تَكُونُوا" مَعَ نَبِيِّكُمْ "كَالَّذِينَ آذَوْا مُوسَى" بِقَوْلِهِمْ مَثَلًا : مَا يَمْنَعُهُ أَنْ يَغْتَسِل مَعَنَا إِلَّا أَنَّهُ آدَر "فَبَرَّأَهُ الله مِمَّا قَالُوا" بِأَنْ وَضَعَ ثَوْبه عَلَى حَجَر لِيَغْتَسِل فَفَرَّ الْحَجَر بِهِ حَتَّى وَقَفَ بَيْن مَلَأ مِنْ بَنِي إِسْرَائِيل فَأَدْرَكَهُ مُوسَى فَأَخَذَ ثَوْبه فَاسْتَتَرَ بِهِ فَرَأَوْهُ وَلَا أُدْرَة بِهِ وَهِيَ نَفْخَة فِي الْخُصْيَة "وَكَانَ عِنْد الله وَجِيهًا" ذَا جَاه : وَمِمَّا أُوذِيَ بِهِ نَبِيّنَا صَلَّى الله عَلَيْهِ وَسَلَّمَ أَنَّهُ قَسَم قِسْمًا فَقَالَ رَجُل هَذِهِ قِسْمَة مَا أُرِيد بِهَا وَجْه الله تَعَالَى فَغَضِبَ النَّبِيّ صَلَّى الله عَلَيْهِ وَسَلَّمَ مِنْ ذَلِكَ وَقَالَ : (يَرْحَم الله مُوسَى لَقَدْ أُوذِيَ بِأَكْثَر مِنْ هَذَا فَصَبَرَ) رَوَاهُ الْبُخَارِيّ

Oh believers, do not perform with disrespect to your Prophet, as did those who abused Moses when they would say, for instance, "The only explanation he does not shower us with is that he has a swelling in his testicles." Therefore, God cleared him of what they were suspicious when Moses placed his clothes on a rock to go to wash. **The rock hurtled apart from him with it** (his robe), until the rock approached to and stopped among a crowd of men from the offspring of Israel. As Moses pursued it and took his robe to cover himself, at same time the Jews saw his testicles and saw that he had no such infection or illness infecting his testicle. And he was honored in the eye of God.

An example of our Prophets being subjected to hurt was when dividing up the spoils a Muslim man said to him, "This is a partition is not meant to please God" (unjust apportionment)! Therefore the Prophet became offended and said, "May God have mercy upon Moses, for truly he was hurt with worse than this, but tolerated."

⚔ Allah will do anything to prove that the testicles of his prophets are the best.

- ⅄ In this story, not even one Jew wondered how the rock ran, as if it's something they witness every day!
- ⅄ If Moses had bad testicles, would that make him unfit for the position as a prophet?
- ⅄ The Muslim man noticed that Muhammad was not dealing justly, and he was not what he claimed to be. In response, Muhammad came up with the story of Moses' testicles, but what does this have to do with dividing the stolen money from the Christian and the Jews?

How Many Times Are Good Deeds Multiplied?

First we read Qur'an 2:261 (Usama Dakdok translation):

مَّثَلُ الَّذِينَ يُنفِقُونَ أَمْوَالَهُمْ فِي سَبِيلِ اللَّهِ كَمَثَلِ حَبَّةٍ أَنبَتَتْ (Al-Ba'qara, 261) , سورة البقرة)
سَبْعَ سَنَابِلَ فِي كُلِّ سُنبُلَةٍ مِّائَةُ حَبَّةٍ ۗ وَاللَّهُ يُضَاعِفُ لِمَن يَشَاءُ ۚ وَاللَّهُ وَاسِعٌ عَلِيمٌ

The parable of those who spend their money for the sake of Allah is like the parable of a grain which produces seven sanabul [ears of corn] and in each ear of corn a hundred grains and Allah will multiply to whom he wills. Allah is large, knowing.

1 good deed = (7 ears of corn x 100 grains) = 700

1 good deed x 700 = 700 good deeds

Now let's check Qur'an 6:160 (Usama Dakdok translation):

Whoever comes with a good deed, so to him there will be **ten** like it...

مَن جَاءَ بِالْحَسَنَةِ فَلَهُ عَشْرُ أَمْثَالِهَا ۖ وَمَن جَاءَ بِالسَّيِّئَةِ فَلَا يُجْزَىٰ إِلَّا مِثْلَهَا وَهُمْ لَا يُظْلَمُونَ
(Al-Ana'am, 160) , سورة الأنعام)

1 good deed x 10 = 10 good deeds

The question now is, is one good deed multiplied by 700 or by 10? To find out let's check Qur'an 4:40 (Usama Dakdok translation):

إِنَّ اللَّهَ لَا يَظْلِمُ مِثْقَالَ ذَرَّةٍ وَإِن تَكُ حَسَنَةً يُضَاعِفْهَا وَيُؤْتِ مِن لَّدُنْهُ أَجْرًا عَظِيمًا

(An-Nis'a, 40 ,سورة النساء)

Surely Allah will not treat unjustly even the weight of the smallest ant. And if there be any good deed, he will **double it**, and he will give from himself a great wage.

In the last verse, Allah will double the reward, so now good deeds are multiplied by 2, not 10 or 700.

Let's recap the guidance in those verses with the following chart:

Qur'an	Deeds	Multiply	Multiply
Qur'an 2: 261	1	700	Seven-hundred
Qur'an 6:160	1	10	Ten
Qur'an 4:40	1	2	Double

I think Allah needs to rethink how he will reward good deeds to make the contract clear.

The Prophet Idris

Qur'an 56: (Source: Louis Ginzberg, Legends of the Jews, [The Jewish Publication Society of America, Philadelphia, 1909], Vol. IV, Chapter V: Solomon)

Furthermore, mention in the Book the case of Idris: he was a truthful man of honesty and was from the prophet-hood.

Let's continue reading and you will see how the Qur'an is identical with the legend of the Jews:

After some time, Solomon received a letter from Adares, the king of Arabia. He begged the Jewish king to deliver his land from an evil spirit, who was doing great mischief, and who could not be caught and made harmless, because he appeared in the form of wind. Solomon gave his magic ring and a leather bottle to one of his slaves, and sent him into Arabia. The messenger succeeded in confining the spirit in the bottle. A few days later, when Solomon entered the Temple, he was not a little astonished to see a bottle walk toward him, and bow down reverently before him; it was the bottle in which the spirit was shut up. This same spirit once did Solomon a great service. Assisted by demons, he raised a gigantic stone out of the Red Sea. Neither human beings nor demons could move it, but he carried it to the Temple, where it was used as a cornerstone.

Through his own fault Solomon forfeited the power to perform the miraculous deed, which the Divine spirit had conferred upon him. He fell in love with the Jebusite woman Sonmanites. The priests of Moloch and Raphan, the false gods she worshiped, advised her to reject his suit, unless he paid homage to these gods. At first Solomon was firm, but, when the woman bade him take five locusts and crush them in his hands in the name of Moloch, he obeyed her. At once he was bereft of the Divine spirit, of his
strength and his wisdom, and he sank so low that to please his beloved he built temples to Baal and Raphan.

Is Intercession Allowed or Not?

Allah said it is allowed in Qur'an 4:85 (Usama Dakdok translation):

مَّن يَشْفَعْ شَفَاعَةً حَسَنَةً يَكُن لَّهُ نَصِيبٌ مِّنْهَا ۖ وَمَن يَشْفَعْ شَفَاعَةً سَيِّئَةً يَكُن لَّهُ كِفْلٌ مِّنْهَا ۗ وَكَانَ اللَّهُ عَلَىٰ كُلِّ شَيْءٍ مُّقِيتًا

(An-Nisa, 85, سورة النساء)

Whoever intercedes a good intercession, a portion of it will be his. And whoever intercedes an evil intercession, a portion of it will be his...

Yet, Muhammad also says it is NOT allowed in Qur'an 74:48:

فَمَا تَنفَعُهُمْ شَفَاعَةُ الشَّافِعِينَ

(Al-Muddathir, 48, سورة المدثر)

No intercession by the intercessor will help them (on Judgment Day).

Allah said intercession will be allowed on Judgment Day, but Muhammad said the opposite. I guess that clears it up!

77

Muhammad Said Intercession is Allowed

Sahih Muslim, Book 1, Hadith 352 (Direct link:
http://www.searchtruth.com/book_display.php?book=001&translator=2&start=0&
number=0352#0352):

> I am your Lord (Allah speaking). The Muslims will say, "Yes, you are our Lord."
> Then the bridge would be established over Hell and intercession would be
> allowed. They would say, "O our Lord, protect us, protect us."

Sahih Muslim, Book 1, Hadith 369 (Direct link: https://sunnah.com/muslim/1/378

> I asked the Messenger of Allah, if Allah would take out people from the hell Fire
> by the intercession. He the prophet answered: "Yes."

> The Prophet (ﷺ) said, "Some people will be taken out of the Fire through
> the intercession of Muhammad they will enter Paradise and will be called
> Al-Jahannamiyin (the Hell Fire people)
https://sunnah.com/bukhari/81/155

Muhammad's Nation Needs Intercession

Sahih Muslim, Book 1, Hadith 385 (Direct link:
http://www.searchtruth.com/book_display.php?book=001&translator=2&start=38
5&number=0385):

> The Messenger of Allah said, "There is for every messenger a prayer with
> which he would pray. I wish I could save my prayer for the intercession of my
> nation on the Day of Resurrection."

If Muhammad will be the intercessor for Muslims, why is he asking them to be
his intercessor by praying for him?

Sahih Al-Bukhari, Page 2374 (Arabic):

2374 - عن عائشة عن النبي صلى الله عليه وسلم قال سددوا وقاربوا وأبشروا - ص
فإنه لا يدخل أحدا الجنة عمله قالوا ولا أنت يا رسول الله قال ولا أنا إلا أن يتغمدني

'Aisha reported: "The Prophet, may Allah pray on him and salute him, said, 'Shoot and join together and get ready for the good news, because no one will enter heaven because of his work.' They said, 'Not even you?' The Prophet said, 'Even me but only if Allah bestows his mercy on me by his mercy and forgiveness.'"

Muhammad Needs Muslims to Intercede for Him So He Can Get the Top Rank

This hadith presents perfectly the selfishness that is Muhammad's, it's all about him and what he wants, whomsoever prays for Muhammad gets ten blessings (Sahih Muslim Book 4, Hadith 747):

Allah's apostle said, "Whenever you hear the muezzin (one who does the call for prayer) shout the call for prayer, restate what he says. Subsequently, call upon Allah for a blessing on me, for everyone who calls upon a blessing on me will receive ten blessings from Allah; **afterwords beg from Allah Al-Wasilah [the top high rank in heaven] for me**, which is a rank in Paradise made for only one of Allah's servants, and I hope that I may be that one who gets it. If anyone of you who asks for me to be given the top rank, he will be provided my intercession."

This is something that we really should look at carefully, because it shows that Muhammad is supposed to be the greatest of men—so great that Allah and his angels pray on him. (Qur'an 33:56):

إِنَّ اللَّهَ وَمَلَائِكَتَهُ يُصَلُّونَ عَلَى النَّبِيِّ ۚ يَا أَيُّهَا الَّذِينَ آمَنُوا صَلُّوا عَلَيْهِ وَسَلِّمُوا تَسْلِيمًا
(سورة الأحزاب , Al-Ahzab, 56)

Allah and his angels pray on the prophet. O whom you believe, pray on the prophet and salute him a high salute.

How is it that Muhammad's god and his angels pray on Muhammad? Allah orders Muslims to pray on Muhammad also, and Muhammad even asks Muslims to do more. He asks them to pray on him (Muhammad) each time they pray so that he can get the top rank in Paradise.

I think Muhammad is showing how self-centered he is. By asking Muslims to pray *on* him instead of *for* him, he makes himself equal to Allah. We will discuss this more in **Muhammad, the God.**

Muhammad is the Top Intercessor

Sahih Muslim, Book 30, Hadith 5655:

> Abu Huraira said: "Allah's Messenger, may Allah pray on him, said, 'I shall be first to be raised (from the grave) of the descendants of Adam on the Day of Resurrection, and I will be the top intercessor and the first whose intercession will be accepted by Allah.'"

Muhammad Cannot Intercede for His Mother

After Muhammad took all the time and effort to tell Muslims that his intercession is the way to be saved on Judgment Day, he then contradicts himself in a hadith, where it tells the story about how he cannot intercede for his mother. (Sahih Muslim, Book 4, Hadith 2129):

> Abu Huraira reported: "Allah's Apostle, may Allah pray on him, said: 'I appealed to Allah's permission for the forgiveness for my mother, but He did not permit it to me. I asked approval from Him to visit her grave, and He gave permission to me.'"

No Intercession Will Be Accepted on Judgment Day

Sahih Muslim, Book 30, Hadith 5655:

> Abu Huraira said: "Allah's Messenger, may Allah pray on him, said, 'I shall be first to be raised (from the grave) of the descendants of Adam on the Day of Resurrection, and I will be the top intercessor and the first whose intercession will be accepted by Allah.'"

وَاتَّقُوا يَوْمًا لَا تَجْزِي نَفْسٌ عَن نَفْسٍ شَيْئًا وَلَا يُقْبَلُ مِنْهَا شَفَاعَةٌ وَلَا يُؤْخَذُ مِنْهَا عَدْلٌ وَلَا هُمْ يُنصَرُونَ

(سورة البقرة , Al-Baqara, 48)

Qur'an 2:48 tells a different story:

> Protect yourself from that day (Day of Judgement) when no soul can be useful to another soul and no intercession will be accepted, and no help will come from anyone.

Muhammad said he is the top intercessor, but then we find out that he cannot intercede for his mother. In fact, no one can intercede for anyone. Muhammad clearly contradicts himself all the time and that shows us that he is making up his own "revelations" and attributing them to God.

Ideological Contradictions

In Qur'an 2:23, Allah is challenging the Arabs to make something of the quality of his Qur'an:

> And if ye are in doubt concerning that which We reveal unto [Muhammad], then produce a chapter of like [quality as] this Qur'an, and call your God to help you [besides Allah] if you are truthful.

The same challenge was made by Allah in Qur'an 17:88:

> Say: "If all of mankind and the jinn do gather together to produce the like of this Qur'an, they can not!"

We will not talk for now about the Arabic mistakes in the Qur'an, of which the Qur'an is full. I know most of you don't speak Arabic, so there is no point in exposing the errors which are so clear in Arabic. But, I will get proof from Allah's words himself, that anyone can make a Qur'an. Including Mr. Satan (Qur'an 22:52-53):

> 52 We never sent before thee any messenger or prophet but that when he recited [the scripture] Satan cast into his recitation (his words), but then Allah abrogates, whatever Satan had cast, then Allah will confirm His revelations, and Allah is all Know-er, Wise.
> 53 Allah makes what Satan has cast, a trial for those in whose hearts has sickness and those whose hearts are hardened, for truly the Oppressors are in disagreement.

These verses are very well known as the satanic verses!

In Qur'an 2:23, Allah said, "Who can make a Qur'an like this?" However, in Qur'an 22:52-53, Allah is saying he will take what Satan threw in the mouth of Muhammad as Qur'an. What's funny, is that Muhammad himself was reciting the Qur'an of Satan. Muhammad did not even notice the difference between Allah's Qur'an and Satan's Qur'an, even to the point he said that Satan did that to all of Allah's prophets before Muhammad!

We can understand from this all the following:

1. Satan always made the Qur'an. No one recognized that it was not from Allah.

2. Satan did this to all of Allah's prophets and was successful. Muslims say it is true of all the prophets of Islam, like 'Isa and Moses that Satan corrupted their books and Allah couldn't do anything about it. This is especially disturbing since we are to believe that Allah sent to mankind 124,000 Muslim prophets!

3. This means Satan did this 124,000 times, casting words and chapters to Allah's prophets and not one of his prophets even noticed.

4. Then Allah has a solution for what Satan casts (then Allah abrogates, whatever Satan had cast), Allah will abrogate! What a funny solution. This doesn't match with Muhammad's claim of all the other prophets' corruptions. Why didn't Allah abrogate Satan's verses for the other prophets?

5. The Qur'an is challenging both mankind and jinn to make a Qur'an like it. Muslims cannot say the challenge is made for only the humans, as we see in Qur'an 17:88:

Say: "If the mankind and the jinn were together to produce the like of this Qur'an, they could not produce the like thereof, even if they helped one another."

Therefore, we must ask the Muslims that if Allah is god, doesn't he know that Satan is from the jinn (Qur'an 18:50, "...So they prostrated except Iblis {Satan}. He was one of the jinn") as Islam tells? Satan will do it and has done it for the last 124,000 prophets as verse Qur'an 22:52 says:

We never sent before thee any messenger or prophet but that when he recited [the scripture] Satan cast into his recitation (his words), but then Allah abrogates, whatever Satan had cast...

Allah said he will abrogate what Satan throws, but he never told the Muslims what verses he will abrogate, nor which ones were sent from Satan. How can Muslims find out the bad satanic verses if he did not point to them one by one?! Maybe Allah will abrogate them in his sky book (Qur'an 85:22, **"On a guarded tablet."**)! What's the benefit of this protection if Satan's teachings are still in the Muslim's hands?

How would we know that verse 22:52 itself is not from Satan as long as Satan can cast verses into Muhammad's mouth? Couldn't he cast one more? So, Allah would just say, 'Don't worry about the filthy wrong teaching that has been given so far. I will take it off!'

6.   Finally, when this verse was cast to Muhammad, he not only recited Satan's words, but he bowed down to idols. This means that Satan had control of Muhammad physically, for the story says in Tafsir Ibn Kathir, 1999 Printing, Kingdom of Saudia Arabia, V5, Page 442:

قَرَأَ رَسُولُ اللهِ صَلَّى اللهُ عَلَيْهِ وَسَلَّمَ بِمَكَّةَ النَّجْمَ فَلَمَّا بَلَغَ هَذَا الْمَوْضِعَ " أَفَرَأَيْتُمُ اللَّاتَ وَالْعُزَّى وَمَنَاةَ الثَّالِثَةَ الْأُخْرَى " قَالَ فَأَلْقَى الشَّيْطَانُ عَلَى لِسَانِه : تِلْكَ الْغَرَانِيقُ الْعُلَى وَإِنَّ شَفَاعَتَهُنَّ تُرْتَجَى قَالُوا مَا ذَكَرَ آلِهَتَنَا بِخَيْرٍ " قَبْلَ الْيَوْمَ فَسَجَدَ وَسَجَدُوا فَأَنْزَلَ اللهُ عَزَّ وَجَلَّ هَذِهِ الْآيَةَ "

When the prophet was doing recitation of the chapter of Al Najem (The Star, Qur'an 53) Satan cast in his mouth, "Do you see Al-Lat and Al-'Uza and Manat the third one, it's a must to praise them and their Intercession should be asked for." And the pagan said, "Muhammad never did praise our gods as today." And he (Muhammad) bowed down and they (the pagans) did bow down with him (to the idols, the three daughters of Allah).

This leads us to other reasons to reject Muhammad as a prophet of God, because this is a major contradiction for the Qur'an in many ways, as we will see in Qur'an 15:42:

Over my slaves, you, Satan have no authority over them (I protect them), **except the bad ones** who follow you (Satan)!

•   This means Muhammad must be from the bad one.

•   Muhammad can't be a prophet.

•   He is not protected by Allah.

•   Allah's protection is a false one and it does not even exist. This is why nothing is working with Muhammad.

•   How was Satan able to make Muhammad bow? Was he in full control of this man? Maybe Muhammad and Satan are one and the same! In the best case, Muhammad must be possessed by Satan; therefore, he isn't suitable to be a prophet by any means.

Muhammad: Possessed With Devils.

Some might say I am trying to drive to that conclusion, but the fact is, it's what Muslims believe (Sahih Bukhari, Book 53, Hadith 400):

حدثني محمد بن المثنى حدثنا يحيى حدثنا هشام قال حدثني أبي عن عائشة
أن النبي صلى الله عليه وسلم سحر حتى كان يخيل إليه أنه صنع شيئا ولم يصنعه

Reported by 'Aisha: "The Prophet was bewitched so that he started fantasizing that he had done a thing, which, in fact, he had never done."

Muhammad, as Muslims and his wife said, was possessed. But this is against what Qur'an 15:42 tells and promises:

Over my slaves, you, Satan, have no authority over them (I protect them), except the bad ones who follow you (Satan)!

Muhammad was bad once again or how else was Satan placing his black magic over him as we see in Bukhari, Book 71, Hadith 658; Bukhari, Book 73, Hadith 89; Bukhari, Book 7, V 71, Hadith 661:

Described by 'Aisha: "Bewitching did activate on Allah's prophet (Muhammad) so that he started to imagine that he had done something which he had not."

You will see how funny the story is and how Muhammad's life was full of fairy tale stories. As always, the Jews are to blame or a Jewish man did it. Look how this Jewish man, as Muhammad claimed, was able to control Muhammad "by a comb and the hair stuck to it and a skin of the pollen on a male date palm tree." How small is the brain of a human to believe in such a story.
We need to ask why Muhammad is making up these lies.

- First, to give himself an excuse for his strange behavior.
- The lies he always made up and claimed that he was under the influence of black magic (as Muslim call it, but for me, he was possessed). This way no one would judge him for his filthy behavior.
- One of Muhammad's lies was this hadith (Sahih Muslim Book 23, Hadith 5081):

'Amir bin Sa'd bin Abu Wa'qas reported that Allah's Apostle said: He who eats seven palm date fruits in the morning, poison and bewitching will not harm him until the end of the day.

He was teaching them lies, infected by magic, and he died by poison! Later we will talk about his death, for sure.

To gain some understanding of just how badly Muhammad was possessed, we can look at the opening line of Sahih Al-Bukhari, Book 73, Hadith 89:

Narrated 'Aisha (Muhammad's child-wife): "The Prophet continued for such-and-such period imagining that he has slept (had sexual intercourse) with his wives, and in fact he did not!"

It does not actually matter how much Muslims try to cover up for this man and his madness. Still, nothing can explain how badly he was living in delusion and illusion, to the point he did not know if he truly was having real sex with his nine wives, or imagining it. After all of this, there are some important questions we need to ask:

- How can we trust Muhammad saying he saw an angel, and that his name is Jibreel (Gabriel), when we have just seen the proof that he was living in a delusion? Who knows? Maybe the angel story was one of them.

- Why wasn't Allah able to protect him from Satan when the Qur'an says that Allah protected Maryam and her son from Satan? Qur'an 3:36:

I have named her Maryam (Mary), and I protected her and her offspring by Allah protection from the Evil One, the cursed.

- Does that mean 'Isa (the wrong name of Jesus) was beloved more than Muhammad? Wasn't he the one Allah promised he would protect? The verse says that Allah will protect the good Muslims. To answer this, we consider that either:
    - The Qur'an is a book of lies, Allah made a false prophet, and he is just a fake name made by Muhammad and his gang (Waraqa Ibn Naofal and the monk Buhira) or;
    - Muhammad is not a Muslim, and that verse is meant for a real Muslim! Either way, that will make Islam a false religion made by a man, for the man.

The Killing of an Innocent Boy, How and Why

Moses meets with the prophet Al Khader, Qur'an 18:65:

فَوَجَدَا عَبْدًا مِنْ عِبَادِنَا آتَيْنَاهُ رَحْمَةً مِنْ عِنْدِنَا وَعَلَّمْنَاهُ مِنْ لَدُنَّا عِلْمًا

He did meet one of our slaves who we gave him mercy and from our knowledge, we gave him a lot of it from our self (Allah).

We understand from this verse that this man (Al Khader) is a prophet of god to whom Allah gave mercy and so much knowledge that even Moses asked him, as we see in the following verse (Qur'an 18:66), to be his student:

قَالَ لَهُ مُوسَى هَلْ أَتَّبِعُكَ عَلَى أَنْ تُعَلِّمَنِ مِمَّا عُلِّمْتَ رُشْدًا

Moses said to him, "May, I follow thee, so I can learn from your knowledge and wisdom?"

As we see here, this Al Khader is a big deal as a prophet. Please remember for later, that verse 18:65 said that Allah gave him "mercy" and "knowledge." This prophet has a special gift of mercy and knowledge.

In this story, we learn that as they go along their way, he (Al Khader) saw a young boy, and he killed him! So Moses asked him how he could kill an innocent boy. Al Khader said, "I told you that you might not be able to put up with me!" The story begins in Qur'an 18:74:

فَانْطَلَقَا حَتَّى إِذَا لَقِيَا غُلَامًا فَقَتَلَهُ قَالَ أَقَتَلْتَ نَفْسًا زَكِيَّةً بِغَيْرِ نَفْسٍ لَقَدْ جِئْتَ شَيْئًا نُكْرًا

Then they went (prophet Moses and Al Khader) until they found a young boy, so he killed him! Moses said, "You just did something evil!"

The story continues through verse 18:80 where Al Khader says:

وَأَمَّا الْغُلَامُ فَكَانَ أَبَوَاهُ مُؤْمِنَيْنِ فَخَشِينَا أَنْ يُرْهِقَهُمَا طُغْيَانًا وَكُفْرًا

The boy, his parents were good Muslims, and "We were afraid that when he grew, he might be unjust and an infidel!"

In Sahih Muslim, Book 033, Hadith 6434, we find an interpretation of the story:

The prophet of Allah said: "The youth whom the prophet Al- Khadir murdered was an infidel by his nature, and if he was not butchered, he would have been involving his parents in disobedience and disbelief."

Now let us study this story and find out what is wrong with it:

- The boy is a Muslim boy who has done nothing wrong. Both prophets of Islam agree that he was innocent!

- How can you judge someone for a crime he hasn't done yet? He was just a kid who didn't even know what he did, or is that would have done? Actually, he had not done anything yet!

- Verse 80 said that Al Khader was afraid the boy might be unjust.

- He's not even sure that he would be leaving Islam or not.

- The most important question is that, if Allah is telling us a true story, why are there millions of kids who grow up and become adult atheists, and many insult their parents, but Allah does not cause their death in childhood? Only this one boy!

- The way the prophet of Islam, Al Khader, killed the boy was so evil.

- From the Al Jalalayn interpretation of verse 18:74, we see this excerpt:

فَانْطَلَقَا" بَعد خُرُوجِهمَا مِنْ السَّفِينَة يَمْشِيَانِ "حَتَّى إذَا لَقِيَا غُلَامًا" لَمْ يَبْلُغ الْحِنْث يَلْعَب مَعَ الصِّبْيَان أَحْسَنهمْ وَجْهًا "فَقَتَلَهُ" الْخَضِر بِأَنْ ذَبَحَهُ بِالسِّكِّينِ مُضْطَجِعًا أَوْ اقْتَلَعَ رَأْسه بِيَدِهِ أَوْ ضَرَبَ رَأْسَهُ بِالْجِدَارِ

●

- He went and he saw a boy, he slew him with a knife and he picked his head off and started smashing it against the wall!

- Why would anyone kill someone in such a way? Especially playing with his body after death. Remember, we are not talking about an adult who did something wrong. If he was, we could say that the prophet (Al Khader) was seeking revenge! However, he was just a boy and he was brutally killed. What was the point of beheading him then smashing his head in the wall?

- At the end, we can say this is a fairy tale story showing an ugly face of Islam. Killing someone for doing nothing, just because you fear he might do something in the future. If this story were true, all mankind should be killed before they get older, because all of us are guilty of sin. This story is one mad tale of Muhammad.

Allah Misguides the One He Likes and Guides the One He Likes

For one of Allah's positions on guidance we turn to Qur'an 4:88:

فَمَا لَكُمْ فِي الْمُنَافِقِينَ فِئَتَيْنِ وَاللَّهُ أَرْكَسَهُمْ بِمَا كَسَبُوا أَتُرِيدُونَ أَنْ تَهْدُوا مَنْ أَضَلَّ اللَّهُ وَمَنْ يُضْلِلِ اللَّهُ فَلَنْ تَجِدَ لَهُ سَبِيلًا

Why you become two parties about the hypocrites? Allah damns them for what their hands did. Do you want to guide who
Allah misguides? The one who Allah deceives, no guidance is for them and you will not find a way to guide these!

We gain more insight in Qur'an 6:39:

وَالَّذِينَ كَذَّبُوا بِآيَاتِنَا صُمٌّ وَبُكْمٌ فِي الظُّلُمَاتِ مَنْ يَشَأِ اللَّهُ يُضْلِلْهُ وَمَنْ يَشَأْ يَجْعَلْهُ عَلَى صِرَاطٍ مُسْتَقِيمٍ
And those who accuse the Qur'an of lies are deaf and dumb, in darknesses, and who Allah will deceive, no guidance to them for the straight way.

Qur'an 6:125 reads:

فَمَنْ يُرِدِ اللَّهُ أَنْ يَهْدِيَهُ يَشْرَحْ صَدْرَهُ لِلْإِسْلَامِ وَمَنْ يُرِدْ أَنْ يُضِلَّهُ يَجْعَلْ صَدْرَهُ ضَيِّقًا حَرَجًا كَأَنَّمَا يَصَّعَّدُ فِي السَّمَاءِ كَذَلِكَ يَجْعَلُ اللَّهُ الرِّجْسَ عَلَى الَّذِينَ لَا يُؤْمِنُونَ

And he whom Allah made his fate, guide to Islam, he opens his chest to Islam and from those whom he likes to mislead he makes their chest in narrow, as if he is mounting to the sky. And he put more sin on them (Allah will cause more sin on them).

1. In Islam, the one who leads to evil is Allah, as you see, not Satan!

2. If Allah does this, what is the job of Satan?

3. If this verse is clearly saying that Muhammad doesn't have the right to guide them nor is he allowed, then why is Muhammad called a messenger of God? What is his job?

4. Why is Allah angry at him for trying to guide these people?

Qur'an 7:178 tells us:

مَنْ يَهْدِ اللَّهُ فَهُوَ الْمُهْتَدِي وَمَنْ يُضْلِلْ فَأُولَئِكَ هُمُ الْخَاسِرُونَ

He who Allah guides, he is guided, and those who Allah misguides are the losers.

1. Look at this god! How can Allah guide and then misguide, and then punish them for being misguided?

2. Islam is about luck. If you're lucky you will be one of those whom Allah whimsically chooses, and if you're not lucky, you will be one of those whom Allah rejects! You don't even know what your fault was!

Allah Misguides the Christians and Jews

All of us are aware that the Muslims keep telling us that Jesus was NEVER crucified. Christ's crucifixion is a very important thing to believe in, to the point that, if you don't believe in it, you are not a Christian.

But the story in the Qur'an is kind of strange and makes no sense. Let us see the logic of Allah's and Muhammad's work, when it comes to Jesus' crucifixion by reading Qur'an 4:157:

وَقَوْلِهِمْ إِنَّا قَتَلْنَا الْمَسِيحَ عِيسَى ابْنَ مَرْيَمَ رَسُولَ اللَّهِ وَمَا قَتَلُوهُ وَمَا صَلَبُوهُ وَلَكِنْ شُبِّهَ لَهُمْ وَإِنَّ الَّذِينَ اخْتَلَفُوا فِيهِ لَفِي شَكٍّ مِنْهُ مَا لَهُمْ بِهِ مِنْ عِلْمٍ إِلا اتِّبَاعَ الظَّنِّ وَمَا قَتَلُوهُ يَقِينًا

And those who said we murdered 'Isa the son of Maryam (Mary) the messenger of Allah. They murdered him not, nor they crucified him, but it was made to appear to them, as if he was, and they are in argument about that, but they believe in what they think, they are not sure of it.

The book of Jame' Al Baiyan fe Tafsir Al Qur'an, Year 310, Islamic

(هـ310تفسير جامع البيان في تفسير القرآن)/ الطبري (ت)
عن ابن إسحاق، قال: أن عيسى حين جاءه من الله إنّى رَافِعُكَ إِلىَّ قال: يا معشر الـحواريين: أيكم يحبّ أن يكون رفيقي في الـجنة حتـى يشبه للقوم في صورتي فيقتلوه مكانـي؟ فقال سرجس: أنا يا روح الله قال: فاجلس في مـجلسي فجلس فيه، ورُفع عيسى صلوات الله عليه، فدخـلوا عليه فأخذوه، فصلبوه، فكان هو الذي صلبوه وشُبِّه لهم به. وكانت عدتهم حين دخلوا مع عيسى معلومة، قد رأوهم فأحصوا عدتهم، فلما دخلوا عليه ليأخذوه وجدوا عيسى فيما يرون وأصحابه وفقدوا رجلاً من العدّة، فهو الذي اختلفوا فيه. وكانوا لا يعرفون عيسى، حتـى جعلوا لـيودس زكريايوطا ثلاثين درهماً على أن يدلهم عليه ويعرّفهم إياه، فقال لهم: إذا دخلتـم عليه فإنـي سأُقبِّله، وهو الذي أُقَبِّل فخذوه فلـما دخلوا عليه، وقد رُفع عيسى، رأى سَرْجِس في صورة عيسى، فلـم يشكّ أنه هو عيسى، فأكبّ عليه فقبله، فأخذوه فصلبوه.

From Ibn Ishaq, he said: When 'Isa revealed to him, from Allah that, "I will raise you above O 'Isa." Then Jesus said to his apostles, "Who of you will take my place to be killed, and he will be my companion to go to heaven and Allah will put my image and look on him, so he will look like me and they will kill him instead of me!" One of the apostles, his name is Sarjes! He said to Jesus, "Me, the Spirit of Allah!"

89

Then Jesus said unto him. "Then sit on my chair." And he sat on it. Then Allah raised Jesus to heaven unto him. The Jews entered the house, and they took Sarjes and they crucified him, for he is the one that looked like Jesus after Allah made him look like Jesus. When they entered the house they counted that there were 12 in it and one was missing from the total number (13). For Jesus, Allah raised him up. Because they didn't know what Jesus looked like, (The Jews didn't know what Jesus looked like?!) this was why they offer to Youdos Zakria Youta thirty pieces of silver to lead them to Jesus. He told them, "When I enter, I will kiss him so you will know which one is Jesus." So when they entered the house, Jesus was raised, but he saw Sarjes that looked like Jesus, so he kissed him, as he told them, and then they crucified him.

As we consider this story, nothing in it makes sense:

1. Allah is asking Jesus to order his men to lie so that he can run!

2. Allah misleads the Jews and the Christians. The story of the twelve being there or not doesn't make me understand why Allah would make me see Jesus on the cross instead of that man Sarjes, who looked exactly like him. If 100,000 men told me that it wasn't him, I wouldn't accept their stories if I saw him on the cross with my own eyes! Also, how can you make his mother, Mary, accept that he was not the one on the cross, when he has the same look and the same voice (as a clone)?

3. Why didn't any of the twelve apostles of Jesus repeat this story or even a word about the other person being Jesus' clone?

4. What's the point of saving Jesus and then making some other good man die for me? This is a cowardly act of 'Isa, the Muslim, to run and ask someone else to die for him! This is not how heroes act. The real heroes die for others, not ask others to die for them.

5. Didn't Allah know, if he is a real god, that this cloning was going to cause the biggest deception in the history of mankind for more than three billion who have accepted Christianity today?

6. This makes Allah the top deceiver ever in the history of mankind.

7. This would mean that Allah is Satan. Only Satan deceives.

8. The Qur'an's story proves that what the Bible is reporting to us, that Jesus was crucified, is a true story. The Bible reports what the eye witnesses saw, and it **would be a big fraud if they had reported something other than what they saw** with their own eyes.

9. The coming question is so important: What is the point of cloning when Allah already raised Jesus before they arrived to kill him? If Allah had

taken Jesus up to heaven to save him, why couldn't he also save all of Jesus' apostles, or is Allah all out of tools and tricks? What about making all twelve men look like Jesus, or make all the Jews look like Jesus, too? How about making the whole world look like Jesus? Then there would be no way to find who and where he is!

10. This is the most stupid story ever. At the same time it shows us the mentality of Muhammad, who created this fairy tale story, by showing how deception is accepted in this belief, as long it's Allah or the Muslims doing it.

> Since we have proven that Allah lies, we should remember what Christ said in John 8:44:

Ye are of your father the devil, and the lusts of your father ye will do. He was a murderer from the beginning, and abode not in the truth, because there is no truth in him. When he speaketh a lie, he speaketh of his own: for he is a liar, and the father of it.

I think, after reading that verse, I have no further comment on this topic. The Christ gave us the answer.

The Coming Back of the Messiah

Since I have shown you how the Jesus ('Isa) in Islam is now in heaven, and that he is still alive, from 2000 years ago until now, the story is not over yet. In Sahih Bukhari Book 34, Hadith 425 we read:

Allah's Messenger said: "I pledge by Him in Whose hand is my life, the Son of Mary will soon come down among you as a just and ruler-judge. He will tear crosses, slaughter the swine and abolish jizyah (penalty Christians have to pay, or they will be murdered) and the wealth will flow forth to such a measure that no one will halt to take it."

1. Here we see a new image of Christ in Islam. Remember, Muhammad is the greatest prophet ever among all the prophets of Allah, but he is dead! Jesus is a prophet, but his book is corrupted! He couldn't even make one person in this world today follow him! He is the one who ran for his life, and asked someone else to die for him, and after all these bad things that the Qur'an said about him, he is still the savior of the world!

2.   He will come back to be the one who will rule the earth! As you see, Muhammad said their "just and ruler" would be for the whole world.

3.   Then we need to ask why the Messiah was not Muhammad.

4.   Even in all the movies, everyone dies except the hero. He is the one at the end who saves the good one and brings victory. According to the above hadith, the one who brings victory is Jesus Christ, not Muhammad the dead!

5.   This means that we, the Christians, are doing the logical and right thing. If someone said to you, "We have two people to choose to follow. One is dead and one is alive." Who should we go after?

6.   If Jesus is going to be the "just and ruler-judge," doesn't this make Jesus God? No man is good, but God, as in Qur'an 6:57:

قُلْ إِنِّي عَلَى بَيِّنَةٍ مِنْ رَبِّي وَكَذَّبْتُمْ بِهِ مَا عِنْدِي مَا تَسْتَعْجِلُونَ بِهِ إِنِ الْحُكْمُ إِلَّا لِلَّهِ يَقُصُّ الْحَقَّ وَهُوَ خَيْرُ الْفَاصِلِينَ

"For me, I am knowledgeable of my Lord, but ye rejected what I have. What ye would see hastened for a punishment, is not in my power. The orders in the hand of Allah only: He judges by the Truth, and He is the best of judges.

7.   As we see, the best of Judges is Allah, because he is the only one who has the truth. Having the truth means that he knows the unseen. To be a perfect judge, you have to know each one's sins, lies and truth! This makes Jesus a person who knows the unseen and the unknown as in Qur'an 3:149:

وَرَسُولًا إِلَى بَنِي إِسْرَائِيلَ أَنِّي قَدْ جِئْتُكُمْ بِآيَةٍ مِنْ رَبِّكُمْ أَنِّي أَخْلُقُ لَكُمْ مِنَ الطِّينِ كَهَيْئَةِ الطَّيْرِ فَأَنْفُخُ فِيهِ فَيَكُونُ طَيْرًا بِإِذْنِ اللَّهِ وَأُبْرِئُ الْأَكْمَهَ وَالْأَبْرَصَ وَأُحْيِي الْمَوْتَى بِإِذْنِ اللَّهِ وَأُنَبِّئُكُمْ بِمَا تَأْكُلُونَ وَمَا تَدَّخِرُونَ فِي بُيُوتِكُمْ إِنَّ فِي ذَلِكَ لَآيَةً لَكُمْ إِنْ كُنْتُمْ مُؤْمِنِينَ

And a prophet from the children of Israel, "I came with a sign of your God. I create a figure of a bird. I breathe into it and it will become alive, by the leave of Allah. And make the dumb talk and I heal those that are born blind, and the lepers, and I raise the dead ones, and I declare to you what ye eat, and what ye store in your houses. Surely therein is a Sign made for you. So believe."

8.   As you see, Jesus knows what we eat and what we store in our houses. This means he must be:

⅄ Jesus is just and ruler.

⅄ Everywhere (omnipresent).

⅄ With every person in this earth.

⋏ Nothing can be hidden from him. It does not matter how much we try.

⋏ Don't forget his ability to create life!

⋏ Gave eyes (created them anew) and vision to the one born blind by saying a word!

⋏ Now the funny part is that the Jesus in the Qur'an did all of these things to make us believe in Allah! But these things make us believe on Him!

⋏ Here we go again. Allah is playing stupid by giving a man what he shouldn't have, because only God can do these things as documented in Qur'an 22:6:

ذَلِكَ بِأَنَّ اللَّهَ هُوَ الْحَقُّ وَأَنَّهُ يُحْيِي الْمَوْتَى وَأَنَّهُ عَلَى كُلّ شَيْءٍ قَدِيرٌ

This is, because Allah is the truth. It is he who gives life to the dead ones, and it is he who has power over all things.

Allah is telling Muhammad what to say about himself as a man, in Qur'an 7:188:

قُلْ لا أَمْلِكُ لِنَفْسِي نَفْعًا وَلا ضَرًّا إِلا مَا شَاءَ اللَّهُ وَلَوْ كُنْتُ أَعْلَمُ الْغَيْبَ لاسْتَكْثَرْتُ مِنَ الْخَيْرِ وَمَا مَسَّنِيَ السُّوءُ إِنْ أَنَا إِلا نَذِيرٌ وَبَشِيرٌ لِقَوْمٍ يُؤْمِنُونَ

Say, "I am not useful or harmful to myself, except what Allah decided for me and if I knew the unseen I will take a lot of the good of it to me and nothing can harm me then, but I am just a messenger to tell and warn!"

1. Here Muhammad is giving us the real image of himself. Look! He is saying, "If I knew the unseen I would save it for my own benefit!" He did not say, "I will help you with it." The first thing he thought about was himself!

2. He is clearly saying that he knew nothing about the unseen and gave proof of it. We need to ask why Allah's Qur'an says that Jesus can tell us what we eat, and what we hide and store in our houses, but Muhammad cannot?! Was Muhammad a left over and Allah didn't want to make him look like a prophet for a second? We've learned one more thing that proves the disability of Muhammad and his god. He had no choice but to claim that the miracles of Jesus came from his god, by giving Allah the credit for it. At the same time, Allah couldn't support Muhammad with one miracle, as Qur'an 17:59 says:

We refrain from sending any miracles for former generations refused them as true miracles!

3. Allah clearly said he refrained from giving Muhammad any miracles. This is just a false excuse for Muhammad because he couldn't do any. On top of that, who is the former generation that rejected the miracles of Jesus or Moses? All of the Christians believe in it, so simply, it's false and bad. Muhammad is just trying to get away from those who keep asking him why he can't do what Jesus or Moses or others did! Later we will go more into detail about this topic.

    ⅄ Allah wanted to prove to us that he is God by giving Jesus the ability to do what only God should or can do!

    ⅄ Did Allah know that these kinds of miracles would make the Christians believe in Jesus, that he is above all mankind, and that they would make him their God?

    ⅄ To explain my point, if Jesus cannot raise anyone from death, create a bird, give eyes to the blind, heal the lepers, tell us what we hide in our houses, tell us what we eat; if He is not son of a virgin, still alive for more than 2000 years; if he cannot be touched by Satan, as Muhammad said; if He is not holy, as Qur'an 19:19 says; and if He is not judge and ruler of the world at the end of time, then I have no reason to make him my God! So from the Islamic logic of miracles, Allah made us worship Jesus, and here we go again, Allah gave Jesus power to guide or to misguide!

    ⅄ Now if we look at Qur'an 3:49 Jesus said, "I create a figure of a bird, I breathe into it and it will become alive!"

    This leads to another question. If it's by the leave of Allah, why does the verse say, "I create?" This would mean that "the leave of Allah" is just an approval of his action. As anything we do in life, it might be against Allah's leave or permission. For example, a Muslim can rape his wife, because it's approved by Allah (by Allah's leave). Getting the permission to do that does not mean he can physically do it if the man is weak. In some Muslim countries, one Muslim woman might be able to beat ten men! We will go to Qur'an 55:33:

O company of jinn and humans, if you are able to pass through the Range of the heavens and the earth, then pass through! You will not pass through except with Authority.

    ⅄ As you see, Allah is challenging us to leave the zone of the earth without his permission. Did the Russians and Americans go out of the zone of the earth? According to this it was done without Allah's leave. As is also true of our Lord Jesus Christ when he returned to heaven!

My point is? Muslims might try to use that word to explain why Jesus has that ability. As an example, they may say to you, "In the time of Jesus, medicine was so advanced! This is why Jesus' miracles were about healing!"

⚔ All of us know that what Jesus did was 600 years before Muhammad. Science is more forward now, not backward.

⚔ Today, even 2,000 years after Christ, can the scientific knowledge of mankind altogether do even one of the miraculous things which Jesus did?!

⚔ Remember, Jesus never gave medicine, he gave orders! The difference is so huge!

To Make a Poetic Sound, We Exaggerate With Lies!

Let's go to Qur'an chapter 97:3

لَيْلَةُ الْقَدْرِ خَيْرٌ مِنْ أَلْفِ شَهْرٍ

Qur'an 97:3

It's the night of power that is better than one thousand months.

Let us study this verse carefully. This is supposed to be the night when Allah sent down the first verse of the Qur'an. Let's address some questions concerning this night of power:

1.   Why is this night, or more specifically prayer on this night, better than 1,000 months?

If you speak Arabic, you see that Muhammad is just trying to match words up. Let's take a look. The four phrases in this verse end with these words قدر شهر أمر فجر (qader, shaher, amr, fajer). The Qur'an of Muhammad does not really care about the meaning. He is just trying to match the rap that he has going. This is clear for all of them and does not make any sense any way you try.

One night of prayer = 1,000 months = 83 years and 33 days of praying on other nights!

2. Is that fair? Me praying one night is better than someone else praying for 83 years? Let's look at Al Jalalayn Tafsir (interpretation), V1, Page 815, year 864 (Islamic), of Qur'an 97:3:

هـ) { لَيْلَةُ ٱلْقَدْرِ خَيْرٌ مِّنْ أَلْفِ شَهْرٍ } ليس فيها 864تفسير تفسير الجلالين/ المحلي و السيوطي (ت المحلي
ليلة القدر فالعمل الصالح فيها خير منه في ألف شهر ليست فيها

The deeds of this night and the good work in this night are better than one thousand nights compared to other nights.

Qur'an 2:82:

وَالَّذِينَ آمَنُوا وَعَمِلُوا الصَّالِحَاتِ أُولَئِكَ أَصْحَابُ الْجَنَّةِ هُمْ فِيهَا خَالِدُونَ

And those who did believe, and good they got, the heaven of Allah with rivers running underneath of them.

3. Let's say we have two Muslims. One prayed one night during the night of power. Is he going to be better than the one who prayed for 83 years, but didn't pray that night? Are they going to end up in the same heaven? If they have the same reward, why is this night (the night of power) better? Will the one get 1,000 times more reward?

If the reward is the same, this means that this is just rap talk. It means nothing, said for nothing. As we have seen, Allah is about justice and he will not reward anyone for one night of prayer the same, or even better as the verse says, as someone who has prayed for 83 years. This would be a kind of madness. Either way, Muhammad proved to us again that he created the Qur'an and it is made up to fit with rap (rhymes), but its words have no meaning or real value.

Allah Guards the Revelation

Allah said in the verses that he protected his revelation. Let's examine this and see if this is true. All of us know that Muslims practice stoning to death for illegal sexual intercourse, but where is the order of Allah for it? We will look at Sahia Bukhari, Volume 8, Book 82, Hadith 816:

> Reported by Ibn 'Abbas: Omar said, "I am fretful that later a long time from now, the people might say, We cannot recognize the Verses of the Rajam (stoning to death) in the Holy Book, and therefore, they possibly will go astray by leaving liability that Allah has revealed. Therefore, I confirm that the punishment of Rajam be practiced on him who commits illegal sexual intercourse, if he is already married and the crime is proven by witnesses or pregnancy or confession." Sufian added, "I have memorized this recitation in this way." 'Umar added, "Surely Allah's Apostle exercised the penalty of Rajam, and so we are following him."

What do we understand from this hadith? It's a very strong, approved hadith by all Muslims, with no exceptions. This would mean:

1. There is a missing chapter or verses in the Qur'an.
2. The Muslims couldn't put it in the Qur'an!
3. What Muslims say to us, that they know the Qur'an by heart, is a false statement. If they know what is missing, why didn't Uthman the Khalif add it in his Qur'an when he made or collected it?

This takes us to another point. We read in the interpretation of Al Jalalayn, V1, Page 338:

{ إِنَّا نَحْنُ نَزَّلْنَا ٱلذِّكْرَ وَإِنَّا لَهُ لَحَافِظُونَ }
{ وَإِنَّا لَهُ لَحُفِظُونَ } من التبديل والتحريف والزيادة والنقص .

We promise to protect the book now and later from any corruption or adding or missing!

⁂ As we see, the promise of Allah is not true and that makes the Qur'an a book of false promises and false prophecy.

Where do we find the first verse that was revealed to Muhammad in the night of power (Al Qader Night)? The Qur'an is not in chronological order. But it is accepted by Muslims that it is Qur'an 96:1:

Read in the Name of Allah, the One Who Created!

Didn't Allah call changing location of verses a corruption? Let us see the proof in Qur'an verses 4:46, 5:3, 41. First within Qur'an 4:46:

> From the Jews who changed the locations of words from its location and the claim that they did obey God! ...

- ⅄ It's clear that the one who changes locations of words is doing corruptions. Do not forget that when the Qur'an was made, verse numbering or naming did not exist.

- ⅄ Let us take a look at one more of the endless examples; Qur'an 5:3:

> I prohibited you to eat dead meat, blood, the flesh of swine, and that on which hath been prayed the name of other Gods than Allah or which hath been destroyed by choke or by a violent blow, or by a Horn hit, or by being beaten to death; or some which have been eaten by a lion, unless ye are able to butcher it before it dies; that which is sacrificed for the idols, or from which you claim an oath or divining of arrows, has no feathers or head. Today, those who reject Islam have given up all hope of your religion: yet fear them not, but fear Me. Today I perfected your religion for you, completed My gracefulness upon you, and have selected for you Islam as your religion. However, if any is forced by hunger, not intentionally to transgression of my orders, Allah is indeed Forgiving, Most Merciful.

- ⅄ Look at this part of the verse; "Today I perfected your religion for you, completed My gracefulness upon you, and have selected for you Islam as your religion."

As you see, it says, "today Islam became perfect!" But we have a problem here. If "today Islam became perfect," then how can it be said in Chapter 5:3? This is after "today." There is no need for more chapters or verses in the Qur'an, but as we know there are more than 109 chapters after this one! Did someone add them or did someone move this verse from the end of Qur'an to the front of the Qur'an? Furthermore, what does forbidden food have to do with perfection anyway? The Qur'an is an empty book that has a lot of missing teachings. If we would do an examination of the entire Qur'an, 90% of what Muslims practice is not even in it!

The Qur'an even teaches a lot of things which Muslims cannot practice anymore, like in verse 11:114 where the Qur'an orders them to pray three times:

> And do demonstrate the ordinary prayers at the two ends of the day and at the arrival of the night.

The Qur'an never gives the definition for what the word Zakat means, which is the part of the money the Muslims have to pay either from what they make from work or what they got from stealing from the Christians and the Jews.

Muhammad did not forget how much his share was from stealing. He and Allah got a fifth and the rest went to those who fought with him (the thieves). The Qur'an never said:

- ▲ How to do hajj?
- ▲ How to pray?
- ▲ Where can we find in the Qur'an how to do ablution (washing)?
- ▲ How to fast?
- ▲ When to fast?
- ▲ When to stop fasting?
- ▲ How much Zakat to pay (money to Muhammad's State)?

On the other hand, which verses are the abrogated ones? How can we know which ones to practice and which ones not to practice when the Qur'an is full of both? This is one of the reasons for its confusion.

Qur'an 8:41 tells how the spoils of war were to be divided:

And know that whatever ye take as spoils of war (what they steal from kafir), the fifth thereof is for Allah, and for the messenger and left for the poor men and orphans (of these who die killing and fighting for Muhammad) and the needy.

Later we find the Muslims accusing Muhammad of stealing some stolen red underwear as in Qur'an 3:161 (Dakdok translation):

وَمَا كَانَ لِنَبِيٍّ أَن يَغُلَّ وَمَن يَغُلْلْ يَأْتِ بِمَا غَلَّ يَوْمَ ٱلْقِيَامَةِ ثُمَّ تُوَفَّىٰ كُلُّ نَفْسٍ مَّا كَسَبَتْ وَهُمْ لاَ يُظْلَمُونَ

161And it was not to a prophet to cheat (in dividing the spoils), and whoever cheats will bring what he cheated (dishonestly gained) on the day of the resurrection. Then every soul will be paid what it has earned, and they will not be dealt with unjustly.

Tafsir Al Jalalayn, sura Al-Imran, elaborates on this verse (Qur'an 3:161):

When Muslims started dividing the booty, some red velvet clothes went missing on the Day of Badr, and some Muslims began to say, possibly the Prophet hides it for himself. The following was revealed you should know, "It is not for a prophet to steal."

Imagine the apostles of Christ accusing him of stealing stolen clothes! For sure this is impossible. This behavior would be expected from a criminal gang, not from men of God. But at the same time, this is telling us who Muhammad is and who those were who associated with him!

Challenge to Mankind and the Jinn To Produce the Like of This Qur'an

Qur'an 17:88:

> Say (Muhammad) If the humans and the jinn get together to produce the same as this Qur'an, they cannot produce the like thereof, even if they both work in it together.

- ⌖ The challenge is so clear to both the jinn and humans that they cannot make the same as this Qur'an.
- ⌖ I think if we find any that can make a Qur'an the same or better, Allah has lost his challenge.

In the coming Hadith (The Book of 'Ol-It'qan Fee 'Olum Al-Qur'an, V1, Page 137), from Omar, the companion of Muhammad, and one for the four Islamic Khalifs after Muhammad, Omar said:

الإتقان في علوم القرآن
[النوع العاشر137الجزء الأول [ص]:
وأخرج البخاري وغيره ، عن أنس قال : قال عمر : وافقت ربي في ثلاث : قلت : يا رسول الله لو اتخذنا من
[وقلت : يا 125] [البقرة : 138مقام إبراهيم مصلى ؟ فنزلت : واتخذوا من مقام إبراهيم مصلى [ص]:
رسول الله ، إن نساءك يدخل عليهن البر والفاجر ، فلو أمرتهن أن يحتجبن ؟ فنزلت آية الحجاب . واجتمع
على رسول الله ـ صلى الله عليه وسلم ـ نساؤه في الغيرة ، فقلت لهن : عسى ربه إن طلقكن أن يبدله أزواجا
[فنزلت كذلك5خيرا منكن [التحريم :

Reported by Annas, the Omar bin Al Khatab said: "My almighty agreed with me in three things:
(First), I said, 'Oh Allah's Apostle, I wish if [you would] take as your place of worship the place where Abraham did [have his] place to pray. It so came, the Divine Inspiration: (page 137) (Qur'an 2:125) And take you (Muslims) the place of Abraham as a place of prayer.'
(Second), And I said to the Prophet, to the prophet of Allah, 'Good and bad ones talk to your wives, therefore order them to veil themselves!' So Allah sent

down the concerning the veiling of the women (Qur'an 24:31).

(Third), the wives of the Prophet made a coalition against the Prophet, and I said to them, 'Maybe if his, the lord of the Prophet, divorced you, (all the wives) and exchange you with better wives than you.' So the verse revealed (Qur'an 66:5) **the same as I had said."**

You can see the same story in Sahih Al-Bukhari (Book 8, Hadith 395).

- We see that Allah's challenge is fake! How can he ask the human kind and jinn kind to make a Qur'an, if they can, but yet he is copying Omar's words!

- This hadith shows Allah copying Omar three times. I wonder how many verses Allah has copied from others also, but we do not know about them!

- Even Omar Said: "So the verse (66:5) revealed, **the same as I had said."**

- It's so clear that there is no Allah or revelation. It was Omar talking to Muhammad. Muhammad heard what Omar said, loved it, and then he adopted the ideas of Omar! As we see, Allah is in the service of Muhammad, as usual!

We showed how Omar, as a "human," made the Qur'an, and even Allah copied from him; so what about the jinn? Remember the verse was challenging both jinn and human together. Is there any Qur'an made by the jinn?

I think many of us are aware of satanic verses, like in Salman Rushdie's book, The Satanic Verses. So what is the satanic verse?

The Satanic Verses.

Satanic verses are described in Qur'an 22:52:

We send not before you (Muhammad) any messenger or prophet but that when he recited, Satan cast scripture into his recitation (what is not from the Qur'an). However, Allah abrogates. Whatever Satan had cast, then Allah will fix his revelations. And Allah is Knower, and Wise.

To see what the story is, we will go to the interpretation of this verse (Qur'an 22:52) by Ibn Kathir, 1999 Printing, V5, Page 441:

وَمَا أَرْسَلْنَا مِنْ قَبْلِكَ مِنْ رَسُولٍ وَلَا نَبِيٍّ إِلَّا إِذَا تَمَنَّى أَلْقَى الشَّيْطَانُ فِي أُمْنِيَّتِهِ فَيَنْسَخُ اللَّهُ مَا يُلْقِي الشَّيْطَانُ {52}
ثُمَّ يُحْكِمُ اللَّهُ آيَاتِهِ وَاللَّهُ عَلِيمٌ حَكِيمٌ
قَدْ ذَكَرَ كَثِيرٌ مِنَ الْمُفَسِّرِينَ هَهُنَا قِصَّةَ الْغَرَانِيقِ وَمَا كَانَ مِنْ رُجُوعِ كَثِيرٍ مِنَ الْمُهَاجِرَةِ إِلَى أَرْضِ الْحَبَشَةِ ظَنًّا
مِنْهُمْ أَنَّ مُشْرِكِي قُرَيْشٍ قَدْ أَسْلَمُوا وَلَكِنَّهَا مِنْ طُرُقٍ لَهَا مُرْسَلَةٍ وَلَمْ أَرَهَا مُسْنَدَةً مِنْ وَجْهٍ صَحِيحٍ وَاللَّهُ أَعْلَمُ قَالَ
ابْنُ أَبِي حَاتِمٍ حَدَّثَنَا يُونُسُ بْنُ حَبِيبٍ حَدَّثَنَا أَبُو دَاوُدَ حَدَّثَنَا شُعْبَةُ عَنْ أَبِي بِشْرٍ عَنْ سَعِيدِ بْنِ جُبَيْرٍ قَالَ : قَرَأَ
رَسُولُ اللَّهِ صَلَّى اللَّهُ عَلَيْهِ وَسَلَّمَ بِمَكَّةَ النَّجْمَ فَلَمَّا بَلَغَ هَذَا الْمَوْضِعَ " أَفَرَأَيْتُمُ اللَّاتَ وَالْعُزَّى وَمَنَاةَ الثَّالِثَةَ الْأُخْرَى
" قَالَ فَأَلْقَى الشَّيْطَانُ عَلَى لِسَانِهِ : تِلْكَ الْغَرَانِيقُ الْعُلَى وَإِنَّ شَفَاعَتَهُنَّ تُرْتَجَى قَالُوا مَا ذَكَرَ آلِهَتَنَا بِخَيْرٍ قَبْلَ الْيَوْمِ
" فَسَجَدَ وَسَجَدُوا فَأَنْزَلَ اللَّهُ عَزَّ وَجَلَّ هَذِهِ الْآيَةَ

(Ibn Kathir) Said: "Many of the commentators mention here the story of (Al Qaraniq) the three daughter of Allah, and it became known, to the point that many of Muslims who went to Ethiopia came back for they thought the pagans converted to Islam and that story, from Ibn Hatem narrated from Ibn Younis from Ibn Habib told from the apostle of Allah that when he recited the chapter of Al Najem in Mecca, he, the Satan, cast into his mouth, 'Have you considered the goddesses (Al-Lat and Al-'Uza, and Manat, the third one? {Qur'an 53:19-20}), for sure their intercession is to hope for,' and then the prophet did bow down, and the pagans did bow with him."

I will not go into too much detail with this story, for it has become so well known, but I will make a short summary of it:

1. Satan (who is from the jinn) made part of the Qur'an, as this verse explains.

2. Allah, himself, approved it to the point that he will "take what Satan cast." So Muslims cannot say that they do not accept this story. If they do say that, it means this verse is a lie and the Qur'an cannot be considered a real source of information.

3. When Muhammad recited these satanic verses, he proved to us a few things. Such as:

⚔ Satan's Qur'an is not of less quality than Allah's Qur'an.

⚔ Muhammad did not notice it was from Satan, for it looked exactly the same!

⚔ The Arabic language is very clear here in its meaning. It's as follows.

⚔ It means that Satan made the Qur'an. By Muhammad's judgment it was so good that he said it and announced it as Allah words. If it was bad, why did Muhammad do such a thing?

⚔ When Allah made the challenge to us to make a Qur'an, he said, "produce like this Qur'an." Let's say I am going to be the one who will challenge Allah in making a Qur'an. After I make this Qur'an, I will go to Muhammad and appoint him for the job of judging the scriptures made by me or the one made by Satan. I don't think the Muslims would say that Muhammad is not a good judge for the quality of the Qur'an or scriptures I would make!

ᴧ   Therefore, as long as Muhammad is accepted, and he already confirmed the cast of Satan, it would mean that the Judge (Muhammad) **said**, "**These are great verses.**" To the point that he thought they were from God!

ᴧ   Saying that Allah's verse is challenging mankind and jinn is unintelligent and exposes the weakness of the Qur'an's maker. Whoever he is.

After proving 'Oman made the Qur'an and that Satan did too, we have a problem. The fact is, it's not us who has the problem—it's Allah! In the verse after the cast of Satan, we read this (Qur'an 22:53):

لِّيَجْعَلَ مَا يُلْقِي الشَّيْطَانُ فِتْنَةً لِّلَّذِينَ فِي قُلُوبِهِم مَّرَضٌ وَالْقَاسِيَةِ قُلُوبُهُمْ ۗ وَإِنَّ الظَّالِمِينَ لَفِي شِقَاقٍ بَعِيدٍ

That He, Allah, will make what Satan has cast a trial for those in whose hearts is a sickness and those whose hearts are harsh, for these, the unjust ones, are far from accepting the truth.

This verse gives Muslims many problems:

1.   Satan is not **bad,** but he is a tool and an obedience servant used by Allah.

2.   Why did Allah just say in verse 52 that he would take these satanic verses out, but now Allah says he will use the verses to "cast a trial" (provoke rebellion)? This would mean that he took out nothing at all, because if Allah had taken it away, no one would be affected by something that does not exist anymore!

3.   How can the satanic verses be a trial if Muhammed said it and the pagans liked it? They were already lost and were unchanged by these verses. They still worshiped pagan gods!

4.   How do these verses affect the unjust ones (pagans)? If these verses are in the Qur'an, the ones who will read and accept it are the Muslims!

5.   Why did Allah allow such a falsehood to go into the mouth of his prophet?!

6.   If Allah knows the future, why did he let such a thing occur?

7.   What's the point of guidance, when the one guiding is happy with

spreading falsehoods? Allah is clearly saying that he loves this to be the way to increase the turmoil of mankind for those he calls unjust! I thought the point of establishing Islam was to make the unjust, just!

I will move on, but this story has one more problem. Things are getting much stinkier, as you will see. When someone makes a lie, he needs to tell one thousand more to cover the first one. Let's go to Qur'an 15:42 where Allah is speaking:

إِنَّ عِبَادِي لَيْسَ لَكَ عَلَيْهِمْ سُلْطَانٌ إِلَّا مَنِ اتَّبَعَكَ مِنَ الْغَاوِينَ
(سورة الحجر، 42 Al-Hijr,)

From my slaves (The Muslims), over them you (Satan) have no authority, **except the lost one who follows you, Satan**.

This verse is clearly saying that Satan cannot control any of the good ones (the Muslims) and he (Satan) can only control and deceive the lost ones (the infidels).

1.   If this is the case, how can Satan control Muhammad and cast satanic verses into his mouth? See this excerpt from Sahih Al-Bukhari, Book 71, Hadith 658:

'Aisha said: "There is a man called Labid bin Al A'sam from the tribe of Bani Zaraiq, who worked magic on Allah's Apostle to the point the messenger was imagining that he had done things that he had not really done. ..."

2.   How was Satan able to control Muhammad by what Muslims call black magic, when Satan has authority over the bad ones only? Was Muhammad a bad one?

How Bad Was Muhammad's Case?

We will see this in the following in a hadith from Bukhari (Book 73, Hadith 89):

'Aisha revealed that: "The Prophet continued for an undefined period, fantasizing that he had slept (had sexual relations) with his wives. However, indeed he did not. ..."

How do Muslims answer this?

1.   Muhammad is living in delusion to the extent that he is losing the

ability to distinguish reality from fantasy. He isn't even sleeping during this!

2. Muhammad could not distinguish between reality and fantasy, even when it came to having sexual intercourse with his 13 wives. How can we trust him about seeing a real angel (Gabriel)? Maybe it was fantasy too? Was he also imagining that?

3. What's wrong with this man? Everything wrong in the world happened with him, from black magic, sex with children, taking his son's wife, dying by being poisoned—the list is endless!

In a quick look at Islam, we find that Muslims love to attack those who are pagans, commit idolatry, or practice polytheism. But the fact is, Islam is one of the religions that promote idolatry and polytheism.

The Kaaba in Islam: What is the Kaaba?

The Kaaba was a Christian Church!

The Kaaba used to have an icon of Mary (Christ's mother) as documented in a number of books:

⚔ Akhbar Mecca by Al-Azraqi, 2004 Printing, V1, Page 205.

⚔ Al-Ma'gazi by Al-Waqidy, 1989 Printing, V1, Page 833:

دخل النبي صلى الله عليه وسلم فرأى فيها صورة الملائكة وغيرها ، ورأى صورة إبراهيم صلى الله عليه
وسلم قال قاتلهم الله جعلوه شيخا يستقسم بالأزلام ثم

رأى صورة مريم ، فوضع يده عليها ثم قال امسحوا ما فيها من الصور إلا صورة إبراهيم

"When the prophet entered the Kaaba, he found many pictures; one of them was of Mary and one of Abraham, so he put his hand over Abraham's picture and said wipe all save this one (meaning Abraham)."

The Kaaba used to have statue of Jesus and his mother.

Akhbar Mecca by Al-Azraqi, 2004 Printing, V1, Page 200:

وحدثني جدي ، قال : حدثنا داود بن عبد الرحمن ، عن ابن جريج ، قال : سأل سليمان بن موسى الشامي
عطاء بن أبي رباح وأنا أسمع : أدركت في البيت تمثال مريم وعيسى ؟ قال : نعم ، أدركت فيها تمثال مريم
مزوقا ، في حجرها عيسى ابنها قاعدا مزوقا . قال : وكانت في البيت أعمدة ست سوار ، وصفها كما نقطت
في هذا التربيع « قال : وكان تمثال عيسى ابن مريم ومريم عليهما السلام في العمود الذي يلي الباب . قال
ابن جريج : فقلت لعطاء : متى هلك ؟ قال : في الحريق في عصر ابن الزبير

"I have been told by my grandfather, he said we have been told by Dawood Ibn Abd-Al-Rahman from the son of Gorieej and Suliman bin Mousa AL-SHami 'Ata bin Rabah, I did hear that you witness that the Kaaba used to have the statue of Mary and her son Jesus in her lap, and both were covered with beauty things? He said yes, the Kaaba use to have six columns and the statue of Mary and Jesus in the top of it, He said do you know when it's destroyed, he said by fire in the time of Ibn Al-Zubir (war between Muslims)."

In the coming list, we will see how The Tribe of Khoza'a, the polytheists, did defeat the Christians and turn the Kaaba again into a pagan worship place, and made it revert to the old days of idol worshipers.

First we will see what the Muslims believe about the building of the Kaaba. According to Muslims, the Kaaba was first built by:

1. The Angels.

2. Adam.

'Irshad AL-'Aqel Al-Salem Fe Al-Qur'an Mazayia A, Beirut, 1999, V1, Page 160, (إرشاد العقل السليم إلى مزايا القرآن الكريم.):

أنها بنيت عشر مرات منها بناء الملائكة عليهم السلام وذكره النووي في تهذيب الأسماء واللغات والأزرقي في تاريخه وذكر أنه كان قبل خلق آدم عليه السلام ومنها بناء آدم عليه السلام

"Kaaba was built ten times first time by the angels pace of themselves and stories mentioned by Imam AL-Nwawi, in the book of Tahzeb Al-'Asma' wa A-Lu'gat and mentioned too in the book of Al-Azra'qi that it was built before Adam and then Adam built it too."

3. Seth, the son of Adam.

'Euon Al-Ather Fe Funun Al-Ma'gazi Wal-Shama'el Wal-Sear by AL-Safi'e, V1, Page 77, 1977, Beirut:

الشافعي عيون الأثر في فنون المغازي والشمائل والسير
وكانت الكعبة قبل ان يبنيها شيث عليه السلام خيمة من ياقوتة حمراء يطوف بها آدم ويأنس بها لانها أنزلت إليه من الجنة وكان قد حج إلى موضعها من الهند.

"The Kaaba before it was built by Seth son of Adam, it was a tent made of rubies, and Adam used to enjoy visiting it, and **it was at that time in Inola.**"

1. Abraham and Ishmael. Described in a very long hadith; Sahih Al-Bukhari, Book 55, Hadith 583.

2. The Giants. Fateh AL-Bari Fe Shareh Sahih Al-Bukhari, V6, Book of Ahadith, Beirut Lebanon 1953, Page 464:

3. According to the story of 'A'ah Bin Al-Sa'eb, their roots go back to Jurhum Tribe.

وَفِي رِوَايَةِ عَطَاءِ بْنِ السَّائِبِ " وَكَانَتْ جُرْهُمٌ يَوْمَئِذٍ بِوَادٍ قَرِيبٍ مِنْ مَكَّةَ ، وَقِيلَ إِنَّ أَصْلَهُمْ مِنَ الْعَمَالِقَةِ

The tribe of Jurhum (they became Christians before Islam), according to the book of Fateh AL-Bari Fe Shareh, Sahih Al-Bukhari, Beirut Lebanon, 1953, V6, Page 548, Book of Maqeb. Bukhari, Book 40, Hadith 556:

> The Prophet said, "May Allah be generous to the mother of Ishmael! If she had left the water of Zam-Zam spring as it was, or said, 'If she had not used that spring,' it would have been a flowing stream. Jurhum tribe came and asked her, 'May. We settle at your dwelling?' She said, 'Yes. However, you have no right to possess the water.' They accepted."

The tribe of Khoza'a, who had kicked the tribe of Jurhum out of Mecca and took over the Kaaba for more than 300 years. Fateh AL-Bari Fe Shareh, Sahih Al-bukhari, Printing 2,02, Beirut Lebanon, 1953, V10, page 32:

- للإمام ابن حجر العسقلاني2.05فتح الباري، شرح صحيح البخاري، الإصدار
548المجلد السادس << كِتَاب الْمَنَاقِبِ >> باب قِصَّةِ خُزَاعَةَ ص
فهيرة بنت عمرو بن الحارث بن مضاض الجرهمي وكان أبوها آخر من ولي أمر مكة من جرهم فقام بأمر البيت سبطه عمرو بن لحي فصار ذلك في خزاعة بعد جرهم، ووقع بينهم في ذلك حروب إلى أن انجلت جرهم عن مكة، ثم تولت خزاعة أمر البيت ثلاثمائة سنة

"Fahera, daughter of Umaro Ibn Al-Hareth Bin Mu'da'd Al-Jurhum, her father was the last one of the tribes of Jurhum as a ruler of Kaaba, and there was a war between Jurhum and Khoza'a until the war ended with Khoza'a winning and kicked them out of Mecca therefore Khoza'a took over the Kaaba for three hundred years."

- Qusai, The Son of Dogs (Muhammad's forefather), who kicked Khoza'a (first man of the Qurish tribe) out of Mecca. Book of
Fateh AL-Bari Fe Shareh Sahih Al-Bukhari, Beirut Lebanon, 1953, V6, Page 548, Book of Maqeb:

فغلب قصي حينئذ على أمر البيت، وجمع بطون بني فهر وحارب خزاعة حتى أخرجهم من مكة؛

"Qusai did win and took over the Kaaba and he gathered all the clan of the sons of Faher (tribe) and forced them out of Mecca."

Qusai, The Son of Dogs added two Statues to worship next to the Kaaba. Sahih Muslim-Beshar'h Al-Nawawi, V9, Book of Haj, Beirut Lebanon, 2006, Page 401:

فَالرَّجُلُ اسْمُهُ إِسَافُ بْنُ بَقَاءٍ ، وَيُقَالُ ابْنُ عَمْرٍو ، وَالْمَرْأَةُ اسْمُهَا نَائِلَةُ بِنْتُ ذِئْبٍ ، وَيُقَالُ بِنْتُ سَهْلٍ ، قِيلَ :
كَانَا مِنْ جُرْهُمَ فَزَنَيَا دَاخِلَ الْكَعْبَةِ ، فَمَسَخَهُمَا اللَّهُ حَجَرَيْنِ ، فَنُصِّبَا عِنْدَ الْكَعْبَةِ ، وَقِيلَ : عَلَى الصَّفَا وَالْمَرْوَةِ
لِيَعْتَبِرَ النَّاسُ بِهِمَا وَيَتَّعِظُوا ، ثُمَّ حَوَّلُهُمَا قُصَيُّ بْنُ كِلَابٍ فَجَعَلَ أَحَدَهُمَا مُلَاصِقَ الْكَعْبَةِ وَالْآخَرَ بِزَمْزَمَ ، وَقِيلَ
: جَعَلَهُمَا بِزَمْزَمَ ، وَنَحَرَ عِنْدَهُمَا وَأَمَرَ بِعِبَادَتِهِمَا

"The man, his name was 'Isaf Bin Ba'qa' or Bin 'Umar, and the woman was Na'elah Bent Ze'eb or Bent Sahel, they [were] both from Jurhum, and they commited inside the Kaaba adultery so Allah turned them both to two statues, so they were placed next to the Kaaba, and it was said placed on the Safa & Al-Marwa (two places Muslim have to visit in hajj pilgrimage—see Qur'an 2: 158), so Qusai, The Son of Dogs, placed them both next to the Kaaba and sacrificed to them (the two statues) and forced people to worship them."

- The tribe of Qurish built the Kaaba five years before Muhammad became became a prophet! Book Titel Faid Al-'Qader, Printed in 2000, Egypt, V1, Page 639:

إعادة بنائها في زمن المصطفى صلى الله عليه وسلم وله من العمر خمس وثلاثون سنة

The Kaaba was rebuilt when the prophet was thirty five years old

- Abdu Allah Ibn Al Zobeir in the Islamic year 65 (684 AC). (Book of Al-Kamel Fe Al-Tari'kh page 362 by Ibn 'Ather).

- Al Hajaj Ibn Yousef Al Thaqafi, who destroyed the Kaaba totally and rebuilt it again! The Kaaba was covered by garbage. (Book of Al-Bidayiah Wa Al-Nihayia, by Ibn Kather, V8, Page 246.)

- The Ottoman sultan Murad, year 1630 AC

But the Muslim's claim that the Kaaba is the first house built in the world by the angels of God can be easily refuted by reading some of the Muslims texts such as Tafsir Al-Lebab by Ibn 'Adel Al-'Aanbali, V4, Page 225:

وعن علي : أن رجلا قال له : هو أول بيت؟ قال : لا ، كان قبله بيوت ، أول بيت وضع للناس ، مباركا ، فيه الهدى والرحمة والبركة ، أول من بناه إبراهيم ، ثم بناه قوم من العرب من جرهم ، ثم هدم ، فبنته العمالقة ، وهم ملوك من أولاد عمليق بن سام بن نوح ، ثم هدم فبناه قريش .

According to Ali, a man said to him, "This is the first house?" (He replied), "No, there was before it houses, but this is the first house that was made for mankind. And it has guidance and mercy and blessing. And the first who built it is Abraham, then the people of the Arab, from them the tribe of Jurhum.Then it was destroyed, then it was built by the giants, and they are kings from the children of Amliq, the son of Sam, the son of Noah. And then it was destroyed again and built by the tribe of Qurish.

The point of showing you how and what Muslims think about their Kaaba, is to gain an understanding of why they think it's holy!

Notice here that as long as they agree the Kaaba was rebuilt many times, it means it was destroyed many times too! At the same time, the Qur'an claims that Allah always guarded the Kaaba, according to the story in the Qur'an, the chapter of the Elephant (Qur'an 105:1-5):

[1] Had not they seen how your Lord treated the people of the Elephant?

[2] Did He not make their plan fail?

[3] And send against them army of fighting birds,

[4] Which throw at them stones of baked clay,

[5] And made them like green leaf that has been eaten by cattle.

This story is about an army of Christians, sent by the king of Ethiopia under the command of Abraha (a Christian ruler of Yemen), who wanted to destroy the Kaaba. Allah sent fighting birds to destroy this army who were armed with hundreds of elephants. Even the Muslims call that year the Year of the Elephant (570 AC). As we see by the date, this story claims to be not long before Muhammad's birth. The story doesn't make a lot of sense. Let us look at it together and see why.

1. There were never any elephants in the Arabian Peninsula.

2. Neither in Yemen.

3. The only possibility is that elephants were brought to what is present day Saudi Arabia through the Red Sea! This is impossible, because no one at that time could have built such a huge number of large ships to carry hundreds of elephants, especially not thousands as the story claims!

4. Are we to assume that they had American aircraft carriers to fly them over and the elephants landed safely in Yemen!

5. How could they feed them in the dessert? An adult elephant can consume 140–270 kg (300-600 lbs.) daily, but this number can change based on the work they do! If they do not work, less food is needed in one day. However, in this case they would need more than normal, for they were walking in a very hot desert and carrying all the war equipment and/or men on top of them. You should know that after you leave Yemen, the land is just a plain desert. Nothing is green. Ever! The only way for them to make it would be to carry the food for each elephant with them. That would also be impossible because the elephant would only be able to carry enough for maybe one day!

6. Then we've got the water issue. How will they serve the elephants'

need of water? They drink from 100 to 300 liters a day and that's based on zoo life or wildlife. The elephants in our story need a lot more for they are walking in one of the hottest deserts. How can the army provide them with the water they need to drink?

7. Where will they get the elephants enough water to spray themselves? As we know, elephants do not have a cooling system (they do not sweat), so they need to cool themselves, either by staying in water during the heat of the day or by spraying themselves with water. Remember that the desert of Saudi Arabia does not have trees to provide shade during their trip.

8. Why does this king need the elephants anyway? The Kaaba can be destroyed by two men. Even one man is enough to do the job! It's very easy to destroy a room. It was not made of anything as substantial as concrete at that time!

9. Maybe this Ethiopian king was a fool. He is an African who had never been in the desert before!

10. If the Kaaba was destroyed many times, as we showed that Muslims agree about, why did Allah want to protect it this time?

11. The Muslims might say it was destroyed by wind, or an earthquake, before! The fact is, this is false.

I will ask some very serious questions if this later assertion is true.

Where was Allah's Army?

1. Year 63 Islamic, 682 AC, when Yezed Ibn Mo'awiah attacked the Kaaba led by Muslim Ibn 'Oqbah and his army! To fight Abdulah Ibn Al Zubier, they attacked Mecca and the Kaaba by catapult, and leveled the Kaaba to the ground! After Abdulah Ibn Al Zubier's men sought refuge in it!

2. A few years later in the year 692 AC, 73 Islamic, Abed Al-Malik Ibn Mrwan sent Al-Hajah Ibn Yousef Al Saqafi to kill Abdulah Ibn Al Zubier because they had destroyed the Kaaba in the last attack. However, he took over Mecca again, and the Kaaba was destroyed again in less then ten years fighting the same person (Abdulah Ibn Al Zubier). His men again sought refuge in the Kaaba, then he (Al-Hajaj) hit the Kaaba by catapult again and destroyed it!

3. In the book of Ibn Kathir, Al-Bidaiah & Nihayiah, V11, Page 135/137. In the year 317 Islamic, 929 AC, book of Ibn Khaldon V2, Page 84/258,

هـ حيث هاجموا الحجاج يوم التروية واستباحوا دماءهم وأموالهم وقتلوهم في جوف الكعبة وقلعوا باب 317 الكعبة وكسوتها والحجر الأسود وحملوه إلى بلادهم ومكث عندهم اثنتان وعشرون سنة. انظر فضائح .. وانظر الموسوعة 137-135/11الباطنية للغزالي ص تحقيق عبد الرحمن بدوي، وانظر البداية والنهاية، 194/5. الأعلام، الزركلي، 395الميسرة في الأديان المعاصرة، الندوة العالمية، مرجع سابق، ص

When Abu Taher Al Qurmty (Qurmoti) from Iraq, attacked Mecca killing more than 30 thousand Muslims, destroying the Kaaba, and taking the most holy stone in it (the black stone), they kept it for more than 20 years using it as bathroom stone (urinating on it). On top of that, when his men were busy destroying the Kaaba, he was screaming to the sky saying, "I am the creator! Where are your birds Allah? Where are you Allah?" The black stone did not come back to the Kaaba

until the Khalif of the Fatmeen (الخليفة المنصور بن المعز لدين الله الفاطمى) Al-Mansour Le Deen Allah Al-Fatimy interceded and asked them (Al-Qaramita) nicely to return the black stone."

You can find the same story in Al-Mausu'a Al-'Alamia Al-Misarah Fe Al-Adian, Page 395; and book of Al-'Alam, V5, Page 194, by Al-Zarkaly.

The important and unique thing about **Abu Taher Al-Qurmty** is that he proved the lies of the Qur'an, not only by the destruction of the Kaaba, but also in challenging Allah by screaming, "Where is Allah? Where are the birds who are loaded with stones?" As if he was trying to:

⚔ Prove that there is nothing holy about the Kaaba.

⚔ The Qur'an is a book of legend and false fairy tale stories.

⚔ Muslims worship idols that are useless and harmless.

⚔ The black stone is nothing more than a meteorite that Arabs used to worship before Islam. They worshiped a lot of them because they thought they came from God. Later, the black stone was put in a cover that was shaped as a vagina.

⚔ Allah did not do anything to save his most holy stone, nor was anyone able to force them by war to get it back. It was only returned after intercession to them for it.

I will add to all of this one simple question: Why did Allah protect the Kaaba when the elephant army came? Remember that at that time the Kaaba was:

1. Not holy, for it was full of idols.

2. Not controlled by Muslims.

3. Not a place of worship—it was only a business location!

4. Protected by Allah when the Kaaba was dirty (unclean by the infidels and full of their gods), but he did not make a move when it was under control of the clean, good believers—the Muslims!

5. Today, where are the birds of Allah while the American military aircraft are flying over? Not even one of his birds has shown its head yet!

One Kaaba or Many Kaaba!

Many do not know that there were 26 Kaaba in the Arabian Peninsula and that the Meccan Kaaba was just one of them. There was nothing unique about it. Did you know that all of them were built over one holy stone, and they all look exactly the same in height and width? Sahih Al Bukhari, book of Al Magazi Hadith 4117:

حدثنا الصلت بن محمد قال سمعت مهدي بن ميمون قال سمعت أبا رجاء العطاردي يقول كنا نعبد 4117
الحجر فإذا وجدنا حجرا هو أخير منه ألقيناه وأخذنا الآخر فإذا لم نجد حجرا جمعنا جثوة من تراب ثم جئنا
بالشاة فحلبناه عليه ثم طفنا به فإذا دخل شهر رجب قلنا منصل الأسنة فلا ندع رمحا فيه حديدة ولا سهما فيه
حديدة إلا نزعناه

Abu Raja said, "We used to worship stones and if we found a stone better than the other stone, we would leave worshiping the first one, and we started worshiping the new one."

From this hadith we understand the following:

1. Stones were their gods.
2. It was the look of the stone that made them like it more.
3. This stone is not their god forever, but it is present and the best that is in their hands.

The black stone is not the only holy stone! Sahih Al-Bukhari, Book 26, Hadith 676:

Ibn 'Omar. He revealed, "I have never forgotten to touch, the two stones of Kaaba, the **black stone** and the **Yemen Corner stone,** both in the existence and the nonexistence of public ever since I saw the Prophet touching them. I asked Naf'e, "Did Ibn 'Omar used to tour between the two corners?" Naf'e responded, "He used to walk because it was easier for him to touch it."

If Islam is against paganism, why did Muhammad copy the pagans and take the Kaaba as a prayer station? We talked before, if you remember, about Omar Ibn

Al-Khatab saying (Bukhari, Book 8, Hadith 395):

> The Book of 'Olum Al-Qur'an, V1, Page 137, Omar bin Al Khatab said: Reported by Annas that Omar bin Al Khatab said: "My God agreed with me in three things:
>
> **(First)**, I expressed 'Oh Allah's missionary, I desire as your place of worship the place where Abraham did [have a] place to worship. So it came, the heavenly revelation (Page 137), (Qur'an, 2:125). And take you (Muslims) the home of Abraham as a place of worship.'
>
> **(Second)**, And I said, To the Prophet, to the prophet of Allah, 'Good and bad singles talk to your wives. Therefore, instruct them to veil their identity.' Therefore Allah sent down the verse of the veiling of the women, as well as the Qur'an concerning the veiling of the women (Qur'an 24:31).
>
> **(Third)**, The wives of the Prophet performed a compact against the Prophet, and I said to them, 'Maybe if His Almighty, the Prophet, divorced you, (all the wives) and exchanged you with
>
> better wives than you.' So the verse (Qur'an, 66:5) (the same as I had said) was revealed."

If you look at this hadith closely, you will notice that Muhammad was trying to make those who loved the Kaaba happy. It had been their prayer station for hundreds of years. Muhammad knew he needed to make those that were Muslims happy. He also knew that it would make Islam more accepted for those who had refused him. He knew they didn't want to change the way of life they were accustomed to!

The fact is, it wasn't only that he wanted to make them happy, but it was for economic reasons also. After Muhammad killed all the Jews and the Christians in Mecca, business in this city died and no one was coming into the city to trade. Everyone was afraid of Muhammad and his army because they knew he would have them killed (they were infidels). Muhammad needed to create a trade movement into the city, and since he liked what Omar asked for, he got a great idea.

1. If I make Mecca a centerpiece for Muslims, the city will be busy with believers who will have to come and visit.
2. If they visit, they have to sleep in hotels and buy food and gifts.
3. At the same time, they will bring things with them to sell.
4. That will make the city a business center, more than a religious or holy city.
5. On top of that, it's a decision that will give Muhammad's tribe the power

over all the Arabs.

6. To prove all these points, we will go to the Qur'an and see for ourselves how it's not really the Kaaba that Muhammad wanted. In Qur'an 2:142 we read:

سَيَقُولُ السُّفَهَاءُ مِنَ النَّاسِ مَا وَلَّاهُمْ عَنْ قِبْلَتِهِمُ الَّتِي كَانُوا عَلَيْهَا قُلْ لِلَّهِ الْمَشْرِقُ وَالْمَغْرِبُ يَهْدِي مَنْ يَشَاءُ إِلَى صِرَاطٍ مُسْتَقِيمٍ

The stupid (fools) from the people will say: "What made them replace the Qibla (prayer direction, which, at the time, was Jerusalem) to which they were used to?" Say: "To Allah tie up East and West: He leads whom He wants to the true way."

➤ As we see here, Muhammad already had a direction that he prayed towards. It had always been, from the first day he claimed to be a prophet, towards Jerusalem. But the verse says he doesn't really need one!

➤ As the verse says, all directions are to Allah. What's the point? In the coming verse, Muhammad is trying to explain why he changed the direction. Some were making fun of him, because he kept changing the directions for prayers. Qur'an 2:143:

وَكَذَلِكَ جَعَلْنَاكُمْ أُمَّةً وَسَطًا لِتَكُونُوا شُهَدَاءَ عَلَى النَّاسِ وَيَكُونَ الرَّسُولُ عَلَيْكُمْ شَهِيدًا وَمَا جَعَلْنَا الْقِبْلَةَ الَّتِي كُنْتَ عَلَيْهَا إِلَّا لِنَعْلَمَ مَنْ يَتَّبِعُ الرَّسُولَ مِمَّنْ يَنْقَلِبُ عَلَى عَقِبَيْهِ وَإِنْ كَانَتْ لَكَبِيرَةً إِلَّا عَلَى الَّذِينَ هَدَى اللهُ وَمَا كَانَ اللهُ لِيُضِيعَ إِيمَانَكُمْ إِنَّ اللهَ بِالنَّاسِ لَرَءُوفٌ رَحِيمٌ

Plus, therefore, We have made you a medium fair-minded nation so you may be the bearers of witness to the people and that the Messenger may be a bearer of witness to you; and We did not make that which you would have to be the 'Qibla (direction of prayer) but that We might differentiate him who follows the Messenger from him who goes round back upon his heels, and this was certainly hard except for those whom Allah has guided aright; and Allah was not going to make your faith to be worthless most certainly Allah is kindness Merciful to the people.

It says here the reason for changing the direction of the prayer from Jerusalem to Mecca was to distinguish between Muslims and non-Muslims. There is something very wrong here!

Note with me that this would mean that the Kaaba is not a holy place at all. **It's just a way for Allah to know who is a Muslim or not!**

If this is the case, why did Allah say that we are dirty, and that we (Non-Muslims) cannot enter the city of Mecca anymore, when it's not holy at all? Why did Muhammad kiss the black stone, when the Kaaba itself, is not holy? As a result, the black stone isn't holy either, which means the Kaaba is not important. This means the same for the Hajj (pilgrimage to Mecca).

If the infidels and pagans prayed in the direction of the Kaaba, and the Muslims do the same, how would we know which were Muslims?

It's so clear that this is a faulty excuse, and not even a smart one! The next verse even shows that the one who made this excuse was not smart at all. Qur'an 2:144:

قَدْ نَرَى تَقَلُّبَ وَجْهِكَ فِي السَّمَاء فَلَنُوَلِّيَنَّكَ قِبْلَةً تَرْضَاهَا فَوَلِّ وَجْهَكَ شَطْرَ الْمَسْجِدِ الْحَرَامِ وَحَيْثُمَا كُنتُمْ فَوَلُّوا وُجُوهَكُمْ شَطْرَهُ وَإِنَّ الَّذِينَ أُوتُوا الْكِتَابَ لَيَعْلَمُونَ أَنَّهُ الْحَقُّ مِن رَّبِّهِمْ وَمَا اللَّهُ بِغَافِلٍ عَمَّا يَعْمَلُونَ

We saw you (Muhammad) rotating your face around looking for solutions. Now We will turn thee to a direction that shall please thee. Turn then your face in the direction of the protected Mosque. Anywhere ye are, turn your faces in that direction. The people of the Book know well that is the truth from their Lord, and Allah is not unconscious of what they are doing.

1. Look here! Allah is just pleasing Muhammad. It was Muhammad's wish that he copy Omar's idea.

2. Muhammad was looking for a solution. What was he trying to solve? The Muslims never complained about the direction of the prayer. They already had one!

3. Allah is choosing the direction that everyone was used too!

4. The one they were used too was the perfect one. It was Muhammad that was doing the wrong one!

5. On top of this, the verse is clearly saying that Muhammad used to pray to the Kaaba too, which means he was a pagan all his life. He had been doing what his tribe had always done before he claimed to be prophet of Allah.

The Black Stone in Islam

For some background reference, we will take a quick look at how Muhammad was creating a new religion by mixing up old belief systems and religions. Al-Bukhari, Book 26, Hadith 679 tells us:

أربعة ومشى أشواطة ثلاثة و سعى النَّذ بي سعى ـ الْحَجّ كِتَاب ـ الـ بخاري صحيح ه ي ل ع مـلـس و ة ـالـث طا و ش

حَدَّثَنَا سَعِيدُ بْنُ أَبِي مَرْيَمَ أَخْبَرَنَا مُحَمَّدُ بْنُ جَعْفَرِ بْنِ أَبِي كَثِيرٍ قَالَ أَخْبَرَنِي زَيْدُ بْنُ أَسْلَمَ 1528 ـ «ص582»

عَنْ أَبِيهِ أَنَّ عُمَرَ بْنَ الْخَطَّابِ رَضِيَ اللَّهُ عَنْهُ قَالَ لِلرُّكْنِ أَمَا وَاللَّهِ إِنِّي لَأَعْلَمُ أَنَّكَ حَجَرٌ لَا تَضُرُّ وَلَا تَنْفَعُ وَلَوْلَا
أَنِّي رَأَيْتُ النَّبِيَّ صَلَّى اللَّهُ عَلَيْهِ وَسَلَّمَ اسْتَلَمَكَ مَا اسْتَلَمْتُكَ فَاسْتَلَمَهُ ثُمَّ قَالَ فَمَا لَنَا وَلِلرَّمَلِ إِنَّمَا كُنَّا رَاءَيْنَا بِهِ
الْمُشْرِكِينَ وَقَدْ أَهْلَكَهُمُ اللَّهُ ثُمَّ قَالَ شَيْءٌ صَنَعَهُ النَّبِيُّ صَلَّى اللَّهُ عَلَيْهِ وَسَلَّمَ فَلَا نُحِبُّ أَنْ نَتْرُكَهُ

Stated by Zaid's bin Islam that his father said: "I saw that 'Omar's bin Al Khattab was kissing the black stone, and then he said to the stone while kissing it, 'If I had not seen Allah's Apostle kissing you (stone), I would never have kissed you.'"

Sahih Al-Bukhari Book 26 (Hajj), Hadith 1520, (Arabic Print):

صحيح البخاري - كِتَاب الْحَجِّ - بَاب مَا ذُكِرَ فِي الْحَجَرِ الْأَسْوَدِ
بَاب مَا ذُكِرَ فِي الْحَجَرِ الْأَسْوَدِ

حَدَّثَنَا مُحَمَّدُ بْنُ كَثِيرٍ أَخْبَرَنَا سُفْيَانُ عَنْ الْأَعْمَشِ عَنْ إِبْرَاهِيمَ عَنْ عَابِسِ بْنِ رَبِيعَةَ عَنْ عُمَرَ رَضِيَ اللَّهُ 1520
عَنْهُ أَنَّهُ جَاءَ إِلَى الْحَجَرِ الْأَسْوَدِ فَقَبَّلَهُ فَقَالَ إِنِّي أَعْلَمُ أَنَّكَ حَجَرٌ لَا تَضُرُّ وَلَا تَنْفَعُ وَلَوْلَا أَنِّي رَأَيْتُ النَّبِيَّ صَلَّى
اللَّهُ عَلَيْهِ وَسَلَّمَ يُقَبِّلُكَ مَا قَبَّلْتُكَ

Reported Muhammad Ibn Kathir, and Sufian from Ibrahem, from 'Abe's bin Rabi'ah that 'Omar Said: 'Omar walk toward the front the black stone and kissed it, and he said "I know that you are a stone and cannot in either case give a benefit to anyone nor harm anyone. If I had not seen Allah's Apostle kissing you, I would not under no circumstances have kissed you."

1. As we see in here, Omar did not like kissing the stone, because he knew it was a pagan act, but he had no choice but to do so, for Muhammad the big boss did!

2. Omar even said that it's harmless and useless, but Muhammad had something else to say. This means Omar knew Muhammad was a liar and not a prophet.

Muhammad said in Al-Tirmidhi, Hadith 877, page 226:

سنن الترمذي - كِتَاب الْحَجِّ عَنْ رَسُولِ اللَّهِ صَلَّى اللَّهُ عَلَيْهِ وَسَلَّمَ - بَاب مَا جَاءَ فِي فَضْلِ الْحَجَرِ الْأَسْوَدِ وَالرُّكْنِ
وَالْمَقَامِ

- «بَاب مَا جَاءَ فِي فَضْلِ الْحَجَرِ الْأَسْوَدِ وَالرُّكْنِ وَالْمَقَامِ226ص -»

حَدَّثَنَا قُتَيْبَةُ حَدَّثَنَا جَرِيرٌ عَنْ عَطَاءِ بْنِ السَّائِبِ عَنْ سَعِيدِ بْنِ جُبَيْرٍ عَنْ ابْنِ عَبَّاسٍ قَالَ قَالَ رَسُولُ اللَّهِ صَلَّى اللَّهُ 877
عَلَيْهِ وَسَلَّمَ نَزَلَ الْحَجَرُ الْأَسْوَدُ مِنْ الْجَنَّةِ وَهُوَ أَشَدُّ بَيَاضًا مِنْ اللَّبَنِ فَسَوَّدَتْهُ خَطَايَا بَنِي آدَمَ قَالَ وَفِي الْبَاب عَنْ عَبْدِ اللَّهِ
بْنِ عَمْرٍو وَأَبِي هُرَيْرَةَ قَالَ أَبُو عِيسَى حَدِيثُ ابْنِ عَبَّاسٍ حَدِيثٌ حَسَنٌ صَحِيحٌ

"This black stone has come down from Heaven and it was whiter than milk, but sins and mistakes of mankind turned it dark black."

3. It says here that Muhammad claimed the black stone to be a holy stone sent by and from God. He also said that it had a job, which was sucking the sin of mankind. He claimed that as time went by, sin had changed the white color of the stone to black! This means Muhammad's story was not at all convincing to Omar, because Omar did not accept it, but he had to accept it to gain the benefit of being with this gang leader. One of these men was right. It can't be both. I think we all agree that Omar was right on this one.

4. Muhammad even claimed that the black stone was a white ruby and that it would witness to Allah on the judgment day for each Muslim's sin, as seen in Sunan Al-Tirmidhi, Hadith 961, page 294:

سنن الترمذي - كِتَاب الْحَجِّ عَن رَسُولِ اللَّهِ صَلَّى اللَّهُ عَلَيْهِ وَسَلَّمَ - بَاب مَا جَاءَ فِي الْحَجَرِ الْأَسْوَدِ

- «بَاب مَا جَاءَ فِي الْحَجَرِ الْأَسْوَدِ294ص -»

961 حَدَّثَنَا قُتَيْبَةُ عَنْ جَرِيرٍ عَنْ ابْنِ خُثَيْمٍ عَنْ سَعِيدِ بْنِ جُبَيْرٍ عَنْ ابْنِ عَبَّاسٍ قَالَ قَالَ رَسُولُ اللَّهِ صَلَّى اللَّهُ عَلَيْهِ وَسَلَّمَ فِي الْحَجَرِ وَاللَّهِ لَيَبْعَثَنَّهُ اللَّهُ يَوْمَ الْقِيَامَةِ لَهُ عَيْنَانِ يُبْصِرُ بِهِمَا وَلِسَانٌ يَنْطِقُ بِهِ يَشْهَدُ عَلَى مَنْ اسْتَلَمَهُ بِحَقٍّ قَالَ أَبُو عِيسَى

Narrated by Qutiba from Jareer from Ibn Abbas: The prophet said the black stone in the judgment day Allah will make him alive and resurrect him! It has eyes, it sees by them; and ears, hearing by them! In addition to that, a tongue, to witnesses by it (the stone) by the truth, to each one who had held it with his hands.

Where are the Muslims concerning this story? I have not seen one video or claim about the science of the talking stone that has eyes and ears! It's clear that they choose whatever makes Islam look better just to fool us. If Muhammad speaks science, is he right some of the time and a dummy some of the time? The fact is, the ones that he was right about, he just took from others books.

Where did Muhammad get this idea that stones talk, take the sins of humans, and work for God?

Qur'an Says All Prophet-Hood is From Jacob (Israel), So Was Muhammad One of Them?

Qur'an 45:16:

> And truly we gave the children of Israel the scripture and the command and the prophet-hood, and provided them with the delicious sustenance and preferred them above all mankind!

Muhammad is not from the children of Israel.

The verse says clearly that Allah gave the commands and the prophet-hood to the **children of Israel**! You need to remember that the **children of Israel** means the **children of Jacob** as in Genesis 32:28:

And he said, Thy name shall be called no more Jacob, but Israel: for as a prince hast thou power with God and with men, and hast prevailed.

1. Muslims might say that Allah is only speaking about Israel, and that is why he did not give more details. If you read that chapter, you will see that Muhammad's god jumped into this for no reason! If Allah knew that it was not only Jacob's (Israel's) children that had prophet-hood, what's the point of saying something not true? Especially, since the Muslims believe in many prophets who are not even Arab, like Alexander the Great or the prophets Idress, Saleh or Shuyeb, and add to them, Muhammad. This means he did not really make the prophet-hood through them.

2. This has not only been proven to be a contradiction, but it also shows that Muhammad cannot be a prophet, because he is not from Israel. He is actually their worst enemy.

3. To make our point more clear, we should go to Qur'an 29:27:

4. And to [Abraham] We gave him Isaac and Jacob, and made Exclusively among his Offspring the Prophet-hood and Revelation...

5. Now Muslims can play with the translation as much as they like, but in the end, it's so clear where the prophet-hood has to be from; the offspring of Isaac and Jacob.

6. One more chapter to make things clearer is Qur'an 37:112-113:

112 To Abraham, We gave him the good news of Isaac, who will be a prophet, one of the law-abiding,
113 We blessed him and Isaac, and from among his Offspring are, and their descendants are, he who is incorruptible good and bad to their own souls.

7. If Ishmael is older and a prophet, why did Allah forget his name? This verse would be more accurate with Islam's belief if Allah had put the name of Ishmael there. A very simple question, why isn't it?

⮦ Ismael is the oldest.

⮦ Ishmael is a prophet in Islam.

⮦ Muslims claim that Muhammad is of Ishmael's offspring. I don't agree with this claim at all, but will go with the Muslims and say, if Ishmael is important, why does Allah, verse after verse, keep forgetting his existence? But later, he made a verse saying, "Oh, Ishmael is a prophet too!"

⮦ For me, Muhammad cannot be from Ishmael. Sadly, even some Christians think he is from Ishmael, which is a big mistake. They just repeat and say in churches what someone else has told them. There is a very simple explanation.

(a) Arabs existed before Ishmael, so how can he be their father?

(b) Abraham is Aramaic. Hagar was Egyptian. The son is an Arab?

(c) Even the Muslims books (Book of Al-Sirah Al-Nabwiah by Ibn Hisham, V1, Page 5) say that Ishmael married one of their daughters from the tribe of Jarhom (Her name was Ra'lah, daughter of 'Amro Al-Johrimy according to Muslims). The Jarhom tribe became Christians about 400 years before Islam (Book of Al-Agani 13:109). Muhammad's is not from that tribe, which means he can not be from Ishmael.

(d) Many might say, well doesn't the Bible say God will make his offspring as numerous as the stars in heaven or the sand on the sea shore? Genesis 22:17 (KJV):

That in blessing I will bless thee, and in multiplying I will multiply thy seed as the stars of the heaven, and as the sand which is upon the sea shore; and thy seed shall possess the gate of his enemies;

(e) But they forgot that the real Arabs today (not those who speak Arabic) are not even 40 million in number. Are the Indonesians Arab? Are the Pakistanis? Or numerous other peoples we could name? So, this is very wrong information being propagated in our churches. By doing this, we are helping the Muslims to spread a lie. On top of that, ask yourself why Muhammad wanted to be claimed as the offspring of Ishmael! It's simply because he wanted to have legal relation and lineage to the father of prophets, so he could have a legitimate claim.

(f) Muhammad said in Sahih Bukhari, Book 55, Hadith 596:

Reported of Ibn 'Omar: "The Prophet said, 'The honorable man is the son of the honorable man, the honorable, mirroring the honorable Joseph, the son of Jacob, the son of Isaac, the son of Abraham.'"

(g) Did you notice here that Muhammad dropped the name of Ishmael? The fact is this hadith opens doors for more questions!

"The honorable is the son of the honorable!" As you see, Muhammad sometimes, or most of the time, does not think carefully about his own words. Let's look again at Sahih Bukhari, Book 55, Hadith 596:

Reported of Ibn 'Omar: "The Prophet said, **The honorable man is the son of the honorable man**, the **honorable, mirroring the honorable** Joseph, the son of **Jacob**, the son of **Isaac,** the son of **Abraham.**"

1. According to Muhammad, to be honorable, you have to be the son of an honorable person! But Muhammad forgot that his father and his mother were both infidels, and Allah said infidels were dirty.

2. Remember the word "honorable" has only a religious meaning.

3. Also, Muhammad did not add the name of Ishmael to that hadith as an honorable son. Look at Qur'an 9:28:

O you who believe, the polytheist is for sure filthy [they are] filth, on narrative of their inner wickedness so do not let them come near the Sacred Mosque after this year...!

4. This is what the Qur'an said about Muhammad praying to his family who were infidels. Qur'an 9:113:

It is not accepted for the Prophet, and those who believe, to pray for the forgiveness for infidels even though they are <u>relative with</u>, after it hath become obvious that they are people of hell-fire.

5.   This verse shows us many things. Muhammad's family is in the hell fire, because they are not honorable.

6.   Muhammad cannot be an honorable man, because he is not the son of an honorable man according to his own word. The Qur'an, or Allah, said that whoever was like his parents, were filthy and dirty! We see this in Sahih Muslim, Book 001, Hadith 0398:

صحيح مسلم - كِتَاب الْإِيمَانِ - باب بَيَانِ أَنَّ مَنْ مَاتَ عَلَى الْكُفْرِ فَهُوَ فِي النَّارِ وَلَا تَنَالُهُ شَفَاعَةٌ وَلَا تَنْفَعُهُ قَرَابَةُ الْمُقَرَّبِينَ

حَدَّثَنَا أَبُو بَكْرِ بْنُ أَبِي شَيْبَةَ حَدَّثَنَا عَفَّانُ حَدَّثَنَا حَمَّادُ بْنُ سَلَمَةَ عَنْ ثَابِتٍ عَنْ أَنَسٍ أَنَّ رَجُلًا قَالَ يَا رَسُولَ 203 اللَّهِ أَيْنَ أَبِي قَالَ فِي النَّارِ فَلَمَّا قَفَّى دَعَاهُ فَقَالَ إِنَّ أَبِي وَأَبَاكَ فِي النَّارِ

'Anas stated. "Truly, an individual said: 'Ambassador of Allah, where is my father?' The prophet said: 'Your father is in the hell fire.' When he turned away, <u>The Prophet of Allah, called him and said: 'Truly, my father and your father are in the Hell Fire.'"</u>

Sahih Muslim, Book 004, Hadith 2129:

Abu Huraira reported that Allah's Messenger did say: "I asked Allah's permission to allow me to beg for the forgiveness of my

mother, but He refused to grant it to me. I sought permission from Him to visit her grave, and He granted that to me."

-     Muhammad asked Allah to forgive his mother for not being a believer in Allah. Did you notice that he never asked for forgiveness for his father? He never met his real dad, and the fact is he didn't really know who he was. How could he ask for forgiveness for him? Now some will say, "Well, Muhammad's father was Abduallah." As we have discussed elsewhere in this book, the truth is, no one knows who his father was, for Muhammad was born four years after the death of his supposed father (Abdu Allah). How could he be his father?

-     The discrimination and prejudice of Islam is, if you are not of them, you are considered dirty and filthy! It is taken to the point that non-Muslims can't enter many cities in Saudi Arabia, and if you do, even by mistake, you should be killed. Imagine if there was a sign saying, "Muslims are not allowed to enter New York, for they are not clean!" Everyone would say how ugly the Christians are! I don't see anyone making the same accusation against Muslims for this same action!

⤵ In John 3:16, the Bible says:

For God so loved the world, that he gave his only begotten Son, that whosoever believeth in him should not perish, but have everlasting life.

⤵ In Christ's words, we see how he opens his arms, not only for those who accepted him, but for the world. Matthew 5:44 says:

But I say unto you, love your enemies, bless them that curse you, do good to them that hate you, and pray for them which despitefully use you, and persecute you;

Compare this to the "honorable" being accused by Muslims of stealing red underwear! Muhammad never accepted the Qur'an's rules on himself, not even his own hadith (order or speech).

Muhammad is An Arab—Was Ishmael Arab Too?

Abraham is Aramaean (Aramaic) + Hagar is Egyptian = Ishmael is Arab?

What many people do not know that Arab is not an Ethnic but its a word mean the inhabitants of the dessert, **Arbat** mean dessert in other word who ever live in the dessert used to be called with such name or description even he would be living in Arizona desert in the USA.
However even if assume that the word Arab is meant for an ethnic group was Ishmael an Arab?

Many, even in our churches, teach that Ismael is an Arab and often Christians repeat this myth without investigating the information. I will show you that even Muslims themselves do not make such a claim in their books (Bukhari, Book 55, Hadith 583):

"She (Ishmael's mother) lived in that way until some community from the tribe of Jurhum or a family from Jurhum crossed by her and her child, as they (the Jurhum people) were coming through the road of Kada'. They landed in the further down part of Mecca where they saw a bird that had the habit of flying around water and not going away. They said, 'This bird must be flying in a loop over water, even though we experience that there is no water in this valley.' They sent one or two messengers, which discovered the source of water, and returned to notify them of the water. So, they moved towards the water." The Prophet added, "Ishmael's mother was seated near the water. They asked her, 'Do you allow us to [put our] tents here? She responded as Yes, but you will have no right to own the water.' They accepted to that." The Prophet in addition said, mother of Ishmael was delighted with the situation as she used to love to take pleasure in the accompany of the people. Therefore, they settled over there, and later they sent for their families who came and settled with them so that some families became permanent residents nearby. The child (Ishmael) grew up between them and **learnt Arabic** from them (Jurhum people), and they liked him as he grew up, and when he reached the age of maturity they made him marry a woman from among them.

⋏ "The child (Ishmael) grew up between them and **learnt Arabic** from them (Jurhum people)"

⋏ He is Arab but he does not know Arabic!

⋏ He married a woman of them, so does this make his kids Arab like the mother?

⋏ The answer is no, in Arab tradition you belong to the father not to the mother. And remember the ones reporting the story are the Arabs.

⋏ This is means that Abraham and Ismael's mother both do not speak Arabic. This is why he learned it from Jurhum tribe as we read in the book of AL-Fateh, V6, Page 403, by Al-Hafez Ibn 'Hajer, printed in Beirut Lebanon, 1991:

(6/403)قال الحافظ ابن حجر في الفتح(
(قوله (وتعلم العربية منهم
فيه اشعار بأن لسان أمه وأبيه لم يكن عربيا

He said, "He learned Arabic from them (Jurhum) this is inform us that Ishmael mother and father both do not know Arabic"

⋏ Then how old was Ismael when he started speaking Arabic? We find the answer in many Islamic books.

We will find out from Ali (Muhammad's cousin) in his own words. Book of Sahih Al-Jame', V1, Page 435, Hadith Number 2581:

- عشرة سنة435أول من فتق لسانه بالعربية المبينة إسماعيل و هو ابن أربع الجزء الأول ص
الشيرازي في الألقاب) عن علي) .
في صحيح الجامع2581قال الشيخ الألباني : (صحيح) انظر حديث رقم :

He said, "The first who spoke perfect Arabic is Ishmael and he spoke it at the age of fourteen years." And the Imam Albani said it's a correct hadith.

Based on this, Muslims agree that Ishmael is not of Arabic ancestry; his parents, both mother and father, are not Arabs; they both do not speak Arabic; he learned Arabic from the Arabs; and he spoke it at the age of fourteen—so how does that make him Arab!

The important question we need to ask is does a person's ethnic group change by learning a language? Of course that is ridiculous. Some might say that Allah made Ishmael as the first man who was Arabic. But this is false as we proved from their own books, which say that he learned Arabic from the Jurhum tribe. But for the sake of argument, even if Allah taught him Arabic, that still does not make him an Arab.

To make it more clear, Zipporah is a Midianite woman she was the daughter of Reuel, priest of Midian, who becomes the wife of Moses. Why no Christina says that Moses children's are Midianite?

16 Now the priest of Midian had seven daughters: and they came and drew water, and filled the troughs to water their father's flock... 21 And Moses was content to dwell with the man: and he gave Moses Zipporah his daughter.Exodus 2

The fact The Midianites not long after they had war with Israel, and came under attack back by Moses, Num 31, so getting married to a woman makes you and your children's sons of that nation so how they go into war with Moses, and Moses went in war with them?

Therefor I would like to ask every Christian not to take what his priest speaks for granted, until he question and studies how accurate his teaching is for many speak of their ignorance.

Who can be called Arab according to Muhammad?

Al-'Khasa'es Al-Kubra, author Al-Seu'ti, Beirut Lebanon, 1985, V1, Page 66:

الكتاب : الخصائص الكبرى
المؤلف / أبو الفضل جلال الدين عبد الرحمن أبي بكر السيوطي
- بيروت - 1405هـ - 1985م.دار النشر / دار الكتب العلمية
/ عدد الأجزاء 1
قال رسول الله {صلى الله عليه وسلم} إن الله خلق الخلق فاختار من الخلق بني آدم واختار من بين آدم العرب
واختار من العرب مضر واختار من مضر قريشا واختار من قريش بني هاشم واختارني من بني هاشم فأنا
من خيار إلى خيار

The prophet said: "Allah created his creation and chose from them sons of

Adam, and from sons of Adam, he chooses the Arab, and from the Arab, he chose Mudar (tribe), and from Mudar, he chose sons of Hasim (clan), and from Hashim, he chose me, finest of the best."

Here we see clear proof in Muhammad's own words about how Allah divided between mankind, separating them by ethnic groups and tribes, not by languages. You will notice the frequent use in Arabic of the word "Ibn," which means "son of." In the last hadith, Allah chose by "the son of," not by the language; which is by the blood line rather than by the language they speak. This proves that being an Arab is not the one who speaks Arabic only, but the one who is from an Arab father. In all the names, only the father will be used to prove who you are. Not your mother as long your father is known.

Therefore, Ishmael cannot be called Arab because he at some point spoke Arabic, neither in the Arab tradition nor in Islamic law as Muhammad stated in the reference we presented above.
But Muhammad badly needed to link himself to Ishmael in order to make himself one of seeds of Abraham, thus enabling him to be accepted as a prophet.

⋏   One more point; Ismael's twelve sons were named Aramaic names. But he is Arab!

Genesis 25 (King James Version):

> 12 Now these are the generations of Ishmael, Abraham's son, whom Hagar the Egyptian, Sarah's handmaid, bare unto Abraham:
> 13 And these are the names of the sons of Ishmael, by their names, according to their generations: the firstborn of Ishmael, Nebajoth; and Kedar, and Adbeel, and Mibsam,
> 14 And Mishma, and Dumah, and Massa,
> 15 Hadar, and Tema, Jetur, Naphish, and Kedemah:

⋏   Where did Ishmael and his sons live? Genesis 25:16-18:

> 16 These are the sons of Ishmael, and these are their names, by their towns, and by their castles; twelve princes according to their nations.

> 17 And these are the years of the life of Ishmael, an hundred and thirty and seven years: and he gave up the ghost and died; and was gathered unto his people.
> 18 **And they dwelt from Havilah unto Shur, that is before Egypt,** as thou goest toward Assyria: and he died in the presence of all his brethren.

If you would like to see for yourself where **Shur** is located, visit this site and you will see it's on the other side of the red sea and has nothing to do with Mecca: www.bible.ca

Muhammad and Morality

(Muhammad is willing to sleep with all Muslim women)

In the book of Jame' Alsag'er (Imam Al-Soiuty), Hadith 2994 Muhammad said:

الجامع الصغير للسيوطي حديث رقم2994
عن معاذ قال النبي صلعم أيما امرأة زوجت نفسها من غير ولي فهي زانية.

Any women, [if] she gives herself to a man to marry him without her father's, or man of the house's permission, she is a whore!

Compare this to Qur'an 33:50 where we read:

... And a believing woman if she gives herself unto the Prophet (to sleep with her) and the Prophet desires her, he has a privilege for thee only (so no other man can sleep with her after Muhammad) ...

1. How can the woman, who gives herself to marry a man, be a whore, but the woman that gives herself to Muhammad be a good woman?

2. Why would a woman do that? Muslim women loved to share their bed with Muhammad to show their love to Allah?

3. Why is Muhammad's god making it as a law? Was it something so bad to be doing in front of the Muslims and the Arabs, that

    Muhammad needed a verse from his false god to make it as if it was his god's wish and not his own desire?

4. If it's Allah wish, shouldn't we ask why? Muhammad had many wives according to Muslims. Thirteen wives! Wasn't it enough to have 13 wives, and all the slaves he wanted, but he still had to have more sexually aggressive women?

5. If we ask Muslims about women giving themselves to Muhammad, they translate it as saying that this is about women asking Muhammad to marry them! To expose their lies, I will ask them to give me one name of

a woman, just one of the 13 wives of Muhammad, who became a wife to him by giving herself to him! Their answer would be zero. Not even one of his wives was one of those who gave herself to Muhammad. This is proof that this is not about marriage. It's all about sex, and sex only! Let's take a look at 'Aisha (Muhammad's child-wife) and how she expressed her anger about Muhammad's lust. Read with me what 'Aisha herself said. Muslims try to play with the translation and change the real meaning of what she said. Here we read from Sahih Bukhari, Book 60, Hadith 311:

Narrated 'Aisha: "I used to look downward upon those females which had granted themselves to Allah's prophet, and I used to state 'How can a woman not be shamefaced to offer herself (to a man for sex)?'"

6.   Why is 'Aisha saying this if it's normal? Remember, Muhammad was the one who said that the woman who gives herself to a man is a whore!

We can read the same story in these books:

49. Sahih Muslim book of breast ‏صحيح مسلم، كتاب الرضاع، ص‏ 1065 ‏الحديث‏ feeding (nursing) page 1065 Hadith 49 or Sahih Al Bukhari, Book of tafsir, Chapter of Al Ahzab V3, Page 118, 163, 164:

‏قَالَ كَانَتْ خَوْلَةُ بِنْتُ حَكِيمٍ مِنَ اللاِّئِي وَهَبْنَ أَنْفُسَهُنَّ لِلنَّبِيِّ صلى الله عليه وسلم فَقَالَتْ عَائِشَةُ أَمَا تَسْتَحِي الْمَرْأَةُ أَنْ تَهَبَ نَفْسَهَا لِلرَّجُلِ فَلَمَّا نَزَلَتْ {تُرْجِئُ مَنْ تَشَاءُ مِنْهُنَّ} قُلْتُ يَا رَسُولَ اللهِ مَا أَرَى رَبَّكَ إِلاَّ يُسَارِعُ فِي هَوَاكَ.‏

Muhammad tried to rape Umaima bint An-Nu'man bin Sharahil. This woman was the daughter of Al Nu'man, who was ruler of his people, but with Muhammad's army growing, his tribe came under Muhammad's command. How would anyone dare to say no to Muhammad. She was very brave and did say no.

If you look at the Qur'an, it says "a woman gave herself to the prophet," but Muhammad couldn't stop there. Despite all the women he had, and the ones that gave themselves to him, it was not enough, for he was never ashamed to rape anyone he could!

Bukhari, Volume 7, Book 63, Hadith 182:

‏[صحيح البخاري]‏
‏الكتاب : الجامع الصحيح المختصر‏
‏المؤلف : محمد بن إسماعيل أبو عبدالله البخاري الجعفي‏

الناشر : دار ابن كثير ، اليمامة - بيروت

1407 - 1987الطبعة الثالثة ،

تحقيق : د. مصطفى ديب البغا أستاذ الحديث وعلومه في كلية الشريعة - جامعة دمشق

6عدد الأجزاء :

Sahih Al-Bukhari Kitab Jame' Al-Sahih Al-Mu'khtaser, 1987 printing, V6, Hadith 4957:

4957 دَخَلَ عَلَيْهَا النَّبِيُّ صَلَّى اللَّهُ عَلَيْهِ وَسَلَّمَ قَالَ هَبِي نَفْسَكِ لِي قَالَتْ وَهَلْ **تَهَبُ الْمَلِكَةُ نَفْسَهَا لِلسُّوقَةِ** قَالَ
فَأَهْوَى بِيَدِهِ يَضَعُ يَدَهُ عَلَيْهَا لِتَسْكُنَ فَقَالَتْ أَعُوذُ بِاللَّهِ مِنْكَ فَقَالَ قَدْ عُذْتِ بِمَعَاذٍ ثُمَّ خَرَجَ عَلَيْنَا فَقَالَ يَا أَبَا أُسَيْدٍ
اكْسُهَا رَازِقِيَّتَيْنِ وَأَلْحِقْهَا بِأَهْلِهَا

Al-Bukhari, Volume 7, Book 63, Hadith 182:

> ...When the Prophet entered upon her, he said to her, "Give me yourself! (to sleep with her) as a hand out. She said, "**How can a queen give herself to a savage man?**" The Prophet raised his hand to <u>beat</u> her so that she might become composed. She said, "I seek refuge with Allah from you." So he said, "You did seek refuge with one who can rescue you."

This same story can be found in many other Islamic books including the Book of Al-Sirah, V4, 588/599, Beirut, 1952; and Tafsir Al-Qur'tbi, V14, Page 167, Beirut, 1973.

I put the Arabic and English text in bold where she said to him, "**How can a queen give herself to a savage man?**" I did this because in the English translations Muslims try to cover this shameful hadith, by altering the words and make it appear as if he asked her to marry him, when he asked her for sex, and she called him **a savage man**.

1. In this story we see how this sex addicted man, the prophet of Allah, has no limits to where he can or should stop. After reading this hadith, just look at what he is asking her to do. To give herself as a gift! It's very clear she took that as a big insult. It is a huge insult for any lady that respects herself. Imagine a man entering the house of a woman that he never met before and on the first second he enters, he asks her for sex, and to give herself as a gift to him. If we would ask any Muslim if it's acceptable in Islam for a man to enter the house of a strange woman and ask her for sex as a gift, he would say, "No way!" For Muhammad it was okay! It's clear that Muslims today have a lot more morality than Muhammad. I am sure if Muhammad would try to do today what he did back then, the Arabs themselves would fight him as they did before.

The Prophet was preferred above all mankind in 16 issues:

(هـ671تفسير الجامع لاحكام القرآن/ القرطبي (ت

Tafsir Al Qur'an (Al jame' Le Ahkam, Al Qur'an) by Imam Al-Qur'tubi, Beirut, 1992, V14, Page 212:

فجملته ستة عشر: الأوّل: صَفِيّ المغنم. الثاني: الاستبداد بخمس الخمس أو الخمس. الثالث: الوصال. الرابع: الزيادة على أربع نسوة. الخامس: النكاح بلفظ الهبة. السادس: النكاح بغير وليّ. السابع: النكاح بغير صداق. الثامن: نكاحه في حالة الإحرام. التاسع: سقوط القَسم بين الأزواج عنه؛ وسيأتي. العاشر: إذا وقع بصره على امرأة وجب على زوجها طلاقها؛

Here are some of the **sixteen ways** in which Muhammad was preferred:

1. Prescribed the best of spoils.
2. The fifth of the best of spoils.
3. Reached out by sex (with any woman without marriage).
4. Increase of wives: more than four wives!
5. Sex by word (women who offer themselves), as a gift!
6. Marriage without a guardian.
7. Marriage without a dowry.
8. The marriage in the case of I'hram (Muhammad was the only Muslim that could have sex during the practice of hajj)!
9. If he took an oath with his wives, he could break it!
10. **If his eyes fall onto a married woman, her husband had to divorce her, so the prophet could have her!**

We will stop here and take a look at the last ten things Muhammad had above all mankind:

1. Notice all that Allah favored him was about one of two things: sex or money!
2. He is above all that Allah rules. It's assumed that what Allah ruled for mankind was perfect, as Muslims claim, but it's clear that those rules are not suitable for Muhammad. He needs more!
3. There is Allah and Muhammad who are above any law. The law of Allah was made in two ways. One to be practiced by Muslims and another to give advantage to Muhammad. This makes Muhammad above all mankind. This is in contradiction to Qur'an 49:13:

O mankind! We have created you male and female, and have made you nations and tribes that ye may know one another. Lo, the best of you is the one who obeys Allah. For Allah is all Knower.

➤ So the best is the one that obeys Allah's rules, but as we see, Muhammad does not obey Allah. The Qur'an said four wives, but Muhammad keeps marrying as many as he wants!

➤ Allah said you need a guardian to ask a woman for her hand in marriage to be legal. Muhammad didn't like that.

➤ According to the Qur'an you have to pay women money to marry them. Muhammad wanted women for free!

➤ Allah ordered men not to go after married women, but Muhammad was ordering men to leave their wives if he wanted them. Yes, even if she was married!

After all of this, he is the best man. And the prophet!

➤ Christ said in Matthew 5:28:

But I say unto you, That whosoever looketh on a woman to lust after her hath committed adultery with her already in his heart.

➤ Where is Muhammad concerning Christ's teaching?

Muhammad's Death Proved Him To Be a False Prophet.

Allah's punishment for anyone who lies about the real God: (...*had forged a false saying concerning Us (Allah)... We certainly would have cut off his life artery (aorta)...*

In this case, we will see amazing proof from the Qur'an about Muhammad as a false prophet in Qur'an 69. Allah is saying that the one who lies about him, he will cut off his life artery (aorta). Read with me please, Qur'an 69:44-47:

44 And if he (Muhammad) had a counterfeit statement concerning Us (Allah),
45 We surely would have confiscated him by his right hand (or with force and strength).
46 And then We certainly would have cut off his life artery (aorta),
47 and none of you can hold back Us from punishing him.

This is Allah's promise, to kill, in a specific way, the one who lies about him. Things would have seemed normal if Muhammad had not died the same way Allah determined to kill the one who would make fraudulent sayings about him (Allah)!

In the book of Sahih Al Bukhari, we find this story of a Jewish woman who sought revenge for her family's death by the hands of Muhammad and his men. From Sahiah Bukhari, Book 47, Hadith 786; Sahih Muslim, Book 026, Hadith 5430 and 5431:

> Reported by Anas bin Malik: "A Jewish woman delivered a poisoned goat for the Prophet to eat from it, as a result he did eat from it. She was seized and brought to the Prophet, and he was asked, 'Shall we kill her?' The Prophet answered, 'No, don't.' As well as, I continued to watch the outcome of the poison on the roof of the mouth of Allah's Messenger."

Later the woman was beheaded, but Muhammad's initial hesitation was waiting to see if she had a cure for the poison.

We read in Sahih Bakhari, Volume 5, Book 59, Hadith 713:

> ...Narrated 'Aisha: "The Prophet in his ailment in which he died, used to say, 'O 'Aisha! I still feel the pain caused by the food I ate at 'Khaibar, and now, I feel as if my aorta is being cut from that poison.'"

1. Notice 'Aisha said this happened: "The Prophet in his ailment in which he died," and also that she said that Muhammad "used to say." So, according to 'Aisha, Muhammad never complained in his death about anything but the poisoned food that he ate in 'Khaibar.

2. This means the only cause of Muhammad's death was the poisoned food.

3. Remember in Qur'an 69:44-46, it says clearly that the one who will lie about the god, Allah will cut his artery (aorta). Qur'an 69:46: "And then We certainly would have cut off his life artery (aorta)."

4. By poisoning, this is exactly what happened to Muhammad!

5. As long as this was the way of death chosen by Muhammad's god, for the one who lies about him (Allah), then how can Muslims explain that Allah watched Muhammad die in such a way? According to the verse, this is what Allah does only for those who do bad to him.

6. If you remember, Muslims believe in what they call "Al Qadar, القدر,"

which means <u>destiny</u> or <u>divine predestination</u>, where Allah is the only one who will decide how anyone will die, with no exception.

7. This would surely mean that it was Allah who wanted Muhammad to die in such a way. It must have been a punishment for Muhammad's lies!

8. I say it's the real God who did this, not Muhammad's god. He wanted to show us that He would make come true what Muhammad wished for the one who lied about the real God, and at the same time to expose Muhammad with all his lies.

9. One last thing. If the Muslims claim that Allah saved Jesus Christ from death by not allowing Jesus to die by Jewish hands, then why did Allah allow Muhammad to be killed by Jewish hands? Does that mean Allah loved Jesus more than Muhammad? Doesn't the Qur'an say that Muhammad is the best creation of Allah?

Muhammad, The God or The Man.

We read in Qur'an 33:45-46

وَدَاعِيًا إِلَى اللَّهِ بِإِذْنِهِ وَسِرَاجًا مُّنِيرًا (Al-Ahzab, Verse 46) سورة الأحزاب)

(Al-Ahzab, Verse 45) سورة الأحزاب)

45 you The Prophet! We have assigned you as a Witness, a messenger a reporter of good news and Warner,
46 missionary of Allah by His permission and as a lamp with luminosity light.

Al-Tabari (V4, Page 501) in his commentary said:

قال الإمام الطبري رحمه الله : [{ من الله نور } يعني بالنور محمدا صلى الله عليه وسلم الذي أنار الله به الحق وأظهر به الإسلام ومحق به الشرك فهو نور لمن استنار به...] تفسير الطبري ج4صـ501ـ

That is, 'light' refers to Muhammad because people are guided by him as they would be with light...

In another verse, in Qur'an 5:15 we find this:

يَا أَهْلَ الْكِتَابِ قَدْ جَاءكُمْ رَسُولُنَا يُبَيِّنُ لَكُمْ كَثِيرًا مِّمَّا كُنتُمْ تُخْفُونَ مِنَ الْكِتَابِ وَيَعْفُو عَن كَثِيرٍ قَدْ جَاءكُم مِّنَ اللَّهِ نُورٌ وَكِتَابٌ مُّبِينٌ

O believers of the Book (Christians and Jews)! Certainly, Our Messenger has come to you making clear to you much of what you're hiding of the Book (Bible)

and forgive much more; truly, over there has come to you as light and an explained Book (Qur'an) from Allah.

As we see in this verse, Allah sent two things; light and a book. The light can't be meant to be the book, for it says there clearly a "light and a book," not a light of the book. Also, note that the verse is talking about Muhammad and that he is coming to them. Both the Shi'a and the Sunni Muslims believe that Muhammad is made from light for them, even though he is a human at the same time. When the Muslims believe that Muhammad is a light, this means he is MAN *and* GOD at the same time! Muslims will say, "We do not believe he is God." Then how is he "light," when the Qur'an clearly says that Allah is light too?

Muhammad Was Created Before Adam!

In the book of Tafsir Ibn Kathir, V3, P470 we read:

عن أبي هريرة -رضي الله عنه- عن النبي -صلى الله عليه وسلم- في قوله تعالى: قال النبي -صلى الله عليه وسلم-:
كنت أوّل النبيين في الخلق وآخرهم في البعث فبدأ بي قبلهم وَكِتَابٌ مُبِينٌ

That the Prophet said, "I was the first of the Prophets to be created and the last of them to be sent."

⅄ Look at Muhammad! He sounds like he is copying the words of Jesus. Looks like Muhammad is the alpha and the omega! John 9:5:

As long as I am in the world, I am the light of the world.

⅄ The Qur'an says Muhammad is light to the world, but how can he be light when he does wrong? The Qur'an tells in many chapters that he committed sin. Even the Qur'an tells that Muhammad was asked by Allah to ask for forgiveness, as in Qur'an 47.19:

You should know, that there is no god but Allah, and ask forgiveness for your sin [Muhammad], and for the sin of men and women who believe.

⅄ Have you ever thought that the light of the world needed to be guided?

⅄ This verse shows how Muhammad's memory is, and it's the same as his honor. It's like the weather, changeable, to the point he contradicts other verses in a very clear way. Like Qur'an 9:80:

[Muhammad] if you ask for forgiveness for them, O Muhammad, or if you do not ask forgiveness or even if you ask for it **seventy times** for them, Allah will not forgive them!

If we go to the Hadith (Sahih Muslim, Book 4, Hadith 2129) we read:

Abu Huraira reported: "Allah's Apostle, may Allah pray on him, said: 'I appealed to Allah's permission for the forgiveness for my mother, but He did not permit it to me. I asked approval from Him to visit her grave, and He gave permission to me.'"

Also, in the book of Tuhafat Al A'hwazi Fe Shareh Al-Turmizi, Tafsir Al-Qur'an, 1953 printing, page 401:

تحفة الأحوذي شرح سنن الترمذي ـ كتاب تفسير القرآن ـ استغفار النبي صلى الله عليه وسلم لأبى طالب
ـ قوله : (وهما مشركان) جملة حالية (أوليس استغفر إبراهيم لأبيه) أي أتقول هذا أوليس استغفر401ص
إلخ ماكان للنبي والذين آمنوا أن يستغفروا للمشركين

Muhammad was asking Allah for forgiveness for his uncle (Abu Talib), Ali (Muhammad's cousin) said (exclaimed), "You [are] asking for forgiveness of infidels!" Muhammad said, "Did not Abraham ask for his father's forgiveness?"

The same story can be found in many other books like Asbab Al-Nuzul, 1963 Printing, V1, Page 176.

Abraham's Father's Name

⅄ Well this is funny. Where did Muhammad get the information about Abraham's father's name? Don't forget that even the name of Abraham's father is wrong in the Qur'an which claims it was Azar (Qur'an 6:74). Who then was Terah?

Joshua 24:2 (KJV):

And Joshua said unto all the people, Thus saith the LORD God of Israel, Your fathers dwelt on the other side of the flood in old time, even Terah, the father of Abraham, and the father of Nachor: and they served other gods.

Luke 3:34:

Which was the son of Jacob, which was the son of Isaac, which was the son of Abraham, which was the son of <u>Terah</u>, which was the son of Nachor,

As you see, we can add this as one of many mistakes in the Qur'an. If the Muslims say the Bible is corrupted, and that the Bible is wrong, not the Qur'an, then can you give me one reason for the Jews to change the name of Abraham's father?

⚔ The funny thing about Muhammad in the Qur'an is that he created stories as if they were real. You can tell that this man would make a great movie script writer. In one instance Muhammad was trying to fool the tribe of 'Abdullah Ibn Ubayy', who was a powerful leader of the tribes of Al-Aws and Al-Khazraj. When Ibn Ubayy died, Muhammad prayed on his grave. He was being a hypocrite to his tribe. Later he noticed that it did not give him any benefit. In fact, it did just the opposite for the Muslims. They started wondering, why he asked for the enemy of Allah to be forgiven when Allah says in the Qur'an 4:48:

Allah forgives not that partners Gods with him. He forgives all sin but not for who ascribe partners to Allah, he hath indeed invented a tremendous sin.

In Qur'an 9:80, Muhammad is doing what he should not be doing, trying to please the pagan because he was a man without an army. Therefore, he played soft and nice to the point he would pray over the grave of the infidel.

فتح الباري شرح صحيح البخاري

أحمد بن علي بن حجر العسقلاني

دارالريان للتراث

م 1986 /هـ 1407 :سنة النشر

--- :رقم الطبعة

ثلاثة عشرجزءا :عدد الأجزاء

باب قوله استغفر لهم أو لا تستغفر لهم إن تستغفر لهم سبعين مرة فلن يغفر الله لهم

لما توفي عبد الله بن أبي جاء ابنه عبد الله بن عبد الله إلى رسول الله صلى الله 4393 عليه وسلم فسأله أن يعطيه قميصه يكفن فيه أباه فأعطاه ثم سأله أن يصلي عليه فقام رسول الله صلى الله عليه وسلم ليصلي عليه فقام عمر فأخذ بثوب رسول الله صلى الله عليه وسلم فقال يا رسول الله تصلي عليه وقد نهاك ربك أن تصلي عليه فقال رسول الله صلى الله عليه وسلم إنما خيرني الله فقال استغفر لهم أو لا تستغفر لهم إن تستغفر لهم

THE DECEPTION OF ALLAH

سبعين مرة وسأزيده على السبعين قال إنه منافق قال فصلى عليه رسول الله صلى الله
عليه وسلم فأنزل الله ولا تصل على أحد منهم مات أبدا ولا تقم على قبره

Book title Fateh Al-Bari Fe Shareh Sahih Al-Bukhari, AL-Raian Publishing, 1896 Printing, V8, Page 334, Hadith 4393:

At the same time, as Abdulah Ibn 'Ubai passed away his son Abdualah Ibn Abdualah came to the prophet asking him if he can give him his shirt, so he can shroud his father with it, therefore the prophet gave him his shirt, and he asked to pray on him so the messenger of Allah stood-up to pray for him (the dead man), and right away Omar stood-up and snatched the clothes of the prophet and said to Muhammad: "How do you pray on him and Allah forbid thee from praying on him?" The prophet answer saying: "Allah told me if you pray to them or not to pray to, then if you pray seventy times or even more, Allah still will not forgive them. The prophet continued saying he is Hypocrite, but he said (the Narrator) the prophet did pray on him! So Allah sent a verse saying do not pray every on any of them nor stand on their graves.

In Qur'an 9:113, Muhammad broke his god's law again because the dead man was his uncle as we see in the interpretation of Sahih Al-Bukhari Tafsir Al-Qur'an, 1993 Printing, Page 1718, Hadith 4398:

When the death came to Abu-Talib, the prophet entered upon him, and Abu-Jahel (Muhammad's uncle) was there, then the prophet said, "Oh my uncle why do you not say that there is not god except Allah ? So I can use it as an intercession in-front of Allah." Abu-Jahel said: "Abu-Talib are you going to leave your father's faith?" Muhammad said, "I will intercede for you in-front of Allah, asking for his forgiveness," therefore the verse came down saying [to] you, "It may not for a prophet to intercede for the pagans."

As you see, Muhammad knew that he should not pray over the enemy of Allah, whom he knew to be a hypocrite, and all Muslims knew how bad this man was to Islam. Omar knew that it was against Allah's teaching and command, but still Muhammad decided to be a hypocrite, praying over the one whom Allah will not accept. Muhammad's prayed anyway. So why is Muhammad praying?

The point is that the law of Allah is changeable and fixable, dependent upon Muhammad's deceptive plans and needs. When he wants Allah to forgive infidels, he played that role. When that didn't work out, or he didn't need that anymore, or these actions were no longer helping him, he would then create a verse as if Allah was upset with him. This way he is granted a clear way in front of Muslims showing that, "Yes, Allah is the one who guides me and as you see, if I do wrong, Allah is watching over us!"

This takes us to Muhammad the Sinner and the Open License from Allah for Muhammad to Commit Sin!

Qur'an 47.19:
You should Know, that there is no god but Allah, and ask forgiveness for your sin [Muhammad], and for the sin of men and women who believe. Allah knew what is changing on you.

1. Qur'an 48:2:
That might God pardon thee [Muhammad] the sins of the previous and those to follow, to complete Allah's sympathy to thee, and to guide thee to the Straight Way.

⅄ As you see here Allah is giving Muhammad an open door for all kinds of sin, and he granted him forgiveness even for the coming sins! Even without the need for Muhammad to ask to be forgiven.

⅄ At the same time you see the verse says, "and guide thee on the Straight Way." Allah forgives Muhammad for the coming sin and he completes his favor upon Muhammad by guidance! What was this kind of guidance that was not enough to stop Muhammad from being a sinner? On the top of that, he is the light of the world. Muhammad said in the hadith Sahih Al-Bukhari, V9, Page 403; and Sahih Bukhari, Book 93, Hadith 534:

...So Allah please forgive the previous sins or the ones I will do in the future, and also those sins which I did in under cover or in public, and that which You know better than I. None has the right to be praised but you.

Here we go again! Why is Muhammad even asking to be forgiven, when he is granted forgiveness for the coming sin?!

⅄ Things do not stop or end here. Even Muhammad created rules and law that was not from Allah, as Qur'an 66:1 tells:

O Prophet, why [do] you forbid which Allah hath made lawful for thee, seeking to please your wives? Allah is forgiving, and merciful.

⅄ In this chapter Muhammad was found having sex with one of his slaves in the house of one of his wives (Hafsa). He got into a big fight with his wife. She and his other wives cannot take Muhammad's degradation. Then Allah, himself (no kidding, Allah is always ready for whatever Muhammad wants, even inside the home), sends a chapter threatening the wives of Muhammad that if they don't stop bothering Muhammad's sexual life and his favorite entertainment as in Qur'an 66:5:

Perhaps his (Muhammad's) Lord, if he divorces all of you, he will give him instead of you better wives than you, who they are submissive, believing, pious, penitent, devout, who travel! And fast, virgins and divorced.

▲ I wonder how big the fight was, to the point god in his heaven is making a chapter about it?! Also, why is Allah taking the side of Muhammad against his wives, when all they are asking is for Muhammad to have sex with no one but his wives? If you noticed, Muhammad made a promise not to do it again, but later when he gained more power, he missed the good time with all these women around. He then made verse 66:1, presenting it as if it was Allah who wanted him to have sex with other women. To shut up his wives and to be sure they will never, ever complain again, he made verse 66:5.

The fact is, Muhammad took this for the Qur'an from Omar Ibn Al Khatab because he liked it, as we see in the following hadith (The Book of 'OL-It'qan Fee 'Olum Al-Qur'an, V1, Page 137):

Reported by Annas, the Omar bin Al Khatab said: "My almighty agreed with me in three things:
[First,] I said, 'Oh Allah's Apostle, I wish if take as your place of worship the place where Abraham did place to pray. It so came the Divine Inspiration: (page137) (Qur'an 2:125) And take you [Muslims] the place of Abraham as a place of prayer.'
[Second,] And I said, To the Prophet, to the Prophet of Allah, 'Good and bad ones talk to your wives therefore order them to veil themselves!' So Allah sent down the concerning the veiling of the women (Al-Noor (24):31).
[Third,] The wives of the Prophet made a coalition against the Prophet, and I said to them, 'Maybe if His, the Lord of the Prophet, divorced you (all the wives), and exchange you with better wives than you.' So the verse was revealed (Qur'an 66:5), the same as I had said."

You can see the same story in Sahih Al-Bukhari (Book 8, Hadith 395.)

Later we will go more in depth into this hadith, but for now, just notice that Omar said, "Allah used my words exactly!" It's so clear that Muhammad's inspiration was not effected by God, but by the opinion of men around him, even to choosing the Kaaba. It was the choice made by Omar, not Allah!

Muhammad just hijacked words, ideas, plans, poems, names, and even stories as we will see in further reading and researching. Let's again read the verse of Qur'an 66:5:

> Perhaps his (Muhammad's) Lord, if he divorces all of you, he will give him instead of you better wives than you, who they are submissive, believing, pious, penitent, devout, who travel! And fast, virgins and divorced.

Notice the following:

⊿ When all of a man's wives go against him, with no exception, it's very clear proof that Muhammad was not a good man to his wives, as Muslims try to fool us into believing.

⊿ Why is Allah involved in family matters? If I have a fight with my wife, will Allah send a verse against her?

⊿ Have you ever heard about a one shot divorce from 11 wives? All of them are wrong, but only Muhammad is right?

⊿ The idea of exchanging the wives came from Omar. Why did Muhammad need an *exchange* and not to remarry again? Exchange here means that women in Islam are the same as machine parts. They have no value as a person, only the value of a job or a function. Nothing more.

This explains why Islam looks down on women.

Women in Islam

I've seen many articles written by Muslims, and even Muslim women. They all try to fool us saying that we need to separate Islam and the culture of Muslims! We are not going to talk about culture, and to make it clear from the start, we will not mix Islam and culture. Remember, Muslims who read my words, the coming reference is not from culture, but from:

1. Qur'an verses on women.
2. Muhammad's Hadith, or sayings, about women.
3. Muhammad's laws and orders over women.
4. Zero cultural talk.
5. Islamic references and Islamic courts approve.

Women Should Not Remove Facial Hair, Or They Will End in Hell-Fire.

From Sahih-Al-Bukhari, Vol. 6, Book 60, Hadith 408:

> Allah curses those women.... who remove their facial hair, In order to look more pretty trying to change Allah's creation.

Does that mean all Muslim women will end in hell? All Arab women are hairy, as are Arab men; so to make Allah happy women have to grow a beard and mustache?

The funny thing is that Muhammad's excuse was that these women were changing the look which Allah gave to them, but then Muhammad turned around and ordered them to shave their vaginas. Muhammad even colored his own hair with henna making it red.

See Sahih Al-Bukhari, Book 56, Hadith 668; and Sahih-Al-Bukhari, Book 72, Hadith 786:

> Abu Huraira reported: Allah's messenger said, "The Jews and the Christians, they do not dye their gray hair, so you Muslims have to do the opposite of what they do, so dye your gray hair and beards..."

Why is Muhammad doing something just to be opposite of the Christians and the Jews? He cursed women who tried to change their look by removing their facial hair, but at the same time it was okay for the men to dye theirs!

This hadith proves that Muhammad was creating rules, not because they were righteousness, or about wrong or right, but just to oppose the Christians and the Jews.

Sahih Muslim, Book 024, Hadith 5243:

> ...His head and his beard were so white, alike as hyssop. Therefore, He, Allah's Messenger, instructed the women whom the color of his hair should be changed, so they are ordered to do something about it and change it.

Why is Muhammad's beard color so important to a man whose main focus in life is supposed to be Islam and Allah?

Women as Witnesses

First of all, I need to inform you that women in Islam can be witnesses in court only in cases of a money contracts or agreements, but this does not include witnessing for any kind of inheritance or crime. This means **women are NOT accepted as witnesses in court in <u>all</u> of the following cases**:

1. Crime: (killing, theft, etc.) Book of Badae' Al-Sanae' V9 Page 4079: "Women are not accepted as witnesses in all kinds of crimes that come with punishment."

بل وقد ذهب جماعة من الفقهاء الى ان المرأة يجوز لها تولي كل اشكال وكل افرع وهذا الرأي نادي به احد فقهاء المذهب الحنفي ..القضاء بما فيها الحدود والقصاص وايده في ذلك عديد من (4079 ص9, بدائع الصنائع ج)وهو محمد بن حسن الشيباني , وابن حزم, الامام الحسن البصري:كبار الفقهاء الذين يعدون مرجعا فقهيا معتمدا مثل ص9, بدائع الصنائع ج. وابن القاسم,وابن جرير الطبري

2. Adultery: Qur'an 24:4, interpretation of Al-Qurutbi; He said, in his interpretation: "of the all mighty saying and bring four witnesses on them (in case of adultery) he said the witnesses must be males only, and all the nation agree about that."

وقال القرطبي في تفسير قوله تعالى (فَاسْتَشْهِدُواْ عَلَيْهِنَّ أَرْبَعَةً مّنكُمْ): ولا بد أن يكون الشهود ذكوراً؛ لقوله منكم، ولا خلاف فيه بين الأمة

3. Idolatry

4. Divorce or Marriage: Book of Al-Mugni by Ibn 'Qudama V7/8: "...no marriage is accepted by one man witness and two women agreed with that Nukha'ee, and Al-Shafe'e and Al-Oza'e."

) : " ولا ينعقد النكاح بشهادة رجل وامرأتين . وهذا قول 8/7قال ابن قدامة في "المغني" (, والأوزاعي , والشافعي . النخعي

5. Inheritance: Qur'an 5:106: "O you believers, authorize the testimony between you, when death come to you, at the time of an inheritance be that of <u>two men</u> witness of among you.

تفسير ابن كثير تفسير القرآن
إسماعيل بن عمر بن كثير القرشي الدمشقي
دار طيبة
م2002هـ / 1422سنة النشر:

وقال ابن جرير : حدثنا عمرو بن علي ، حدثنا أبو داود ، حدثنا صالح بن أبي الأخضر ، عن الزهري قال :
[217مضت السنة أنه لا تجوز شهادة كافر في حضر ولا سفر ، إنما هي في المسلمين . [ص:

Tafsir Ibn Kather, Publisher Tibah, 2002, V3, Page 217:

محمد بن إدريس الشافعي دار المعرفة فروع الفقه الشافعي سنة النشر: 1410هـ/1990م والآيتان بينتان أنهما
[ص: 17] في المؤمنين وإنما قلت في الأحرار المؤمنين خاصة بتأول ونحن بالآيتين لا نجيز شهادة أهل
الذمة فيما بينهم (قال الشافعي) رحمه الله تعالى : فرجع بعضهم إلى قولنا فقال لا تجوز شهادة أهل الذمة .

Ibn Jareer Said: "It's not allowed or accepted to have non-Muslims as witness either in the city or in travel."

Book Fro' Al-Fiqh Al-um by Imam Muhammad Ibn Idres Al-Shafi'e, 1990 Printing by D.'T., Page 17:

It meant the free believers (not slaves) and the two verse's interpretation, it's forbidden to accept the witnessing of Christians and Jews.

Fatwa (Answers According to Islamic Law)

Date 6-19-2001, from www.islamweb.net, Fatwa # 591:

The question: Can women be witnesses for marriage one man and two women or four women?

The answer:

وأنه لا تجوز شهادة النساء في ذلك، لما روى أبو عبيد في الأموال عن الزهري أنه قال: (مضت السنة أن لا
تجوز شهادة النساء في الحدود ولا في النكاح ولا في الطلاق).

It's not allowed for women to be witnesses in case of marriage or any criminal case (cases needing punishment) or marriage or divorce.

You can see the Islamic Answer in this link (Arabic):
http://www.islamweb.net/ver2/fatwa/ShowFatwa.php?Option=FatwaId&lang=A&Id=591
Mohsin Khan's translation Qur'an 5:106:

O you who believe! When death approaches any of you, and you make a bequest, [then take] the testimony of two *just men* of your own folk or two others from outside, while you are traveling through the land and death befalls on you. Detain them both after As-Salat (the prayer), [then] if you are in doubt (about their truthfulness), let them both swear by Allah [saying]: "We wish not for any worldly gain in this, even though he (the beneficiary) be our near relative. We shall not hide testimony of Allah, for then indeed we should be of the sinful."

I can cite many other similar examples showing how Muslims have been ordered to reject a woman being a witnessing person in anything, except the case of a **contract for a debt for a fixed period in writing, or things for which men cannot be witnesses because they're only about women, such as in a women telling about her period.**

This means that in Islam, Muslim women are not accepted as witnesses in 99% of cases. She is perceived of very lowly as a person, but better than a Christian man. In Islam all non-Muslims are unacceptable as witnesses, not trusted, nor to be taken as a friend, as we see in Qur'an 3:28, 118; 5:51; and 60:1.

Remember, Muslims who read my words, the coming reference is not from culture, but from Qur'an 2:282:

"Whenever you Muslim's contract with each other, in money trades...get two witnesses, out of your own men. Moreover, if there are not two men, then a man and two women, such as ye select for witnesses, so that if one of them (women) is misguided the other can remind her."

From this verse we learn that two men are the norm for witnessing in Islam. In case there is only one man and women to witness, then the rule is as follows:

A. 10,000,000,000 women will not be accepted as witnessing persons, for they must have at least one man with them. This clearly reveals how Islam looks at women. It's as though they are not fit for the simple task of witnessing! It does not matter how many there are, if there's not at least one male witness, then the number of women does not count, even if there are 10 million women!

B. Also notice that there are no conditions for the man, or men, that are accepted as witnesses. This means that any two men are good to do the job, but in the case of women, they have to be approved. Most women are not approved in Islam. In other words, "We have to choose the ones we think are the best of the junk of women kind!"

Let us look at the hadith and see how Muhammad used this verse to proclaim his judgment over women as bad and **"deficient in intelligence."** Notice what he says in Sahih Bukhari, Book 6, Hadith 301:

Reported by Abu Said Al-Khudri: "Once before the Prophet went out to the mosque to pray on the holy day which [is the] end of fasting month of Ramadan prayer. Then he walked by some women and said to them, 'You women. Give

THE DECEPTION OF ALLAH
THE DECEPTION OF ALLAH

charity, for I have seen that the majority of the residents of Hell-Fire was you women.' The women said: 'Why is that, Allah's Prophet? He answered, 'You do curse frequently and are ungrateful to your husbands, and I have never seen any deficient in intelligence of brain and religion more than you. You influenced the faithful man astray.' Afterwards the women asked, 'O Allah's prophet, what is our deficiency in our intelligence and religion?' He said answering, 'It is not correct that the evidence of two women is equal to the witness of one man?' (Qur'an 2:282) They replied confirming, agreeing. He said, 'This is the deficiency in her intelligence. Isn't it true that a woman is not permitted in either case to pray nor to fast during her period?' The women replied in the confirming. He said, 'This is the deficiency in her religion.'"

In this hadith, things are getting uglier, and from it, we learn the following:

A. All women are suffering from deficiency in their intelligence, with no exceptions.

B. The majority of women who are in hell-fire are there because they are bad, they always curse a lot and they are not grateful to their husbands. This means that women are always to blame for the bad, and the men are the ones that are always good. To the point that most of hell's occupants are women, not men!

C. Women should not fast or pray because they have menses (menstruation or period). This makes women lower than men, because women will not be able to do the duty of worshiping Allah?

D. After he mentioned the disability of women to pray and to fast in their menses, he says, "This is the deficiency in her religion."

It's time for me to ask Muslims a few questions.

1. If Allah is the one who created women the way they are, why would Allah punish them by sending them to hell fire? If they are not given equal brains, as the Qur'an claims, to do the same task as men, is that justice, or is it a claim made for the benefit men? **Islam is made by man for the man! If the claimed imperfection is Allah's fault, why do the women have to pay for it?**

2. Is not being bad part of their imperfection or because of their design? Why are they to blame for it?

3. Did Allah know about this deficiency of women when he created them or did he find out later? Same as Toyota Motor Company, if he is God, can't he make a recall and fix them all? Change the brain maybe?

145

4. On top of that, all I have to say to Muhammad and his followers is; if Islam teaches you to respect your mother, how <u>dare</u> you say such a thing to your mother who risked the loss of her life to give birth to you!

5. If we ask a husband and a wife, after they come back from a party, to describe for us the details of the food and clothes, or whatever may have happened during that night, we would see that the man might not even remember what he ate on his dinner plate, but the woman could give all the amazing details that the man would not have even noticed!

6. That's a proof, without reading books of science, that the Qur'an is man-made. Made by the man, for the man.

7. Science teaches there are differences, for sure, between men and women. Like for example, men are good in some things and women are better in something else. I will quote this from sciencedaily.com: http://www.sciencedaily.com/releases/2008/02/080220104244.htm

"Psychologists Agneta Herlitz and Jenny Rehnman in Stockholm, Sweden asked an even more complicated question of human predisposition: Does one's sex influence his or her ability to remember every day events? <u>Their surprising findings did in fact determine significant sex differences in episodic memory, a type of long-term memory based on personal experiences, favoring women.</u>"

This means even science proves Allah wrong. Do you remember that Allah said the woman is not good in witnessing in court? Being a witness in the court requires long-term memory. Science says women are better than men in that task!

Majority in Hell-Fire are Women

Sahih Muslim, Book 036, Hadith 6596:

قال رسول الله صلى الله عليه وسلم "قمت على باب الجنة. فإذا عامة من دخلها المساكين. وإذا أصحاب الجد محبوسون. إلا أصحاب النار. فقد أمر بهم إلى النار. وقمت على باب النار. فإذا عامة من دخلها النساء".

Allah's messenger said: "I stopped at the gate of heaven, and I saw the greatest majority of those who boarded therein was that of poor ones and the rich persons were restrained to get into that. The residents of hell were commanded to get into hell, and I stopped in front the gate of fire and <u>the majority among them who entered there was that of women.</u>"

Muwatta Malik, Book 48, Hadith 48.4.7:

موطأ مالك » كتاب الجامع
427 426ص
وحدثني عن مالك عن مسلم بن أبي مريم عن أبي صالح عن أبي هريرة أنه قال نساء كاسيات عاريات
مائلات مميلات لا يدخلن الجنة ولا يجدن ريحها وريحها يوجد من مسيرة خمس مائة عام

Ya'hyia said to me reporting Malik saying as Muslim Ibn Aby Marriam from Abu Salih that Abu Hurayra said, "Women, are naked, even though they are wearing clothes, go amiss and make others go amiss, and they will not enter heaven, and they will not smell its perfume and its sense is conscious of similarly far as the distance of five hundred years."

If Eve Did Not Exist, Wives Would Never Betray their Husbands.

Sahih Al-Bukhari Volume 4, Book 55, Hadith 547:

Abu Huraira Reported: "The Messenger said, 'If there were no Jews existing, meat would never spoil and if Eve did not exist, wives would never cheat (betray) their spouses.'"

⅄ What we understand from this hadith, or speech of Muhammad, is that he blamed the Jews for the meat decaying. Another way to say this is anything bad in this world must be done by the Jews, insomuch that they were the root cause of even the meat in your closet decaying. That explains how much Muhammad hated the Jews and how the seed of hate was planted. The Arabs never hated the Jews before Muhammad. Arab Christians were living in peace with them.

⅄ If there was no Eve, no wives would betray their husbands! I've seen many articles written by Muslims saying the Bible blamed Eve for the sin of Adam. The fact is, the Bible blames both Adam and Eve. Both were punished. Our Lord never blamed Eve alone nor Adam alone, for both agreed together to disobey God. It was not Eve alone or Adam alone. In the above hadith, we see Muhammad making it clear that if there was no Eve, all the women in the world would be good to their husbands. He did not mention the name of Adam at all for having the blame of anything.

⅄ How could Muhammad accuse Eve of betraying her husband, when even the Qur'an did not say a word about Eve doing that? This is one way the Muslims deceive the Christian women. They say, "See! Our book never named Eve, but your Bible did." The fact is the Qur'an is an empty book without the hadith (the words and works of Muhammad), and as always, if you want to know the story, you find it in the hadith. Not in the Qur'an.

⚔ What was Eve's crime exactly? Did she sleep with another man in heaven, when there is no other man than Adam there? Also, why is Muhammad accusing her with the word "betray"?

The Evil of Eve

Tafsir Al-Qur'anAl-Ba'ghawi, 1993, Beirut, V1, Page 84:

تفسير القرآن تفسير البغوي
الجزء الأول تفسير البغوي » سورة البقرة » تفسير قوله تعالى " وإذ قلنا للملائكة اسجدوا لآدم فسجدوا إلا إبليس أبى واستكبر وكان من الكافرين
وكان سعيد بن المسيب يحلف بالله ما أكل آدم من الشجرة وهو يعقل ولكن حواء سقته الخمر حتى إذا سكر قادته إليها فأكل . [ص: 84]

The son of Moseb said that Eve dunked Adam and made him lose his mind (to make him eat from the tree).

- للإمام القرطبي2.02الجامع لأحكام القرآن، الإصدار
{وقلنا يا آدم اسكن أنت وزوجك الجنة وكلا منها رغدا 35 من الطبعة >> سورة البقرة >> الآية: 1الجزء
} حيث شئتما ولا تقربا هذه الشجرة فتكونا من الظالمين

إن أول من أكل من الشجرة حواء بإغواء إبليس إياها - على ما يأتي بيانه - وإن أول كلامه كان معها لأنها وسواس المخدة، وهي أول فتنة دخلت على الرجال من النساء، فقال: ما منعتما هذه الشجرة إلا أنها شجرة الخلد، لأنه علم منهما أنهما كانا يحبان الخلد، فأتاهما من حيث أحبا - "حبك الشيء يعمي ويصم" - فلما قالت حواء لآدم أنكر عليها وذكر العهد، فألح على حواء وألحت حواء على آدم، إلى أن قالت: أنا آكل قبلك حتى إن أصابني شيء سلمت أنت، فأكلت فلم يضرها، فأتت آدم فقالت: كل فإني قد أكلت فلم يضرني، فأكل فبدت لهما سوآتهما وحصلا في حكم الذنب

In the explanation book, Jame' of Ahkam Al-Qur'an by Imam Al-Qur'tubi, Vol.1, Chapter 2:35, we find these words:

"And we said to Adam and his wife, go and live in heaven and eat from it and enjoy it..."
That the first who ate from the tree was Eve and Satan whispered to her in her sleep, and it was the first act of misleading of women against men, and then Satan said, "He (God) forbid thee from the tree for it is the tree of eternal life." For he, Satan, knew that they (Adam and Eve) loved eternal life. So Satan came to them from where they loved and where you love is where you are deaf and blind, so when Eve asked Adam to eat from it, Adam rejected her request and he told her, "Did you forget the promise we made [to Allah]?" Eve insisted to make him eat and then she said, "What if I eat first and if nothing happens to me, nothing will happened to you!" So she ate and nothing happened to her and then she said, "See nothing hurt me." So he ate too and then they became under the sin!

148

⚞ Now we have a better understanding of why Muhammad is blaming Eve for everything ugly that happened before, or will happened later to a man. It must be from women for they are evil and full of deceptions in the eyes of Muhammad!

Book of Jame' of Ahkam Al Qur'an by Imam Al-Qur'tubi, V1, Page 352:

فدخل آدم في جوف الشجرة فناداه ربه : أين أنت ؟ فقال : أنا هذا يا رب قال : ألا تخرج ؟ قال استحي منك يا رب قال : اهبط إلى الأرض التي خلقت منها ولعنت الحية وردت قوائمها في جوفها وجعلت العداوة بينها وبين بني آدم ولذلك أمرنا بقتلها على ما يأتي بيانه وقيل لحواء : كما أدميت الشجرة فكذلك يصيبك الدم كل شهر وتحملين وتضعين كرها تشرفين به على الموت

Then Adam entered inside of a tree, then his Lord called him saying, "Adam where are you?" Adam answered, "I am ashamed before you Lord." Then Allah said: "Get down from heaven to earth where you have been created from! And I curse the snake and I make her feet disappear inside her, and I make enmity between you and all seed of Adam for this we order to kill it (the snake)," and to Eve Allah said: "As you made the tree bleed, you will be bleeding too, once every month, and you will be pregnant and you will deliver when you hate it, and face death doing that!"

⚞ I see here some of the story as it's written in the Bible, though the Bible never said Eve was the reason for sin. A lot of what Muhammad taught is copied from the books of others, for he was a corrupt man trying to corrupt stories.

⚞ Rather, the Bible tells us that Eve was deceived by the snake. Genesis 3:1-6 (KJV):

¹ Now the serpent was more subtle than any beast of the field which the LORD God had made. And he said unto the woman, Yea, hath God said, Ye shall not eat of every tree of the garden? ² And the woman said unto the serpent, We may eat of the fruit of the trees of the garden: ³ But of the fruit of the tree which is in the midst of the garden, God hath said, Ye shall not eat of it, neither shall ye touch it, lest ye die. ⁴ And the serpent said unto the woman, Ye shall not surely die: ⁵ For God doth know that in the day ye eat thereof, then your eyes shall be opened, and ye shall be as gods, knowing good and evil. ⁶ And when the woman saw that the tree was good for food, and that it was pleasant to the eyes, and a tree to be desired to make one wise, she took of the fruit thereof, and did eat, and gave also unto her husband with her; and he did eat.

⚞ As we see, Eve in the Biblical story was rejecting the evil, but she was deceived in the end; as all of us do sin today. Adam was not rejecting anything. He accepted so fast! The fact is, she was fighting back more than

Adam. Contrast this with the Qur'an and hadith story, where it was Adam fighting back. He did not want to eat. In the Bible it was Eve trying to keep God's order. Anyway, the point is, Muslims try to portray Eve as an evil person and then project that onto every woman on this earth.

Evil Ominous (Omen)

شروح الحديث
شرح النووي على مسلم
يحيي بن شرف أبو زكريا النووي
دار الخير
سنة النشر: 1416هـ / 1996م
عدد الأجزاء: ستة أجزاء
وحدثنا عبد الله بن مسلمة بن قعنب حدثنا مالك بن أنس ح وحدثنا يحيى بن يحيى قال قرأت على مالك عن ابن 2225
شهاب عن حمزة وسالم ابني عبد الله بن عمر عن عبد الله بن عمر أن رسول الله صلى
الله عليه وسلم قال الشؤم في الدار والمرأة والفرس

Al-Bukhari V4, Book 52, Hadith110:

Narrated 'Abdullah bin 'Omar: I heard the Prophet saying, "Evil omen is from three things, the female horse, the woman and the house."

⚐ This is a very clear and sad view of the deviance of Muhammad's look towards women. The strange thing is that women are the **Evil Ominous, but at the same time he has 13 wives and hundreds of slave women for sex! He must be a man who loves evil so much that he wanted his house to be full of it!**

Sahih Al Bukhari Hadith: 4/336

Narrated Abdullah: The Prophet stood up and delivered his speech and pointed his finger to the house of 'Aisha, and expressed "Evil is right here," repeating that three times.

Sahih Muslim, Arabic book, the Chapter of Sedition's, Vol l4, Page 2229:

الباري شرح صحيح البخاري
أحمد بن علي بن حجر العسقلاني
دار الريان للتراث
سنة النشر: 1407هـ / 1986م
عدد الأجزاء: ثلاثة عشر جزءا
الكتب » صحيح البخاري » كتاب النكاح » باب الوصاة بالنساء
حدثنا إسحاق بن نصر حدثنا حسين الجعفي عن زائدة عن ميسرة عن أبي حازم عن أبي 160ص 4890
هريرة عن النبي صلى الله عليه وسلم قال من كان يؤمن بالله واليوم الآخر فلا يؤذي جاره واستوصوا بالنساء
خيرا فإنهن خلقن من ضلع وإن أعوج شيء في الضلع أعلاه فإن ذهبت تقيمه كسرته وإن تركته لم يزل أعوج

فاستوصوا بالنساء خيرا

Muhammad said, concerning his wife Hafsa (the daughter of Omar), "The master of Blasphemy."

The story can be found in many books like Fateh Al-Bari Fe sharih Sahih Al-Bukhari, 1986 Printing; Book of Nukah, Chapter taking care of women, Page 160, Hadith 4890.

Sahih Muslim, Book 008, Hadith 3467:

Abu Huraira said: The Woman has been originated from a rib bone, and it's impossible to straighten her for you in any way; so if you desire to take advantage of her, then use her while corruption remains in her. And if you try to straighten her, you will break her, and breaking her is by divorcing her.

Women Are Created the Same as an Animal

In the book which I reference in this section, I will translate only that portion which is relevant to our topic, but I am posting all the text as it is so that Muslims who speak Arabic will not say it's out of context. On

top of this, I will post a link for their Islamic Jordanian government website so they can see it there for themselves.

In the book of Tafsir Al Kaber, Mafateeh Al Gaeeb, by Iamam Al Razi, Qur'an 30:21:

هـ) المسألة الأولى: قوله: { خَلَقَ لَكُمْ } **دليل على أن** 606تفسير مفاتيح الغيب ، التفسير الكبير/ الرازي (ت
:**النساء خلقن كخلق الدواب والنبات وغير ذلك من المنافع**، كما قال تعالى
{ خَلَقَ لَكُم مَّا فِى ٱلأَرْضِ }

Also see what Allah is saying Qur'an 30:21: "We created to yourselves," is a proof that Allah created women the same as he created animals (for the need of men).

] وهذا يقتضي أن لا تكون مخلوقة للعبادة والتكليف فنقول خلق النساء من النعم علينا وخلقهن لنا 29البقرة: [
وتكليفهن لإتمام النعمة علينا لا لتوجيه التكليف نحوهن مثل توجيهه إلينا وذلك من حيث النقل والحكم والمعنى،
أما النقل فهذا فهذا وغيره،، وأما الحكم فلأن المرأة لم تكلف بتكاليف كثيرة كما كلف الرجل بها، وأما المعنى فلأن
المرأة ضعيفة الخلق سخيفة فشابهت الصبي لكن الصبي، لم يكلف فكان يناسب أن لا تؤهل المرأة للتكليف،
لكن النعمة علينا ما كانت تتم إلا بتكليفهن لتخاف كل واحدة منهن العذاب فتنقاد للزوج وتمتنع عن المحرم،
ولولا ذلك لظهر الفساد.

Him (Allah) saying in the Qur'an 30:21 "created for you," is proof that women were created the same as animals and plants and other useful things. Allah also said in Qur'an 2:29: "He created for you what is on earth," and that need of the woman not to be created for worship or be charged with divine orders. We say creating the women is one of the favors bestowed upon us (men) and that charging them with divine commands is to complete the favor bestowed upon us, not that they are charged as we (men) are charged. For women are not charged with a lot of commands as we (men) are charged, because the woman is made weak, absurd (silly). In other words she is like a kid and no commands are charged upon children, but for the favor of Allah upon us to be complete, women had to be given obedience; charged so that each one of them (women) may be afraid of punishment so she obeys her husband, and refrains from what is forbidden, otherwise immorality would occur."

Women are Sex Toys

In the book of Sahih Al-Bukhari, Book 54, Hadith 460:

Reported by Abo Huraira: Allah's prophet said: "If the husband calls his wife to his bed for sex, and she refuses and made him sleep in anger, the angels of Allah will keep cursing her until morning."

You can find this understanding of women's duty all over Islamic books like the book of Al Qurtoby /Jame' Ahkam, Beirut, 1993, Al Qur'an 30:21, V 13, Page 17:

(هـ671تفسير الجامع لاحكام القرآن/ القرطبي (ت
والذي نفسي بيده ما من رجل يدعو امرأته إلى فراشها فتأبى عليه إلا كان الذي في السماء ساخطاً عليها حتى
يرضى عنها " وفي لفظ آخر: " إذا باتت المرأة هاجرة فراش زوجها لعنتها الملائكة حتى تُصبح

The prophet said, "By the one who my soul is in his hand, if a man asked his wife for sex and she refused, the one who is in the sky (meaning Allah) He will be embittered until her husband is satisfied with her." (Qurtoby adding to this) In other words, if the wife did not go to bed for him, angels of Allah will curse her until the morning.

I will go to every well-known book used by all Muslim courts of law to provide judgment for Muslim's arguments or cases.

Book title "The Treasure of Workers on Legislation and Words and Deeds," by Imam Al Mutaqi Al Hindi, Section five in the Wife and Husband Rights, Chapter one (The Rights of Man Over the Woman):

من حق الزوج على الزوجة أن لو سال منخراه دما وقيحا وصديدا فلحسته بلسانها ما أدت حقه، ولو- 44801

.كان ينبغي لبشر أن يسجد لبشر لأمرت الزوجة أن تسجد لزوجها إذا دخل عليها لما فضله الله عليها

The prophet Muhammad said:
44801 - Right of the husband over his wife, that if the mucus, blood, pus and filth pour from his nose and she did lick it with her tongue, that will not be enough to give the man his right over her! As long as I am not allowed to order a human being to prostrate to a human being, I would like to order the wife to prostrate to her husband when he enters to her home, upon the virtues of God.

44821- .إذا تزوج البكر على الثيب أقام عندها سبعا، وإذا تزوج الثيب على البكر أقام عندها ثلاثا

If a man marries a virgin above non-virgins, he should stay with her seven days, and if he marries a non-virgin above the virgin, he should stay with her three days!

44824- .للحرة يومان، وللأمة يوم

44824 - For the free women two days (he should stay with her), and for the slave one day.

44842- .إذا رأى أحدكم امرأة حسناء فأعجبته فليأت أهله، فإن البضع واحد، ومعها مثل الذي معها

44842- If a man liked a woman (he got sexually aroused), go and do your wife, for both have the same tools!

Commentary of Imam Al-Nawawi on the Hadith of Sahih Muslim, Book 003, Number 0684:

Our companions have said that if the penile head has penetrated a woman's anus or men's anus, or an animal vagina or her anus, then it is necessary to wash whether the one being penetrated is alive or dead, young or old.

Qur'an 2:223:

Your women are a tillage for you, so do to your tillage as ye will, and when as you like...

(ت) التفسير الكبير/ الرازي ، تفسير مفاتيح الغيب606هـ)
.ابن عمر أنه كان يقول: المراد من الآية تجويز إتيان النساء في أدبارهن

{ أَنَّىٰ شِئْتُمْ } والمشهور ما ذكرناه أنه يجوز للزوج أن يأتيها من قبلها في قبلها، ومن دبرها في قبلها والثاني: }
أن المعنى: أي وقت شئتم من أوقات الحل: يعنى إذا لم تكن أجنبية، أو محرمة، أو صائمة، أو حائضاً والثالث:
.أنه يجوز للرجل أن ينكحها قائمة أو باركة، أو مضطجعة

In the book of Tafsir Al Kaber, Mafateeh Al Gaeeb, 2004 Printing, Beirut, by Iamam Al Razi, Qur'an 2:223, Page 61:

Ibn Omar said this verse is about how it's fine to have sex by the woman's anus:

> (ana sh'tom), it's allowable for men to do his woman from front or back, from her vagina, or from front or back position with her anus, and the second issue is to do them whenever you want or like, any time of your choice, he can f___ her (do nikah) standing or sitting or on her back.

⅄ Notice how the word Nikah, which Muslims try to present as being about marriage, is used to describe how to perform sex positions while the man is doing Nikah.

⅄ I think my commentary is not important anymore. Their words are more than enough to explain how Islam views women, and how male sexual gratification is so important and takes up a huge part of this cult. Do not forget that Muslims do not really love Allah. They love the sex Allah will give them in heaven. This is why they would love to die. No more work, hard life will be history, a new era of sex and to win life.

⅄ Muhammad did everything in his power to be sure that women were under slavery rules, and to give the man all the law or legal right to do that.

⅄ The Muslims might say that the prophet said, "The best of your men is he who is the best to his wives!"

⅄ This is only after all the conditions on women are met, and then the duty of man is to provide food and shelter. If the woman is of full obedience, he has no reason to be bad to her. We can see this in the coming verse:

Qur'an 4:34:

> Men are in control of women, because Allah hath made the one of them to be superior over the other, and because they spend of their money on women. So the good women are the full obedient, keeping in secret what Allah order to be kept. As for those from whom you may fear their submissiveness, admonish them and lock up them to their beds, and <u>scourge them</u>. Then if they obey you, punish them no more. For Allah is high, great.

You will hear Muslims say, regarding this verse, that it's about beating women *lightly*. The fact is, this verse shows:

1. The word lightly does not even exist in the verse. Not even in any interpretation of the Qur'an. You see, it's only in the English books to

sell Islam to westerners. Just as Obama and others try to tell us by saying that Islam is peace.

2. Even if the word does not mean tough beating, at the end of the day, beating is beating. Regardless of how harsh or tough it is.

3. How light can a beating be? Lighter than a spit? It's about humiliation, not only the physical harm. Women are human. No one has the right to do such a thing to another human being.

4. Dogs in America have more rights than Muslim women. If you beat a dog in the USA, you go to jail, but if you beat a woman in an Islamic land, you are a hero who is teaching his wife how to behave!

5. What about jailing the wives in their rooms? Even the man can rape them as part of their punishment. There was a case of which you might not have heard, where a mad man, American judge (New Jersey judge) let a Moroccan husband in the U.S. rape his wife without punishment, because he believed his Muslim religion permitted it. Muhammad said

تحفة الأحوذي
سنن الترمذي كتاب الرضاع باب ما جاء في حق الزوج على المرأة
[فإني لو كنت آمرا أحدا أن يسجد لغير الله لأمرت المرأة أن تسجد لزوجها ، والذي نفس محمد بيده لا 272ص:
تؤدي المرأة حق ربها حتى تؤدي حق زوجها ، ولو سألها نفسها ، وهي على قتب لم تمنعه أخرجه أحمد

6. Book title Tu'hfet Al-A'hawazi Suana Al-Turmzi, book name Al-Rida', page 272:

The prophet Muhammad said, "If [you] would like to order to bow to someone other than Allah, it would be ordering the woman to bow down to her husband. By him in Whose Hands hold my soul, a woman cannot carry out the right of her Lord, until she carries out the right of her husband. And if he asks her to surrender herself [to him for sexual intercourse] she should not refuse him even if she is on top of a camel's hump."

. فيض القدير، شرح الجامع الصغير 7الجزء الثاني ص
أعظم الناس حقا على المرأة زوجها) حتى لو كان به قرحة فلحستها ما قامت بحقه ، ولو أمر أحد أن يسجد لأحد)
لأمرت بالسجود له فيجب أن لا تخونه في نفسها ومالها ، وأن لا تمنعه نفسها وإن كانت على ظهر قتب ، وأن لا
.تخرج إلا بإذنه ولو لجنازة أبويها

Book title Faed Al-Qadeer fe Sharih AL-Jame' Al-Sa'ger, Printed in Cairo, 1974, V2, Page 7:

The prophet said, "The most who have right over a woman is her husband, as well as if her husband has an ulcer (pus), and she did lick it. She did not give him his right over her yet, and if an order someone to bow to someone other than Allah it would be ordering the woman bowing to her husband, and she should not cheat on him or forbid him from her money or herself sexually, even if she is on the top of the camel hump, and she should not go out of his house without his permission, even if it's her parent's funeral."

In the BBC NEWS Wednesday, 14 January, 2004, 14:57 GMT, http://news.bbc.co.uk/2/hi/europe/3396597.stm :

> 'Imam rapped for wife-beating book.
> Mustafa reportedly says he opposes violence against women. A Muslim cleric who wrote a book that advised men how to beat up their wives without leaving incriminating marks has been sentenced by a Spanish court.
> In his defense, the imam said he was interpreting passages from the Koran.

As you see, it's not how I am translating it or that maybe I am trying to make it look bad! That's how ugly and savage it really is.

In the coming hadith, we will see how the real beating in Islam is.

Her Skin Is Greener Than Her Clothes

Bukhari Book 72, Hadith 715 in Arabic book of AI-LIBAS (book of clothes/green clothes), Hadith 5487:

> Reported by Ekrema: "That Rifa'a divorced his wife and Abd Al-Rahman bin Al Zobair married her. 'Aisha said that she came to her wearing green clothes and showed her her skin and it was greener than her clothes from beating. And it's normal that women take the side of each other, so when Allah's Apostle came, 'Aisha said: 'I have not met any woman tortured as much as Muslim women. Look at **her skin, it's greener than her clothes** (speaking to the Prophet)!'
> But When 'Abd Al-Ra'hman heard that his wife went to the Prophet to complain, he came with his two sons from another wife.
> She (his wife) said, 'I swear by Allah! I have done nothing bad to him, but he is sexually disabled and is as useless to me as this,' holding and showing the side of her garment. Abd Al-Ra'hman said: 'I swear By Allah, Prophet, what she claims is a lie! I do shag her, same as if I am shagging the ground, but she is disobedient and wants to go back to Rifa'a (ex-husband).' Allah's Apostle said, to her: 'If that is your aim (to go back to your ex-husband) then you should know that it is unlawful for you to remarry Rifa'a, unless Abdur-Rahman has had sexual intercourse with you, and he tasted your juice.' When the Prophet saw two men with Abd Al-Rahman so the Prophet asked him, 'Are these your sons?' 'Abd Al-Rahman said, 'Yes.'
> The Prophet said (to the man's wife), 'You made an allegation, and you insist

that he cannot have sex? However, I swear by Allah, his male children resemble him as a crow resembles a crow.'"

صحيح البخاري ـ كِتَاب اللِّبَاس ـ بَاب ثِيَابِ الخُضْرِ

5487 حَدَّثَنَا مُحَمَّدُ بْنُ بَشَّارٍ حَدَّثَنَا عَبْدُ الوَهَّابِ أَخْبَرَنَا أَيُّوبُ عَنْ عِكْرِمَةَ أَنَّ رِفَاعَةَ طَلَّقَ امْرَأَتَهُ فَتَزَوَّجَهَا عَبْدُ الرَّحْمَنِ بْنُ الزَّبِيرِ القُرَظِيُّ قَالَتْ عَائِشَةُ وَعَلَيْهَا خِمَارٌ أَخْضَرُ فَشَكَتْ إِلَيْهَا وَأَرَتْهَا خُضْرَتَهَا بِجِلْدِهَا فَلَمَّا جَاءَ رَسُولُ اللَّهِ صَلَّى اللَّهُ عَلَيْهِ وَسَلَّمَ وَالنِّسَاءُ يَنْصُرُ بَعْضُهُنَّ بَعْضًا فَجَاءَ وَمَعَهُ ابْنَانِ لَجِلْدُهَا أَشَدُّ خُضْرَةً مِنْ ثَوْبِهَا قَالَ وَسَمِعَ أَنَّهَا قَدْ أَتَتْ رَسُولَ اللَّهِ صَلَّى اللَّهُ عَلَيْهِ وَسَلَّمَ فَجَاءَ وَمَعَهُ ابْنَانِ لَهُ مِنْ غَيْرِهَا قَالَتْ وَاللَّهِ مَا لِي إِلَيْهِ مِنْ ذَنْبٍ إِلَّا أَنَّ مَا مَعَهُ لَيْسَ بِأَغْنَى عَنِّي مِنْ هَذِهِ وَأَخَذَتْ هُدْبَةً مِنْ ثَوْبِهَا فَقَالَ كَذَبَتْ وَاللَّهِ يَا رَسُولَ اللَّهِ إِنِّي لَأَنْفُضُهَا نَفْضَ الأَدِيمِ وَلَكِنَّهَا نَاشِزٌ تُرِيدُ رِفَاعَةَ فَقَالَ رَسُولُ اللَّهِ صَلَّى اللَّهُ عَلَيْهِ وَسَلَّمَ فَإِنْ كَانَ ذَلِكِ لَمْ تَحِلِّي لَهُ أَوْ لَمْ تَصْلُحِي لَهُ حَتَّى يَذُوقَ مِنْ عُسَيْلَتِكِ قَالَ وَأَبْصَرَ مَعَهُ ابْنَيْنِ لَهُ فَقَالَ بَنُوكَ هَؤُلَاءِ قَالَ نَعَمْ قَالَ هَذَا الَّذِي تَزْعُمِينَ مَا تَزْعُمِينَ فَوَاللَّهِ لَهُمْ أَشْبَهُ بِهِ مِنَ الغُرَابِ بِالغُرَابِ

⅄ Maybe some of you do not know yet what this woman is trying to do! Muhammad created a crazy rule. It decreed that if a Muslim man divorced his wife three times, he could not have her back unless she has married and divorced someone else.

Then after the second husband divorced her, she could remarry her ex-husband again! This is seen in Qur'an 2:230:

> And if he hath divorced her three time, then she is not lawful unto him, until she marry another husband. Then if he (the new husband) divorce her, it is no problem for both of them that both (wife and her ex) come back together again if they like to do that.

⅄ What the woman was trying to do was to save her family. Her husband had divorced her three times already, but she could not go back to her ex-husband unless she married another man. As we see, she thought that this was an old man, he would marry her, and then she would make him hate her, maybe by refusing to have sex, then she might be able to go back to her family and kids, but the man was using his right as a Muslim man to beat her for refusing to be obedient to him and the refusal of sharing the bed. This was why this story had occurred.

⅄ Here are the important issues of this story:

1. Muhammad did not say one word against the husband beating her to the point that her skin became greener than her clothes!

2. Muhammad took the side of the man. As a result, humiliating the woman.

3. It's so clear that this woman does not want to share the bed with this man anymore. She is looking for any way to get out of this marriage, but Muhammad told her that if she wanted to go back to her ex-husband, she had to have sexual intercourse with her second husband.

4. Muhammad was proving to her that she was telling a lie about him being

impotent, for he had two grown sons from another wife! Although I wonder what this has to do with a man's ability for sex. Impotency can happen anytime, because of illness to a man, even after having ten kids or more. Many men, even at a young age, not old as this man in the story, might not be able to perform the sexual relationship at all.

5. On top of that, Muhammad gave this man Qur'an 4:34, to empower all men over women in Islam forever.

A Woman, a Donkey and a Dog Defile the Prayer

Sahih Muslim Book 004, Hadith 1034:

> Abu Horaira reported: That the Messenger of Allah said: "A woman, donkey and a dog defiles the prayer, but something like a packsaddle protects against that!"

➤ In this hadith we see that women, dogs and donkeys are all the same, and the men are the only humans!

➤ This is proof that Muhammad viewed women as animals.

➤ Muslims might say to cover this hadith, "Oh, it's about having sex. If you have sex, you need to do ablution." The answer for this lie is the hadith itself:

1. It says **woman**, not wife. This includes **any** woman; mother, sister, or daughter. Do Muslims have sex with these?

2. Muhammad listed women along with animals in the same line. Does that mean Muslims will have sex with donkeys and dogs? The sad fact is many of them do.

3. Why did Muhammad forget the pig?

4. What about all other animals? Don't they destroy the Muslim prayer? Like, what about the mule? Or, the horse? Is the rat fine?

5. The most clear proof that it's not about sex with these three, women, dogs and donkeys, that would destroy the Muslim prayer, is because Muhammad said that the "packsaddle protects against that." This means that if the Muslim man has a packsaddle between him and the three, or any of the three, he is still clean!

6. Now, do not ask me why Muhammad chose a packsaddle for protection and not anti-virus. Only Allah knows! As Muslims say when you corner them.

Teach Not Women How to Read and Write

Tafsir Al-Qu'tobi, Al-Jame' Le Ahkam, Al-Qur'an, chapter of Al-Noor page 146:

تفسير القرطبي

عائشة ـ رضي الله عنها ـ : لا تنزلوا النساء الغرف ولا ص 146 الجامع لأحكام القرآن » سورة النور تعلموهن الكتابة وعلموهن سورة النور والغزل

'Aisha said: "Do not give women rooms alone and teach them not how write but teach them chapter of Al-Noor and spinning, sewing."

'Aisha reported this from Muhammad. This is why the Taliban forbids females from going to schools in Afghanistan.

How to Choose the Right Women in Islam

In the book of Majdy Al Said Ibrahim, The Cult and Legend of Women (Cairo 1922), page 61, Chapter of The Duty of Woman to Service Her Husband:

The Duty of Woman to Service Her Husband:

1. She cannot stay out in windows or a balcony;
2. She has to hide from men in the front doors (in the house);
3. She should not go out wearing perfume;
4. She shouldn't wear short dresses, as infidels;
5. She shouldn't walk in the middle of the street;
6. She shouldn't speak in loud voice;
7. She shouldn't associate with men;
8. She shouldn't talk to men.

The writer of the book also explains what women should do / not do:

1. Speak with a low and weak voice;
2. Walk on the side of the street;
3. Do not ever expose yourself in your house door when there is a visitor;
4. Do not go out, if not necessary;

5. Do not ever leave your veil off for any reason;

6. Be sure of what you are wearing, when getting close to a balcony;

7. Do not ever shake hands with men (not with any man forbidden to you to marry);

8. Do not travel without a guardian of your male family members, for these are one of the cults of these days;

9. Do not spend your time in stupid things, but in praising Allah when you walk in street. No one should hear your voice and;

10. Do not look left and right, but always look down.

Is Nikah a word meaning Marriage? The Answer, No!

Let us prove it with Qur'an 2:230 (Usama Dadok translation):

فَإِن طَلَّقَهَا فَلَا تَحِلُّ لَهُ مِن بَعْدُ حَتَّىٰ **تنكح** زَوْجًا غَيْرَهُ ۗ فَإِن طَلَّقَهَا فَلَا جُنَاحَ عَلَيْهِمَا أَن يَتَرَاجَعَا إِن ظَنَّا أَن يُقِيمَا حُدُودَ اللَّهِ ۗ وَتِلْكَ حُدُودُ اللَّهِ يُبَيِّنُهَا لِقَوْمٍ يَعْلَمُونَ

So if he divorced her [a third time], so it is not lawful for him to take her again until she **has sex (nikah)** with another husband.

Now from this verse we learned that if a woman has been divorced three times she cannot get back with her old husband until she does Nikah with the new husband, the meaning of which is that it is not the marriage with the new husband which will make her able to go back to the old one, but doing of the act of Nikah. We will prove this from this story in Sahih All-Bukhari. We got to go back to the hadith which we posted previously under the topic of Greener Than Her Clothes; Bukhari, Book 72, Hadith 715 in Arabic, book of Al-LIBAS (book of clothes/green clothes), Hadith 5487:

Reported by Ekrema: That Rifa'a divorced his wife and Abd Al-Rahman bin Al Zobair married her. 'Aisha said that she came to her wearing green clothes and showed her her skin and it was greener than her clothes from beating. And it's normal that women take the side of each other, so when Allah's Apostle came, 'Aisha said: I have not met any woman tortured as much as Muslim women. Look at **her skin, it's greener than her clothes** (Speaking to the Prophet)! But When 'Abd Al-Ra'hman heard that his wife went to the Prophet to complain, he came with his two sons from another wife. She (his wife) said, "I swear by Allah! I have done nothing bad to him, but he is sexually disabled and is as useless to me as this," holding and showing the side of her garment. Abd Al-Ra'hman said: "I swear By Allah, Prophet, what she claims is a lie! I do shag her, same as if I am shagging the ground, but she is disobedient and wants to go back to

Rifa'a (ex-husband)." Allah's Apostle said, to her: "If that is your aim (to go back to your ex-husband) <u>then you should know that it is unlawful for you to remarry Rifa'a, unless Abdur-Rahman has had sexual intercourse with you, and he tasted your juice.</u>" When the Prophet saw two men with Abd Al-Rahman so the Prophet asked him, "Are these your sons?" 'Abd Al-Rahman said, "Yes." The Prophet said (to the man's wife), "You made an allegation, and you insist that he cannot have sex? However, I swear by Allah, his male children resemble him as a crow resembles a crow."

Read with me carefully what Muhammad said, "then you should know that it <u>is unlawful for you to remarry Rifa'a, unless Abdur-Rahman has had sexual intercourse with you, and he tasted your juice.</u>"

So in Qur'an 2:230 the word "to do Nikah, تنكح," is the condition which the woman has to fulfill so she can go back to her ex-husband. The story before us is about a woman who is already married to the new husband, but this does not make her lawful to go back to her ex-husband until she does Nikah, which is sexual intercourse, and he has to taste her juice. I will leave tasting the juice with no commentary. Just ask yourselves what kind of prophet speaks to a woman like this?

One more verse from the Usama Dakdok translation of Qur'an 33:50:

> O you prophet, surely we have made it lawful for you, your wives whom you have given their wages and those that your right hand possesses which Allah has granted you and the daughters of your paternal uncle and the daughters of your paternal aunts and the daughters of your maternal uncle and the daughters of your maternal aunts, those who emigrate with you. And a believing

woman if she gives herself to the prophet to have sex (nikah يستنكحها) with her.

وَامْرَأَةً مُؤْمِنَةً إِن وَهَبَتْ نَفْسَهَا لِلنَّبِيِّ إِنْ أَرَادَ النَّبِيُّ أَن يَسْتَنكِحَهَا خَالِصَةً لَّكَ مِن دُونِ الْمُؤْمِنِينَ :Qur'an 33:50

In the Yusuf Ali translation, he translated that last part as "any believing woman who dedicates her soul to the Prophet" This is one of the examples of the Muslims' deception, trying to cover their prophet's sexual gifts to himself. Think about it, "dedicates her soul to the Prophet," What would Muhammad do with her soul and what happened to the word Nikah? If it meant marriage, why do Muslims try to hide it in this verse?

I think things are clearer now, because of all the women who gave themselves to Muhammad as sex gifts, not even one of them was called a wife. The names of some of the women who gave themselves to Muhammad for sex are Khawla Bint Hakim, Zaenab Bint 'Khuzima and Um Shariek.

Sahih Muslim, Book 008, Hadith 3453:

> A'isha narrated. "I used to be jealous of those women who [had] given themselves to Allah's Messenger," and she said: "Then when Allah, the Exalted and Glorious, revealed this: 'You may delay anyone of them, you wish, and take to yourself any you wish; and if you desire any you have seat side.'" Aisha said: "It seems to me that your Lord rushes to satisfy your (sexual) desire."

Muhammad may delay any of these women. It sounds like a long line of women needed Muhammad badly in bed, and watch how Aisha noticed that Muhammad was a false prophet when she said "It seems to me that your Lord rushes to satisfy your (sexual) desire." She knew he is making up the Qur'an just to justify his sexual madness. Ask yourself why a man who already has many wives even allowed such a thing. Were his wives not enough and why was this license given only to Muhammad?

Just think, the lord of the universe is busy making chapters about Muhammad's special sexual needs.

In this Sharia Law order we read this Question

"is doing Nikah to the hand is forbidden in Islam, and the one would do it is cursed?" Fatwas number (3201 book of Fatwa Al-Lajnah Al-Da'emah lil-Buhoth V.4

نكاح اليد وما في حكمه المسمى بالعادة السرية حرام، ولم يثبت فيما نعلم الحكم على من يفعل ذلك بأنه 2:ج
المجموعة الرابعة» فتاوى اللجنة الدائمة للبحوث العلمية والإفتاء :كتاب ملعون،

Answer: " doing Nikah to your hand is forbidden but we have no knowledge that h would be cursed"

So if the word Nikah or Nikah mean marrige, have you ever heard of some one marriying his hand is he is doing masturbation?

Polygamy in Islam

Qur'an 4:3:

> If you fear not to be just to the orphans, have sexual intercourse, whoever you like, two or three or four. And if you fear that ye cannot do justice to them, then one woman only or [the captives and slaves] that your right hands possess. Thus it is more likely you will not be inequitable.

⅄ There are two kinds of women who are free to be slept with as wives, and the third to sleep with are slaves (nikah: sexual intercourse), but not marriage.

⅄ If the orphans are not good for you, because they are poor and you cannot be nice to them for that reason, then go for the others.

⅄ You have the choice of two or three or four. But if you cannot afford it, then just one.

⅄ Muhammad preferred the Muslims to have more than one wife, but, if not, the last choice is one woman.

⅄ The Qur'an indicates that Muslim men can have four wives, but only if they can do justice to them at the same time. The end of the verse says, you cannot be inequitable (unjust or unfair)!

⅄ This would mean that Muslims should not ever marry or have more than four women in bed. Because of the conditions to have them, Muslim men are not able to have even one. This will be shown in other verses in the same chapter, as we see in Qur'an 4:129:

> You will not be able to deal equally in justice between your wives, does not matter how you try to do so!

⅄ It's clear that Muhammad's law contradicts itself. To have four wives, I have to deal justly with them all, but I can't, so why are you saying I can marry four?

Was Muhammad the Best Man of Islam Who Dealt Justly With His Wives?

Sahih Bukhari, Volume 3, Book 47, Hadith 755:

Reported 'Orua that 'Aisha said: "The Prophet's wives were in two parties. First group included 'Aisha, Hafsa, Safiyia and Saoda, and the other group included Om Salama and the rest of the wives of Allah's Apostle. All The Muslims knew that Allah's Messsenger idolized and adored 'Aisha, so if any of them liked to deliver a gift and wished to give it to Allah's Messenger, he would hold over sending it, until Allah's Prophet had moved towards to 'Aisha's house, and then he would deliver his gift to Allah's Messenger in 'Aisha's home. The side of Om Salama discussed the matter meeting together and decided that Om Salama should request Allah's Messenger to tell the Muslims to send their gifts to him in whatever wife's house he is in. Om Salama told Allah's Apostle of what they were asking for and what they said, but he did not reply. Then they (the team of Om Salama) asked Om Salama about it. She said, 'He did not reply or answer and did not say anything to me.' They asked her to try talking to him again. She talked to him again when she met him on her day, but he ignored her and gave no reply. When they asked her (the group of Om Salama), she replied that he had given no reply. They said to her, 'Keep asking him until he gives you a response.' And when it was her turn, she talked to him again. He (Muhammad) said to her: 'Do not harm me regarding 'Aisha, as the Divine Inspirations do not come to me on any (ثوب) dress except the dress of 'Aisha!' With that answer Om Salama said: 'I do repent to Allah for hurting you.' Then the group of Om Salama called Fatima, the daughter of Allah's Apostle and asked her to go to him and sent her to Allah's Apostle to say to him, 'Your wives request to apply to them and the daughter of Abu Baker on equal terms.' Then Fatima delivered the message to him. The Prophet said, 'Oh my daughter! Don't you love whom I love?' Fatima replied in the positive, and went back and told them of the circumstance. However, the group of Om Salama asked her to go to him again, but she rejected. They later sent Zainab bint Jahsh, who went to him and used harsh words saying to (Muhammad), 'Your wives demand you to apply to them with the daughter of Ibn Abu Qo'hafa ('Aisha) on equal rights.' It followed that she raised her voice and yelling at 'Aisha to her face so much so that Allah's Apostle looked at 'Aisha to see whether she would reverse the attack. Subsequently 'Aisha started yelling to Zainab until she silenced her. The Prophet then looked at 'Aisha and said. 'She is for sure the daughter of Abu Baker!'"

1. Muhammad did not practice his god's law for sure. Qur'an 4:129 says, "You will not be able to deal equally in justice between your wives, does not matter how you try to do so!"

2. This is a living example of how ugly it is to have more than one wife.

3. This shows how the wives are gathered in groups, as if it's two armies!

4. What about the kids? Will they then go in groups and hate each other?

5. The wives are not asking too much of Muhammad. I wonder if a woman came to Muhammad complaining about her husband doing the same as

Muhammad was doing, I am sure Muhammad would ask the man to deal fairly and justly! But, Muhammad will not!

6. Notice also how they are acting around him, as if they are cats. When one of them, Om Salama, opened her mouth, she said, "Do not hurt me regarding 'Aisha." This scared the hell out of her, for he said clearly that this was hurting him, not 'Aisha! She answered like a poor cat, "I do repent to Allah for hurting you".

7. The wives keep trying to make him change his mind. This is telling us how extremely angry they are, because all the money and gifts are going to 'Aisha's house only, which is unfair.

8. The Muslims were playing an evil role too. They waited until Muhammad was in 'Aisha's house, because they knew if they sent the gift to any of the other wives houses, 'Aisha would open the doors of hell on them! They totally understood that she was in control. To avoid her wrath, they sent their gifts to 'Aisha's in order to get the benefit of the gift in full.

9. This means that Muhammad was favoring 'Aisha above the others, because she was the youngest (his child-wife)! It was so clear to all the Muslims around. It was not just inside the walls of his house, but it was widespread knowledge!

10. Then we ask ourselves, how seriously unfair was Muhammad with the other wives; to the point that all Muslims, with no exception, sent their gifts to 'Aisha's home only?

11. When the other wives, through Om Salama, asked him for fair treatment, why did it take him forever to answer their request? Don't they even deserve an answer?

12. Muhammad was watching 'Aisha and Hafsa fighting. While watching, he looked at 'Aisha as giving her the green light to do the attack. It's so clear that 'Aisha was a big mouth woman to the point it says, "she silenced her."

13. After that, Muhammad insulted Hafsa by saying to 'Aisha, "She is really the daughter of Abu Baker!" Which means she is really good! Abu Baker is his best friend and partner in the Islam Corporation.

14. Even his daughter Fatima, the one the Shi'a claim is the only real daughter of Muhammad, couldn't help. On top of that, he said, "Don't hurt me regarding 'Aisha for I never received the Qur'an but in her dress!"

➤ The Muslims try to make the word 'dress' mean 'Aisha's <u>house</u>, but when they say this; it means that Muhammad never received the Qur'an in the house of Khadija! This would mean that he lied!

➤ They do not like to envision their prophet wearing women's dresses, even though their many hadith are reporting it. Let's accept their position that the word dress means the house of 'Aisha, but this means that all the revelations Muhammad received when he was married to Khadija were lies. This is especially condemning, because at that time Muhammad only had Khadija as a wife!

Sauda and Muhammad

When Sauda had aged, was fat, and heavy in movement, Muhammad stopped coming to her in her night for sex! Sauda heard that Muhammad might divorce her for she is useless for bed. She couldn't find any solution. She knew that at this age, and because she had no kids, no one would marry her. She talked to 'Aisha and asked her for help, because she knew how powerful 'Aisha was. Then 'Aisha got an idea. We can find the reference concerning what 'Aisha said in many locations. Here is one of them in Suanan Abu Dawood, Book of Nikah (sexual intercourse—that Muslims translate as marriage), Page 243, Hadith 2135:

Reported from 'Aisha: "The prophet used to go and visit all of us each in her day and he had sexual intercourse with each woman in her day only! (Look how fair he was. Remember that the one talking is 'Aisha. There's no way she will complain.)

SUNAN OF Abu DAWOOD

سنن أبي داود ـ كِتَاب النَّكَاحِ

2135 ص -»« عَنْ هِشَامِ بْنِ عُرْوَةَ عَنْ 243حَدَّثَنَا أَحْمَدُ بْنُ يُونُسَ حَدَّثَنَا عَبْدُ الرَّحْمَنِ يَعْنِي ابْنَ أَبِي الزِّنَادِ ـ»« أَبِيهِ قَالَ قَالَتْ عَائِشَةُ يَا ابْنَ أُخْتِي كَانَ رَسُولُ اللَّهِ صَلَّى اللَّهُ عَلَيْهِ وَسَلَّمَ لَا يُفَضِّلُ بَعْضَنَا عَلَى بَعْضٍ فِي الْقَسْمِ مِنْ مُكْثِهِ عِنْدَنَا وَكَانَ قَلَّ يَوْمٌ إِلَّا وَهُوَ يَطُوفُ عَلَيْنَا جَمِيعًا فَيَدْنُو مِنْ كُلِّ امْرَأَةٍ مِنْ غَيْرِ مَسِيسٍ حَتَّى يَبْلُغَ إِلَى الَّتِي هُوَ يَوْمُهَا فَيَبِيتَ عِنْدَهَا وَلَقَدْ قَالَتْ سَوْدَةُ بِنْتُ زَمْعَةَ حِينَ أَسَنَّتْ وَفَرِقَتْ أَنْ يُفَارِقَهَا رَسُولُ اللَّهِ صَلَّى اللَّهُ عَلَيْهِ وَسَلَّمَ يَا رَسُولَ اللَّهِ يَوْمِي لِعَائِشَةَ فَقَبِلَ ذَلِكَ رَسُولُ اللَّهِ صَلَّى اللَّهُ عَلَيْهِ وَسَلَّمَ مِنْهَا قَالَتْ نَقُولُ فِي ذَلِكَ أَنْزَلَ اللَّهُ تَعَالَى وَفِي أَشْبَاهِهَا أُرَاهُ قَالَ وَإِنْ امْرَأَةٌ خَافَتْ مِنْ بَعْلِهَا نُشُوزًا

When Sauda aged and she felt or feared that the prophet might divorce her, she said, "Oh apostle of Allah, I give my day to 'Aisha." So the prophet accepted what Sauda said, and in this event Allah sent Qur'an 4:128:

If a wife fears lack of sexual attraction (نشوزا) or abandonment on her husband's part, there is no chide or reproach on them if they arrange a reconciliation settlement between themselves; and such settlement is best;

even though men's souls are changed by greed. But if you do good and seek protection by obeying Allah, God is all knowledgeable with all that ye do.

The funny word (Nshoze, نشوزا) is the same word used in Qur'an 4:34 which gives the man a reason for his wife-beating, but if the man did it, she has to let it go and do his wishes to please him!

Fateh Al-Bari Fe Shareh Sahih Al-Bukhari, 1986 Printing, Publisher Al-Raian, Page 223:

فتح الباري شرح صحيح البخاري
أحمد بن علي بن حجر العسقلاني
دار الريان للتراث سنة النشر: 1407هـ / 1986م ص: 223
ولقد قالت سودة بنت زمعة حين أسنت وخافت أن يفارقها رسول الله صلى الله عليه وسلم : يا رسول الله يومي
لعائشة ، فقبل ذلك منها ، ففيها وأشباهها نزلت وإن امرأة خافت من بعلها نشوزا الآية
وله نحوه من رواية جرير عن هشام ، وأخرج أبو داود هذا الحديث وزاد فيه بيان سببه أوضح من رواية مسلم

"Sauda she said: I was afraid that the prophet might divorce her, because she was aged, so she said to him, 'Do not divorce me and keep me as one of your wives and I give my day to 'Aisha as return!' So the verse, Qur'an 4:128 revealed," The hadith was narrated to by Jarer from Hisham, and Abu-Dawood, and it's explained in Sahih Muslim.

[سودة كانت امرأة قد أسنت ، ففزعت أن يفارقها رسول الله صلى الله عليه وسلم ، وضنت 428ع] ص:
بمكانها منه ، وعرفت من حب رسول الله صلى الله عليه وسلم عائشة ومنزلتها منه ، فوهبت يومها من رسول
الله صلى الله عليه وسلم لعائشة ، فقبل ذلك النبي صلى الله عليه وسلم .

Tafsir Ibn Kathir Beirut, Published in 2002, V 2, Page 428:

Reported from Ibn 'Abass: "Sauda aged and she was afraid that the prophet might divorce her and she lose her position as a wife, and she knew how much the prophet loved 'Aisha and he favor, she is special to him, so she gave her day to her ('Aisha) and the prophet accepted"

Fakhr Ad-Din Al Razi, *Al Tafsir Al Kaber* (*the big interpretation*) on Qur'an 4:128:

The Prophet wanted to divorce Sauda bint Zam'a, but she offerd him to keep her on the condition that she would give up her day to 'Aisha, and he allowed that and he did not divorce her (Sauda).

The same story can be found in the Book of Mishkat Al Masabih, V2/966, No. 3237/

Sahih Bukhari, Volume3, Book 48, Hadith 853:

...Sauda bint Zam'a gave her day and night (her sexual rights as wife) to 'Aisha, the wife of the Prophet trying to be satisfied and please Allah's Apostle.

Arabic Hadith has a different number; 2454:

البخاري ـ كِتَاب الْهِبَةِ وَفَضْلِهَا وَالتَّحْرِيضِ عَلَيْهَا ـ أما إنك لو أعطيتها أخوالك كان أعظم لأجرك
حَدَّثَنَا حِبَّانُ بْنُ مُوسَى أَخْبَرَنَا عَبْدُ اللَّهِ أَخْبَرَنَا يُونُسُ عَنْ الزُّهْرِيِّ عَنْ عُرْوَةَ عَنْ عَائِشَةَ رَضِيَ اللَّهُ عَنْهَا 2454
قَالَتْ كَانَ رَسُولُ اللَّهِ صَلَّى اللَّهُ عَلَيْهِ وَسَلَّمَ إِذَا أَرَادَ سَفَرًا أَقْرَعَ بَيْنَ نِسَائِهِ فَأَيَّتُهُنَّ خَرَجَ سَهْمُهَا خَرَجَ بِهَا مَعَهُ
وَكَانَ يَقْسِمُ لِكُلِّ امْرَأَةٍ مِنْهُنَّ يَوْمَهَا وَلَيْلَتَهَا غَيْرَ أَنَّ سَوْدَةَ بِنْتَ زَمْعَةَ وَهَبَتْ يَوْمَهَا وَلَيْلَتَهَا لِعَائِشَةَ زَوْجِ النَّبِيِّ
صَلَّى اللَّهُ عَلَيْهِ وَسَلَّمَ تَبْتَغِي بِذَلِكَ رِضَا رَسُولِ اللَّهِ صَلَّى اللَّهُ عَلَيْهِ وَسَلَّمَ

Why did Muhammad want to divorce this poor woman and stop sharing the bed with her? We may learn in Sahih Bukhari, Volume 2, Book 26, Hadith 740:

Narrated 'Aisha: "Sauda asked the Prophet to allow her to leave earlier at the night of Jam', and she Sauda was a fat and very slow woman. The Prophet granted her to leave."

1. I can show more and more references about this story, but all, or a few, is more than enough to explain that Muhammad was never FAIR with his wives.

2. If the best man of Islam is not fair with his wives, can the other Muslims be?

3. The best man is a selfish man. He used this woman for years and years until she is old and fat, then he dumped her in his trash box!

4. Allah always makes chapters fit exactly with Muhammad's sexual lust and he's ready anytime to make it a holy order!

5. Muslims say that a Muslim man should always be fair with his wives, but then they threaten a woman with divorce for no fault other than her age and beauty. Is this fair?

6. Why didn't Allah say to him, "Shame on you to use this old woman when she was young and now you are humiliating her?"

7. Would any Muslim appreciate someone who would do the same as Muhammad did to their mother, sister or daughter?

8. How evil 'Aisha was to jump into the coming opportunity to have more control of the house of Muhammad, which means the authority.

9. In the Qur'an, the verse is saying Allah is okay with women making agreements between each other. Was this for all Muslims or just for Muhammad? The fact is, it was only for Muhammad, as always! Was this really an agreement or was the poor old woman being forced into it only for the exchange of food and shelter?

The Word Noshoze, نشوز

The word **noshoze** in these verses means rejecting the spouse in bed or not liking him or her anymore. It's also about disobedience in the case of the husband ordering the women to go to bed.

The strange thing is this same word is in verse 4:34. نُشُوزَهُنَّ Noshoze is the excuse giving the man the right to beat his wife as punishment, because she does not like her husband in bed very much, or for not obeying him to go to bed (have sex), or any other reason. If the man is the one doing "noshoze" to his wife, because he does not like to sleep with her anymore, Allah does not give the same right he gave to the man (the right of beating) to the women. Even though it's the same word and the same action, everything was changed depending to whom it's done.

1. Male doing noshoze to female = the man is good and Allah is okay with it, to the point that Allah blesses that action and supports it with a chapter.
2. Female doing noshoze to male = beating, jailing, and humiliation is the answer.

It's clear that Allah has two different laws for the same action. The rule changes when the gender changes. It's good and fine, and blessed by Allah, if a man does it, but it's condemned, refused and punishable by beating if the woman is doing it.

Important Point About Qur'an 4:34

In that verse, the Muslims translate the word 'Ohjroin, أهجروهن, as, "leave them in bed as punishment", but we found that the word "noshoze" is a person leaving the bed of the spouse. It is clear Muslims are not telling the truth, because if a woman leaves your bed, this is your problem. So how can you **force her to share the bed by leaving her in bed?**

The fact is, that word is about jailing them, tying them up and raping them as punishment for rejecting the man. I will show the proof, as always, from their Islamic books.

One of the rules Muhammad made was giving the man open choice as to when women deserved to be beaten, and that no one had the right even to question the husband's behavior, as we see in the following hadith.

Sunan Abu Dawood, Book 11, Hadith 2142:

> Narrated mar Ibn Al Khatab: The Prophet said: "No man should be asked or to be questioned as how and why he beat his wife".

Sunan Abu Dawood Book 12, Number 2220:

سنن أبي داود ـ كِتَاب الطَّلَاقِ ـ خذ بعض مالها وفارقها

حَدَّثَنَا مُحَمَّدُ بْنُ مَعْمَرٍ حَدَّثَنَا أَبُو عَامِرٍ عَبْدُ الْمَلِكِ بْنُ عَمْرٍو حَدَّثَنَا أَبُو عَمْرٍو السَّدُوسِيُّ الْمَدِينِيُّ عَنْ عَبْدِ 2228 اللَّهِ بْنِ أَبِي بَكْرِ بْنِ مُحَمَّدِ بْنِ عَمْرِو بْنِ حَزْمٍ عَنْ عَمْرَةَ عَنْ عَائِشَةَ أَنَّ حَبِيبَةَ بِنْتَ سَهْلٍ كَانَتْ عِنْدَ ثَابِتِ بْنِ قَيْسِ بْنِ شَمَّاسٍ فَضَرَبَهَا فَكَسَرَ بَعْضَهَا فَأَتَتْ رَسُولَ اللَّهِ صَلَّى اللَّهُ عَلَيْهِ وَسَلَّمَ بَعْدَ الصُّبْحِ فَاشْتَكَتْهُ إِلَيْهِ فَدَعَا النَّبِيَّ صَلَّى اللَّهُ عَلَيْهِ وَسَلَّمَ ثَابِتًا فَقَالَ خُذْ بَعْضَ مَالِهَا وَفَارِقْهَا فَقَالَ وَيَصْلُحُ ذَلِكَ يَا رَسُولَ اللَّهِ قَالَ نَعَمْ قَالَ فَإِنِّي أَصْدَقْتُهَا حَدِيقَتَيْنِ وَهُمَا بِيَدِهَا فَقَالَ النَّبِيُّ صَلَّى اللَّهُ عَلَيْهِ وَسَلَّمَ خُذْهُمَا وَفَارِقْهَا فَفَعَلَ

'Habibah bent (daughter) of Sahel she was the wife of Thabet, so he did beat her until he <u>broke some of her parts</u>! So she came to the Prophet asking for justice, so the Prophet did call asking for him, when he came the Prophet said to him, "Take some of her money and leave her." Thabet said, "Is that alright?! I gave her two gardens as her dowry." The Prophet said, "Take them back and leave her".

A Final Point About Wife Beating

⚑ Muhammad forced the woman, whose bones were broken from being beaten, to lose the money she had received as payment for this marriage.

⚑ This means he is punishing the woman for marring this man. She is leaving the marriage with broken bones, no money and no house; so she lost everything.

⚑ Muhammad didn't say one word to the man about how severely he had beaten her, nor did he even question the man as to why he did this.

⚑ This means that according to Islam, if a woman takes her husband to court over a bad beating, she will lose everything and he loses nothing. He gets his full money back. He then can **purchase** a new wife!

⚑ This is proof that in Islam man is god over women, and what Muslims say about light beatings being just tapping, is a big fat lie!

Sexuality in Islam

One of the big contradictions in Islam is its orders and teachings about sex. On one hand, Islam teaches that morality is a duty of every Muslim. On the other hand, Islam is a Playboy book.

Muhammad seduces men with sexual promises and sometimes these promises are mere fantasies rather than promises that can be fulfilled in reality.

In Tuhfat Al-Habib 'Ala Share'h el AL-Khateb, Book of Nuka'h (Book of the F-word), p.356, Imam AL-Qurtubi said:

تحفة الحبيب على شرح الخطيب ـ وفائدته

ـ كتاب النكاح356ص

بل صرح القرطبي بأنه يجوز سائر نكاح المحارم في الجنة إلا الأم والبنت ؛ لأن العلة هنا التباغض وقطيعة الرحم وهي منتفية هناك ، لا ما فيه رذيلة كوطء في دبر ومنه وطء الأبعاض كبنته وأمه ؛ وقد ورد : " يعطى

ـ كتاب النكاح قدم العبادات356أحدكم في الجنة ذكرا مثل النخلة السحوق وفرجا يسع ذلك "ص

In summary, the preceding text says that it is lawful to have sex with your family members in heaven, except with your mother and daughter. A sexual relationship between family members is not considered incest, because it will not result in procreation. It is also considered not as bad as having anal sex. Additionally, Muhammad was reported to say that Allah will give each man a penis the size of a palm tree whose end cannot be seen.

As we continue reading the text, a man is permitted to have sex with all the women from his family, except his mother and daughter in the Islamic heaven. This means that Muslim men can have sex with their sisters, grandmothers, aunts and nieces. Muhammad also extended that authority by allowing men to have sex with everyone else. By that, Muhammad is satisfying the sexual fantasies and needs of Bedouin men.

Arab people, who lived in the desert, lived a simple life. Everything in their life was based on wealth (animals, gold and women). By promising endless sexual gratification, Muhammad spoke to their dreams and made these dreams attainable. As a result, he controlled their minds and did not give them enough space to think about these promises—that is, whether they could be fulfilled or not—because they are too good to be ignored.

Penis Like an Endless Palm Tree

Muhammad takes it further by giving Muslim men what they want. They want to have very huge private parts. Men will have a penis the size of palm trees whose end cannot be seen. Muhammad used the word سحوق, which means the end cannot be seen. Additionally, Allah will provide the men with a woman who has a vagina that will fit the man's over-sized penis. References V3. Book of Tuhfat Al 'Habib 'Ala Sharh Al-Katieb P.356:

" تحفة الحبيب على شرح الخطيب » كتاب النكاح " الجزء الثالث - "" - ص 356
بل صرح القرطبي بأنه يجوز سائر المحارم في الجنة إلا الأم والبنت ؛ لأن العلة هنا التباغض وقطيعة الرحم
وهي منتفية هناك ، لا ما فيه رذيلة كوطء في دبر ومنه وطء الأبعاض كبنته وأمه ؛ وقد ورد : " يعطى أحدكم في
" الجنة ذكرا مثل النخلة السحوق وفرجا يسع ذلك

Penis would never go soft Allah promise?

Messenger of Allah (ﷺ) said:

"There is no one whom Allah will admit to Paradise but Allah will marry him to seventy-two wives, two from houris and seventy from his inheritance from the people of Hell, all of whom will have desirable front(big breast) passages and he will have a male member that never becomes flaccid (i.e., soft and limp)".

English reference   : Vol. 5, Book 37, Hadith 4337
Arabic reference   : Book 37, Hadith 4481

مَا مِنْ أَحَدٍ يُدْخِلُهُ اللَّهُ الْجَنَّةَ إِلاَّ زَوَّجَهُ اللَّهُ عَزَّ وَجَلَّ ثِنْتَيْنِ وَسَبْعِينَ زَوْجَةً ثِنْتَيْنِ مِنَ الْحُورِ الْعِينِ وَسَبْعِينَ مِنْ مِيرَاثِهِ مِنْ
" أَهْلِ النَّارِ مَا مِنْهُنَّ وَاحِدَةٌ إِلاَّ وَلَهَا قُبُلٌ شَهِيٌّ وَلَهُ ذَكَرٌ لاَ يَنْثَنِي

Sexual Morality

Let us start with some verses showing the morality found in the Qur'an. Qur'an 23:5-7:

وَالَّذِينَ هُمْ لِفُرُوجِهِمْ حَافِظُونَ
إِلَّا عَلَىٰ أَزْوَاجِهِمْ أَوْ مَا مَلَكَتْ أَيْمَانُهُمْ فَإِنَّهُمْ غَيْرُ مَلُومِينَ 6
فَمَنِ ابْتَغَىٰ وَرَاءَ ذَٰلِكَ فَأُولَٰئِكَ هُمُ الْعَادُونَ 7

5 And those who guard their private parts (from others) 6 except from their women or the slaves that they own 7 and whoever goes beyond these exceptions is against Allah.

What we understand from this is that Muslim men have several ways to satisfy their sexual desires:

- He can marry four wives at the same time and divorce any of them anytime to make room for new wives.

- He can hire a woman for sex in a temporary marriage, known as Mut'a. Mut'a is simply an agreement between a man and woman to share a bed for a period of time wherein the length of contract and amount of payment is prearranged.

- He has the right to have sexual intercourse with all his slaves regardless of their number. They can be in the millions but as long as he owns them, he has the right to sleep with all of them. This is in contrast to the maximum number of wives he is allowed to have.

The point of using the word "marriage" in Islam is simply to legalize extra-marital affairs. It is not a real marriage:

- Women are exploited for sex.
- No loyalty is bestowed on them.
- It is easy for a man to divorce his wife or wives.
- Marriage is loose. It is done according to the man's will, not both (man and woman).
- By law, a contract provides both sides equal rights including starting and ending the marriage contract. However, according to the Qur'an and Muhammad, the right is based only on gender—that is, men receive special treatment. It gives men absolute authority and full control of the contract. This likens the woman to a mere employee who provides service to the man for as long as he requires or wills it. He can void the contract anytime. He can say "I do not need you anymore. Get out!"
- This proves that the whole idea of marriage in Islam is just a way to make the man happy. The woman is simply a sex toy. She has no rights except for what is provisioned in the contract, which is nothing more than the payment.

Muslims claim that Muslim women are given all the rights that no other women had before. However, the fact is the rights they are referring to are nothing more than the same rights given to animals; that is, feeding them and giving them shelter. The man, the "provider," provides the same "rights" to his animals as well.

Also, Islam supposedly provided women the right to inherit, but they do not tell us that she only inherits half of what her male counterpart will inherit. I will discuss this further in the section where I discuss the rights of women in Islam.

This kind of teaching is opposite to what Christ said in Mathew 19:5-6:

> "For this reason a man shall leave his father and mother and be joined to his wife, and the two shall become one flesh. So then, they are no longer two but one flesh. Therefore what God has joined together, let not man separate."

Christian marriage is a unity by God, not a contract for sex.

I will give you an example how this kind of sexual contract has to be done according to the verse, Qur'an 4:24. We have a man and woman discussing a Mut'a arrangement. We'll call the man, Ahmad, and the woman, Fatima.

Ahmad: Salam to you, Fatima.
Fatima: And to you, too! How I can help you?
Ahmed: I feel a great desire for sharing a bed with you **for a half-hour** in accordance to Allah's order to do pleasure marriage (mut'a).
Fatima: I am ready for that, but how much will you pay me?
Ahmed: I will pay **three dollars and 50 cents**.
Fatima: Well, I did a man before you for ten dollars.
Ahmed: Okay. I will make it five. Maybe he was rich. I am not!
Fatima: Fine. We will have a half-hour sex, and you pay me before my sweat dries, as the prophet said.
Ahmed: It's a done deal. Let us go to bed.

When the half-hour agreement is over, the Mut'a marriage automatically ends, which means no divorce proceedure is necessary (i.e. not necessary for the man to recite "I divorce you," three times).
What you may have not noticed here is that Mut'a is a marriage that does not require witnesses. This is an important point because adultery is condemned in Islamic law. If an illicit sexual relationship between a man and a woman is discovered and attested to by four male witnesses (a minimum of four witnesses is required to prove adultery according to Qur'an 24:4), all the couple needs to do is claim that they are engaged in a Mut'a marriage. No one can disprove this, because the couple is not required to have witnesses to this temporary marriage. Let's read about it in Book of Sahih Al Kafi by the Imam Al-Bahbodi, Volume 3, Number 46:

3/46قال البهبودي : صحيح

**) الْحُسَيْنُ بْنُ مُحَمَّدٍ عَنْ أَحْمَدَ بْنِ إِسْحَاقَ عَنْ سَعْدَانَ بْنِ مُسْلِمٍ عَنْ عُبَيْدِ بْنِ زُرَارَةَ عَنْ أَبِيهِ عَنْ أَبِي عَبْدِ اللَّهِ

عليه السلام) قَالَ ذَكَرْتُ لَهُ الْمُتْعَةَ أَ هِيَ مِنَ الْأَرْبَعِ فَقَالَ تَزَوَّجْ مِنْهُنَّ أَلْفاً فَإِنَّهُنَّ مُسْتَأْجَرَاتٌ

Reported by Al-Husin son of Muhammad from Ahmed son of Ishaq from Sa'dan son of Muslim from Aubid son of Zarah from his father from Abdullah, peace be upon him: I mentioned to him the Mut'a asking if it's one of the four (kinds of approved sexual relationships). He said, "Marry from them (women) one thousand. They are women for rent."

What this means is that you can rent as many women as you want for sex. The number, one thousand, mentioned in the verse is used to mean that men have an unlimited license to rent women (read: prostitutes), as long as they have the money.

I also wonder how they can get away with using the word "marry," when they are, in fact, hiring! What Muslims call "marriage," we call "prostitution"—and if their marriage is prostitution, what does that make of their adultery?

If we read carefully you will notice that this is the same as Mut'a; if you have money you can buy women and have sex with them. If she is a free woman, then it's a contract between the two, her and the temporary husband; otherwise it is a purchase contract between slave buyer and seller, but it is all about sex.

From the Sunni Muslim books we get clarification. Book title, Al-Muhalla, Volume 6, Part 9, page 467, Imam of Ahlu-Sunnah, by Ibn 'Hazm he said:

No one is allowed to have together more than four women, but in addition to them, he is allowed to purchase as many women as he wants.

This is just the superficial view of Islamic law on adultery. If we dig deeper, we would find out that it is more complicated than it looks.

What I showed you in the last verse is the definition of legal sexual relationship, but Islam does not forbid a lot of ugly behavior:
Qur'an 4:23, Usama Dakdok translation:

Forbidden to you are your mothers and your daughters and your sisters and your paternal aunts and your maternal aunts and the daughters of the brother and the daughters of the sister and the mothers who nursed you (any woman who feeds a man at least five times becomes his mother) and your sisters in the breast feedings (any girl who has been breastfed by a man's mother at least five times becomes his sister) and the mothers of your women (wives) and your step-daughters who are in your laps, born of your women (wives) which you had entered into (had sex with). So if you were not entered into them (not had sex with them), so you are not at fault, and also the wives of your sons who proceed out of your backbone (this was believed to be the origin of man's sperm) and two sisters together, except where it is already done. Surely Allah was forgiving, merciful.

Qur'an 4:24: (وَالْمُحْصَنَاتُ مِنَ النِّسَاءِ إِلَّا مَا مَلَكَتْ أَيْمَانُكُمْ)

And forbidden to you a married woman except the [captured] slave as Allah has ordained upon you. Except for these, all others are lawful, provided you seek them with agreement of money from your property, without breaking the law of Allah. So for whatever you have enjoyed from them, pay them what you agreed to pay. Allah is all knowing, all wise.

What this means is that Islam legalizes sexual relationship between the Muslim man and his own married female slave. This hadith explains the verse for us; Sahih Al-Bukhari, Volume 7, Book 62, Number 137:

We got women captives from the war spoils, and we used to sleep with them. So we asked Allah's messenger about having sex with them, and he said: "Do you really do that?" Restating the question three times, then he said: "There is no soul that is made (by Allah) to be present but will come into existence until the day of resurrection..."

A sexual relationship with a married woman is forbidden in Islam, that is with a married Muslim woman. Non-Muslim women who are married are fair game. Whether they are kidnapped from their husband first or not, non-Muslim wives are free for the Muslim man to take by force. Kidnapping is optional, because it does not "legalize" the rape. The rape of non-Muslim wives is already legal or approved.
Additionally, Muslims are allowed to force their kidnapped non-Muslim women into prostitution. They are considered their kidnapper's property and, therefore, subject to be used as tools for business.

Slavery of Women in Islam

Islam does not only approve slavery, but makes it a very important part of the economy, military, and sexual life of every Muslim, as we begin to see in Qur'an 30:28:

> He (Allah) has given you a fable from your own life and yourselves. Do you take your slaves as partners, in what We have given you for sustenance, power, respect, and wealth? However, you fear them not to share with you your wealth as you fear each other. Thus do. We make an explanation for people who understand.

In this so-called parable, Allah is forbidding Muslims—who received wealth and power from Allah—to share wealth and respect with their slaves. Allah is making it clear that he is god to Muslims, and Muslims are gods to their slaves. Allah does not want partners to share his power. Therefore, Muslims must not share their wealth and respect with their slaves. You can read Islamic interpretations in English confirming this translation. Go to http://www.altafsir.com; on the left of the screen, select "Tafsir Al-Jalalayn in English;" enter the Tafsir by selecting "Click here" at the bottom of the page; for Sura, select "30 Ar-Rùm" and for Verse No., select "28;" finally select "Display."

Slavery and Christianity

Many try to judge the laws in the Bible by comparing it to the laws of today. I have no problem with that, as long they can name for me one law, that we have been ordered to follow today, which does not fit with the human rights laws of today. What was made thousands of years ago was made appropriate for that period, in a time when all lived by the sword and died by it. The nation of Israel itself (the entire nation) was enslaved. It was the lifestyle at that time; they had to survive within it, but did not have to love it. At that time, one did not have a lot of choices. Whether you did or did not like owning a slave, you might end up being one!

For me, the teaching of Christ is not only a solution for a painful history that humans went through, but it is an all-knowing solution to horrific problems from which humans suffer, like hunger, war, hate, violence and slavery.

This is the teaching of Christ and this is why I am Christian; Matthew 5:44:

> But I say unto you, Love your enemies, bless them that curse you, do good to them that hate you, and pray for them, which despitefully use you, and persecute you;

The Bible provides laws on how to deal with cases concerning slaves. As a matter of fact, these laws protected the slave. Exodus 21:20

> "If a man strikes his male or female slave with a rod and he dies at his hand, he shall be punished."

The Bible provides every reason **to free the slave**, including offenses **such as the master breaking the slave's tooth!** This means, "If you break my tooth, I am free!" Exodus 21:26-27:

> 26 If a man strikes the eye of his male or female servant, and destroys it, he shall let him go free for the sake of his eye.
> 27 And if he knocks out the tooth of his male or female servant, he shall let him go free for the sake of his tooth.

The Bible even orders the protection of the slave who runs from his master seeking freedom. Deuteronomy 23:15:

> You shall not hand over to his master a slave who has escaped from his master to you.

If the slave owner beats his slave to death, he will be punished for his crime. Exodus 21:20:

> "If a man strikes his male or female slave with a rod and he dies at his hand, he shall be punished."

Causing the death of a slave is punishable by death in the Bible. Exodus 21:12:

> "He who strikes a man so that he dies shall surely be put to death."

In the old days, when a man became destitute, he could sell himself as a slave. The Bible also provided protection for such a man. Leviticus 25:39-43:

> If a countryman of yours becomes so poor with regard to you that he sells himself to you, you shall not subject him to a slave's service. He shall be with you as a hired man, as if he were a sojourner; he shall serve with you until the

year of jubilee. He shall then go out from you, he and his sons with him, and shall go back to his family, that he may return to the property of his forefathers. For they are My servants whom I brought out from the land of Egypt; they are not to be sold in a slave sale. You shall not rule over him with severity, but are to revere your God.

The Bible also warns against slave abuse, and whoever commits such a crime will be punished for it. The Bible even encourages familial love towards slaves.

Proverbs 29:21:

He who pampers his slave from childhood will in the end find him to be a son.

Slavery was and is a part of human tragedy. The Jewish nation herself was enslaved by both whites (Babylonians) and Africans (Egyptian). This tells us that slavery was not a crime against color but a crime against other nations. Whites enslaved whites, blacks enslaved blacks, and blacks and whites enslaved blacks and whites.

In the Bible, we find **Exodus 21:16**, which many do not like to mention:

He who kidnaps a man, whether he sells him or he is found in his possession, shall surely be put to death.

This means that it is a crime to kidnap a person to own or sell as a slave. The punishment of death is so clearly stated, but was that enough to stop slavery? For sure it wasn't, because the greed of man is endless.

We can see that the Bible always works in one direction, which is to make humans more human as illustrated in 1 Timothy 6:1-2:

All who are under the yoke as slaves are to regard their own masters as worthy of all honor so that the name of God and our doctrine will not be spoken against. Those who have believers as their masters must not be disrespectful to them because they are brethren, but must serve them all the more, because those who partake of the benefit are believers and beloved. Teach and preach these principles.

Those who hate Christianity try to use the same verse to point out that the Bible is ordering Christians to be good slaves! On the contrary, it is clear that the verse is calling the master and the slave as brothers—as equals. It is telling them to be good to each other. This is what Christ's mission is all about—peace and love. It is totally against fighting.

Some people argue, "If the white man is a Christian, then why does he enslave others?" The simple answer is greed. It is the same reason that made the Africans enslave their fellow-Africans and the Israelites. We need to remember that change in humans goes at a very slow pace, and that's why slavery of all kinds still exists today. Not much has changed. The Bible has said over and over again—that to God, we are all equal. We are all His children. In Galatians 3:28:

> There is neither Jew nor Greek, there is neither slave nor free man, there is neither male nor female; for you are all one in Christ Jesus.

Again in Colossians 3:11:

> A renewal in which there is no distinction between Greek and Jew, circumcised and uncircumcised, barbarian, Scythian, slave and freeman, but Christ is all, and in all.

Christ also spoke about the rich who are ungodly. Matthew 19:24:

> And again I say unto you, it is easier for a camel to go through the eye of a needle, than for a rich man to enter into the kingdom of God.

As we all know, Muslims always try to fool African Americans into believing that Islam is the only religion that is free of prejudice. Muslims are exactly the kinds of people described in Matthew 23:24:

> Ye blind guides, which strain at a gnat, and swallow a camel.

Now we will see how slavery works in Islam.

The source of slavery in Islam

The source of slavery in Islam:

1. **War against non-Muslims.** Christians, Jews, and infidels like Safia and Juria whom Muhammad enslaved after killing their entire tribe.
2. **Gifts, as in the case of Mariah the Copt.** She was sent as a gift, along with her cousins, to Muhammad, and he accepted them.
3. **Buying and selling.** Muhammad sold and bought slaves.
4. **Progeny**. The son of a slave is a slave.
5. **A form of punishment.** The son of a free woman who commits adultery automatically becomes a slave. Muhammad ordered that newborn sons

that result from a woman's adulterous relationship will automatically become a slave.

6. Inheritance.

Out of thousands, a few examples are enough to prove these points.

Slavery from War

Sahih Al-Bukhari, Volume 3, Book 46, Hadith 717:

> ...The Prophet of Allah did unexpectedly attack the tribe of Al-Mus'taliq short of any warning as they were unconcerned and while they were busy watering their animals. Their fighting men were killed, and their women and children were taken as slaves; the Prophet got Jureyah (the daughter of Mus'taliq tribe leader) on that day...

Book of Adau'a Al-Bayean, Volume 3, Number 387:

قال الشيخ الشنقيطي رحمه الله : وسبب الملك بالرق : هو الكفر ، ومحاربة الله ورسوله ، فإذا أقدر اللهُ المسلمينَ المجاهدينَ الباذلين مُهَجهم وأموالهم وجميع قواهم وما أعطاهم الله فتكون كلمة الله هي العليا على الكفار : جعلهم ملكاً لهم بالسبي إلا إذا اختار الإمام المنَّ أو الفداء لما في ذلك من المصلحة للمسلمين . أ.هـ " ("أضواء البيان 3/ 387) .

The reason to own humans as slaves is if Allah gives victory to those who sacrifice their money and their force to fight the kafir (infidels) so if the word of Allah gives victory he, Allah, makes them (the enemy) their slaves except if the leader chooses to accept ransom for them.

After Muhammad defeated his enemies, he enslaved them and forced them to fight for him. He used their strong bodies to win him victory in war. If the slave showed skill and leadership in fighting, Muhammad made him lead the war against the free peoples. Ironically, although the slave warrior was given an honorable position in Muhammad's army, he remained a slave.

In a story found in the Book of Fateh Al-Bary Fee Share'h Sahih Al-Bukhari (p. 131), some of the white Arab men got upset when they heard that Bilal, the Ethiopian, would lead them. When they approached Muhammad, Abu-Zer, who spoke for the group, said, "I refuse to obey a black slave!" Muhammad's answer is found in Sahih Al-Bukhari, Book 11, Hadith 662:

قَالَ النَّبِيُّ صَلَّى اللَّهُ عَلَيْهِ وَسَلَّمَ لِأَبِي ذَرٍّ اسْمَعْ وَأَطِعْ وَلَوْ لِحَبَشِيٍّ وَقَدْ أَخْرَجَ مُسْلِمٌ مِنْ طَرِيقِ غُنْدَرٍ عَنْ شُعْبَةَ بِإِسْنَادٍ آخَرَ إِلَى أَبِي ذَرٍّ أَنَّهُ انْتَهَى

حَدَّثَنَا أَبُو بَكْرِ بْنُ أَبِي شَيْبَةَ حَدَّثَنَا وَكِيعُ بْنُ الْجَرَّاحِ عَنْ شُعْبَةَ عَنْ يَحْيَى بْنِ الْحُصَيْنِ عَنْ جَدَّتِهِ أُمِّ الْحُصَيْنِ
قَالَتْ سَمِعْتُ رَسُولَ اللَّهِ صَلَّى اللَّهُ عَلَيْهِ وَسَلَّمَ يَقُولُ إِنْ أُمِّرَ عَلَيْكُمْ عَبْدٌ حَبَشِيٌّ مُجَدَّعٌ فَاسْمَعُوا لَهُ وَأَطِيعُوا مَا
قَادَكُم بِكِتَابِ اللَّهِ

The Prophet said, "Consider and take orders from your leader, even if he is an
Ethiopian whose head is like a raisin were made to you a leader."

Book of Sahih of Abu Dawood, Hadith 2158 and the hadith approved by the
book of Al-Alabani (Sahih Abu Dawood, Number 1890):

(1890) ، وحسّنه الشيخ الألباني في " صحيح أبي داود " (2158رواه أبو داود)

فعن رويفع بن ثابت الأنصاري قال : سمعتُ رسول الله صلى الله عليه وسلم يقول لا يحل لامرئ يؤمن بالله
واليوم الآخر أن يقع على امرأة من السبي حتى يستبرئها ، ولا يحل لامرئ يؤمن بالله واليوم الآخر أن يبيع
" مغنما حتى يقسم

"The Prophet said that it is not lawful for a Muslim to have sex with a slave
woman until he is sure she is not pregnant."

However, Muhammad, as always, said things he did not mean. In the same day
that he slaughtered the entire tribe of Khaiber, Muhammad himself raped their
women, including Safia. She was a young wife whose husband was killed in the
slaughter. Muhammad didn't wait to find out first if Safia was pregnant before he
raped her.

Attack on the Tribe of Khaiber (Jewish Tribe)

Book of Al-Magazi by Al-Waqidy, Page 708:

Abu Ayoub spent his night standing guard next to the tent of the Prophet
holding his sword. When the morning came, the Prophet came out, so he said
"Allah is Akbar." Muhammad said to him, "What is up Abu Ayoub?" Abu Ayoub
answered, "Oh apostle of Allah, you slept with this slave (Safia) and you just
killed her father and brothers and her husband and all of her tribe, so I was
afraid she might assassinate you. The prophet laughed and said, "I will return
this favor to you."

The same story can be found in book titled Zad Al-M'ad Fe Huda 'Khaer Al-
'Ebad, Printed in 1198, Publisher Dar Al-Risalah, Chapter Attacking the Tribe of
'Khaibar:

زاد المعاد
الإمام شمس الدين أبي عبد الله ابن القيم الجوزية
مؤسسة الرسالة

182

1998م / 1418هـ سنة النشر:

زاد المعاد في هدي خير العباد فصل في ترتيب سياق هديه مع الكفار والمنافقين من حين بعث إلى حين لقي الله عز وجل فصل في سياق مغازيه وبعوثه على وجه الاختصار فصل في غزوة خيبر فصل في القدوم إلى خيبر

مد النافذة لإظهار كل الأبواب بالجزء المختار | نتائج البحثالتالي

ولما بنى بها أبو أيوب ليلته قريبا من قبته ، أخذا بقائم السيف حتى أصبح ، فلما رأى رسول الله صلى الله عليه وسلم كبر أبو أيوب حين رآه قد خرج ، فسأله رسول الله صلى الله عليه وسلم : ما لك يا أبا أيوب ؟ فقال له : أرقت ليلتي هذه يا رسول الله لما دخلت بهذه المرأة ، ذكرت أنك قتلت أباها وأخاها وزوجها وعامة عشيرتها ، فخفت أن تغتالك . فضحك رسول الله صلى الله عليه وسلم وقال له معروفا

Muslims in the West like to quote a hadith where Omar Ibn Al-Khatab is claimed to have said, **"How can you enslave people when their mothers gave birth to them as free people?"** This narrative is, in fact, true. However, it is reported only for the sole purpose of deceiving the listener. We can easily show how the report does not represent any truth about Islam's stance on slavery.

The real context of the story centers on the antagonism between Omar Ibn Al-Khatab and 'Amr Ibn Al-'Aas. When Al-Khatab asked the question quoted above, he was not admonishing Al-'Aas for having slaves—instead, he was trying to humiliate Al-'Ass while making himself look morally superior over Al-'Ass.

Al-'Ass said that he hated slavery, so Al-Khatab was forcing him to explain why he did not have any problem accepting all the verses in the Qur'an regarding slavery. Al-'Ass himself owned thousands of slaves. He raped and beat his slaves and he never freed any of his slaves. Al-Khatab's question was not a question meant to condemn slavery. It was a question meant to attack and expose his deeply hated enemy as a hypocrite.

It is interesting to note that if Al-Khatab's question was meant to condemn slavery, wouldn't that mean that he thought Muhammad was a bad man, since Muhammad himself owned slaves and gladly accepted men and women slaves, not only as spoils of war, but also as gifts? The claim that Al-Khatab's popularly quoted question is an example of Islam's stance against slavery is a joke. When put in its proper context, the question is actually nothing but an expression of hate and jealousy between two men. The narrative itself has nothing to do with freeing slaves.

By the way, Muhammad never gave orders and conditions when to free a slave. When I say never, I mean NEVER! I challenge any Muslim to quote one verse ordering Muslims to free their slaves. Freeing a slave was up to the owner to do or not do. It is optional.

In fact, he re-enslaved a freed slave. Sahih Al-Bukhari Book 85, Hadith 80 (also see Sahih Al-Bukhari Book 41, Hadith 598):

دَبَّرَ رَجُلٌ مِنَ الأَنْصَارِ غُلَامًا لَهُ لَمْ يَكُنْ لَهُ مَالٌ غَيْرُهُ فَبَاعَهُ رَسُولُ اللَّهِ ـ صَلَّى اللَّهُ عَلَيْهِ وَسَلَّمَ ـ ، فَاشْتَرَاهُ ابْنُ
" النَّحَّامِ عَبْدًا قِبْطِيًّا مَاتَ عَامَ أَوَّلٍ فِي إِمَارَةِ ابْنِ الزُّبَيْرِ

An adult male human from the Ansaar gave his youth slave his freedom, and let his slave go free, and he did not have any other property. This news arrived at Allah's Messenger. Moreover, the messenger said, "Who will buy that slave from me?" So Nu'aem bin Abd-Allah Al-Na'ham bought him for 800 Dirhams. Jabir added: It was a Coptic slave who passed away that year.

This hadith shows how Muhammad was in full control of slavery as a business. He could even do things against anyone's will. When a man freed his slave, Muhammad put the slave back into slavery and made money out of him. At the same time, he showed no mercy toward the poor slave who was waiting all his life to be freed. Also see that the slave died after he was sold again. I would not be surprised if this was because of depression. What would Muhammad lose if he had let the man go? He did not even own the man, but money was Muhammad's god.

The slave owner was poor, and his only property was his slave, but he still chose to free his slave. Why did Muhammad cancel the slave's emancipation? He knew that if everybody started freeing their slaves, then the slave market could not continue to thrive?

Sahih Al-Bukhari Book 8 Volume 82 Hadith 822:

Reported by Abu Huraira:
The opinion of Allah's messenger [was] requested when the unmarried slave girl [was] found guilty of unlawful intercourse. On that ground, he responded, "If she performs illegitimate sexual intercourse, then scourge her fifty belts, and if she engages unlawful sexual intercourse another time, after that lash her fifty belts, and if she commits unlawful sexual intercourse for the third time, after that lash her fifty belts and trades her for even for the price of her tie."

By making such a rule, her owner could rape her at the same time, but she cannot have unlawful sexual intercourse. Based on this, if the slave is sick of her master, she is forced now to do such behavior, so she might get out of that master's home to be with a new master.

Bilal the Ethiopian

We always hear Muslims speak about Bilal, the black man who was one of

Muhammad's slaves. Muslims try to fool African Americans into believing that there is no racism in Islam by telling them that Bilal was the first to chant the call for prayer. What the Muslims will not say is that Bilal was simply following orders from Muhammad, his master. Bilal was not given a place of honor as Muslims want us to think. Bilal was just a slave following another order from his master.

Let us see how Bilal had no life. He was a slave who did not have the right to choose what to do.

Bilal and the Call for Prayer

I can show hundreds of hadiths about Bilal doing tasks that **are all ordered for him** to do, including orders for him to do the call for prayer.

Allah's Apostle **orders** Bilal to get up and pronounce the Adhan for prayers:

- Bukhari Book 11, Hadith 578
- Bukhari Book 11, Hadith 579
- Bukhari Book 11, Hadith 580
- Bukhari Book 56, Hadith 663
- Bukhari Book 52, Hadith 297
- Sunan Abu Dawood Book 1, Hadith 0193

    "Then he commanded **Bilal** to call for prayer."

Ask yourself why Muhammad did not call for the prayer himself or why he never ordered Abu Bakr or Ali or anyone else. Only this poor slave had to get up early in the morning and get ready before everyone else, and then scream to wake up all of Mecca! He was selected to do the call for prayer simply because no one wanted to do it. It's the slave's job.

Bilal the News Slave

Sahih Bukhari, Volume 4, Book 52, Hadith 297:

    ...Bilal was ordered to announce the news amongst the people...

May Allah support this religion of Islam with wicked men?

Sahih Bukhari, Volume 8, Book 77, Hadith 603)

> ...Allah's messenger said, "Bilal! Get up and broadcast in the community, none will enter heaven but a worshiper and Allah may. <u>He supports this religion Islam with wicked men</u>."

Bilal the Food Servant at Home and Out

Sahih Bukhari, Volume 5, Book 59, Hadith 524:

> ...The Messenger ordered Bilal to lay out the leather carpets on which dates, dehydrated yogurt and butter were put on it...

Bilal the Money Bag

Sahih Bukhari, Volume 3, Book 38, Hadith 504:

> ...The Prophet of Allah said, "Oh Bilal, pay him the price of the camel and provide him bonus money..."

Even other people ordered Bilal around; Sunan Abu Dawood, Book 2, Hadith 498:

> ...afterwards the Apostle of Allah, may Allah pray on him, said: "O Bilal, stand up, see what Abdullah Ibn Zayed commanded you to do, then do it."

Muhammad also made it clear that a slave, even if he is a Muslim, cannot be a witness in the court as we can see in the Qur'an 5:106, interpretation of Tanwîr Al-Miqbâs min Tafsîr Ibn 'Abbâs:

> O ye who you believe! Let there be witnesses among and between you, in agreement or upon traveling, so when one of you dies, then of the dead person, two witnesses should testify for his will, just men from among you (<u>no women accepted</u>) two free men (<u>no slave accepted</u>).

Bilal is Asking to be Freed From Abu Bakr

In the coming hadith, we see the slave Bilal begging for his freedom after Muhammad's death and he still did not get it (Sahih Bukhari, Volume 5, Book 57, Hadith 99):

Narrated Qais: Bilal said to Abu Bakr, "If you have bought me for own then keep me for yourself to serve, but if you have bought me for the sake of Allah, then free me to do work for Allah."

After all the services this man provided, why did he need to beg for his freedom? Shouldn't he get it right away from the good prophet Muhammad or the good companion Abu Bakr? Why didn't Muhammad order Abu Bakr to do it? This man was a faithful slave to them. He fought and kidnapped for them. He fed the animals and collected money for his masters as a merchant. He did everything. Why did the good men of Allah wait for him to beg for his freedom?

Omar Ibn Al-Khatab and Slavery

As long as we started with the Hadith of Omar Ibn Al-Khatab, I will show some stories about this man and see how ugly his character is. You can find this hadith in the book, The Pact of 'Omar Ibn Al-Khatab. Let's see how this man dealt with slaves. The Imam Al-Beyhaqi records in Al-Sunnan Al-Kobra, Volume 2, page 227:

"عن جده أنس بن مالك قال كن إماء عمر رضي الله عنه يخدمننا كاشفات عن شعور هن تضطرب ثديهن"

Hadith from grandfather of Annas, son of Malik, that the women slaves of Omar Ibn Al-Khatab used to serve us with their hair uncovered and their breasts shaking touching their hair.

You will notice that Omar Al-Khatab owned many female slaves. Not only that, in the following hadith, you will notice that Al-Khatab beat the slave women when they covered themselves. He wanted them exposed for him and his visitors to enjoy watching. Book of Kanes Al-Umal Fee Suanan Al-A'qwal, Hadith 41925:

عن أنس قال: رأى عمر أمة لنا متقنعة فضربها وقال: لا تشبهي بالحرائر، ألقي القناع. -41925

Reported by Anass: "Omar Ibn Al-Khatab saw a slave woman wearing her headscarf so he beat her screaming, 'You should not clothe yourself like a free woman!'"

You can find the same narration in the following books:

- Tabaqat Ibn Saad, Volume 7, Page 127
- Tarikh Damishq, Volume 58, Page 191

Book of Kanez Al-'Umal Fee Suanan Al-A'qwal, Volume 15, Hadith 41928, Page 486:

عن المسيب بن دارم قال: رأيت عمر وفي يده درة فضرب رأس أمة حتى سقط القناع عن رأسها، - 41928
قال: فيم الأمة تشبه بالحرة.

Reported by Al-Museeb Ibn Daram: He said "I saw Omar beating a woman slave on her head with a stick until her cover fell down and he told her not to dress or assume the manner of a free woman."

The link to Hadith in Arabic: http://al-eman.net/Islamlib/viewchp.asp?BID=137&CID=582

'Omar Praises Allah That the Black Son is Not His

Book of Al-Mu'gny by Ibn 'Qudamah, Volume 10, Page 412:

روى سعيد حدثنا سفيان عن ابن أبي نجيح عن فتى من أهل المدينة أن عمر بن الخطاب رضي الله عنه كان
يعزل عن جارية له فجاءت بحمل فشق عليه وقال اللهم لا تلحق بآل عمر من ليس منهم فإن آل عمر ليس بهم
خفاء فولدت ولداً أسود فقال ممن هو فقالت من راعي الإبل فحمد الله وأثنى عليه.. المصدر: كتاب «المغني»
لابن قدامه 10 / 412.

Reported from Sa'id by Sufyian from Ibn Abu Naje'h from a man in the city of Madina: Omar used to pull out his male organ before he had orgasm when he was having sex with a female slave girl. One day, she told him that she was pregnant, then 'Omar, praying to Allah, said, "Allah, do not make in my family one who is not from me, because no one in my family is from a shameful line; then the slave girl gave birth to a black boy. 'Omar asked her who was the baby's father. She said the camel shepherd, then 'Omar thanked Allah (that he is not the father).

In this hadith, we see that the slave girl is nothing but a sex toy. Her master and his friends shared her. It is clear from the narration that Omar used slaves for sex only, not procreation. However, remember that Muslims claim Islam is against adultery, yet we see here that sharing a slave girl is permitted. A slave girl is not considered human enough that a sexual relationship with her would be condemned as adultery.

Sahih Al-Bukhari, Book 58, Hadith 197:

I saw the Messenger of Allah, and in the accompany of him were the only ones who converted to Islam, five slaves, two women, and Abu Bakr.

As always, we see Muhammad owning slaves, and his house is full of them. Notice also in the narration that no one can enter his house without first asking for permission through his slaves.

Sahih Al-Bukhari, Book 72, Hadith 734:

...At the doorway of the room, over there was a black slave to whom I walked and said, I request to me a permission from the prophet to enter. He authorized me and I entered to see the Prophet lying on a carpet that had left its engraving on his side...

Book of Kenz EL-'Omal Fe Sunan Al-Aqual, Hadith 44824 http://islamic-books.org/cached-version.aspx?id=1835-26-33

44824- للحرة يومان، وللأمة يوم.

You give the free women two nights and slave woman one night (for sex).

Book of 'Awen Al-Ma'bud Fe Shareh ab u Dawood, page 190:

عون المعبود شرح سنن أبي داود ـ كِتَاب الطَّهَارَة
قَالَ السُّيُوطِيُّ : : تَصْغِيرُ الْأَمَةِ ضِدُّ الْحُرَّةِ ، أَيْ جُوَيْرِيَّتَكَ ، وَالْمَعْنَى : لَا تَضْرِبِ الْمَرْأَةَ مِثْلَ ضَرْبِكَ الْأَمَةَ

Imam Al-Sui'ty said: "Beat not your wife the same way you beat the slave women".

⅄ This means you can beat them both but you can be harder on slave woman.

Killing someone is not always punishable by death. According to Muhammad, the killer can pay what is called a payback ransom. The victim's life is exchanged with a female slave or a newborn baby male (Sahih Al-Bukhari, Book 83, Hadith 41):

Reported by Abu Horaira: Two adult females from the tribe of Hazeail fought and one of them threw a rock at the other woman causing her a miscarriage. Allah's Apostle gave his judgment that the killer of the fetus should give a slave's newborn baby, male or female, as payback ransom to the woman who had the miscarriage.

This hadith can be found in Arabic in Sahih Al-Bukhari, Hadith 1681, and Sahih Muslim, Hadith 6910:

عن أبي هُرَيْرَةَ رَضِيَ اللهُ عَنْهُ قَالَ : (اقْتَتَلَتْ امْرَأَتَانِ مِنْ هُذَيْلٍ ، فَرَمَتْ 1681) ومسلم (6910البخاري)
إحْدَاهُمَا الأُخْرَى بِحَجَرٍ ، فَقَتَلَتْهَا وَمَا فِي بَطْنِهَا ، فَاخْتَصَمُوا إِلَى النَّبِيِّ صَلَّى اللهُ عَلَيْهِ وَسَلَّمَ ، فَقَضَى أَنَّ دِيَةَ
جَنِينِهَا غُرَّةٌ : عَبْدٌ أَوْ وَلِيدَةٌ).

Let's think about this story for few moments. Imagine yourself a slave woman, and your lady master caused someone to have a miscarriage. Ask yourself these questions:

1. Is it from the mercy of Allah and his prophet that the slave woman, who did no crime, should lose her baby to a strange woman, as if her baby is a puppy to give away at anytime to anyone?

2. Is it fair, from the mercy of Allah and his prophet, that the baby will grow without his biological mother for no crime of his own?

3. If Muhammad was a slave, would he like it if someone took his newborn son or daughter as payment for a crime he did not do?

Muhammad made his judgment regarding the death of the fetus based on the Qur'an (سورة البقرة , Al-Baqara, Qur'an 2:178):

يَا أَيُّهَا الَّذِينَ آمَنُوا كُتِبَ عَلَيْكُمُ الْقِصَاصُ فِي الْقَتْلَى ۖ الْحُرُّ بِالْحُرِّ وَالْعَبْدُ بِالْعَبْدِ وَالْأُنثَىٰ بِالْأُنثَىٰ

O you who believe! It's an order upon yourselves in the case of murder a punishment: free for the free, slave for the slave, and women for the woman

However, Muhammad did not really follow what this verse commanded. The Qur'an had no answer for a case where an adult kills an unborn baby, so he created a new rule. He added to the Qur'an as law, that the payback ransom in such cases is a newborn baby of a slave.
The fact is Muhammad made it clear that there is not punishment for killing a slave.

The Free Man Will Not Be Killed for Murdering the Slave

(Mutta' Malik,Book 43, Hadith 21.15)

According to Qur'an of Allah, the high the glorified in the case of the counter attack it is written for you in the case of murdering. The freeman for the freeman and the slave for the slave. Malik said, the one was murdered, only has the right against the one who murdered him. If the killer who murdered the man, he dies, the one was murdered has no rights against the killers no more, or blood-money. Malik said: There is no punishment arranged against a freeman by a slave for any injury. The slave is killed for the freeman when he purposely murders him. The free man will not be killed for murdering the slave, even if he murders. He did it intentionally. This is the most accurate way I learned.

Notice also that the verse divides the human race into three classes, and the judgment for each class is exclusive. If a free man kills another freeman, the killer is sentenced to death. If a freeman kills a slave, he is not sentenced to death. Instead, one of the freeman's slaves will be killed or he pays the owner of the slave with another slave. If a woman is killed, another woman is killed as payment for her death. What kind of justice is this?

Muslims give us speeches about the merciful Allah and the merciful Muhammad, but narratives like these show just how Islam exemplifies the cruel way slaves are treated, as mere commodities and sex toys.

Slaves are not even allowed to sing, as we see in the following hadith. If a slave owner dies and his slave girl sings for him, Muslims are commanded not to pray for him. Islam forbids singing, so the dead man will be condemned to hell.

Book of Ahkam Al-Qur'an by Ibn Al-'Arabi, Volume 3, Number 525:

سورة لقمان أحكام القرآن الجزء الثالث525ص:
عن عائشة قالت قال رسول الله صلى الله عليه وسلم: (من مات وعنده جارية مغنية فلا تصلوا عليه).

Reported by 'Aisha: She said "The prophet, may Allah pray on him, said,'If a man dies, and he has a slave girl who sings for him, do not pray for him.'"

However, the hypocrisy of Muhammad is endless. Regardless of this forbidden art, he used to order his slaves to sing (Sahih Al-Bukhari, Book 15, Hadith 70):

Allah's Messenger attained to my residence while two slave girls were singing close to me the songs of Bu'ath (which is a song about war before Islam between two tribes, the Khazraj and the Aos). The messenger laid down on the bed and turned his face to the other side. Then Abu Baker came and spoke to me harshly saying, "Musical instruments with flute of Satan near the messenger of Allah?" Therefore, the messenger rotated his face towards him and said, "Leave them." And later I winked at the girls to go out, and they left. It was the holy day...

⚔ As you see, slave girls are singing for Muhammad's entertainment, songs which had nothing to do with Allah or Islam, but still he liked it? And it's very clear that Abu Baker was outraged with Muhammad's behavior and

191

hypocrisy, because if a Muslim listens to songs, he is going to hell as the prior hadith indicated.

Book of Al-Bidayia and Al-Nihayia, Volume 4 page 224:

وقال أبو داود: حدثنا مسدد، حدثنا حماد بن زيد، عن عبد العزيز بن صهيب، عن أنس بن مالك قال: صارت
(224/ 4صفية لدحية الكلبي، ثم صارت لرسول الله صلى الله عليه وسلم. (ج/ص:

Abu Dawood said from Anas Ibn Malik he said "Safia was given away from the share of Da'yia L-Kalbi."

Safia is the Jewish woman that Muhammad took as his wife after slaughtering all the men of her tribe and enslaving the women and children.

Book of Al-Bidayia and Al-Nihayia, Volume 4, Page 229:

وهذا السياق يقتضي أن خيبر بكمالها قسمت بين الغانمين . وبهذا قال الزهري: خمس رسول الله صلى الله
(229/ 4عليه وسلم خيبر، ثم قسّم سائرها على من شهدها، (ج/ص:

The same was done to all of the tribe of Khaiber. Al-Zuhri said the Prophet's share was a fifth of the tribe of Khaiber.

Muhammad took one-fifth (1/5) of the loot from the city of Khaiber, and four-fifths (4/5) went to the rest of the Muslims. If there were 5000 women to be distributed as slaves in that tribe, Muhammad's share would be 1000 women slaves. If there were 20,000 children, Muhammad alone would have gained 4000 child slaves.

Muslim, Sunni or Shi'a, Are No Different When it Comes to Slavery

Book of Bihar Al-Anwar, Volume 101, Number 58:

page [58] [] - [المؤلف : العلامة المجلسي101اسم الكتاب : بحار الأنوار /]
الغالب عن الحسين بن رباح عن ابن عميرة عن محمد بن مروان عن ابن أبي يعفور عن الصادق (ع) قال
ثلاثة لا يقبل الله لهم صلاة عبد أبق من مواليه حتى يرجع إليهم فيضع يده في أيديهم و رجل أم قوما و هم له
كارهون و امرأة باتت و زوجها عليها ساخط

The prayer of three people was not accepted by Allah. A slave who is not obeying his master, until he obey again, an Imam who leads a prayer for [those] who do not like him, and a woman who lets her husband sleep angry.

Book of Al-Istb'sar Volume 3, Page 136:

روى الطوسي عن محمّد عن أبي جعفر عليه السلام قال: قلت:
3/136)الرجل يحل لأخيه فرج جاريته؟ قال: نعم لا بأس به ما له ما أحل له منها) (الاستبصار).

Al-Tosse reported that Abu Ja'far said, "Can a man give his brother the vagina of his slave?" He said, "Yes, it is permissible to do what he allowed him to do to her."

The following hadith illustrate how a man can loan his slave girl for sex (Book of Tahdeeb Al-Ahkam, Volume 7, Page 244; Book of Al-Kafi, Volume 5, Chapter 300, Hadith 16):

A man came and asked Imam Ja'far Al-Sadiq if it was permissible to temporarily loan a woman (slave girl) to another man. The imam said, "It is not allowed," but then he stopped for a moment and Imam J'afar added, "There is no harm if one makes her halal to one of his brothers."

Someone might come to us and say that slavery was widespread at that time and that it was accepted as normal. He will say there's really nothing new. It was normal practice.

I am going to show you a fatwa that shows the Islamic stance on slavery that remains true today. The fatwa is dated May 22, 2005. For those who do not know, a fatwa is an answer given by Muslim leaders that are based on Allah's orders (Sharia Law) from the Qur'an and Sunnah.

Fatwa Number 62344:

Is it permissible to enjoy slave women sexually for the Muslim who has four wives?

May 22, 2005 (equivalent to Saturday, 13th day of the first month of spring in the Islamic year 1426).

The Question:

I need the explanation of the verse "Whatever you own on your right hand, like slave women, from what Allah gave you" (سورة الأحزاب , Al-A'hzab, Qur'an 33:50). Does it mean that it is permissible for a man to marry slave women in addition to his four wives?

The Fatwa (The Answer):

193

Praise be to Allah and prayer on our prophet and his family and friends. It is not permissible to have more than four wives at the same time, but having more than four slave girls for sexual enjoyment is permissible, and having many slaves and enjoying them all sexually is permissible regardless of their number.

The Imam Al-Kasa'y in his book, *Jawame'a Al-Fwaw'ed*, said that there are two reasons for gathering foreign women: one to marry them and another to enjoy them sexually. However, gathering them for marriage is not permissible if you already have four wives. But having more than four foreign women for sex only and not marriage is permissible. This is based on the man's right over them as his slaves. Having many women slaves for sex is always permissible without any conditions that limit the maximum number that a man can own as stated in Qur'an 4:3 (سورة النساء , An-Nis'a, 4:3).

The Islamic Fatwa site in Arabic can be found here:
http://fatwa.islamweb.net/fatwa/index.php?page=showfatwa&Id=62344&Option=Fatwald

رقم الفتوى:62344
عنوان الفتوى : يجوز الاستمتاع بالإماء المملوكات لمن كان عنده أربع زوجات
تاريخ الفتوى 13 ربيع الآخر 1426 / 22-5-2005 : السبت
السؤال
أريد تفسير الآية الكريمة " وما ملكت يمينك مما أفاء عليك الله" فهل للرجل المتزوج بأربع نساء وعنده ملك يمين، فهل يحل ل أن يتزوجهن مع احتفاظة بزوجاته الأربع وشكرا
الفتوى
الحمد لله والصلاة والسلام على رسول الله وعلى آله وصحبه أما بعد:
فلا يجوز أن يجمع الرجل بين أكثر من أربع زوجات، سواء كن حرائر أو إماء، وأما الجمع في الوطء بين
قال الإمام الكاساني الحنفي في . أكثر من أربع إماء دون عقد وإنما بملك اليمين فلا مانع منه إذ لا يتقيد بعدد
بدائع الصنائع: وأما الجمع بين الأجنبيات فنوعان أيضا: جمع في النكاح، وجمع في الوطء ودواعيه بملك
أما الجمع في النكاح فنقول: لا يجوز للحر أن يتزوج أكثر من أربع زوجات من الحرائر والإماء عند . اليمين
وأما الجمع في الوطء ودواعيه بملك اليمين فجائز، وإن كثرت الجواري، لقوله تعالى: فَإِنْ خِفْتُمْ .. عامة العلماء
أَلَّا تَعْدِلُوا فَوَاحِدَةً أَوْ مَا مَلَكَتْ أَيْمَانُكُمْ. أي إن خفتم أن لا تعدلوا في نكاح المثنى والثلاث والرباع بإيفاء
حقوقهن فانكحوا واحدة، وإن خفتم أن لا تعدلوا في واحدة فمما ملكت أيمانكم؛ كأنه قال سبحانه وتعالى: هذا أو
هذا، أي الزيادة على الواحدة إلى الأربع عند القدرة على المعادلة وعند خوف الجور في ذلك الواحدة من
الحرائر وعند خوف الجور في نكاح الواحدة هو شراء الجواري والتسري بهن، وذلك قوله عز وجل: أَوْ مَا
مَلَكَتْ أَيْمَانُكُمْ ذكره مطلقا عن شرط العدد.

What we get from this Fatwa (Number 62344) is that Islam changed nothing. Islam embraced slavery rather than put a stop to it. The humiliation of men and women continued. Not only did Islam approve slavery, it made it legal for Muslims to practice it forever. Slave ownership and abuse is still allowed today, because the Muslims don't have any other source about slavery. They only have the Qur'an and Muhammad's actions and the hadith to follow. It gives a Muslim the perpetual right to kidnap and rape non-Muslim women and use them as sex slaves for as long as they live.

Let me point out that this fatwa alone proves the hypocrisy of Muslims in the West. They convert African-Americans to Islam by pointing to the slavery of blacks by the white man. The Muslims' claim that Islam condemned slavery is quite the opposite of the truth about the Islamic stance on slavery.

Sex With Your Servant is Allowed

Book of Al-Mu'hala by Ibn Hazem. Volume 11, Page 251, published by Dar Al-Fikr by Ahmad Shaker:

(.. إن المخدمة سنين كثيرة لا حد على المخدم ـ بكسر الدال ـ إذا وطئها)
(/ ط دار الفكر بتحقيق أحمد شاكر 251 / ص11المحلى لابن حزم / ج)

...there is no problem if her master did intercourse with her!

A Woman Having Sex With a Woman

The Book of the Four Islamic Sects, by Al-Jazery, book of Al-'Hudood, Chapter Masturbation by Hand, page 1223.

(و من نكح يده ، و تلذذ بها ، أو إذا أتت المرأة المرأة ، و هو السحاق ، فلا يقام حد في هذه الصورة بإجماع)
العلماء ، لأنها لذة ناقصة ، و إن كانت محرمة ، و الواجب التعزير على الفاعل حسب ما يراه الإمام زاجراً له
/ 1223الفقه على المذاهب الأربعة للجزيري / كتاب الحدود – الاستمناء باليد / ص) (. عن المنكر

http://shamela.ws/browse.php/book-9849/page-1954

"If a man did Nukah to his hand (literally F___ his hand / masturbate), or if a woman had sex with a woman who is called lesbian, all scholars agreed there is no punishment over this because the pleasure is partial, even if it's forbidden, but must warn the one is doing it, and warn her that Islam disliked such an action."

Notice here that this is against what the Qur'an said about a woman being with a woman in Chapter 4:15, where women have to be jailed forever, until they die. This proves that Muhammad created a lot of rules, which were totally against his god's orders. Muhammad didn't even remember it, because he was making up a holy book; and thus what he said yesterday was abrogated (forgotten) by what he said or did today.

Having Sex With a Little Girl is Approved in Islam

The Book of Al-Mabsu't, by Imam Al- Sarkhasi, V5/10, Page 155:

(وهذا فيما إذا كانت في حد الشهوة فإن كانت صغيرة لا يشتهى مثلها فلا بأس بالنظر إليها « ومن مسها »
لأنه ليس لبدنها حكم العورة ولا في النظر والمس معنى خوف الفتنة .)
هـ1406 / كتاب الاستحسان ط دار المعرفة 155 / ص10المبسوط ، للإمام السرخسي / المجلد الخامس / ج)
)

And when it's come to the punishment in case of sexual desire with a minor girl who normally no one has sexual desire to her, due to her very young age, it's alright to do that even by touch for her body is not considered full of private part yet.

Al-Mabsu't Al-Sarkhasi, V9, Page 75:

وإن زنى بصبية لا يجامع مثلها فأفضاها فلا حد عليه، لأن وجوب حد الزنا يعتمد كمال الفعل وكمال الفعل لا
(يتحقق بدون كمال المحل فقد تبين أن المحل لم يكن محلاً لهذا الفعل حين أفضاها
(75 / ص 9المبسوط للإمام السرخسي / ج)

If a man did intercourse with a little girl and made her lose her virginity, there is no punishment, for that action was done for a little girl, so the pleasure is not complete (she did not give same pleasure as a woman).

To Marry a Suckling Girl is Fine in Islam

Book Title, Collection of Al-Mabsu't, by Imam Al-Sarkhasi, V15, Page 109:

(ولكن عرضية الوجود بكون العين منتفعاً بها تكفي لانعقاد العقد ، كما لو تزوج رضيعة صح النكاح)
/ كتاب الإجارات / ط دار 109 / ص15المبسوط ، للإمام السرخسي / المجلد الثامن / ج)

...if the man has a benefit from it such as marriage, this will be an enough reason to make the marriage is correct, same, as if he did marry an Infant.

Book of Tahrer Al-Waselah, by Imam Khomeini, Page 241, Question 11/12:

291 الى 241 من صفحة 2من كتاب تحرير الوسيلة جـ

...you can have all kinds of sexual relation with an infant, but without intercourse, like hugs or touch or kissing, and if a Muslim did sexual-intercourse with a girl under the age of nine, there is not punishment on that account.

Qur'an & Scientific Miraculous Discoveries

Answering Harun Yahya
www.harunyahya.com

Mr. Harun has made a lot of claims about the Qur'an. I will show how each are false and that Mr. Harun's false claims are intentionally used to deceive.

The following are some of his claims from his site. I will expose the real meaning of these verses in the Qur'an, which Mr. Harun is trying to fool people with.

As Muslims claim, it's about how their god knew. If he is not God, how would he know the following?

⅄ WE LIVE IN AN EXPANDING UNIVERSE

⅄ THE POINT OF DEPARTURE OF OUR ODYSSEY

⅄ WE ARE CREATED OUT OF NOTHING

⅄ THE UNIVERSE IN GASEOUS STATE

⅄ PERFECT ORBITS

⅄ ATOM AND SUBATOMIC PARTICLES

⅄ BLACK HOLES: MIGHTY OATH

⅄ PULSARS

⅄ ATTRACTION AND MOTION

⅄ ALL AFLOAT IN ORBITS

⅄ CREATION IN PAIRS

⅄ RELATIVITY OF TIME ANNOUNCED 1400 YEARS AGO

⅄ THE SUN ALSO MOVES ALONG

⅄ DIFFERENCE BETWEEN THE SUN AND THE MOON

⅄ THE ORBIT OF THE MOON

- ⅄ JOURNEY TO THE MOON
- ⅄ LAYERS OF HEAVENS, LAYERS OF EARTH
- ⅄ WELL PROTECTED ROOF
- ⅄ RETURNED BY THE SKY
- ⅄ HEAVENS NOT SUPPORTED BY PILLARS
- ⅄ GEOIDAL FORM OF THE WORLD
- ⅄ ROLLING THE NIGHT OVER THE DAY
- ⅄ DIAMETERS OF THE EARTH AND SPACE
- ⅄ THE EARTH DOES ROTATE EVEN THOUGH WE ARE NOT CONSCIOUS OF IT
- ⅄ FECUNDATING WINDS
- ⅄ CLOUDS AND THE PROCESS OF RAIN
- ⅄ DUE MEASURE IN RAIN
- ⅄ UNDERGROUND WATERS AND WATER CYCLE
- ⅄ BARRIER BETWEEN SEAS DARKNESS AND INTERNAL WAVES IN THE SEAS
- ⅄ MOUNTAINS AS PEGS
- ⅄ FAULTS ON THE EARTH'S SURFACE
- ⅄ EARTHQUAKES' MESSAGE AND HEAVY BURDENS
- ⅄ FORMATION OF PETROLEUM
- ⅄ RESPIRATION AND PHOTOSYNTHESIS
- ⅄ DIFFICULTY OF ASCENDING TO THE SKY
- ⅄ MAN AND POLLUTION
- ⅄ SEX IN PLANTS
- ⅄ SOIL THAT VIBRATES AND SWELLS AS IT COMES TO LIFE
- ⅄ FEMALE HONEYBEE, BUILDER OF HER OWN CELL
- ⅄ THE FEMALE HONEYBEE'S ABDOMEN AND THE HEALING POWER OF HONEY
- ⅄ FORMATION OF MILK
- ⅄ COMMUNICATION BETWEEN BIRDS
- ⅄ FEMALE ANT AND COMMUNICATION BETWEEN ANIMALS
- ⅄ MAN CREATED FROM DUST AND WATER

⅄ SEMEN IS A COMPOUND

⅄ CREATION FROM A QUINTESSENCE AND CHILD'S SEX

⅄ HANGING ON THE WALL OF UTERUS

⅄ CHEWED LUMP OF FLESH

⅄ BONE FORMATION AND CLOTHING OF BONES WITH FLESH

⅄ CREATION IN THREE DARKNESSES

⅄ IDENTITY ON FINGER TIPS

⅄ LANGUAGE AND MAN

⅄ SIGNS WITHIN OURSELVES

⅄ TELEOLOGICAL CAUSALITY

⅄ ERROR OF THE UNILINEAR PROGRESSIVE CONCEPT OF HISTORY

⅄ MIRACLES BASED ON ARCHAEOLOGY AND THE PEOPLE OF SABA

⅄ THE AAD PEOPLE AND THE CITY OF ERAM

⅄ MYSTERY BEHIND THE NAME HAAMAAN

⅄ ANCIENT EGYPT AND THE PHARAOH'S BODY

⅄ SIGNS IN THE OLD TESTAMENT

⅄ SIGNS IN THE NEW TESTAMENT

⅄ VICTORIOUS ROMANS AND THE LOWEST SPOT ON THE EARTH

⅄ THE LOWEST SPOT OF THE EARTH

⅄ ELECTRIC LIGHT BULB, ELECTRICITY, RAPID TRANSMISSION OF MATERIAL AND NEW MEANS OF COMMUNICATION

⅄ THOSE WHO DISBELIEVE IN THE END OF THE UNIVERSE, DEATH OF THE STARS AND THE SUN FROM BIG BANG TO BIG CRUNCH

⅄ LIKE LOCUSTS

Now THESE ARE MOST OF THE CLAIMS, OR MAYBE ALL, which the Muslims have come up with. For me to help you to see the truth, I can proceed in one of two ways.

1. Answer each one of these claims, or
2. Show the errors of the Qur'an.

I think the most useful way is showing the errors, because if this is a book of God, it should be perfect. At the same time, showing these errors will expose all the lies they made. So, let us start. We will take the Qur'an from the beginning to the end.

Qur'an errors

A. Qur'an and Science Errors

Earth and Space Sciences

- Astronomy
- Astrophysics
- Geography
- Geology
- Geophysics
- Biology
- Mathematics
- Medicine

B. Qur'an and Historical Errors
C. Qur'an and Fairy Tales

In this book, I will try to keep from making things too complicated. I know that for many of the readers this is the first time to read about this topic and that they really may not know much about Islam I will proceed one step at a time.

Qur'an and Astronomy, Astrophysics, Geography

ANSWERING HARUN YAHAYA

First Muslim claim: THE SKIES WITH 'WOVEN' ORBITS
(Following is the Muslim Argument)

Qur'an, Sura adh-Dhariyat (51), 7: "By heaven furnished with paths;"
The Arabic word "alhubuki," translated as "furnished with paths" in verse 7 of Sura adh-Dhariyat (Chapter 51), comes from the verb "hubeke," meaning "to weave closely, to knit, to bind together." The use of this word in the verse is

particularly wise and represents the current state of scientific knowledge in two aspects.

The first is this: The orbits and paths in the universe are so dense and intertwined that they constitute intersecting paths, just like the threads in a piece of fabric. The Solar System we live in is made up of the Sun, the planets and their satellites and heavenly objects in constant motion such as meteors and comets. The Solar System moves through the galaxy known as the Milky Way, which contains 400 billion stars.1 It is estimated that there are billions of galaxies. Celestial bodies and systems revolving at speeds of thousands of kilometers an hour move through space without colliding with one another.

The science of astronomy was developed with the aim of mapping the positions and courses of stars, while astromechanics was developed in order to determine these complex motions. Astronomers used to assume that orbits were perfectly spherical. The fact is, however, that heavenly bodies are known to follow mathematical shapes, such as spherical, elliptical, parabolic or hyperbolic orbits. Dr. Carlo Rovelli of the University of Pittsburgh says, "Our space in which we live is just this enormously complicated spin network."

The second aspect is that the description in the Qur'an of the sky using a word meaning "woven" **may be** a reference to the String Theory of physics. (Allah knows the truth.) According to this theory, the basic elements that comprise the universe are not point-like particles, but strings resembling miniature violin strings. These tiny, identical and one dimensional strings oscillating in the form of filaments are regarded as being like loops in appearance. It is assumed that the origin of all the diversity in the universe lies in the way these strings vibrate at different vibrations, in the same way that violin strings produce different sounds with different vibrations.

The way that Allah describes the universe as being woven paths and orbits in verse 7 of Sura adh-Dhariyat shows that the Qur'an is in extraordinary agreement with science. As can be seen in a great many other instances, the way that all the information revealed in the Qur'an 1400 years ago is confirmed by modern scientific data is highly thought provoking. This perfect harmony between the Qur'an and scientific developments clearly reveals that the Qur'an is the word of our Lord, the creator of and He who knows best about all things. In one verse Allah states: "Will they not ponder the Qur'an? If it had been from other than Allah, they would have found many inconsistencies in it." (Qur'an, Sura An-Nisa (4), 82)

My answer to this claim

- Mr. Harun's claim is based on "maybe!" And I quote, "the description in the Qur'an of the sky using a word meaning "woven" **may be** a reference to the String Theory of physics." Since when is science is about "maybe?"

- As we read, Mr. Harun made a story out of the word path! It became science and then with the discovery about orbits, Muhammad became an astronomer! All of this is based on the **word "path."**

- The fact is, Muhammad is using the word path, because he thinks that there are roads to heaven made of sand. This is shown in the Islamic Arabic dictionary:

Book of <u>Lisan Al Arab</u>:by Abu-AlFadel print year 2003 page 19/20:

لسان العرب
(أبو الفضل جمال الدين محمد بن مكرم (ابن منظور
دار صادر سنة النشر: 2003م وفي التنزيل: والسماء ذات الحُبُك؛ يعني طرائق النجوم، واحدتها حَبيكة
والجمع كالجمع. وقال الفراء في قوله: والسماء ذات الحُبُك؛ قال: الحُبُك تكسُّر كل شيء كالرملة إذا مرت
عليها الريح الساكنة.

The word "alhubuki" (plural of hubiekah) means "the ways to the stars." (Al Fara') said, "the sky that has alhubuki is hubk, is the same as broken sand (become soft from walking over it), if the wind blows over it, it moves with the wind."

- It's so clear that Muhammad is talking about sandy roads that will take you to the heaven of Allah.

- We read in the Hadith of Al Bukhari, Book 58, Hadith 227, (Original book of Al-Mana'qeb {in Arabic}, Hadith 3467, Page 1410-1412—English translation follows the Arabic):

صحيح البخاري - كِتَاب مَنَاقِبِ الْأَنْصَارِ - بَاب الْمِعْرَاج
بَاب الْمِعْرَاج

3674 حَدَّثَنَا هُدْبَةُ بْنُ خَالِدٍ حَدَّثَنَا هَمَّامُ بْنُ يَحْيَى حَدَّثَنَا قَتَادَةُ عَنْ أَنَسِ بْنِ مَالِكٍ عَنْ مَالِكِ بْنِ صَعْصَعَةَ رَضِيَ اللَّهُ
عَنْهُمَا أَنَّ نَبِيَّ اللَّهِ صَلَّى اللَّهُ عَلَيْهِ وَسَلَّمَ حَدَّثَهُمْ عَنْ لَيْلَةِ أُسْرِيَ بِهِ بَيْنَمَا أَنَا فِي الْحَطِيمِ وَرُبَّمَا قَالَ فِي الْحِجْرِ
مُضْطَجِعًا إِذْ أَتَانِي آتٍ فَقَدَّ قَالَ وَسَمِعْتُهُ يَقُولُ فَشَقَّ مَا بَيْنَ هَذِهِ إِلَى هَذِهِ فَقُلْتُ لِلْجَارُودِ وَهُوَ إِلَى جَنْبِي مَا يَعْنِي بِهِ
قَالَ مِنْ ثُغْرَةِ نَحْرِهِ إِلَى شِعْرَتِهِ وَسَمِعْتُهُ يَقُولُ مِنْ قَصِّهِ إِلَى شِعْرَتِهِ فَاسْتَخْرَجَ قَلْبِي ثُمَّ أُتِيتُ بِطَسْتٍ مِنْ ذَهَبٍ
مَمْلُوءَةٍ إِيمَانًا فَغُسِلَ قَلْبِي ثُمَّ حُشِيَ ثُمَّ أُعِيدَ ثُمَّ أُتِيتُ بِدَابَّةٍ دُونَ الْبَغْلِ وَفَوْقَ الْحِمَارِ أَبْيَضَ فَقَالَ لَهُ الْجَارُودُ هُوَ
الْبُرَاقُ يَا أَبَا حَمْزَةَ قَالَ أَنَسٌ نَعَمْ يَضَعُ خَطْوَهُ عِنْدَ أَقْصَى طَرْفِهِ فَحُمِلْتُ عَلَيْهِ فَانْطَلَقَ بِي جِبْرِيلُ حَتَّى أَتَى
السَّمَاءَ الدُّنْيَا فَاسْتَفْتَحَ فَقِيلَ مَنْ هَذَا قَالَ جِبْرِيلُ قِيلَ وَمَنْ مَعَكَ قَالَ مُحَمَّدٌ قِيلَ وَقَدْ أُرْسِلَ إِلَيْهِ قَالَ نَعَمْ قِيلَ مَرْحَبًا
بِهِ فَنِعْمَ الْمَجِيءُ جَاءَ فَفَتَحَ فَلَمَّا خَلَصْتُ فَإِذَا فِيهَا آدَمُ فَقَالَ هَذَا أَبُوكَ آدَمُ فَسَلِّمْ عَلَيْهِ فَسَلَّمْتُ عَلَيْهِ فَرَدَّ السَّلَامَ ثُمَّ
قَالَ مَرْحَبًا بِالِابْنِ الصَّالِحِ وَالنَّبِيِّ الصَّالِحِ ثُمَّ صَعِدَ بِي حَتَّى أَتَى السَّمَاءَ الثَّانِيَةَ فَاسْتَفْتَحَ قِيلَ مَنْ هَذَا قَالَ جِبْرِيلُ

قِيلَ وَمَنْ مَعَكَ قَالَ مُحَمَّدٌ قِيلَ وَقَدْ أُرْسِلَ إِلَيْهِ قَالَ نَعَمْ قِيلَ مَرْحَبًا بِهِ فَنِعْمَ الْمَجِيءُ جَاءَ فَفُتِحَ فَلَمَّا خَلَصْتُ إِذَا
يَحْيَى وَعِيسَى وَهُمَا ابْنَا الْخَالَةِ قَالَ هَذَا يَحْيَى وَعِيسَى فَسَلِّمْ عَلَيْهِمَا فَسَلَّمْتُ فَرَدَّا ثُمَّ قَالَا مَرْحَبًا بِالأَخِ الصَّالِحِ
وَالنَّبِيِّ الصَّالِحِ ثُمَّ صَعِدَ بِي إِلَى السَّمَاءِ الثَّالِثَةِ فَاسْتَفْتَحَ قِيلَ مَنْ هَذَا قَالَ جِبْرِيلُ قِيلَ وَمَنْ مَعَكَ قَالَ مُحَمَّدٌ قِيلَ وَقَدْ
- »بُوسُفُ قَالَ هَذَا 1411 أُرْسِلَ إِلَيْهِ قَالَ نَعَمْ قِيلَ مَرْحَبًا بِهِ فَنِعْمَ الْمَجِيءُ جَاءَ فَفُتِحَ فَلَمَّا خَلَصْتُ إِذَا - ص
يُوسُفُ فَسَلِّمْ عَلَيْهِ فَسَلَّمْتُ عَلَيْهِ فَرَدَّ ثُمَّ قَالَ مَرْحَبًا بِالأَخِ الصَّالِحِ وَالنَّبِيِّ الصَّالِحِ ثُمَّ صَعِدَ بِي حَتَّى أَتَى السَّمَاءَ
الرَّابِعَةَ فَاسْتَفْتَحَ قِيلَ مَنْ هَذَا قَالَ جِبْرِيلُ قِيلَ وَمَنْ مَعَكَ قَالَ مُحَمَّدٌ قِيلَ وَقَدْ أُرْسِلَ إِلَيْهِ قَالَ نَعَمْ قِيلَ مَرْحَبًا بِهِ
فَنِعْمَ الْمَجِيءُ جَاءَ فَفُتِحَ فَلَمَّا خَلَصْتُ إِلَى إِدْرِيسَ قَالَ هَذَا إِدْرِيسُ فَسَلِّمْ عَلَيْهِ فَسَلَّمْتُ عَلَيْهِ فَرَدَّ ثُمَّ قَالَ مَرْحَبًا
بِالأَخِ الصَّالِحِ وَالنَّبِيِّ الصَّالِحِ ثُمَّ صَعِدَ بِي حَتَّى أَتَى السَّمَاءَ الْخَامِسَةَ فَاسْتَفْتَحَ قِيلَ مَنْ هَذَا قَالَ جِبْرِيلُ قِيلَ وَمَنْ
مَعَكَ قَالَ مُحَمَّدٌ قِيلَ وَقَدْ أُرْسِلَ إِلَيْهِ قَالَ نَعَمْ قِيلَ مَرْحَبًا بِهِ فَنِعْمَ الْمَجِيءُ جَاءَ فَلَمَّا خَلَصْتُ فَإِذَا هَارُونُ قَالَ هَذَا
هَارُونُ فَسَلِّمْ عَلَيْهِ فَسَلَّمْتُ عَلَيْهِ فَرَدَّ ثُمَّ قَالَ مَرْحَبًا بِالأَخِ الصَّالِحِ وَالنَّبِيِّ الصَّالِحِ ثُمَّ صَعِدَ بِي حَتَّى أَتَى السَّمَاءَ
السَّادِسَةَ فَاسْتَفْتَحَ قِيلَ مَنْ هَذَا قَالَ جِبْرِيلُ قِيلَ مَنْ مَعَكَ قَالَ مُحَمَّدٌ قِيلَ وَقَدْ أُرْسِلَ إِلَيْهِ قَالَ نَعَمْ قَالَ مَرْحَبًا بِهِ فَنِعْمَ
الْمَجِيءُ جَاءَ فَلَمَّا خَلَصْتُ فَإِذَا مُوسَى قَالَ هَذَا مُوسَى فَسَلِّمْ عَلَيْهِ فَسَلَّمْتُ عَلَيْهِ فَرَدَّ ثُمَّ قَالَ مَرْحَبًا بِالأَخِ الصَّالِحِ
وَالنَّبِيِّ الصَّالِحِ فَلَمَّا تَجَاوَزْتُ بَكَى فَقِيلَ لَهُ مَا يُبْكِيكَ قَالَ أَبْكِي لِأَنَّ غُلَامًا بُعِثَ بَعْدِي يَدْخُلُ الْجَنَّةَ مِنْ أُمَّتِهِ أَكْثَرُ
مِمَّنْ يَدْخُلُهَا مِنْ أُمَّتِي ثُمَّ صَعِدَ بِي إِلَى السَّمَاءِ السَّابِعَةِ فَاسْتَفْتَحَ جِبْرِيلُ قِيلَ مَنْ هَذَا قَالَ جِبْرِيلُ قِيلَ وَمَنْ مَعَكَ
قَالَ مُحَمَّدٌ قِيلَ وَقَدْ بُعِثَ إِلَيْهِ قَالَ نَعَمْ قَالَ مَرْحَبًا بِهِ فَنِعْمَ الْمَجِيءُ جَاءَ فَلَمَّا خَلَصْتُ فَإِذَا إِبْرَاهِيمُ قَالَ هَذَا أَبُوكَ
فَسَلِّمْ عَلَيْهِ قَالَ فَسَلَّمْتُ عَلَيْهِ فَرَدَّ السَّلَامَ قَالَ مَرْحَبًا بِالِابْنِ الصَّالِحِ وَالنَّبِيِّ الصَّالِحِ ثُمَّ رُفِعَتْ إِلَيَّ سِدْرَةُ الْمُنْتَهَى
فَإِذَا نَبْتُهَا مِثْلُ قِلَالِ هَجَرَ وَإِذَا وَرَقُهَا مِثْلُ آذَانِ الْفِيَلَةِ قَالَ هَذِهِ سِدْرَةُ الْمُنْتَهَى وَإِذَا أَرْبَعَةُ أَنْهَارٍ نَهْرَانِ بَاطِنَانِ
وَنَهْرَانِ ظَاهِرَانِ فَقُلْتُ مَا هَذَانِ يَا جِبْرِيلُ قَالَ أَمَّا الْبَاطِنَانِ فَنَهْرَانِ فِي الْجَنَّةِ وَأَمَّا الظَّاهِرَانِ فَالنِّيلُ وَالْفُرَاتُ ثُمَّ
رُفِعَ لِي الْبَيْتُ الْمَعْمُورُ ثُمَّ أُتِيتُ بِإِنَاءٍ مِنْ خَمْرٍ وَإِنَاءٍ مِنْ لَبَنٍ وَإِنَاءٍ مِنْ عَسَلٍ فَأَخَذْتُ اللَّبَنَ فَقَالَ هِيَ الْفِطْرَةُ الَّتِي
- الصَّلَوَاتُ خَمْسِينَ صَلَاةً كُلَّ يَوْمٍ فَرَجَعْتُ فَمَرَرْتُ عَلَى 1412 أَنْتَ عَلَيْهَا وَأُمَّتُكَ ثُمَّ فُرِضَتْ عَلَيَّ - ص »
مُوسَى فَقَالَ بِمَا أُمِرْتَ قَالَ أُمِرْتُ بِخَمْسِينَ صَلَاةً كُلَّ يَوْمٍ قَالَ إِنَّ أُمَّتَكَ لَا تَسْتَطِيعُ خَمْسِينَ صَلَاةً كُلَّ يَوْمٍ وَإِنِّي
وَاللَّهِ قَدْ جَرَّبْتُ النَّاسَ قَبْلَكَ وَعَالَجْتُ بَنِي إِسْرَائِيلَ أَشَدَّ الْمُعَالَجَةِ فَارْجِعْ إِلَى رَبِّكَ فَاسْأَلْهُ التَّخْفِيفَ لِأُمَّتِكَ فَرَجَعْتُ
فَوَضَعَ عَنِّي عَشْرًا فَرَجَعْتُ إِلَى مُوسَى فَقَالَ مِثْلَهُ فَرَجَعْتُ فَوَضَعَ عَنِّي عَشْرًا فَرَجَعْتُ إِلَى مُوسَى فَقَالَ مِثْلَهُ
فَرَجَعْتُ فَوَضَعَ عَنِّي عَشْرًا فَرَجَعْتُ إِلَى مُوسَى فَقَالَ مِثْلَهُ فَرَجَعْتُ فَأُمِرْتُ بِعَشْرِ صَلَوَاتٍ كُلَّ يَوْمٍ فَرَجَعْتُ فَقَالَ
مِثْلَهُ فَرَجَعْتُ فَأُمِرْتُ بِخَمْسِ صَلَوَاتٍ كُلَّ يَوْمٍ فَرَجَعْتُ إِلَى مُوسَى فَقَالَ بِمَ أُمِرْتَ قُلْتُ أُمِرْتُ بِخَمْسِ صَلَوَاتٍ كُلَّ
يَوْمٍ قَالَ إِنَّ أُمَّتَكَ لَا تَسْتَطِيعُ خَمْسَ صَلَوَاتٍ كُلَّ يَوْمٍ وَإِنِّي قَدْ جَرَّبْتُ النَّاسَ قَبْلَكَ وَعَالَجْتُ بَنِي إِسْرَائِيلَ أَشَدَّ
الْمُعَالَجَةِ فَارْجِعْ إِلَى رَبِّكَ فَاسْأَلْهُ التَّخْفِيفَ لِأُمَّتِكَ قَالَ سَأَلْتُ رَبِّي حَتَّى اسْتَحْيَيْتُ وَلَكِنِّي أَرْضَى وَأُسَلِّمُ قَالَ فَلَمَّا
جَاوَزْتُ نَادَى مُنَادٍ أَمْضَيْتُ فَرِيضَتِي وَخَفَّفْتُ عَنْ عِبَادِي

Muhammad Going to Allah on Top of Flying Mule
(Hadith Translation, Sahih Al-Bukhari, Book 58, Hadith 227)

Allah's messenger said, reporting to them his Night expedition saying, "At the same time as I was resting down in my house, unexpectedly someone came to me and cut my body and slit it from here to over in this place." I asked Al-Jarod, whom was next to me, "What does he (the prophet) mean?" He said, "It means from his throat to his pubic area," or said, "From the throttle valve to his pubic area." The Prophet, He continued saying, "He afterwards grabbed out my heart. Then a gold tray of Belief was brought to me, and he washed my heart. Moreover, my heart was filled with faith and wisdom and after that he restored it to its original place. Next a white animal which was shorter than a mule and larger than a donkey was brought to me." About this Al-Jarod asked, "It was Al Buraq, Abu Hamzza?" I replied in the positive. Then the Prophet disclosed that the animal's step was so sizable to the point that it reached the furthest away point within the reach of the animal's vision. I was carried on it, and Gabriel set out with me on the top of it, until we reached the lowest sky. Over there when he (Gabriel) requested for the gateway to be opened, it was inquired 'Who is it over there?' Gabriel answered, 'It's me, Gabriel.' It was inquired, 'Who is accompanying with you?' Gabriel answered, 'It's Muhammad.' It inquired, 'Muhammad has been requested to come?' Gabriel responded, 'Indeed yes, He was called to come." After words they said: 'He is welcomed. What an extraordinary visitor!' After that, the gateway was opened, as well as next I went up to the first sky, I saw Adam there. Gabriel told to me, saying, 'This is your father, Adam, give him your salute.' So I saluted him, and he saluted me back saying, 'You are welcomed, O sincere son and sincere Prophet.' Then Gabriel ascended with me until we reach the second sky. [Gabriel] asked for the gateway to be opened. It was inquired, 'Who is it over there.' Gabriel responded, 'I am Gabriel.' It was inquired, 'Who is accompanying with you?' Gabriel responded back, 'It's Muhammad.' It was inquired, 'Has been requested to come?' Gabriel responded as, 'Indeed yes, He was requested to come.' Then they said, 'He is welcomed. What an excellent visit his visit is!' Then the gate was opened. When I went over the second sky, there I saw Yahyia (John the Baptist) and '"Isa (Jesus) his cousins. Gabriel said to me, 'These are John and Jesus; salute him with your greetings.' So I saluted them and both replied to my salute to me and said, 'You are welcomed, O sincere brother and sincere Prophet.' Afterwards Gabriel ascended me up to third sky and [Gabriel] asked for the gateway to be opened. It was inquired, 'Who is it over there?' Gabriel answered, 'It's me, Gabriel.' It was inquired, 'Who is accompanying with you?' Gabriel answered back, 'It is Muhammad.' It was inquired, 'Muhammad has been called?' Gabriel answered as, 'Indeed yes, He was called to come.' Then they said, 'He is welcomed. What an extraordinary visitor he is!' The gate was opened, and when I proceeded up to the third sky there I saw Joseph. Gabriel said to me, 'This is Joseph, salute him.' So I did saluted him, and he saluted me back, and he said to me, "You are welcomed, O sincere brother and sincere Prophet." Then Gabriel ascended me up to the fourth heaven and (Gabriel) asked for the gateway to be opened. It was inquired, 'Who is it over there?' Gabriel answered, 'It's me, Gabriel.' It was inquired, 'Who is accompanying with you?' Gabriel answered back, 'It's Muhammad.' It was asked, 'Muhammad has been requested to come?' Gabriel answered as, 'Indeed yes, He was called to come.' Then the angels said, 'He is welcomed, what an extraordinary visitor he is!' It follows the gateway was opened, and when I went up to the fourth sky, there I saw Idris. Gabriel said [to me], 'This is Idris, salute him.' So I saluted him, and he saluted me back and said, 'You are welcomed, O sincere brother and sincere Prophet.' Afterwards Gabriel ascended with me to the fifth sky and [Gabriel] asked for the gateway to be opened. It was inquired, 'Who is it over there?' Gabriel answered, 'It's me, Gabriel.' It was inquired, 'Who is accompanying with you?' Gabriel answered, 'it is Muhammad.' It was inquired, 'Muhammad has been requested to come?' Gabriel answered as, 'Indeed yes, he was called to come.' Then they said, 'He is welcomed. What an extraordinary visitor he is!' The gate was opened. So when I went over up to the fifth heaven, where I saw Harun (Aaron), Gabriel said, to me, 'This is Aaron, salute him with your greetings.' I saluted him and he replied to the salute to me and said, 'You are welcomed, sincere brother and sincere Prophet.' Then Gabriel ascended with me up to the sixth sky. [Gabriel] asked for the gateway to be opened. It was inquired 'Who is it over there?' Gabriel answered, 'It's me, Gabriel.' It was inquired, 'Who is accompanying with you?' Gabriel answered back, 'It is Muhammad.' It was asked, 'Muhammad has been called?' Gabriel answered as, 'Indeed yes, he was requested to come.' Then they said, 'He is welcomed. What an excellent visitor he is!' The gate was opened. When I went over up to the sixth sky, there I saw Moses. Gabriel said to me, 'This is Moses, salute him.' So I saluted him, and he returned the salute back to me and said, 'You are welcomed, sincere brother and sincere Prophet.' When I left him, Moses cried hard. Someone asked him, 'What makes you grieve?' Moses answered, 'I cry seeing that after me there has been sent as Prophet a young man (he means Muhammad) whose followers will enter heaven in larger numbers than my followers.' Then Gabriel took me up to the seventh sky. [Gabriel] asked for the gateway to be opened. It was inquired, 'Who is it over there?' Gabriel responded, 'It's me Gabriel.' It was inquired, 'Who is accompanying with you?' Gabriel responded back, 'It's Muhammad.' It was inquired, 'Muhammad has been requested to come?' Gabriel answered, 'Indeed yes, he was called to come.' Then it was said, 'He is welcomed. What an excellent visitor he is!' So when I proceeded over up to the seventh sky, there I saw Ibrahim (Abraham). Gabriel said to me, 'This is your father, salute him.' So I saluted him, and he returned the salute to me and said, 'You are welcomed, sincere son and sincere Prophet.' Then Gabriel took me up to Sudrat Al-Muntaha (big tree in heaven, tree of Allah). Behold its fruits are the same as the ones in the clay jugs of Hajar (a location in Arabia not far away from Mecca) and its leaves look so big as the ears of elephants. Gabriel said, 'This is Sudrat Al-Muntaha (Allah Tree).' And there were four running rivers; two rivers were underneath and invisible, and two rivers were visible. I questioned Gabriel, 'What are these two rivers?' He answered, 'As for the hidden rivers, they are two rivers in Paradise, and the visible rivers are the Nile and the Euphrates.' After that, Al-Bait Al-Ma'mor (the House of Allah) was lifted up to me, and a container full of wine, and another full of milk, and a third full of honey were brought to me to drink. I drank the milk. Gabriel said, 'This is the Islamic religion which you and who follow are following.' Then the order of prayers was given to me. They were fifty prayers a day. When I came back, I passed by Moses, and he asked me, 'What has Allah given you as a command to do?' I responded, 'I have been commanded to pray fifty prayers a day.' Moses's response back, 'Your followers cannot handle fifty prayers a day, and I swear by Allah, I have tried Allah commands on my people before you, and I have well-tried the best I could with children of Israel. Go back to your Lord and ask for a discount to lighten up your followers' obligation.' As a result I went backward, and Allah reduced ten prayers for me. Then again, I came back to Moses, but he repeated and asked me to do same as he said previously. Then again, I went back to Allah, and He decreased ten more prayers. When I came back to Moses, but he restated and asked me to do same as he said before. I went back to Allah and He commanded me to carry out ten prayers a day. When I came back to Moses he restated and asked me to do the same as he said previously, so I went back to Allah and was ordered to do five prayers a day. As I came back to Moses, he said, 'What are the arrangements Allah gave to you?' I responded, 'I have been ordered to practice five prayers a day.' He said, 'I guarantee you, your followers' cannot stand five prayers a day, and no doubt. I have got my experience of my people before you, and I did the best I could with the children of Israel. Therefore, go back to your Lord and ask for more discount to light up your followers' burden. I said, 'I have requested subsequently much of my Lord that I feel shamefaced, but I am satisfied now and surrender to Allah's wish.' Consequently, when I left, I heard a voice saying, 'I have confirmed My Order and have minimized the commitment of My Worshipers.'"

- As we have seen in this fairy tale story, Muhammad hit the road for heaven on his donkey. (The animal's stride was so long that it reached the farthest point within the animal's sight.) This animal is able to go to heaven so fast, because its' stride goes so far!

- Even the angel is also using the donkey to go to Allah.

- Gabriel set out with me on the top of it until we reached the lowest sky"

- As long as the Muslims are speaking about science, is it scientific to say we can go to the sky by donkey, or is this some kind of discovery that has not yet been achieved? And remember, this is not a metaphorical story. It is supposed to be taken literally!

- The heaven Muhammad is speaking about is not a space, it's a physical heaven. It's even connected physically to the earth, because as we see, there are two rivers that are earthly rivers that he names, the **Nile** and the **Euphrates.** "There were four running rivers, two were underneath and invisible and two were visible, I asked Gabriel, What are these two kinds of rivers? He replied, 'As for the hidden rivers, they are two rivers in Paradise and the visible rivers are the Nile and the Euphrates.'" Can any Muslim tell me what the **Nile and the Euphrates are doing in Allah's heaven and on the earth at the same time? The answer is there are roads connecting them.**

- This means that the path is about normal roads to travel on.

- As long I mentioned this story, I would like you to take a note about the **fifty prayers** and how Muhammad, with the help of Moses, changed the number of the prayers from fifty to five. The strangest part of this story is, why didn't Allah give Muhammad five from the start? Why did he initially choose fifty, then forty, then ten and then five? Doesn't Allah know that Moses is waiting on the road for Muhammad?

- Even Moses wanted Muhammad to go back to get zero prayers!

- I want to be sure to remind you about the funny part, where someone installed in the chest of Muhammad a dish of faith (belief), as we see here: "'At the same time as I was resting down in my house, unexpectedly someone came to me and cut my body and slit it from here to over in this place' I asked Al-Jarod, whom was next to me, 'What does he (the prophet) mean?' He said, 'It means from his throat to his pubic area,' or said, 'From the throttle valve to his pubic area.' The Prophet, He continued saying, 'He afterwards grabbed out my heart. Then a gold tray of Belief was brought to me, and he washed my heart. Moreover, my heart was filled with faith and wisdom and after that he restored it to its original place.'"

- If it's about a dish of faith, why did he cut all the way down to his pubic area?

Note: These are more than one claim, but I will put them all together and answer all of these claims, because all are actually one topic.

Second Muslim Claim:

THE LAYERS OF THE ATMOSPHERE
THE PROTECTED ROOF
THE SKY MADE A DOME
THE RETURNING SKY
THE LAYERS OF THE ATMOSPHERE
(Following is the Muslim claim)

One fact about the universe revealed in the verses of the Qur'an is that the sky is made up of seven layers.

> It is He Who created everything on the earth for you and then directed His attention up to heaven and arranged it into seven regular heavens. He has knowledge of all things. (Qur'an, 2:29)

> Then He turned to heaven when it was smoke. In two days He determined them as seven heavens and revealed, in every heaven, its own mandate. (Qur'an, 41:11-12)

The word "heavens," which appears in many verses in the Qur'an, is used to refer to the sky above the earth, as well as the entire universe. Given this meaning of the word, it is understood that the earth's sky, or the atmosphere, is made up of seven layers.

Today, it is known that the world's atmosphere consists of different layers that lie on top of each other. Based on the criteria of chemical contents or air temperature, the definitions made have determined the atmosphere of the earth as seven layers. According to the "Limited Fine Mesh Model (LFMMII)," a model of atmosphere used to estimate weather conditions for 48 hours, the atmosphere is also 7 layers. According to the modern geological definitions the seven layers of atmosphere are as follows:

1. Troposphere
2. Stratosphere
3. Mesosphere
4. Thermosphere
5. Exosphere
6. Ionosphere
7. Magnetosphere

The Qur'an says, "[He] revealed, in every heaven, its own mandate," in Sura Fussilat (Chapter 41), 12. In other words, Allah is stating that He assigned each heaven its own duty. Truly, as will be seen in following chapters, each one of these layers has vital duties for the benefit of human kind and all other living things on the Earth. Each layer has a particular function, ranging from forming rain to preventing harmful rays, from reflecting radio waves to averting the harmful effects of meteors.

The verses below inform us about the appearance of the seven layers of the atmosphere:

Do you not see how He created seven heavens in layers? (Qur'an, 71:15)

He Who created the seven heavens in layers... (Qur'an, 67:3)

The atmosphere only lets rays required for life reach the Earth. For example, ultraviolet rays make it to the world only partially. This is the most appropriate range to allow plants to make photosynthesis and eventually for all living things to survive.

The Arabic word "tibaqan" in these verses, translated into English as "layer" means "layer, the appropriate cover or covering for something," and thus stresses how the top layer is well suited to the lower. The word is also used in the plural here: "layers." The sky, described in the verse as being in layers, is without doubt the most perfect expression of the atmosphere. It is a great miracle that these facts, which could not possibly be discovered without the technology of the 20th century, were explicitly stated by the Qur'an 1,400 years ago.

The Protected Roof

In the Qur'an, Allah calls our attention to a very important attribute of the sky:

We made the sky a preserved and protected roof yet still they turn away from Our Signs. (Qur'an, 21:32)

This attribute of the sky has been proved by scientific research carried out in the 20th century: The atmosphere surrounding the Earth serves crucial functions for the continuity of life. While destroying many meteors-big and small-as they approach the Earth, it prevents them from falling to Earth and harming living things.

In addition, the atmosphere filters the light rays coming from space that are harmful to living things. The most striking feature of the atmosphere is that it lets only harmless and useful rays-visible light, near ultraviolet light and radio waves pass through. All of this radiation is vital for life. Near ultraviolet rays, which are only partially let in by the atmosphere, are very important for the photosynthesis of plants and for the survival of all living beings. The majority of the intense ultraviolet rays emitted from the Sun are filtered out by the ozone layer of the atmosphere. Only a limited and essential part of the ultraviolet spectrum reaches the Earth.

The protective function of the atmosphere does not end here. The atmosphere also protects the earth from the freezing cold of the space, which is approximately -270°C.

It is not only the atmosphere that protects the Earth from harmful effects. In addition to the atmosphere, the Van Allen Belt-the layer caused by the magnetic field of the Earth-also serves as a shield against the harmful radiation that threatens our planet. This radiation, which is constantly emitted by the Sun and other stars, is deadly to living things. If the Van Allen belt did not exist, the massive outbursts of energy called solar flares that frequently occur in the Sun would destroy all life on Earth.

The magnetosphere layer, formed by the magnetic field of the Earth, serves as a shield protecting the Earth from celestial bodies, harmful cosmic rays and particles. In the above picture, this magnetosphere layer, which is also named Van Allen Belts, is seen. These belts at thousands of kilometres above the Earth protect the living things on the Earth from the fatal energy that would otherwise reach it from space.

All these scientific findings prove that the world is protected in a very particular way. The important thing is that this protection was made known in the Qur'an in the verse "We made the sky a preserved and protected roof" fourteen centuries ago.

On the importance of the Van Allen Belt, Dr. Hugh Ross says:

In fact, the Earth has the highest density of any of the planets in our Solar System. This large nickel-iron core is responsible for our large magnetic field. This magnetic field produces the Van-Allen radiation shield, which protects the Earth from radiation bombardment. If this shield were not present, life would not be possible on the Earth. The only other rocky planet to have any magnetic field is Mercury-but its field strength is 100 times less than the Earth's. Even Venus, our sister planet, has no magnetic field. The Van-Allen radiation shield is a design unique to the Earth.

The energy transmitted in just one of these bursts detected in recent years was calculated to be equivalent to 100 billion atomic bombs, each akin to one dropped on Hiroshima at the end of World War II. Fifty-eight hours after the burst, it was observed that the magnetic needles of compasses displayed unusual movement and 250 kilometres above the Earth's atmosphere, the temperature suddenly increased to 2,500°C.

Most people looking at the sky do not think about the protective aspect of the atmosphere. They almost never think what kind of a place the world would be like if this structure did not exist. The above photo belongs to a giant crater caused by a meteor that fell in Arizona, in the USA. If the atmosphere did not exist, millions of meteoroids would fall to the Earth and the Earth would become an inhabitable place. Yet, the protective aspect of the atmosphere allows living things to survive in safety. This is certainly Allah's protection of people and a miracle proclaimed in the Qur'an.

In short, a perfect system is at work high above the Earth. It surrounds our world and protects it against external threats. Centuries ago, Allah informed us in the Qur'an of the world's atmosphere functioning as a protective shield.

THE SKY MADE A DOME

It is He Who made the earth a couch for you, and the sky a dome. He sends down water from the sky and by it brings forth fruits for your provision. Do not, then, knowingly make others equal to Allah. (Qur'an, 2:22)

The Geminid meteor shower is observed at its highest intensity in the second week of December each year. The short lines in the photograph to the side are traces belonging to stars; the long ones belong to meteors. The meteors in the shower seen in the picture (on website) fall at a density of up to 58 per hour.

Here, the Arabic word for the sky is "assamaa binaan." As well as the meaning of "dome" or "ceiling," this also describes a kind of tent-like covering used by the Bedouin. What is being emphasised here, through mention of a tent-like structure, is a form of protection against external elements.
Even if we are generally unaware of it, a large number of meteors fall to the Earth, as they do the other planets. The reason why these make enormous craters on other planets but do no harm on Earth is that the atmosphere puts up considerable resistance to a falling meteor. The meteor is unable to withstand this for long and loses much of its mass from combustion due to friction. This danger, which might otherwise cause terrible disasters, is thus prevented thanks to the atmosphere. As well as the verses regarding the protective properties of the atmosphere cited above, attention is also drawn to the special creation in the following verse:

Do you not see that Allah has made everything on the earth subservient to you and the ships running upon the sea by His command? He holds back the heaven, preventing it from falling to the earth-except by His permission. Allah is

All-Compassionate to mankind, Most Merciful. (Qur'an, 22:65)

The protective property of the atmosphere we discussed in the preceding section protects the Earth from space-in other words, from external elements. With the word "dome," referring to the sky in the above verse, attention is drawn to this aspect of the sky, which could not possibly have been known at the time of our Prophet (saas). The fact that this information was imparted 1,400 years ago in the Qur'an, when there were no spacecraft or giant telescopes, shows that the Qur'an is the revelation of our Lord, the Omniscient.

My answer

To the Atmosphere and Protected Roof

He claimed how Allah knew about the sky being a protected roof (the Atmosphere). First of all, let's see what the Qur'an says about that, then we will find out if this is really speaking about a miracle, an error, or a lie that the Muslims use to promote their religion.

Now, what is the lowest heaven according to the Islamic miracles claim? From Qur'an 21:32:

> And We made the sky a preserved roof; and yet after these signs, they are ungrateful.

I will show you this is Allah speaking about protecting the heaven, not the earth. I can prove that with more clear evidence as we read this excerpt from Sahih Muslim, Book 4, Hadith 902 (also see Sahih Al-Bukhari, Book 60, Hadith 443)

> Ibn 'Abbas reported: The Messenger of Allah (may Allah pray on him and salute him) in neither case recited the Qur'an to the Jinn, nor did he see any of them. The Messenger of Allah (may Allah pray on him and salute him) went out with some of his associates with the intention of going to the bazaar of 'Ukaz. However, there had been blockages between satans and the information from the Heaven (by spying), and there were flames launched upon them. So the devils went back to their people, and they said: "What has taken place to you?" They said: "There have been created obstructions between us and the news from the Heaven..."

Sahih Muslim, Book 004, Hadith 0902, excerpt in Arabic:

211

صحيح البخاري - أَبْوَابُ صِفَةِ الصَّلَاةِ - بَاب الْجَهْرِ بِقِرَاءَةِ صَلَاةِ الْفَجْرِ

بَاب الْجَهْرِ بِقِرَاءَةِ صَلَاةِ الْفَجْرِ وَقَالَتْ أُمُّ سَلَمَةَ طُفْتُ وَرَاءَ النَّاسِ وَالنَّبِيُّ صَلَّى اللَّهُ عَلَيْهِ وَسَلَّمَ يُصَلِّي وَيَقْرَأُ
حَدَّثَنَا مُسَدَّدٌ قَالَ حَدَّثَنَا أَبُو عَوَانَةَ عَنْ أَبِي بِشْرٍ هُوَ جَعْفَرُ بْنُ أَبِي وَحْشِيَّةَ عَنْ سَعِيدِ بْنِ جُبَيْرٍ عَنْ 739 بِالطُّورِ
عَبْدِ اللَّهِ بْنِ عَبَّاسٍ رَضِيَ اللَّهُ عَنْهُمَا قَالَ انْطَلَقَ النَّبِيُّ صَلَّى اللَّهُ عَلَيْهِ وَسَلَّمَ فِي طَائِفَةٍ مِنْ أَصْحَابِهِ عَامِدِينَ إِلَى
سُوقِ عُكَاظٍ وَقَدْ حِيلَ بَيْنَ الشَّيَاطِينِ وَبَيْنَ خَبَرِ السَّمَاءِ وَأُرْسِلَتْ عَلَيْهِمُ الشُّهُبُ فَرَجَعَتْ الشَّيَاطِينُ إِلَى قَوْمِهِمْ
فَقَالُوا مَا لَكُمْ فَقَالُوا حِيلَ بَيْنَنَا وَبَيْنَ خَبَرِ السَّمَاءِ وَأُرْسِلَتْ عَلَيْنَا الشُّهُبُ قَالُوا مَا حَالَ بَيْنَكُمْ وَبَيْنَ خَبَرِ السَّمَاءِ إِلَّا
شَيْءٌ حَدَثَ فَاضْرِبُوا مَشَارِقَ الْأَرْضِ وَمَغَارِبَهَا فَانْظُرُوا مَا هَذَا الَّذِي حَالَ بَيْنَكُمْ وَبَيْنَ خَبَرِ السَّمَاءِ فَانْصَرَفَ
أُولَئِكَ الَّذِينَ تَوَجَّهُوا نَحْوَ تِهَامَةَ إِلَى النَّبِيِّ صَلَّى اللَّهُ عَلَيْهِ وَسَلَّمَ وَهُوَ بِنَخْلَةَ عَامِدِينَ إِلَى سُوقِ عُكَاظٍ وَهُوَ يُصَلِّي
بِأَصْحَابِهِ صَلَاةَ الْفَجْرِ فَلَمَّا سَمِعُوا الْقُرْآنَ اسْتَمَعُوا لَهُ فَقَالُوا هَذَا وَاللَّهِ الَّذِي حَالَ بَيْنَكُمْ وَبَيْنَ خَبَرِ
- »حِينَ رَجَعُوا إِلَى قَوْمِهِمْ وَقَالُوا يَا قَوْمَنَا إِنَّا سَمِعْنَا قُرْآنًا عَجَبًا يَهْدِي إِلَى الرُّشْدِ 268السَّمَاءِ فَهُنَالِكَ «- ص
فَآمَنَّا بِهِ وَلَنْ نُشْرِكَ بِرَبِّنَا أَحَدًا فَأَنْزَلَ اللَّهُ عَلَى نَبِيِّهِ صَلَّى اللَّهُ عَلَيْهِ وَسَلَّمَ قُلْ أُوحِيَ إِلَيَّ أَنَّهُ اسْتَمَعَ نَفَرٌ مِنْ الْجِنِّ
وَإِنَّمَا أُوحِيَ إِلَيْهِ قَوْلُ الْجِنِّ

1. According to the verse in Qur'an 67:5, the stars exist <u>in the lowest heaven.</u>

2. Qur'an: 67:5:

And We have decorated the lowest sky with lamps (stars), and made them (the stars) missiles against the devils, and We have arranged for them the punishment of the flame.

Did you notice that Mr. Harun did not post this verse in his claim, but he posted a verse before it? "He Who created the seven heavens in layers..." (Qur'an, 67:3). Why? The reason is that he does not like this fact which would destroy his claim.

3. In addition to that, Qur'an, 67:3 does not say seven **layers**, but rather seven **skies**. You can check other Muslim translations and you will note right away the deception of Mr. Harun Yahya. He changed the word **skies** to **layers**, and I am sure you know that the difference is huge.

4. If this is describing the atmosphere, as Muslims claim, it would then mean that all of our stars are in the atmosphere! Specifically, in the lowest sky (layer) of the atmosphere.

5. What about the seven layers of the atmosphere? Are there seven? Here we go again! They also lied in this claim. There are actually only <u>four (4) layers in the atmosphere.</u> Later I will show that with more details.

The following is from NASA: (http://www.nasa.gov/audience/forstudents/9-12/features/912_liftoff_atm.html)

The earth is surrounded by a blanket of air, which we call the atmosphere. It reaches near or over 600 kilometers (372 miles) from the surface of the earth.

1. **Troposphere:** The troposphere starts at the earth's surface and extends 8 to 14.5 kilometers high (5 to 9 miles).

2. **Stratosphere:** The stratosphere starts just above the troposphere and extends to 50 kilometers (31 miles) high.

3. **Mesosphere:** The mesosphere starts just above the stratosphere and extends to 85 kilometers (53 miles) high.

4. **Thermosphere:** The thermosphere starts just above the mesosphere and extends to 600 kilometers (372 miles) high.

It's so clear that the Muslims count their own way to fabricate that the atmosphere is made of seven layers! Qur'an 67:5 says:

And We have decorated the lowest sky with lamps, and made them missiles against the devils, and We have arranged for them the punishment of the flame.

It's clear that Allah will shoot any satan with a star, if he tries to go out of the earth.

Tafsir Al-Jalalayn, Qur'an, Al-Mulk (67): 5:

تفسير

{ وَلَقَدْ زَيَّنَّا ٱلسَّمَآءَ ٱلدُّنْيَا بِمَصَٰبِيحَ وَجَعَلْنَٰهَا رُجُوماً لِّلشَّيَٰطِينِ وَأَعْتَدْنَا لَهُمْ عَذَابَ ٱلسَّعِيرِ }
وَلَقَدْ زَيَّنَّا السَّمَاء الدُّنْيَا بِمَصَابِيحَ وَجَعَلْنَاهَا رُجُومًا لِلشَّيَاطِينِ وَأَعْتَدْنَا لَهُمْ عَذَابَ السَّعِيرِ {5}
وَلَقَدْ زَيَّنَّا السَّمَاء الدُّنْيَا" الْقُرْبَى إِلَى الْأَرْض "بِمَصَابِيح" بِنُجُوم "وَجَعَلْنَاهَا رُجُومًا" مَرَاجِم "لِلشَّيَاطِينِ" إِذَا "
اسْتَرَقُوا السَّمع بِأَنْ يَنْفَصِل شِهَاب عَنْ الْكَوْكَب كَالْقَبَس يُؤْخَذ مِنْ النَّار فَيَقْتُل الْجِنِّيّ أَوْ يَخْبِلهُ لَا أَنَّ الْكَوْكَب يَزُول
عَنْ مَكَانه "وَأَعْتَدْنَا لَهُمْ عَذَاب السَّعِير" النَّار الْمُوقَدَة

As well as We have decorated the lowest heaven, the one nearest to the earth, with lamps, by means of stars, and made them missiles against the satans if they try to listen, to spy, as a meteor of fire detaches itself from the star, as a touch off is taken from a fire, and either kills that jinn or drives him insane. It is not the star itself that will move from its position; and We have prepared for them the punishment of the Blaze, the ignited Fire.

Simply, Allah has his self-defense system against any Satan that will try to spy at his secrets, and that is the protected roof.

Maybe some are still not convinced with my proofs. In that case, I will show additional evidence.

Qur'an 15:16-18:

[16] It is We, Who have set out the zodiacal symbols in the heavens, and beautified them to all viewers.

[17] And in addition <u>We have protecting them from every cursed satan</u>.

[18] Except any (satan) that tries to profit on a hearing by sneakiness (to heaven) is <u>chased by a flaming fire</u>, brilliant and visible.

Qur'an 37:6, 7, 10:

[6] We have indeed adorned the lower sky with beauty, the planets.

[7] In addition we guarded the lower sky against any pig-headed disobedient satan.

[10] With the exclusion of him who kidnaps (spies at Allah) off but immediately, <u>he will be chased by an arrow of flame</u>.

Qur'an 72:8-9:

[8] And we touched the sky; but we found it filled with severe bodyguards and brilliant fires.

[9] And we used to sit on [high] places therein to hearken. However, he who is a listener now and after [spies at Allah] finds a flame in wait for him;

Qur'an 55:33:

O company of jinn and humans, if you are able to pass <u>through the Range of the heavens and the earth</u>, then pass through! <u>You will not pass</u> through except with an authority.

Qur'an 67:5 said clearly that Allah will shoot the one who tries to go to heaven. On top of that, we can take a look at the Muslim Tafsir pertaining to Qur'an 55:33, Al-Jalalayn, Ar-Rahman (55), 33:

تفسير
{ يَمَعْشَرَ ٱلْجِنّ وَٱلإِنسِ إِنِ ٱسْتَطَعْتُمْ أَن تَنفُذُواْ مِنْ أَقْطَارِ ٱلسَّمَٰوَٰتِ وَٱلأَرْضِ فَٱنفُذُواْ لاَ تَنفُذُونَ إِلاَّ بِسُلْطَانٍ }

O kind of jinn and humans, if you are able to pass through, to exit from the Range, of the heavens and the earth, then pass through! A challenge made by Allah to challenge them to what they are incapable of doing (jinn and humans). You will not pass through except with authority, and power, and you have no power for such a thing to do.

From both chapters of the Qur'an we found that this has nothing to do with the atmosphere. The fact is, it proves the ignorance of their god, Allah.

⚔ It's clear that the Qur'an is speaking about protecting the sky, not the earth.

⅄ We know that humans went to the sky and even out of the confines of the earth atmosphere. Where were the missiles of Allah? And what's funny is that the humans who went there were the infidels (Americans and Russians), not the Muslims!

⅄ The Qur'an speaks of an exception to leave the confines of earth (You will not pass through except with an authority).

⅄ This provision is about Allah allowing his prophets, like 'Isa and Muhammad, to go up there, but not the Americans!

Despite these scientific facts, Mr. Harun claims that the lowest sky is the **atmosphere.** His god's science proves that Allah didn't know where the stars are located. He thinks they are in the lowest sky only, when science proves we have many galaxies and each one is another sky. Each is full of billions of stars. Remember what **Qur'an: 67:5** said:

And We have decorated the lowest sky with lamps (stars), and made them (the stars) missiles against the devils, and We have arranged for them the punishment of the flame.

Did Allah Create the World in Six, Seven or Eight Days?

The following narration is an approved hadith that gives an account of the creation of the world (Sahih Muslim, V 4, Page 2150 {Arabic}):

Allah's Messenger told me:

خَلَقَ اللهُ، (عَزَّ وَجَلَّ)، التُّرْبَةَ يَوْمَ السَّبْتِ، وَخَلَقَ فِيهَا الْجِبَالَ يَوْمَ الْأَحَدِ، وَخَلَقَ الشَّجَرَ يَوْمَ الْاثْنَيْنِ، وَخَلَقَ « الْمَكْرُوهَ يَوْمَ الثُّلَاثَاءِ، وَخَلَقَ النُّورَ يَوْمَ الْأَرْبِعَاءِ، وَبَثَّ فِيهَا الدَّوَابَّ يَوْمَ الْخَمِيسِ، وَخَلَقَ آدَمَ، عَلَيْهِ السَّلَامُ، بَعْدَ «الْعَصْرِ مِنْ يَوْمِ الْجُمُعَةِ، فِي آخِرِ الْخَلْقِ، فِي آخِرِ سَاعَةٍ مِنْ سَاعَاتِ الْجُمُعَةِ، فِيمَا بَيْنَ الْعَصْرِ إِلَى اللَّيْلِ

Abu Hurira reported: The Prophet of Allah told me, "Allah created the soil on Saturday, and He created the mountains on Sunday, and He created the trees on Monday, and He created the bad things on Tuesday and He created the light on Wednesday and He created the the walking animals on Thursday and He created Adam on Friday afternoon. He was the last created during the last hour of Friday, between afternoon and night.

Hadith correct and approved as in Al-Alabany, V 4, Hadith 1833; (Also in Book of Al-Mishkat Hadith 5735; Book of Mukhtasar Al-'Olu Al-Zahbi Hadith 73: and Book of 'Qism Al-Mustfrak page 664):

رقم: 1833 المجلد: 4

الحديث: خلق الله التربة يوم السبت وخلق فيها الجبال يوم الأحد وخلق الشجر يوم
الإثنين وخلق المكروه يوم الثلاثاء وخلق النور يوم الأربعاء وبث فيها الدواب يوم الخميس
وخلق آدم بعد العصر من يوم الجمعة آخر الخلق من آخر ساعة الجمعة فيما بين العصر
إلى الليل] . (صحيح) . وليس الحديث بمخالف للقرآن كما يتوهم البعض راجع المشكاة
5735 ثم مختصر العلو للذهبي رقم الحديث 71 . انظر التحقيق المطول في الكتاب قسم
الاستدراك ص 664 . وخلاصته فالتفصيل الذي في الحديث هو غير التفصيل الذي في
القرآن الكريم وأيامه غير أيامه فالواجب في مثل هذا عند أهل العلم أن يضم أحدهما إلى
الآخر وليس ضرب أحدهما بالآخر .

https://sunnah.com/muslim/52/10

For the English translation by Muslims, go to:
www.qtafsir.com or http://tafsir.com/default.asp?sid=7&tid=17982

The same story can be found in Tafsir Ibn Kathir, V 7, Page 168, published by
'Tiba publishing company. http://islamport.com/d/1/tfs/1/27/1244.html

According to the hadith, Allah created the earth in six days. However, we just
read in the quote from Sahih Muslim above that He began on Saturday and
finished the job on Friday, totaling seven days of creation. Still, we find the six-
day creation of the earth affirmed by numerous verses in the Qur'an, such as
Sura 7:54, 10:3, 11:7, 25:59, 32:4, 50:38, and 57:4.

Let's examine the account in Qur'an 41:9-12 (Pickthal translation):

9 Say (O Muhammad, unto the idolaters): Disbelieve ye verily in Him Who
created the earth in two Days, and ascribe ye unto Him rivals? He (and none
else) is the Lord of the Worlds.
10 He placed therein firm hills rising above it, and blessed it and measured
therein its sustenance in four Days, alike for (all) who ask;
11 Then turned He to the heaven when it was smoke, and said unto it and unto
the earth: Come both of you, willingly or loth. They said: We come, obedient.
12 Then He ordained them seven heavens in two Days and inspired in each
heaven its mandate; and We decked the nether heaven with lamps, and
rendered it inviolable. That is the measuring of the Mighty, the Knower.

It tells us that Allah created soil in two days; the trees, water, and mountains in
four days; and the skies in two days. If we add the number of days it took Allah to
create the earth, we get a total of eight days, not six. What does that tell us?

The complete account of creation in Sura 41:9-12 clearly contradicts the several verses I mentioned above, which say that creation was completed in six days. It also contradicts the hadith, even though they somewhat match in the order of creation.

Before we finish this topic, Muslims make many claims about the age of the earth, and I heard some of them saying that the Qur'an is more accurate than the Bible when it comes to six (6) days creation because the Qur'an does not give how long these days are. The fact is that Muhammad as always helps us to expose the Muslims false science.

In Sahih AL-Bukhari (Book 59, Hadith 688), "The Prophet of Allah said, 'The time has gotten its **existent looks and shape** which it has now, since Allah created the Heavens and the Earth....'"
It's so clear from Muhammad's words that time at the period of creation is the same as today. Moreover, they expose their false claim that Islam never said the six days of Allah creation is the same as today's days, as you see its exactly the same. By the way, according to science, days that the beginning of the earth were shorter than today and the day is getting longer. See: http://helios.gsfc.nasa.gov/qa_earth.html#earthslow

But on the other hand, Muhammad said one day for Allah is equal to one thousand year of our reckoning, as we see in Qur'an 22:47; "Nevertheless, they ask thee to quicken on the Punishment! However, Allah will not fail in His Promise. Verily, a Day in the sight of your Lord is same as a thousand years of your reckoning."

So if time never changed, it was in the same shape as Muhammad said in the hadith above ("The time has gotten its **existent looks and shape** which it has now, since Allah created the Heavens and the Earth..."), Allah named them the same names we have, and he called them days, this proves more contradictions in Muhammad's words and his god's words. So one of them is telling a lie which means ultimately they are both telling a lie, because the first one (Muhammad) told a lie so all that Allah said is also a lie because it was told by a false witness (Muhamad).

Muslims claim

The Exploration Of Space

Humanity's exploration of space was accelerated with the Soviet satellite Sputnik on 4 October 1957, which carried aloft the first man to ever leave Earth's atmosphere: Soviet cosmonaut Yuri Gagarin. On 20 July 1969, the American astronaut Neil Armstrong became the first human being ever to set foot on the Moon.

In fact, the Qur'an revealed that such developments and achievements would one day be realized. For instance, Allah draws our attention to this in the following verse:

O company of jinn and human beings. If you are able to pierce through the confines of the heavens and Earth, pierce through them. You will not pierce through, except with a clear authority. (Qur'an, 55:33)

The Arabic word sultan, translated here as "a clear authority," has other meanings as well: force, power, sovereignty, dominion, law, path, permission, give leave, justify, and proof.

Careful examination reveals that the above verse emphasizes that humanity will be able to move into the depths of Earth and sky, but only with a superior power. In all likelihood, this superior power is the superior technology employed in the twentieth century, for it enabled scientists to achieve this great feat.

THE SPUTNIK RISING TO THE SKIES

The first ever satellite, "Sputnik 1," was launched in 1957. Verse 19:57 (Surah Maryam, 57) of the Qur'an amazingly refers to rising and being raised.

We raised him up to a high place. (Surah Maryam, 57)

The term "Refa'nahu" in this verse is derived from the verb "refea," meaning "to raise, lift up or elevate." On the other hand, the word "aliyyen" in the verse bears the meaning of "high, very high" in addition to "great." When we consider this verse by itself, therefore, it means "being raised into a very high place." In that respect, verse 19:57 may be a reference to the launching into the sky of the spacecraft Sputnik 1 in 1957. (Allah knows the truth.)

Verse 19:57 of the Qur'an speaks of "raising to a high place."
"Sputnik 1," the first unmanned satellite, was launched in 1957.

My Answer
Allegation: Allah Predicts the Humans Going to Space

This is what Mr Harun said: "Verse 19:57 of the Qur'an speaks of 'raising to a high place.' 'Sputnik 1,' the first unmanned satellite, was launched in 1957." He equates verse 19:57 to the year 1957.
I cannot believe how desperate the Muslims are to find a proof for Islam. This is my answer.

1. The verse speaks about a Muslim prophet named Idres. It says, "**we raised him.**" **This is in the past, not the future.** It was already done to him. Is Idres the prophet a satellite?

2. The verse speaking about raising him refers to a human, but Sputnik 1 was a satellite! So is Allah calling him a satellite? Well I say to Mr. Harun, does your Allah think a satellite is a man?

Yusuf Ali translation, Qur'an 19:56, 57:

56 Also mention in the Book the case of Idris: He was a man of truth (and sincerity), (and) a prophet:
57 And We raised him to a lofty station.

تفسير Tanwîr Al-Miqbâs min Tafsîr Ibn 'Abbâs:

$$\{ \text{وَرَفَعْنَاهُ مَكَاناً عَلِيّاً} \}$$

(And We raised him to high Location) in Paradise.

• The words 'we raised' appears more than 29 times.

Here's just one example about 'Isa (Jesus) in Qur'an 3:55:

Behold! Allah said: "Oh 'Isa! I will take thee and raise thee to myself…

Using Mr. Harun's logic, does that mean that a satellite also went up into space

219

in the year 355 = verse 3:55? And notice this verse would make more sense for Mr.Harun to choose because it's about the future.

- If indeed verse 19:57 is about the first time something goes out from the earth, shouldn't this match with verse 3:55 in the Qur'an speaking about raising up?

- What's even funnier is to ask, did Allah send these verses in this order anyway? Was it not Uthman, the Successor of Muhammad, who by his order made it this way? Or Allah?

- Uthman significantly changed the order of the verses. As an example, the first verse that was given to Muhammad was, "Read." But it's in Qur'an, chapter 96! The verses of the Qur'an were never given numbers by Allah, or even Muhammad!

- This then, must be proof that Uthman is god.

- On the top of this, the Qur'an is contradicting itself, because it says that the bad one can't go out of the zone of the earth, as in chapter 55:33.

As long as we are speaking about chapter 55, I would like to add another claim Harun Yahya made about the moon in this chapter.

Qur'an 55:33, 35, Mohsin Khan Translation:

> 33 O assembly of jinn and men! If you have power to pass beyond the zones of the heavens and the earth, then pass beyond (them)! But you will never be able to pass them, except with authority (from Allah)!
> 35 There will be sent, against you both, heat of fire and flash of brass, and ye will not escape.

As we see in the same chapter, Allah is saying you cannot escape or break free from His fire against both (humans and jinn). Then how can we go out of the earth's atmosphere if Allah will shoot us? Didn't he say in very clear words that you **cannot escape**?

I must not forget to mention that the ones who went to the sky were those who would certainly be considered by Islam as the bad ones, because they are the infidels (Russian, American and Chinese). This is not a miracle as Muslims try to make it look like. It's the opposite, and a big mistake. Humans have already been able to go out to the space, in spite of Allah's claim. And now these who follow him compound the error by making false claims.

Harun's claim

The Voyage To The Moon

Qur'an, 84:18-20:

> And [I swear by] the moon when it is full, you will mount up stage by stage! What is the matter with them, that they have no faith?

After referring to the moon, the above verses then say that people will mount up stage by stage. The term tarkabunna comes from the verb rakiba, (to mount, walk on a path, follow, embark upon, set about, participate, or rule). In the light of these meanings, it is very likely that the expression "you will mount up stage by stage" refers to a vehicle to be boarded.

Indeed, the astronauts' spacecraft pass through each layer of the atmosphere one by one, and then begin to pass through the Moon's gravitational field. Thus, the Moon is reached by moving through individual layers. In addition, the swearing by the Moon in Sura Al-Inshiqaq 18 further strengthens this emphasis, meaning that the verse **may well be a sign** that humanity will travel to the Moon. (Allah knows best.)

(The end of Muslim claim)

My Answer

Let us read from the end of the claim and you will see how false it is. Mr. Harun said; **"may well be a sign,"** so this is the science of Maybe!

Harun used this translation of these verses to make it fit his claim, but even his translation proves that the claim is false. How?

Qur'an 84:19 reads: **"you will mount up stage by stage."**

Let us read the Al-Jalalayn Tafsir (interpretation) of this verse:

لَتَرْكَبُنَّ طَبَقًا عَنْ طَبَقٍ {19}
لَتَرْكَبُنَّ " أَيّهَا النَّاس أَصْله تَرْكَبُونَنْ حُذِفَتْ نُون الرَّفْع لِتَوَالِي الْأَمْثَال وَالْوَاو لِالْتِقَاء السَّاكِنَيْنِ " طَبَقًا عَنْ طَبَق "
" حَالًا بَعْد حَال , وَهُوَ الْمَوْت ثُمَّ الْحَيَاة وَمَا بَعْدهَا مِنْ أَحْوَال الْقِيَامَة

You shall be reconstructed stage to stage, state after state, namely, death, afterlife, then what comes afterwards of the states at the Resurrection.

⅄ If we study all the interpretations of the Qur'an, they all would say the same as Al-Jalalayn is saying. Where did the Muslims today came up with this claim? It's just a game of deception to mislead those who do not speak Arabic!

First, this is saying "**you** go up state after state." It's about the heaven of Allah in the afterlife. It's a promise to go to heaven. Actually, it's the same as Qur'an 67:3 about the seven heavens, where Muhammad clearly said that the heaven of Allah has seven floors. Read the entire chapter and you will see that Allah is issuing a warning to you. Believe and you go to heaven, but if not, Allah will punish you. This has nothing to do with going to the moon.

All right, for the sake of argument we will agree with Mr. Harun's translation and interpretation, but then we have a big problem if this is about going to the moon. The chapter afterwards is speaking about going to heaven and going to hell. Now we face the situation where Allah is mistaken and Mr. Harun is right!

Now let's look at Qur'an 84:1-20 (Ibn Kathir interpretation):

1 When the heaven is split asunder, (All Muslims agreed this is the day which refers to the Day of Judgment),
2 and hears to and surrenders to its Lord when the time is up.
3 And when the earth is spread forth,
4 and has to discharge out all that was inside it and turned out to be empty.
5 And attends to and obeys its Lord, and its obligation to do so.
6 O mankind Verily, you are reconstructing towards your Lord with your records, and actions, a sure coming back, and you will meet your Lord with your deeds.
7 He (the good one) surely will receive worry-free judgment.
8 And will go back to his family in great pleasure (he will be living again in heaven with his family).
9 Except whosoever is given his Record behind his back,
10 he will supplicate for his destruction,
11 and he shall penetrate a blazing fire, and burn in it.
12 Verily, he was living in great pleasure with his family.
13 Verily, he thought that he would certainly not come back to Allah.
14 So I pledge by the afterglow sunset;
15 and by the night and whatever it inside in its darkness,
16 and by the moon when it is at the full.
17 You shall certainly travel from a period to a period.
18 And whenever the Qur'an is proclaimed to them. They do not bow down.
19 So reveal to them a miserable suffering.
20 Guard those who believe and do righteous good deeds, for them will be a

reward, grateful rewards.

See for yourselves in the Ibn Kathir interpretation on the Muslims site
(Ibn Kathir interpretation): www.qtafsir.com

I think the **proclaimed** miracle is exposed, because the chapter explains itself clearly. It's about something that **will occur on the judgment day**. **Harun Yahya made it appear as if it's about going to the moon**. Believe me, I am one hundred percent sure that they know the real meaning of the chapter, but Muslims believe the war with the truth can be won by subjecting science and mixing it with a false presentation of Islam. This is why I called my book <u>The Great Deception</u>.

As long we are addressing the heaven of Allah, I will explain more about it, and at the same time, show more strong evidence answering this claim.

Allah Created the Heaven as Floors; Seven Heavens

Qur'an 15:44:

سورة الحجر , Al-Hijr, 44
لَهَا سَبْعَةُ أَبْوَابٍ لِّكُلِّ بَابٍ مِّنْهُمْ جُزْءٌ مَّقْسُومٌ

To it (heaven) are seven gates: for each of those gates is divided for each by his sin.

This means the better Muslims will go to a higher floor and a better heaven. For example, Al-Qaida might be on the 6th floor, which is closer to Allah than the normal Muslims. We can find the same thing in Qur'an 23:86:

سورة المؤمنون , Al-Mumenon, 86

He is the lord of the seven heavens.

1. So, there are seven divisions (levels), but all are still heaven.

2. In Qur'an 67:3 we see the word (طباقا, tbaqan):

سورة الملك, Al-Mulk, 3
الَّذِي خَلَقَ سَبْعَ سَمَاوَاتٍ طِبَاقًا

3. It's he who created the heaven as <u>floors</u>; seven heavens, one above another.

4. Note here the word translated "floors" is 'tbaqan in Arabic.

5. The verse is not about going to the moon, because Allah's heaven is not in the moon.

6. Read again (Sahih Al-Bukhari, Book 58, Hadith 227) about Muhammad's going to up to seven heavens on page 225 and you will see each one of these heavens has a gate with guards.

7. Some might ask, "Why did Allah swear by the moon in the verses (Qur'an 84:18-20) translated by Mr. Harun Yahya?"

8. The answer is, Allah swears when the moon is full you will go to heaven after life. Read carefully. Allah did not just swear by the moon, but he swore by the *full moon*, as it says in Harun's translation. Not mine. **"And [I swear by] the moon when it is full, you will mount up stage by stage."**

9. This will happen when the moon is full for the after-life, because as long as Allah said, "when the moon is full," this means we cannot go there unless the moon is full! Is it about a one time trip and never again, or about the dates when these trips start? For sure, Muslims will say it's about the start!

10. Allah says that this happens when the moon is full. That makes the claim funny.

11. When did the first spaceship go to the moon?

12. We can find this from NASA: Luna 1, Launch Date: 1959-01-02. Luna 1 was the first spacecraft to reach the moon, and the first of a series of Soviet automatic interplanetary stations successfully launched in the direction of the moon.

13. The date of January 2, 1959, when this spaceship launched, was **not** a full moon! The date of the full moon for January 1959 was *__January 24th__*.

14. As we see, the prediction of Allah about going to space (as they claim), does not match the date of the full moon!

15. Muslims might say, "Oh, it's about man going there, not a spaceship!" Fine. Let us see when the first man went to the: moon. Here is the link http://nssdc.gsfc.nasa.gov/planetary/lunar/apollo11info.html

Apollo 11
Launched: 16 July 1969 UT 13:32:00 (09:32:00 a.m. EDT)
Landed on Moon: 20 July, 1969 UT 20:17:40 (04:17:40 p.m. EDT)
Landing Site: Mare Tranquillitatis - Sea of Tranquility (0.67 N, 23.47 E)
Returned to Earth: 24 July 1969 UT 16:50:35 (12:50:35 p.m. EDT)
Neil A. Armstrong, commander
Michael Collins, command module pilot
Edwin E. Aldrin, Jr., lunar module pilot

As we see, it: "Landed on Moon: 20 July," but the date of the full moon for
July 1969 was July 29th. You can use a moon calculator yourself at:
http://www.webmagician.com/cgi-bin/fullmoon_calc.pl

- Allah lost again. On the top of this, the Muslim's claim contradicts the
  Qur'an as you'll see in Qur'an 55:33:

O company of jinn and humans, if you are able to pass through the Range of
the heavens and the earth, then pass through! You will not pass through except
with Authority.

We see this affirmed by Islamic scholars in interpretation, Tafsir Al-Jalalayn, for
Qur'an 55:33:

Tafsir Al-Jalalayn تفسير

{ يَمَعْشَرَ ٱلْجِنّ وَٱلإِنسِ إِنِ ٱسْتَطَعْتُمْ أَن تَنفُذُواْ مِنْ أَقْطَارِ ٱلسَّمَٰوَٰتِ وَٱلأَرْضِ فَٱنفُذُواْ لاَ
تَنفُذُونَ إلاَّ بِسُلْطَانٍ}

O kind of jinn and humans, if you are able to pass through, to exit from the
range, of the heavens and the earth, then pass through! A challenge made by
Allah to challenge them as to what they (jinn and humans) are incapable of
doing. You will not pass through except with authority, and power, and you have
no power to do such a thing.

As usual, the ones who beat Allah were the infidels. Right up to the present
time, Muslims can't make an airplane. The only thing they have is the flying
carpet that was mentioned in the Qur'an.
It's so clear that Muhammad and his false god never thought about man ever
going to the moon. If we could ask Muhammad to rewrite his Qur'an, he would
add the name of Neil A. Armstrong as a prophet of Allah!

Muslims claim

I will present two claims at the same time sense they both address the same topic.

(Following are the Muslim claims.)

The Earth's Geoid Shape & The Helio-Centric System

After that He smoothed out the earth. (Qur'an, 79:30)

In the above verse, the word "daha" is used in the original Arabic. It, translated as "smoothed out," comes from the word "dahv," meaning "to spread." Although the word "dahv" also means to cover or to set out, the meaning of the verb is more than just a prosaic setting out, since it describes setting out in a circle.

The concept of roundness is also present in other words derived from "dahv." For example, the word "dahv" also refers to children dropping a ball into a hole in the ground, games involving throwing stones into holes and games played with walnuts. Words derived from that root are also used for an ostrich making a nest, cleaning stones from where it is about to lie down, the place where it lays its eggs and the egg itself.

Indeed, the Earth is round, in a manner reminiscent of an egg. The slightly flattened spherical shape of the Earth is known as geoid. From that point of view, the use of the word "daha" contains important information about the shape that Allah has given to the Earth. For hundreds of years, people imagined the Earth to be completely flat and only learned the truth thanks to technology. Yet, this fact was revealed in the Qur'an fourteen centuries ago.

(The second claim which is connected with this one is)

The Helio-Centric System

He created the heavens and the Earth with truth. He wraps the night around the day and wraps the day around the night, and has made the Sun and Moon subservient, each one running for a specified term. Is He not indeed the

Almighty, the Endlessly Forgiving? (Sura az-Zumar, 5)

In the above verse the movement of the Earth is described by the word "yukawwiru," which comes from root verb "takwir," meaning "to cover up a spherical body," in the way that the rotation of the Earth gives rise to night and day, like the winding of a turban. In addition to the spherical shape of the Earth the word is also the most accurate expression of its movement around the Sun. Because of the Earth's spherical shape and its movement around the Sun, the Sun always illuminates one side of the Earth while the other is in darkness. The side in shadow is shrouded by the darkness of night, to be replaced by the brightness of day when the Sun rises. The positions of the Sun and Earth are revealed as follows in Sura Ya Sin:

> And the Sun runs to its resting place. That is the decree of the Almighty, the All-Knowing. And We have decreed set phases for the Moon, until it ends up looking like an old palm spathe. It is not for the Sun to overtake the Moon nor for the night to outstrip the day; each one is swimming in a sphere. (Sura Ya Sin, 38-40)

The movements of the Sun and Moon in verse 40 of Sura Ya Sin are described by the Arabic word "yasbahoona," meaning "flowing, passing or swimming." This word refers to an action performed by someone on their own. Someone acting according to this verb continues to perform it alone, with no intervention from anyone else. The above verses may therefore be referring to the Sun's independent movement in the universe, independent of any other celestial body. (Allah knows the truth.) It is impossible for us to see or follow the movement of the Sun with our own eyes. It is only possible to determine that movement using special technological equipment. As stated in verse 39 of Sura Ya Sin, in addition to rotating around its own axis once every 26 days, the Sun also moves through its own course.

The verse also reports that the Sun is not allowed to "overtake the Moon," and the Qur'an thus states that the Sun and Moon do not revolve around the same body, as astronomers put it. At the same time, the verse makes it clear that there is no connection between the motion responsible for night and day and the movement of the Sun and Moon. (Allah knows the truth.)

Until the 16th century it was thought that the Earth was the center of the universe. This view is known as the "geocentric model," from the Greek words geo (earth) and centron (center). This belief was questioned by the famous astronomer Nicolaus Copernicus in 1543 in his book De Revolutionibus Orbium Coelestium (Of the Revolutions of Heavenly Spheres), in which he suggested that the Earth and the other planets revolve around the Sun. But as a result of observations using a telescope performed by Galileo Galilei in 1610, it was scientifically established that the Earth revolves around the Sun. Since it had hitherto been thought that the Sun revolved around the Earth, most scholars of the time rejected Copernicus' theory. The famous astronomer Johannes Kepler's views setting out the movements of the planets confirmed the heliocentric model in the 16th and 17th centuries. In this model, whose name comes from the words Helios (Sun) and centron (center), the Sun is the center of the universe, rather than the Earth. Other heavenly bodies also revolve around the Sun. Yet this was all revealed 1400 years ago in the Qur'an.

By saying that the Earth was the center of the universe, the ancient Greek astronomer Ptolemy was responsible for the geocentric idea of the universe that prevailed for hundreds of years. For that reason, at the time of the revelation of the Qur'an, nobody knew that the Earth-centered model that accounted for the formation of day and night in terms of the movement of the Sun was incorrect. On the contrary, all the stars and planets were regarded as revolving around the Earth. Despite these prevalent errors of the time, the Qur'an contains many expressions that agree with the scientific facts regarding day and night:

> By the Sun and its morning brightness, and the moon when it follows it, and the day when it displays it, and the night when it conceals it (Sura ash-Shams, 1-4)

As set out in the above verse, day, the brightness of the Sun, is the result of the movement of the Earth. It is not the movement of the Sun that is responsible for night and day. In other words, the Sun is immobile in terms of night and day. The information in the Qur'an refutes the thesis that the Earth is fixed while the Sun revolves around it. The Qur'an is clearly descended from the presence of our Lord, He Who is unfettered by space and time. As science and technology advance more and more examples of the compatibility between the Qur'an and science are coming to light. This is set out in another verse from the Qur'an:

> There is instruction in their stories for people of intelligence. This is not a narration which has been invented but confirmation of all that came before, a clarification of everything, and a guidance and a mercy for people who believe. (Sura Yusuf, 111)

The above manuscript (seen on website) dating from the 1750s shows the geocentric (Earth-centered) model of the universe. It took many years for this to be abandoned and replaced by the heliocentric model.

My Answer
The Roundness of the Earth

First, is the earth round in the Qur'an? We can take a look at the verse that Mr. Harun gave, Qur'an 36(Ya Sin):38-40.

> And the <u>sun runs to its resting place</u>. That is the decree of the Almighty, the All-Knowing. And We have <u>decreed set phases for the moon</u>, until it ends up looking like an old palm spathe. It is not for the Sun to overtake the moon nor for the night to outstrip the day; each one is swimming in a sphere.

In the above verse is a clear mistake: the sun goes and rests to sleep. To understand more of what this verse really means, we should continue to read this verse (Qur'an, 39:5):

خَلَقَ السَّمَاوَاتِ وَالْأَرْضَ بِالْحَقِّ يُكَوِّرُ اللَّيْلَ عَلَى النَّهَارِ وَيُكَوِّرُ النَّهَارَ عَلَى اللَّيْلِ وَسَخَّرَ الشَّمْسَ وَالْقَمَرَ كُلٌّ يَجْرِي لِأَجَلٍ مُسَمًّى أَلَا هُوَ الْعَزِيزُ الْغَفَّارُ

> It's He who created the heavens and the earth by truth. He wraps the night up on the day, and wraps the day up on the night...

Muslims claim this is mentioning the roundness of the earth. Look at the word "wraps" that Muslims choose to use in most of their translations. If the night and the day do not physically exist, how can we wrap them? The word wrap can be only used for something that has a physical size. On top of that, one of them has to be bigger than the other to be able to wrap one with the other. I'm not sure if you understand my point yet. As an example, if you have to wrap a 7" x 7" box, you will need wrapping paper at least 8" x 8". It's not paint that is brushed on!

Also, even if the day and night were both physical objects, they do not have the same length! They can't wrap each other. To prove that Allah thought that the day was a physical object, as well as the night, let us read the flowing.

The Day and The Night are Physically Created

In Sahih Al-Bukhari, Book 59, Hadith 688:

> The Prophet of Allah said, The time has gotten its <u>existent pattern shape</u> which it has, since Allah created the heavens and the earth...

Maybe the words of Muhammad are not enough. Let's see what the Qur'an says about this (Qur'an 21:33):

It's He, it is Who created <u>the night</u> and <u>the day</u>, and <u>the sun</u> and <u>the moon</u>. <u>They float</u>, each of it, in an orbit.

When the Muslims speak about this verse they try to ignore the fact which is clearly shown:

1. **Does the night need to be created?** Who created the night? Allah start by creating the night, but the night is nothing but the darkness, and darkness is the **absence of light**. So as long as Allah did create the day after the night, does this then lead us to conclude that there was light before the day was created? Moreover, what is the creation of day except light creation? This contradicts the verse itself and that is a clear scientific mistake.

2. But in the Bible we see that coming perfectly clear. God did not create darkness, because it does not need to be created, it is just the **absence of light** as we see in Genesis 1:1-5:

3. *¹ In the beginning God created the heaven and the earth. ² And the earth was without form, and void; <u>and darkness was upon the face of the deep</u>. And the Spirit of God moved upon the face of the waters. ³ And God said, Let there be light: and there was light. ⁴ And God saw the light, that it was good: and God divided the light from the darkness. ⁵ And God called the light Day, and the darkness he called Night. And the evening and the morning were the first day.*

4. Notice in Qur'an 21:33 above, I underlined the words, "**they float**." Read it again please, and notice that the words "<u>they float</u>" refer to all four **(night + day + sun + moon).**

5. This means Allah is saying that the **day** and the **night**, <u>they float</u> too! This clearly means that Allah thinks that the day and the night were created as physical objects. The same as the sun and the moon! It's a clear mistake and misunderstanding of how the day and the night occur.

Mohsin Khan translation, Qur'an 16:12 reads as follows:

And He has subjected to you the night and the day, and the sun and the moon; and the stars are subjected by His Command. Surely, in this are proofs for people who understand.

If the day and the night do not physically exist, how can they be subjected? This is how easy it is to expose these false claims.

The Sun and the Moon.
The Day and The Night.
They don't catch each other.

Qur'an 36:40:

It's not allowed for the sun to catch up with the moon, nor may the night come before the day, and each of them is in an orbit, swimming.

- ⚓ Notice in here, the night (darkness) cannot come before the day, when the fact is that the night is the original stage and the day always come afterwards.

- ⚓ If this is really true, does the word "catch" mean physically? We can take it in two possible ways.

   A.   The sun, moon, day, and night can't catch each other **physically.**

This would mean that the day and the night do not catch each other, physically. This proves the verse we spoke about just prior to this one, which shows the Qur'an is wrong again. If it means not physically happening, then Allah must have forgotten something called the eclipse! Maybe he does not know that during an eclipse, day and night meet in the same time! Do not forget that the eclipse involves all four of the names (day + night + moon + sun).

   B.   If the words "*they float*" do not relate to physically catching, this means that the sun and the moon are not physically created, and that would be wrong again.

1.   Either way, there is a big mistake there. Did Allah know about the eclipse? It's so clear what the Allah of Islam (Muhammad) is saying. He is making it up, that the day and night can't catch each other. In the case of the eclipse, this is not true.

2.   Remember, when the eclipse occurs, the day and the night do catch up with one another.

3.   This is what prompted Muhammad to say in Qur'an 54:1 that the judgment day was near. The moon had split and he was ignorant about the fact that it was an eclipse. He thought the moon was splitting and made a false prophecy that the judgment day had started, thinking that the eclipse was a sign of it.

Saying this, we have proven a few more of the Qur'an's mistakes including the false story of splitting of the moon.

In the book of Fateh Al-Bari, Page 105-106:

"Prophet Muhammad mentions the word eclipse 4000 times or more."

ابْنِ عَبَّاسٍ قَالَ : خَسَفَتِ الشَّمْسُ عَلَى عَهْدِ رَسُولِ اللَّهِ ـ صَلَّى اللَّهُ عَلَيْهِ وَسَلَّمَ ـ فَذَكَرَ قِصَّةَ صَلاَةِ الْخُسُوفِ ثُمَّ خُطْبَةِ النَّبِيِّ ـ صَلَّى اللَّهُ عَلَيْهِ وَسَلَّمَ ـ وَفِيهَا الْقَدْرُ الْمَذْكُورُ هُنَا ، فَمَنْ أَرَادَ عَدَّ الأَحَادِيثِ الَّتِي اشْتَمَلَ عَلَيْهَا الْكِتَابُ يَظُنُّ أَنَّ هَذَا الْحَدِيثَ حَدِيثَانِ أَوْ أَكْثَرُ لاِخْتِلاَفِ الاِبْتِدَاءِ ، وَقَدْ وَقَعَ فِي ذَلِكَ مَنْ حَكَى أَنَّ عِدَّتَهُ بِغَيْرِ تَكْرَارٍ أَرْبَعَةُ آلاَفٍ أَوْ نَحْوُهَا

However, Allah is mentioned in the Qur'an 2,690 times, so without a doubt an eclipse is very scary to Muhammad. So scary that he even ordered Muslims to free slaves if they could to get Allah to stop his anger.

It is documented that the Prophet of Allah ordered the public to free slaves during the solar eclipse. (Sahih Al-Bukhari, Book 18, Hadith 163)

Additionally, Muhammad used to offer a special prayer during the eclipse, because he thought it was something God was doing as a warning, as we see in Sahih Al-Bukhari, Book 18, Hadith 158:

Allah's messenger said: "The sun and the moon are two miracles among the miracles of Allah, and they do not eclipse on account of the death of someone but Allah frightens His followers with them."

Again in Sahih Muslim, Book 4, Hadith 1985 we read:

Ibn 'Abas reported that the messenger of Allah did practice eclipse prayer. He recited the Qur'an and stood up, and then bowed. Then he again recited Qur'an on the other hand, he bowed. Afterwards the prophet did again recite and again bowed and again recited and again bowed, and then after that he was exhausted, and the second bowing, and it was as you see.

Why did the science of Muhammad make him pray when he saw the eclipse? It's very clear that Muhammad had no idea what the eclipse was about.
I wonder why Muslims do not do what Muhammad did during the eclipse. I would like to see Muslims practice this now. They now know it's based on ignorance, so they do not do that prayer anymore!

Muslims keep going on with their claims opening more and more eyes to the mistakes in the Qur'an, as we will see in the coming claim.

Muslims Claim

The Relativity of Time

Today, the relativity of time is a proven scientific fact. This was revealed by Einstein's theory of relativity during the early part of the 20th century. Until then, it was not known that time was relative, nor that it could change according to the circumstances. Yet, the renowned scientist Albert Einstein proved this fact by discovering the theory of relativity. He showed that time is dependent on mass and velocity.

However, the Qur'an had already included information about time's being relative! Some verses about the subject read:

> ... A day with your Lord is equivalent to a thousand years in the way you count. (Qur'an, 22:47)

> He directs the whole affair from heaven to earth. Then it will again ascend to Him on a Day whose length is a thousand years by the way you measure. (Qur'an, 32:5)

> The angels and the Spirit ascend to Him in a day whose length is fifty thousand years. (Qur'an, 70:4)

The fact that the relativity of time is so definitely mentioned in the Qur'an, which began to be revealed in 610, is more evidence that it is a divine book.

My Answer

If this proves the relativity of time, then it means Christians had it long before Islam existed. Based on this Muslim's own words, he cannot claim any credit for their book as long as this same information existed in many other older books. It's so clear Muhammad is copying the Bible again. Muslims claim that the Qur'an speaks of the relativity of time. Is that true? Here's their proof.

Qur'an 22:47:

وَيَسْتَعْجِلُونَكَ بِالْعَذَابِ وَلَن يُخْلِفَ اللَّهُ وَعْدَهُ ۚ وَإِنَّ يَوْمًا عِندَ رَبِّكَ كَأَلْفِ سَنَةٍ مِّمَّا تَعُدُّونَ

A day for your Lord is equivalent to a thousand years in the way you count.

After this, the Muslims will post for you references of science telling how time can be changed, or it's relativity to location. I am not in any way opposing what science says about this subject, but rather pointing out that Muslims, in their effort to prove that their verses are scientific, put themselves in a bad trap by making their verses non-metaphorical. Let's see how:

- First of all, here are the verses Muhammad stole from the Bible:

  2 Peter 3:8: But, beloved, be not ignorant of this one thing, that one day is with the Lord as a thousand years, and a thousand years as one day.

  Psalm 90:4: For a thousand years in thy sight [are but] as yesterday when it is past, and [as] a watch in the night.

  The Bible is just telling us how time means nothing for God. It does not really mean that God has a day and his day is equal to anything specific, for he is our Lord and outside of time. As the Bible says in John 1:1-3:

  1 In the beginning was the Word, and the Word was with God, and the Word was God. 2 The same was in the beginning with God. 3 All things were made by him; and without him was not any thing made that was made.
  The words, "in the beginning," are the same words as in Genesis 1:1:

  In the beginning God created the heaven and the earth.

  "The beginning" here represents the beginning of time for His creation. Before that point, there was no time. Even science agrees about that. Let me make it clear, our Lord is outside of our time frame, and he is not controlled by it. The start of time began for his creation, not for him.

- If a day for Allah is equal to 1,000 years of our time not in a metaphorical meaning, it means Allah is inside the time system.

- As long as Muslims are counting time for Allah, this would mean that Allah did not exist before the beginning of time, because he is controlled by time. Remember, I am not the one who took this out of metaphorical context, it was the Muslims. They cannot change their claim any more.

- Following their own premise that their verses relate to the relativity of time, which is based on location change and physical existence of objects, this means that Allah *physically* existed and exists in a location, and time is moving very slowly for him there!

- This would also mean that Allah is under the law of physics. Does this provide evidence that he is a creature rather than creator?

- This would also mean that if we moved Allah to the earth he would grow old faster and he would have the same 24 hour day as we have. He would then be part of the experiment and time would be changeable for him too!

- As long as Allah has normal days, and has nothing to do with our day, it means he also has a month and a year. He is not outside the bounds of the beginning of time.

- The Bible says in Genesis 1:1:

- *In the beginning God created the heaven and the earth.*

- It was the beginning of time, as we know it, when God created everything; but he existed before that beginning. By contrast, we see that Allah is within the bounds of time. He cannot be the creator! Moreover, if Allah understood physics, why are the Muslims trying to fool us by saying that the words *"seven heavens"* mean seven layers of the atmosphere?

- If the *seven heavens* are layers of the atmosphere, does science say that time changes if we go to the atmosphere? Then it's clear, Muslim's lied when they said the seven heavens were the atmosphere!

I will now further expose the liars by reading their prophet's words about how time works for Allah.

Clear Errors in Muhammad's Teaching.

How Many End of Nights Are There on Earth?

Qur'an 11:114 And establish regular prayers at the two ends of the day and at the approaches of the night:

Sahih Al Bukhari, The Book of the Night Prayer, No.1081, Narrated Abu Huraira (or read Sahih Al-Bukhari, Book 21, Hadith 246):

عَنْ أَبِي هُرَيْرَةَ رَضِيَ الله عَنْهُ، أَنَّ رَسُولَ اللَّهِ صَلَّى اللَّهُ عَلَيْهِ وَسَلَّمَ قَالَ: "يَنْزِلُ رَبُّنَا تَبَارَكَ وَتَعَالَى كُلَّ لَيْلَةٍ إِلَى السَّمَاءِ الدُّنْيَا حِينَ يَبْقَى ثُلُثُ اللَّيْلِ الْآخِرُ فَيَقُولُ مَنْ يَدْعُونِي فَأَسْتَجِيبَ لَهُ مَنْ يَسْأَلُنِي فَأُعْطِيَهُ مَنْ يَسْتَغْفِرُنِي فَأَغْفِرَ لَهُ". أخرجه ، 1/521) ، ومسلم (1094 ، رقم 1/384) ، والبخاري (10318 ، رقم 2/487) ، وأحمد (498 ، رقم 1/214مالك) وقال : حسن صحيح . وابن ماجه 3498 ، رقم 5/526) ، والترمذي (1315 ، رقم 2/34) وأبو داود (758رقم) 1366) ، رقم 1/435)

This hadith is verified accurate. As I show with the Arabic text above, it is correct according to:

- Al-Bukari 1/384, No. 1094 (Arabic)
- Musnad Ahamd 2/487, No. 10318 (Arabic)
- Sahih Muslim 1/521, No. 758 (Arabic)
- Abu Dawood 2/34, No. 1315 (Arabic)
- Al-Tirm'zi 5/526, No. 3498 (Arabic)
- Ibn Majah 1/435, No. 1366 (Arabic)

English translation of Sahih Al-Bukhari, Book 21, Hadith 246:

> Muhammad said, "Our Lord, the great, comes every night down to the lowest Heaven to us by the last third period of the night, calling, 'anyone in attendance to call upon Me, so that I may answer to his intercession? Is there any attendance anyone to ask Me, so that I may grant him what he is asking me for? Is there anyone struggling for My forgiveness, so that I may forgive him?'"

1. How many last "third of the nights" are on this earth? You can ask any Muslim and he will tell you that each city in the world has its own five times of prayer!
2. How will Allah come down at the third part of the night?
3. To make it clear let's say the third part of the night is at 2 a.m. in the morning.
4. How many 2 a.m.s do we have around the world? There are 24 Time Zones.
5. So Allah must come down 24 times a day!
6. Where does Allah come down? To the lowest heaven.
7. This would mean that Allah never left to come down! He is always down during the last third part of the night. He would have to be down around the clock!
8. The only answer for this story is that the earth, according to Islam, has only one time set and one last third of the night (i.e. the earth must be flat).
9. Allah Time is not different from our time anymore, because remember, Muslims believe in "the relativity of time," and Allah is so close to us because he comes down physically.

With that being said, does Allah go inside his creation? We know that Muslims claim that God can't be inside his creation. This claim is normally being presented for one reason, which is to prove that Jesus can't be Allah (God).

As long as Allah cannot be inside his creation, then how is Allah moving inside and between his seven heavens, as we saw in the past hadith?

Again, let's read Bukhari, <u>The Book of Night Prayer</u>, Hadith 1081:

> Narrated Abu Huraira: Muhammad said, "Our Lord, the great, <u>comes every night down</u> to the <u>lowest Heaven to us</u> by the <u>last third period of the night</u>, calling, 'anyone in attendance to call upon Me, so that I may answer to his intercession? Is there any attendance anyone to ask Me, so that I may grant him what he is
>
> asking me for? Is there anyone struggling for My forgiveness, so that I may forgive him?'"

1. Allah is moving between two locations; A and B.
2. A is the seventh (highest) heaven.
3. B is the lowest heaven.
4. He has to go through the seven heavens and then stops in the lowest heaven.
5. This means that the Muslim claim about God not being inside of his creation is absolutely false. How he is going between the seven heavens if he is not inside them

Allah's Shape

Allah is Inside His Leg or Outside His leg!

Qur'an 68:42: The day when Allah uncovers his shin...

I have asked Muslims many times if Allah has a shin or a leg. They answer, "Yes, he does, but his leg is not like ours."

1. As long as Allah has a leg, hand, face and fingers, this is a physical attribute. **Not a metaphor**.
2. I ask, "Is Allah inside his body?" If the answer is "Yes," this means Allah can be inside of his creation. If the answer is "No, Allah is not inside his body," then how can we call it his body if he is outside of it?
3. Does that mean Allah and his body are separated? That would make Allah two persons. Allah the spirit and Allah the body. Each of them is Allah!
4. If Allah is one, and the two (the body and the spirit) are one, why can't the Muslims accept the three (the Father, Son, and Holy Spirit) as one?
5. It's fine for them to accept Allah having a form of a real body, but they cannot accept that God can be in the man of Christ.

The Body of Allah and His Single Likeness

As long as Allah cannot be inside his creation, although I have already proven that this was false, and that he must be inside his leg, hand, fingers and face, in which case we would be multiplying Allah's numbers, I will agree with them for the sake of argument. This would mean:
1. Allah's body cannot be created by Allah for he cannot be inside his creation.
2. There is a Creator who created Allah's body!
3. If Allah's body is not created by anyone, maybe Allah is the big bang itself!

4. Anyway, why does Allah need to have a body?

5. When he says, "I have a leg," regardless of the way it looks or the material it's made from, it's still a leg! Since Allah described it by the word *leg,* then it's a leg. Remember, Allah is the one who named things in this earth according to Qur'an 2:31:

وَعَلَّمَ آدَمَ الْأَسْمَاءَ كُلَّهَا ثُمَّ عَرَضَهُمْ عَلَى الْمَلَائِكَةِ فَقَالَ أَنْبِئُونِي بِأَسْمَاءِ هَؤُلَاءِ إِنْ كُنْتُمْ صَادِقِينَ

And He, Allah, taught Adam the names of all things...

6. As long as these names were made by Allah for the way they are used, this means Allah is calling his body part a leg for the way it is used, regardless of the look. As an example; the leg of a donkey is not the same as the leg of an ant, but both are called a leg because of the functionality, not the look.

Meaning, Allah called it leg because it is used as a leg!

7. Then I have to ask, if Christ cannot be God because he has a body, or legs or hands, and he used them, then why is Allah using his leg to walk with? Isn't this a problem for Muslims?

When Allah moves between the heavens, does he take his leg with him, or does he leave it up there? The leg, face, hand and the finger are tools. They exist for a need. They are physical. Any physical body takes and occupies a space or area. This means:

1. Allah has size, which means he can be measured!

2. If he has size and can be measured, it means he is smaller than something bigger than him, because you cannot be of a physical size without being capable of being contained inside of something else!

3. As long as Allah is not two, but one, yet he is body and spirit; then to be everywhere, he would have to be everywhere with his body! But that is impossible, because if he has size, can be measured and is everywhere, we should be able to see him, feel him, and even touch him.

4. At the same time, if Allah is everywhere and cannot be inside his creation, this means that the Qur'an is wrong about the nature of Allah. Either way, the one who claims he is saying Allah's words as god, is false.

The Chair of Allah Is the Size of The Earth and the Sky

Book of Fateh Al-Bari fe Shareh, Sahih Al-Bukhari, Book of Tawhid (Chapter 112), Page 425:

فتح الباري شرح صحيح البخاري - كِتَاب التَّوْحِيدِ - إنجاز ما وعد به من الثواب وهو لا يخلف الميعاد
عَنْ ابْنِ مَسْعُودٍ قَالَ : بَيْنَ السَّمَاءِ الدُّنْيَا وَالَّتِي تَلِيهَا خَمْسُمِائَةِ عَامٍ ، وَبَيْنَ كُلِّ سَمَاءٍ خَمْسُمِائَةِ عَامٍ ، وَفِي رِوَايَةٍ
وَغِلَظُ كُلِّ سَمَاءٍ مَسِيرَةُ خَمْسِمِائَةِ عَامٍ ، وَبَيْنَ السَّابِعَةِ وَبَيْنَ الْكُرْسِيِّ خَمْسِمِائَةِ عَامٍ ، وَبَيْنَ الْكُرْسِيِّ وَبَيْنَ الْمَاءِ
خَمْسُمِائَةِ عَامٍ ، وَالْعَرْشُ فَوْقَ الْمَاءِ وَاللَّهُ فَوْقَ الْعَرْشِ وَلَا يَخْفَى عَلَيْهِ شَيْءٌ مِنْ أَعْمَالِكُمْ

Ibn Mas'ud (preeminent Qur'an collector) said: The distance between the lower sky and the sky in the top of it is 500 years, same distance between each until the seventh sky. The thickness of each sky is 500 years, as well as between the seventh sky and Allah's chair is 500 years. Moreover, between Allah's chair and the water is 500 years, and nothing is hiding of what you do to Allah.

According to the above, we can imagine the following image:

Allah's Chair is round & around us.

WATER

The Earth

7 Sky Space

500 X 7=3500 year

3500 years Speed of Donkey? Or maybe Camel

As long as Allah's chair is around us, We are inside Allah's chair.
If the chair must be round, this means Allah himself is also round. And as long we are in the chair of Allah, then we are sharing Allah's chair with him! This is indeed getting messed up.

But we know Muhammad's was speaking about a flat earth. Also we have many chapters in the Qur'an saying that with clear words, like in Qur'an 79:30, which reads: And after that, he flattened the earth. Considering this fact, this is how the image will appear:

Seven skies x 500 years distance each = after 3500 years we will be out of space, then the water!

Now bear with me and we will do some calculations to see what this all means.

In Muhammad's time they measured distance by days using camels.
A camel's maximum speed is **40 mph**.

Distance between Allah's throne and water is 500 years, therefore:

$$Time = \frac{Distance}{Speed} \qquad Time \times Speed = Distance$$

- 3500 years distance + 500 years to the top of the water = 4000 years and you will be visiting Allah.
- A camel's max speed of 40 mph x 24 hrs = 960 miles per day.
- The Muslim lunar calendar is **354** days **x 960** miles per day = 339.840 miles we can travel per year.
- 339.840 miles x 4000 years = 1,359,360,000 miles to Allah.
- The distance between the sun and the earth is about 92,935,710 miles.
- 1,359,360,000 miles to Allah / 92,935,710 (sun to earth) = 15
- The distance between Allah and us is 15 times the distance to the sun.

Now let's consider the distance to the nearest galaxy. According to Frank H. Shu in The Physical Universe: An Introduction to Astronomy (California: University Science Books, 1982: 291):
"The modern value for this distance is 2 million light years away, which places it

well outside the confines of the Milky Way."
That is **two (2) million light years** to the Andromeda Galaxy.

- ⅄ One year light speed is equal to 5,865,696,000,000 miles.
- ⅄ This means that from earth to **Andromeda** is;
2 light years x 5,865,696,000,000 miles.
- ⅄ Again this proves **Islam is false** with evidence from science.

Is it really 500 years between each sky as we just read, or is it seventy-one, seventy-two, **or** even seventy-three years?
Sunan Abu-Dawood, Book 40, Hadith 4705:

Allah's messenger said: "...Do you know the distance between heaven and earth?" They answered, "No. We do not know." After that He said: "The distance between them and the earth, is seventy-one, seventy-two, or seventy-three years. The heaven, which is above it, is at a similar distance going on up to the time of, he counted all the seven heavens. Above the seventh heavens, over there is a sea, the distance between whose top and bottom is like that between one heaven and the nearest Above that eight mountain goats, the distance between whose hoofs and haunches are like the distance between one heaven and the next, then Allah, the great, is above that."

- ⅄ Notice here Muhammad changed the numbers and he is using OR!
- ⅄ Did Allah say to him "Or?" Allah himself is also unsure!
- ⅄ **"Above the seventh heavens, over there is a sea."**

Sahih Al-Bukhari, Book 60, Hadith 236:

The Prophet, furthermore, said, "By Him in Whose Hand my soul is, the distance between every two gateways of Paradise is like the distance between Mecca and Busra (city in southern Syria)."

Notice this is clearly a false statement, because the distance between Mecca and Busra in Syria is just 821 miles (1,321 Km). As a result, there is one of two options:

- The roadway to heaven's gates is on flat ground.

- On the other hand, the roadway to heaven's gates is going up to the next sky, as often indicated by Muhammad who frequently expressed the words "**above therefore the direction is going up.**"

- So how will it take 500 years as he said in Al-Tirmidhi,   Hadith 5735, or seventy-three years as he said in Suana   Abu   Dawood,

Book 40, Hadith 4705?

$$Time = \frac{Distance}{Speed} \qquad Time \times Speed = Distance$$

The distance between sky gates is 821 miles. Therefore;

- ⚔ 821 miles x 7 sky gates = 5,747 miles is the total height.
- ⚔ The distance between the earth and moon is 238,854 miles (384,399 km).
- ⚔ 238,854 miles / 5747 miles = 41
- ⚔ So the moon is 41 times further than Allah!
- ⚔ So the moon is way behind Allah.
- ⚔ So can we be with Allah by traveling a relatively short distance?
- ⚔ 821 miles / 500 years = 1.642 miles **per year** speed of travel to cover that distance in one year.
- ⚔ At that rate, Muslims will move about 136 meters a day!
- ⚔ A three-toed sloth moves much faster than Muslims!

We have learned the distance, and once we had the distance we could calculate the location. Now the location is a physical place and in that physical place, Allah is sitting on the top of his chair, which is a physical item.

Qur'an chapter 2:255:

...The Chair of Allah in the width and height of the skies and earth.

Does Allah have a physical Chair? Let's ask Muhammad!

Sahih Al-Bukhari, Book 58, Hadith 227:

...Then Gabriel took me up to Sudrat Al-Muntaha (big tree in heaven, tree of Allah). Behold its fruits are the same as the ones in the clay jugs of Hajar (a location in Arabia not far away from Mecca) and its leaves look so big as the ears of elephants. Gabriel said, "This is Sudrat Al-Muntaha (Allah's Tree)." And there were four running rivers, two rivers were underneath and invisible and two rivers were visible. I questioned Gabriel, "What are these two rivers?" He answered, "The invisible rivers. They are two rivers in Paradise, and the visible rivers are the Nile and the Euphrates." After that Al-Bait Al-Ma'mor (the House of Allah)...

Sahih Al-Bukhari Book 52, Hadith 48:

...The Prophet as well revealed, "Above it (the paradise) there is the throne of Allah, and from it run out the rivers of Paradise."

The word above means a specific place and is the opposite of under. This hadith gives Allah an exact location. This is physical and not metaphorical, because the Qur'an says in another verse that the throne of Allah will be carried by eight angels (caribou).

Qur'an 69:17:

وَالْمَلَكُ عَلَى أَرْجَائِهَا وَيَحْمِلُ عَرْشَ رَبِّكَ فَوْقَهُمْ يَوْمَئِذٍ ثَمَانِيَةٌ

And the angels will be around the sides of throne, and eight [caribou] will that day, carry the Throne of thy Lord above them.

الجزء الثالث والعشرون تفسير الطبري » تفسير سورة الحاقة « القول في تأويل قوله تعالى "وانشقت 583ص:
السماء فهي يومئذ واهية

حُدِّثْتُ عَن الْحُسَيْن , قَالَ : سَمِعْت أَبَا مُعَاذ يَقُول : ثنا عُبَيْد , قَالَ : سَمِعْت الضَّحَّاك يَقُول فِي قَوْله : { - 26970
وَيَحْمِل عَرْش رَبّك فَوْقهمْ يَوْمَئِذ ثَمَانِيَة } قَالَ بَعْضهمْ : ثَمَانِيَة صُفُوف لَا يَعْلَم عِدَّتهنَّ إِلَّا اللَّه . وَقَالَ بَعْضهمْ : ثَمَانِيَة
أَمْلَاك عَلَى خَلْق الْوَعْلَة

Tafsir Al-Tabari interpretation, V 23, Page 583, Hadith 26970:

Narrated by Al-Husain, he said, "I have been informed by Abu-Ma'az from 'Aubid from Al-'Dahak he said: 'His mighty saying {in that day the throne of your Lord will be carried by eight angels and Allah above them}, some of them said its eight rows of angels, they got the look of caribou."

Tafsir Al-Jalalayn interpretation of Qur'an 69:17:

In addition to the angels will be all on the sides of its borders, theborders of the heavens, and above the angels that have been spoken of, on that day eight who are from the best of Allah's angels, will carry the Throne of your Lord Allah,and He will be on it.

To prove that Allah's throne physically exists, we can read this:

تفسير جامع البيان في تفسير القرآن/ الطبري
حدثنا عبّاد بن يعقوب الأسدي، قال: ثنا ابن فضيل، عن ليث، عن مـجاهد، فـي قـوله: { عَسَى أَنْ يَبْعَثَكَ رَبُّكَ
مَقَامًا مَحْمُودا } قال: يُجْلِسه معه علـى عرشه.

Tafesser Jami' Al-Bayian by Al-Tabari, V2, Page 24:

Reported from Mujahed about the Lord saying, "May the Lord give him the location of rank;" he said, "Allah will make the Prophet sit with him over his throne."

Sahih Al-Bukhari,Book 54, Hadith 414:

"...At the same time, as I was with the Prophet, some people from Bani Tamim approached. Therefore, they said: "We ask you what the beginning of this universe was." The Prophet said, "There was Allah and nothing else before Him and His Throne was above the water, and He afterwards created the Heavens and the Earth and wrote everything in the Book..."

Book of Fath UL-Bari. explanation of Al-Bukhari, The Beginning of Creation, page 334

رواية الباب أصرح في العدم ، وفيه دلالة على أنه لم يكن شيء غيره لا الماء ولا العرش ولا غيرهما ، لأن
كل ذلك غير الله تعالى " ويكون قبله " وكان عرشه على الماء " معناه أنه خلق الماء سابقا ثم خلق العرش
على الماء ، وقد وقع في قصة نافع بن زيد الحميري بلفظ كان عرشه على الماء ثم خلق القلم فقال : اكتب ما
هو كائن ، ثم خلق السموات والأرض وما فيهن فصرح بترتيب المخلوقات بعد الماء والعرش

There was nothing but Allah, no water or throne or anything else, and his throne was over the water, meaning that he did create first the water then he created the throne over the water, the meaning of this is that he created the water first then he created the throne then he created the pen! And he said to the pen write everything being then he created the sky and the earth!

Based on Muhammad's words and Bukhari's explanation, we arrive at this conclusion:

1. The Throne of Allah was created, so it is a physical throne.
2. As long as Allah is above a physically existing throne, he is physical. Therefore, he is above and he has a body, as I have proven.
3. Sitting or standing above it does not matter, but it's very clear now that he is contained in the chair. When Allah is above it, whatever its size, it's still a chair and has size. As I showed you, eight angels will carry it, which would mean that the throne of the god of Islam is bigger than Allah himself.
4. Since Allah is above the throne and not under the throne, he is not everywhere as Muslims claim.
5. He is above it. Not on the right side, left side, back or front, but above the throne.

6. Then I have to ask, why does Allah need a physical throne? The answer:

7. Because he is physical too. Since Allah *IS* a physical god, Muslims have no claim or fair reasoning for rejecting God in the person of Jesus Christ.

8. All of Islam is nothing but false claims based on a false god, and false accusations against Christianity are made just to fight His name, the only Lord, The Christ.

9. Based on the hadith I presented, there are some points that cannot be ignored. Read it again, please, if you have a short memory. You will find a very interesting line of words in the explanation of the book of Fath-Ul-Bari, Page 334:

He created the water first, then he created the throne, then he created the pen! And he said to the pen write everything being, then he created the sky and the earth!

What do we get from this explanation?

1. First to be created was water.

2. Shouldn't Allah have created space for water first? Where would the water be located?

3. As long as Allah did not need to create a space for the water, and the first thing he created was water, there had to have been space created by someone else. Not Allah, for sure. The hadith says in clear words what was first, but this shouldn't be created first without having a space or something to contain it.

4. This would mean that there must be another creator who created things, like the space, before Allah created anything.

5. Since Allah created the water first and then the chair, or the throne, was the next in his chain of creation, then I have to ask: Why did Allah create water first? He needed it?

6. Why did he create the throne? He likes fantasy? Is he lonely? He was tired? Possibly to show his power? But to whom?

7. If Allah created the water first, this means a story in the Qur'an is false, for the Qur'an says in 79:31:

He brought out its (the earth's) water and substances.

8. The verse says so clearly that the earth was without water and then Allah created water over it.

9. This proves that Muhammad is a story maker and not a prophet, because he is creating tales which are contradicting his Allah's words. If Allah really ever spoke at all.

Then We Go to the Creating of the Pen

Fath Ul-Bari fe Sharh, Sahih Al-Bukhari, Page 334:

He created the water first then he created the throne then he created the pen! And he said to the pen write everything being, then he created the sky and the earth!

*   Why did Allah create the pen?

*   Why does he need a pen?

*   Why does he need to write anything?

*   Is this pen a living creature, which has brain? How can the pen write everything, when he, the pen, has been told nothing yet! In what way do Allah and the pen understand each other? Did Allah order the pen to write in Arabic? Does the pen speak Arabic? Does this pen make mistakes? On the other hand, is he perfect the same as God! So is Allah going to do the proofreading?

*   Muhammad is the best of Allah creation as we mention before in the following book titled Al-'Khasa'es Al-Kubra, Beirut, Lebanon, Author Al-Seu'ti, V1, Page 66:

*   The prophet said: "Allah created his creation and chose from them sons of Adam, and from sons of Adam, he chooses the Arab, and from the Arab, he chose Mudar (tribe), and from Mudar, he chose sons of Hasim (clan) and from Hashim, he chose me, finest of the best."

*   But Muhammad is a sinner as in Qur'an 48:2: "Let it be that Allah may forgive your sin [Muhammad], of the previous and those to follow; fulfill His favors to thee; and lead thee to the straight path."

*   Qur'an 40:55: "Be persistent and patient because the Promise of Allah is truthful and ask forgiveness for your sin and glorify the Praises of, thy Lord in the nightfall and in the dawn."

- Yusuf Ali translation, Qur'an 94: "¹ Have We not expanded thee thy breast? ² And removed from thee thy burden ³ The which did gall thy back?"

- Qur'an 47:19: "Be aware that there is no god but Allah, and ask for your forgiveness sin and the sin of the men and women who believe; for Allah knows how ye action about and where you go."

- If Muhammad is the best of Allah's creation, and he did sin, which means he was in error, then what about the pen never having erred? That would make Allah's pen better than Muhammad, but this will contradict Muhammad's words about himself. If Muslims accept that the pen is not better than Muhammad and that pen of Allah does error, this means that Allah's manuscript has errors because it's written by the pen which is not perfect.

- Didn't Muhammad notice that he forgot that Allah created the pen and then ordered it to write? My question is, write on what?

- If there was nothing created but water and a chair, where did the pen write Allah's order?

- We, as humans, write for one of two reasons:

A. To transfer knowledge and ideas to others and other generations.
B. To keep information from being lost because of memory loss.

- Did Allah think he would die, so he wanted to write his orders?

- Also, since no one can see the book that Allah wrote, was the only reader Allah?

- In that case, I ask, why did Allah read back his orders?

- It must be that he is short on memory, and afraid of dementia and memory loss.

- The Muslims say Allah protected the book from corruption, which is why he wrote his words and orders.

- Does that mean the book of "Isa" (Jesus) is preserved?

- Why doesn't he send us a copy?

- This would mean the gospel has never been corrupted, because it is up there with Allah, therefore Muhammad lied.

- Why didn't Muhammad ask his god for an extra copy of Christ's book?

- Maybe Allah's copy is corrupted too?

- As long as Allah wrote everything before he created the universe, would that mean he wrote his destiny for us on this earth?

Muslims Claim

THE TRUTH OF DESTINY

Qur'an, 76:30:

But you will not will unless Allah wills. Allah is All-Knowing, All-Wise.

As a result of experiments he performed in 1973, Professor Benjamin Libet, a neurophysiologist at the University of California, revealed that all our decisions and choices are set out beforehand, and that consciousness only comes into play half a second after everything has been determined. This is interpreted by other neurophysiologists as meaning that we actually live in the past and that our consciousness **is like a monitor which shows us everything half a second later.**

Therefore, none of the experiences we perceive are in real time, but are delayed by up to half a second from the real events themselves. Libet carried out his research by making use of the fact that brain surgery can be performed without the use of narcosis, in other words while the subject is fully conscious. Libet stimulated the brains of his subjects with small electrical currents, and when they experienced a perception that their hands had been touched the subjects said that they had felt that "touch" almost half a second before. As a result of his measurements, Libet arrived at the following conclusion: All perceptions are normally transmitted to the brain. As these are subconsciously evaluated and interpreted, the ego is unaware of anything. The information that appears before our minds, in other words that we can be aware of, is transmitted to the cortex, the seat of consciousness, after a certain delay.
The conclusion from this may be summarized as follows: The decision to move a muscle takes place before that decision reaches the consciousness. There is always a delay between a neurological or perceptual process and our becoming aware of the thought, feeling, perception or movement it represents. To put it another way, we can only be aware of a decision after that decision has been taken.

In Professor Libet's experiments, this delay varies between 350 and 500 milliseconds, although the conclusion that emerges is in no way dependent upon those figures. Because, according to Libet, whatever the length of that delay-it makes no difference whether it is great or small, whether it lasts an hour or a microsecond-our material life is always in the past. This demonstrates that every thought, emotion, perception or movement happens before reaching our consciousness, and that proves that the future is entirely outside our control.

In other experiments, Professor Libet left the choice of when the subjects would move their fingers up to them. The brains of the subjects were monitored at the moment their fingers moved, and it was observed that the relevant brain cells went into action before the subjects actually took the decision. To put it another way, the command "do!" reaches the individual, and the brain is readied to perform the action; the individual only becomes aware of this half a second later. He or she does not take a decision to act and then performs that action, but rather performs an action predetermined for him or her. Yet, the brain makes an adjustment, removing any recognition that the individual is actually living in the past. For that reason, at the moment we refer to as "now," we are actually living something determined in the past. As already discussed, these studies manifest the fact that everything happens by the will of Allah, as revealed in Sura Al-Insan 30.

My Answer

We should make a point clear, we as Christians live and will be judged by our free will choices. But, as everything around us, we are under the law of nature or universal laws which are made by God.

However, can we stay alive forever by our freewill only? The answer is no, it's by **God's will**. Then what we will talk about is not the universal laws like death and getting older, but rather about our actions in our lives as being good or bad, obedient to law or disobedient, faithful to others or unfaithful.

I am glad that Harun Yahya made this claim, because now Muslims can no longer say that they do not believe Muslims are **slaves to fate**. Before I talk about fate in Islam, let's see what the study is really about. Before we address that issue however, we should know that determinism is a family of theories, not a scientific fact. Webster's Dictionary says it's "the doctrine that all events, including human choices and decisions, have sufficient causes." Even this theory has nothing to do with Harun's claim.

If we read the study of Dr. Benjamin Libet, we will notice how Muslims quote from it in their own way. The study is talking about a claim or theory, not a fact, in which the mind is ahead of the brain. Another way to say it is there are two operating systems; the self-conscious (nonphysical) mind and the brain.

In addition, there are things you can make happen as an experiment, but that does not mean that this is how things happen normally.

I quote from Mr. Harun; "Libet stimulated the brains of his subjects with small electrical currents, and when they experienced a perception that their **hands had** been touched the subjects said that **they had felt that 'touch'** almost half a second before."

Therefore, this is about reaction not action. It has nothing to do with destiny. When they try to fool us with the half-second delay, it's not about us making a big physical move. In fact, it's not about moving at all, it's about feeling, it's about things happening inside our system. Like skin might act before the brain signal arrives to the skin, not that the hand will move or maybe strike, or any such thing!
You can go and read more by visiting this link about Dr. Libet's study: www.learningmethods.com

You can read this article; "Free will is not an illusion," Dr. Raymond Tallis, September 13, 2007: http://www.spiked-online.com

You can also go search for the topic yourself if you like philosophers and philosophy. Here is a name you can search for and read some of his study: Ted Honderich (born 30 January 1933) is a Canadian-born British philosopher, Grote Professor Emeritus of the Philosophy of Mind and Logic, University College London and Visiting Professor, University of Bath. I quote from his words:

> "The principle of free will has religious, ethical, and scientific implications. For example, in the religious realm, free will implies that an omnipotent divinity does not assert its power."

But anyway, let us assume that the biggest philosopher in the world said that you have no free will. And he bases that on moving a finger! I can prove him wrong in just a few moments. Right now, I get the idea to go and buy a ticket to fly to London and I reserve my plane for a year from now! I have not flown yet. What will the half-second of Dr. Benjamin Libet do?

I might receive a call from someone, like a family member, saying that he is ill one second before I take my airplane. I would then make a decision whether or not to cancel my trip! Then all this determinism does not exist. It's simply a joke.

You do not just wake up in the morning and do what you are destined to do. Al-Qaida trained for about six years to commit the 9/11 atrocity, it was not half-second decision. They had to make extensive plans, get visas, go to flight school, get tickets, board the plane and then take action.

Destiny would allow a person to justify every act by saying it was not me, it was Allah's destiny. What is the point of Allah sending laws if it is predetermined that you will not obey them? If they truly believe in destiny, which Muslims accept as fact, then why do they punish a person for not praying, or for leaving Islam? It is outside of their control. Remember, Mr. Harun said, and I quote:

"This demonstrates that every thought, emotion, perception or movement happens before reaching our consciousness, and that proves that the future is entirely outside our control."

1. Notice this is not what Dr. Libet said, this is Mr Harun's discovery!
2. Then why is a Muslim rewarded when it's not even his choice?
3. Why will I convert to Islam if it is Allah who will convert me anyway? It's his choice, not mine?
4. Why will a Christian be sent to hell, as Islam teaches, because it's Allah's will?
5. If it's all based on destiny, why should a Muslim pray? The answers are already predestined decisions.

I call this the injustice and madness of the Islamic religion. According to this belief of destiny, Allah is behind all the crimes in the world including rape, theft, hate, killing and child abuse. Then they say Allah is god! That makes him a control maniac. This is saying that Allah is playing a game of chess by using us as his victims. What an ugly, selfish god he is!

The Destiny in Islam

Allah decides who becomes a Muslim and who does not.

The Qur'an makes it clear that Allah made the infidels into unbelievers or that he causes people to become unbelievers.

Sahih Al-Bukhari, Book 55, Hadith 549:

صحيح البخاري - كِتَاب بَدْءِ الْخَلْقِ - فأتيت بطست من ذهب ملئ حكمة وإيمانا فشق من النحر إلى مراق

البطن ثم غسل البطن بماء زمزم

حَدَّثَنَا الْحَسَنُ بْنُ الرَّبِيعِ حَدَّثَنَا أَبُو الْأَحْوَصِ عَنْ الْأَعْمَشِ عَنْ زَيْدِ بْنِ وَهْبٍ قَالَ عَبْدُ اللَّهِ حَدَّثَنَا رَسُولُ اللَّهِ 3036
ـ أَحَدَكُمْ يُجْمَعُ خَلْقُهُ فِي بَطْنِ أُمِّهِ أَرْبَعِينَ1175صَلَّى اللَّهُ عَلَيْهِ وَسَلَّمَ وَهُوَ الصَّادِقُ الْمَصْدُوقُ قَالَ إِنَّ «- ص
يَوْمًا ثُمَّ يَكُونُ عَلَقَةً مِثْلَ ذَلِكَ ثُمَّ يَكُونُ مُضْغَةً مِثْلَ ذَلِكَ ثُمَّ يَبْعَثُ اللَّهُ مَلَكًا فَيُؤْمَرُ بِأَرْبَعِ كَلِمَاتٍ وَيُقَالُ لَهُ اكْتُبْ
عَمَلَهُ وَرِزْقَهُ وَأَجَلَهُ وَشَقِيٌّ أَوْ سَعِيدٌ ثُمَّ يُنْفَخُ فِيهِ الرُّوحُ فَإِنَّ الرَّجُلَ مِنْكُمْ لَيَعْمَلُ حَتَّى مَا يَكُونُ بَيْنَهُ وَبَيْنَ الْجَنَّةِ إِلَّا
ذِرَاعٌ فَيَسْبِقُ عَلَيْهِ كِتَابُهُ فَيَعْمَلُ بِعَمَلِ أَهْلِ النَّارِ وَيَعْمَلُ حَتَّى مَا يَكُونُ بَيْنَهُ وَبَيْنَ النَّارِ إِلَّا ذِرَاعٌ فَيَسْبِقُ عَلَيْهِ
الْكِتَابُ فَيَعْمَلُ بِعَمَلِ أَهْلِ الْجَنَّةِ

Allah's Messenger said: "As about the issue of your creation, of each one of you are placid in the womb of his mother (as a sperm) for the first **forty days**, and after that he comes to be a clot, and then you **will be a clot for the coming forty days**, and after that will be transformed to a piece of meat for an another forty days. Afterwards Allah sends an angel, and he will be ordered by four words, to write, four destinies; he writes his (the baby's) deeds, time of his death, means of his subsistence and whether he will be miserable (infidel) or blessed in a religious meaning. Afterwards, it will be breathed the soul into his body. So a man will do the deeds of people of heaven and only the distance of an arm is between him and the heaven, then what has been written by the angel supersedes, and so he starts doing deeds of the people of hell fire and enters hell fire. Identical a person may do deeds and work of hell fire subsequently the deeds which are written to him by the angels will be in command to surpass, so he will change to do the work of the people of paradise, so he enters paradise.

⅄ I think this is a clear explanation, made by Muhammad himself, showing that what is written concerning you is what will take effect over what you do all your life. No matter how bad or how decent you were as a person, at the end it's what is written for you that will be the final design, not your bad or good deeds. This is one madness of this belief. Who would trust Allah after reading this? Where is the justice?

⅄ What is the benefit of praying, giving to charity or doing good, when the order of Allah is to kill the Christian, Hindu, Buddhist and the Jew? At the end it is not what you do, it is what Allah likes.

Qur'an 6:148 (Usama Dakdok translation):

سَيَقُولُ الَّذِينَ أَشْرَكُوا لَوْ شَاءَ اللَّهُ مَا أَشْرَكْنَا وَلَا آبَاؤُنَا وَلَا حَرَّمْنَا مِنْ شَيْءٍ ۚ كَذَلِكَ كَذَّبَ الَّذِينَ مِنْ قَبْلِهِمْ حَتَّى ذَاقُوا
بَأْسَنَا ۚ قُلْ هَلْ عِندَكُم مِّنْ عِلْمٍ فَتُخْرِجُوهُ لَنَا ۖ إِن تَتَّبِعُونَ إِلَّا الظَّنَّ وَإِنْ أَنتُمْ إِلَّا تَخْرُصُونَ

Those who are polytheistic will say, "If Allah willed, we did not become polytheists nor our fathers, nor were we forbidden anything." Likewise those who came before them lied until they had tasted our severity. Say, "Do you have any knowledge that you bring it out to us? You only follow but the conjecture, and you only lie."

So according to this verse, the people who believed in many gods—the polytheists—were saying that it was Allah who made them and their fathers polytheistic, and they were accused of lying. However, the following verse in Qur'an 6:107 (Usama Dakdok translation) says exactly the opposite:

وَلَوْ شَاءَ اللَّهُ مَا أَشْرَكُوا ۗ وَمَا جَعَلْنَاكَ عَلَيْهِمْ حَفِيظًا ۗ وَمَا أَنتَ عَلَيْهِم بِوَكِيلٍ

And if Allah willed they would not become polytheists. And we have not made you a keeper over them, and you are not a guardian over them.

I'm sure this is kind of shocking to you. How can this be from God? In Qur'an 4:82, Allah himself said that if this book was not from Him, you should find a lot of contradictions. The contradictions keep going in the same chapter. Qur'an 6:111 (Usama Dakdok translation):

وَلَوْ أَنَّنَا نَزَّلْنَا إِلَيْهِمُ الْمَلَائِكَةَ وَكَلَّمَهُمُ الْمَوْتَىٰ وَحَشَرْنَا عَلَيْهِمْ كُلَّ شَيْءٍ قُبُلًا مَّا كَانُوا لِيُؤْمِنُوا إِلَّا أَن يَشَاءَ اللَّهُ وَلَـٰكِنَّ أَكْثَرَهُمْ يَجْهَلُونَ

And if we had sent down the angels to them and the dead had spoken to them and we had gathered everything before them, <u>they were not to believe, except if Allah wills</u>, but most of them are ignorant.

Qur'an 6:125 (Usama Dakdok translation):

فَمَن يُرِدِ اللَّهُ أَن يَهْدِيَهُ يَشْرَحْ صَدْرَهُ لِلْإِسْلَامِ ۖ وَمَن يُرِدْ أَن يُضِلَّهُ يَجْعَلْ صَدْرَهُ ضَيِّقًا حَرَجًا كَأَنَّمَا يَصَّعَّدُ فِي السَّمَاءِ ۚ كَذَٰلِكَ يَجْعَلُ اللَّهُ الرِّجْسَ عَلَى الَّذِينَ لَا يُؤْمِنُونَ, Al-Anaam, 125) (سورة الأنعام

So whomever Allah desires to guide, he opens his chest to Islam, and whomever he desires to mislead, he will make his chest extremely narrow as though he is only ascending to the heaven. Likewise Allah made the uncleanness on those who do not believe.

Qur'an 4:88:

What do you want from the hypocrites? Allah damned them for what <u>their hands did. Do you want to guide those whom Allah misguided</u>? There is no guidance for those whom Allah deceived, and you will not find a way for them.

Look at this: "Allah damned them for what their hands did. Do you want to guide those whom Allah misguided?" How can Allah say he damned the hypocrites for their deeds when he admits that he was the one who misguided them in the first place? Notice that Allah contradicts himself in one breath.

Furthermore, Allah gets angry with Muhammad for trying to guide the hypocrites. So what is Muhammad's job? Allah does not allow him to guide those who are misguided, which means Muhammad has no business being a prophet. He has no authority from Allah to call back those who become unbelievers. Allah made it clear Muhammad cannot find a way to save them, because it was Allah himself who rejected them.

An even more important question is, why did Allah refuse to give Muhammad the authority to guide people to the truth? It is because it was against Allah's plan, and we know this because it angered him that Muhammad tried to reverse Allah's rejection of the hypocrites.

The idea that Islam, the Qur'an, and Muhammad are sent to people to guide them to salvation is false and meaningless. Once Allah decides that you are not worthy to become a Muslim, your chance of salvation is zero.

In the coming verses, I will show you how this book is made by an unbalanced, mad man. He did not hear his own words.

Qur'an 81:28-29:

> 28 To whomsoever of you wanted to walk in the correct direction (to be Muslim).
> 29 And ye will not, unless it be the desire of Allah, the Lord of the two worlds (human and jinn).

Therefore, this verse is saying it's up to you to be Muslim or not. That is good, and smart, but in the very next verse Allah said the opposite!

This god is out of his mind. **Is it up to us or up to him**? If it's up to him, why did he say in the previous verse it was up to us? In simple words, Allah is saying it is up to Allah, you idiot. It does not matter what you would like it to be!

Who Made Satan an Enemy? It is Allah.

In this coming reading, you will notice that even Satan is a victim of Allah's **destiny**. Qur'an 43:36 (Muhammad Pickthal translation):

> And he whose sight is dim to the remembrance of the Beneficent, We assign unto him a devil who becometh his comrade;

Allah is making a clear threat, that if you do not pray to him and worship him, he will assign Satan for you. However, did you notice exactly what that means? It means that before that point (Allah sending his Satan against you), you didn't have Satan in your life! This means you are a good guy. If you have Satan in your life already, why would he send him to you? If you are wrong already, and you do not worship Allah, then what more can Satan do? As a result, Satan will be against you. This would mean that he would try to change you from leaving Allah to the acceptance of Allah. He would make you do worse for the benefit of whom? Mankind, maybe! Actually, this means Allah saying, "My Satan is my ambassador, and my best tool to drive you to me." Wouldn't this make Allah, Satan himself, and maybe the king of devils?

Qur'an 6:112 (Usama Dakdok translation):

وَكَذَلِكَ جَعَلْنَا لِكُلِّ نَبِيٍّ عَدُوًّا شَيَاطِينَ الْإِنسِ وَالْجِنِّ يُوحِي بَعْضُهُمْ إِلَى بَعْضٍ زُخْرُفَ الْقَوْلِ غُرُورًا ۚ وَلَوْ شَاءَ
رَبُّكَ مَا فَعَلُوهُ ۖ فَذَرْهُمْ وَمَا يَفْتَرُونَ (Ana'am, 112-Al , سورة الأنعام)

And likewise we make for every prophet enemies, satans of human and jinn; they reveal one to another with zukhruf (highly embellished) speech to deceive. And if your lord willed, they would not have done it. So leave them in what they forge.

The following is what we understand from this verse:

- There are two kinds of satans or devils: human and jinn. (Note: Muslims believe in many satans, not just one.)
- It is Allah who made them an enemy to the prophets.
- This means that the created devils are not the evil ones. Allah, who created them, is the evil one. The devils are simply doing the duty which Allah himself sent them to do. This makes them obedient to Allah, and good servants.
- Also, if it were up to them, they could have chosen not to be enemies to the prophets.
- These devils have one job—to say things to deceive by uttering words of zukhruf (highly embellished words of gold).

If Allah carefully chose his beloved prophets, why did he intentionally target them with evil influences?

256

Allah Protects the Prophets

The following verses make Allah's intentions with the prophets more unclear:

Qur'an 15:42 (Usama Dakdok translation):

> Surely my servants, you have no authority over them except those who follow you from the seduced.

Qur'an 16:98-100 (Usama Dakdok translation):

> [98] So when you recite the Qur'an, so seek refuge with Allah from the stoned Satan. [99] Surely he has no authority on those who believed, and they depend on their lord. [100] Surely his authority is only over those who befriend him and those who partner with him.

We will see that Allah and his Prophet Muhammad's words make things so funny. Read this hadith with me from Sahih Al-Bukhari (Al-Bukhari, Book 60, Hadith 260)(Also see Sahih Muslim, Book 033, Hadith 6411):

> Reported Abu Horaira: Allah's Messenger said: "Adam and Moses came together. As a result Moses told Adam, 'You are the person who caused people to live with misery and kicked them out of heaven.' Afterwords Adam replied to Moses, 'You are the one which Allah chose for His message, and whom He favored for Himself, and above and beyond whom He revealed the Torah too.' Moses answered, 'As Yes.' After that Adam said, 'Did you find that written in my destiny before my creation?' Moses said, 'Yes.' So Adam defeated Moses with this reasoning."

In Sahih Al-Bukhari, Book 77, Hadith 611, Adam and Moses are talking again:

> Reported Abu Huraira: Allah's Messenger said: "Adam and Moses debated with each other. Moses said to Adam, 'To You Adam! You are our ancestor who displeased us and fired us out of heaven.' After that, Adam said to Moses, 'You Moses! Allah preferred you, so He talked to you (by his voice, not by an angel), and He wrote in the tablet the Torah, for you with His Hand. Therefore, how do you disapprove me for actions which Allah had written in my destiny forty years earlier to the time of my creation?' So Adam refuted Moses. Adam debunked Moses the Prophet. So Adam was saying again his allegation three times."

Sahih Al-Bukhari, Book 93, Hadith 606:

> Reported Abu Huraira: Allah's Messenger said, that Adam and Moses argued with each other and Moses said, "Your offspring is out of heaven because of You Adam." Adam answered, "You are Moses, whom Allah favored and selected for His

257

message and talked to you. One to one, even so, you blamed me about my wickedness, which had been determined for me even before my creation?" Therefore, Adam overwhelmed Moses, with his reasoning.

- ⚑ Adam did not disobey Allah, but it was Allah's plan for Adam to do every single action Adam did?
- ⚑ Allah planned Adam's destiny forty years before his creation.
- ⚑ Based on this fact, why would anyone be punished for doing what Allah wanted!
- ⚑ Welcome to the stupidity of Islam.

In Qur'an 15:42, Allah tells his servants—the satans—that they do not have power over Allah's good followers, which include the prophets. In Qur'an 16:98-100, the prophets are further assured that they are safe from the evil influences of Satan as long as they stay close to Allah and depend on him for protection.

Allah Cancels His Own Actions

Allah created an enemy (Satan) for each prophet, and the job of Satan is to deceive the prophet (Qur'an 6:112). However, Allah puts himself between Satan and the prophet, and tells Satan that he does not have power over Allah's prophet (Qur'an 15:42). Allah creates enemies with specific duties, but he does not give them any real influence over the prophets. It sounds like Allah created enemies for himself, or he just created Satan so he could say that he is a protector—but the protector of whom and from whom? He is protecting his creation from his own creation.

Allah's Protection is For Damage Control, Not Prevention

If Allah made it so that Satan has no power over Allah's good followers, how was it that Satan was able to put black magic on Muhammad? In Qur'an 53:19-23, Satan was able to make Muhammad recite satanic verses, where he praised the three daughters of Allah. Doesn't that mean that Muhammad is not one of Allah's good followers? If Muhammad is a good follower, why didn't Allah's protection work on him? Allah failed to prevent Satan from overpowering Muhammad. The only thing Allah could do was make corrections.
Qur'an 22:52 (Usama Dakdok translation):

And we did not send before you any messenger or prophet except that when he recites, Satan casts in his recitation, so Allah abrogates what Satan cast. Then Allah fixed his verses. And Allah is knowing, wise.

Either Allah has no real power over Satan, or his promise of protection is a lie.

Allah Does Not Protect

Muhammad is not the only prophet that Allah failed to protect. Allah also failed to protect Abraham from believing that the planets, the moon, and the sun are his "Lord."

- In Qur'an 6:75, Abraham thought that the planets in the sky must be his Lord, because they were **akhbar** (bigger).

- In Qur'an 6:77, Abraham changes his mind when he saw the moon. He thought the moon must be his Lord, because it is **akhbar** or bigger than the planets.

- In Qur'an 6:78, Abraham again changes his mind when he saw the sun rise, and thought that surely this time the sun is his Lord, because it is **akhbar** or bigger than the moon.

Now remember, by calling the planets, the moon, and the sun, "my Lord," Abraham took them as partners of Allah. The fact is that Abraham was committing idolatry, worshiping the moon as a god, in the same way that Muhammad committed idolatry by praising the three daughters of Allah (Qur'an 53:19-20. See the explanation of Ibn Kathir). Also, remember that according to the Qur'an Abraham and Muhammad are both prophets of Allah. As prophets and beloved ones of Allah, why were they not prevented from committing the unforgivable sin of "making partners with Allah?"

According to Qur'an 16:100, Allah tells us that only those who become friends with Satan will fall under Satan's power.

Qur'an 16:100 (Usama Dakdok translation):

> Surely his authority is only over who befriend him and those who partner with him.

Since Abraham and Muhammad fell under Satan's power, they must have befriended Satan, which means they willingly disobeyed Allah's command not to associate him with any partners. However, if they did not willingly disobey Allah's command, it means that they fell into Satan's power because Allah failed to protect them. Whichever explanation you choose, Allah loses to Satan. How can Allah, who created Satan, be so weak against his own creation? This is additional proof that Allah's **Destiny IS FALSE as one important pillar of Islam.**

Allah's Prophets are His Own Enemies

Surely Allah will not forgive partnering with him. On the other hand, **he will forgive whom he wills**.

Qur'an 4:48 (Usama Dakdok translation):

Surely Allah will not forgive partnering (worshipping other gods) with him. But other than this, he will forgive whom he wills. And who partners with Allah, so indeed he forged a great sin.

Qur'an 4:116 (Usama Dakdok translation):

Surely Allah will not forgive the partnering with himself. And he will forgive other than that to whom he wills. And whoever partners with Allah, so indeed have strayed far away astray.

We have established that Muhammad and Abraham committed the ugly sin of "partnering with himself," so based on the two verses, Muhammad and Abraham will not be forgiven. They will end up in Hell, because they are Allah's enemies.

Allah is a False God

Allah created evil beings to be the enemies of his prophets (Qur'an 6:112), but he also promised his prophets that he would protect them

from Satan (Qur'an 15:42 and 16:98-100). Nevertheless, we have seen that Allah is not capable of providing the protection that he promised.

The Qur'an proclaims that Allah is all-powerful, as we see in the following verse. (Qur'an 6:73, Usama Dakdok translation):

And he is who created the heavens and the earth, in the truth and on the day he says, "Be," so it will be. His word is the truth and to him the kingdom..."

If Allah's word is as powerful as the Qur'an claims, why can't he defeat Satan, who is his own creation? Allah should be able to simply say, "Stop," or say any other command to order Satan away from the prophets, and Satan would be defeated very easily, but this is not what happens. Either Allah chooses not to protect his prophets, which makes him a liar; or Allah is not really as powerful as the Qur'an claims, which makes him weak—even weaker than Satan. Again, whichever explanation you choose, you will see that Allah is a false god. The true God is not a liar, and He is truly all-powerful.

We are going to expose more about **Destiny; one of the Six Pillars of Faith** which is taken from Sahih Muslim, Book of Eman, Beirut, Year 1993, V1, Page 37.

"When the prophet was asked about the meaning of faith he said: to believe in Allah and his angels, books, messengers, last day, and to believe in your destiny good or bad."

ولما سئل النبي عن معنى الإيمان قال: {أن تؤمن بالله وملائكته وكتبه ورسله واليوم الآخر, وتؤمن بالقدر خيره وشره}(رواه مسلم والبخاري).

Qur'an 10:22:

It's Allah who drives your way and path in land and sea.

Qur'an 57:22:

{ مَآ أَصَابَ مِن مُّصِيبَةٍ فِي ٱلْأَرْضِ وَلَا فِي أَنفُسِكُمْ إِلَّا فِي كِتَٰبٍ مِّن قَبْلِ أَن نَّبْرَأَهَآ إِنَّ ذَٰلِكَ عَلَى ٱللَّهِ يَسِيرٌ }

No disaster happened on the earth or on yourselves but it's written to yourselves, from before your creation, for Allah this is so easy.

We can also see in Qur'an 18:74, where a prophet named Al-Khadir, killed a boy because he was going to grow up to be an infidel. It was his destiny to be an infidel. We see that explained in the coming hadith.

Every Child Born Muslim Fitra

Sahih Muslim, Book 033, Hadith 6434:

The prophet of Allah said: "The young youth which the prophet Al-Khadir killed was an <u>infidel by his nature</u>, and if he was not killed, he would have been participating in his parents' disobedience and disbelief."

However, this is a big contradiction from what Qur'an 7:172 says:

> Remember when your Lord took out their offspring, from the back bone of the children of Adam, and made them bear witness about themselves by inquiring of them, "Am I not your Lord?" They answered, "Of course, You are our Lord, we bear witness," so do not claim or say on the Day of Judgment, "we were unconscious of this,"

In that verse Allah (Muhammad) claims that all children in the world are conceived to Islam when they are sperm. That means before their birth, even before their fathers are born, and before they say the Sahada (Converting to Islam); even fifty thousand years before Adam was created, as we see in the coming hadith (Sahih Muslim, Book 033, Hadith 6416):

. قدر الله مقادير الخلائق قبل أن يخلق السماوات والأرض بخمسين ألف سنة ، وعرشه على الماء

> Abdullah's bin 'Amero reported: "I heard Allah's apostle speaking: 'Allah ordained the measures' destiny of his creation fifty thousand years before He created the heavens and the earth, as His Throne was on the water.'"

Therefore, Muslims believe in the concept of everyone being born Muslim by nature (Fitra).

So, based on the Hadith and Qur'an 18:74, and I quote Muhammad's words, "The young youth which the prophet Al-Khadir killed was an **infidel by his nature**," this means he was an infidel by birth. Therefore, **fitra** (every baby born as a Muslim) is false by Muhammad's own contradictions.

Sahih Muslim, Book 033, Hadith 6436:

> 'Aisha, the mother of the believers, revealed that Allah's Messenger was appointed to lead the funeral prayer of a child of the Ansar. I ('Aisha) said: "O Allah's Messenger, there is gladness for this child who is a bird from the birds of heaven for he committed no sin nor has he procured the age of committing sin." He said: "'Aisha, take no hazards it may be in other ways because God created for heaven those who are fitted for it at the same time as they were yet in their father's loins and created for hell those who are to go to hell. He created them for hell while they were yet in their father's loins."

The Arabic text of this quote is found in Sahih Muslim, Book of Al-'Qadar, V 4, Page 46, Hadith 2662:

صحيح مسلم ـ كِتَاب الْقَدَر ـ أن الله خلق الجنة وخلق النار فخلق لهذه أهلا ولهذه أهلا

حَدَّثَنَا أَبُو بَكْرِ بْنُ أَبِي شَيْبَةَ حَدَّثَنَا وَكِيعٌ عَنْ طَلْحَةَ بْنِ يَحْيَى عَنْ عَمَّتِهِ عَائِشَةَ بِنْتِ طَلْحَةَ عَنْ عَائِشَةَ أُمِّ الْمُؤْمِنِينَ 2662 قَالَتْ دُعِيَ رَسُولُ اللَّهِ صَلَّى اللَّهُ عَلَيْهِ وَسَلَّمَ إِلَى جَنَازَةِ صَبِيٍّ مِنْ الْأَنْصَارِ فَقُلْتُ يَا رَسُولَ اللَّهِ طُوبَى لِهَذَا عُصْفُورٌ مِنْ عَصَافِيرِ الْجَنَّةِ لَمْ يَعْمَلْ السُّوءَ وَلَمْ يُدْرِكْهُ قَالَ أَوْ غَيْرَ ذَلِكَ يَا عَائِشَةُ إِنَّ اللَّهَ خَلَقَ لِلْجَنَّةِ أَهْلًا خَلَقَهُمْ لَهَا وَهُمْ فِي أَصْلَابِ آبَائِهِمْ وَخَلَقَ لِلنَّارِ أَهْلًا خَلَقَهُمْ لَهَا وَهُمْ فِي أَصْلَابِ آبَائِهِمْ

This is proof that Muhammad's words about Fitra are a lie again. If, as indicated in this quote, each person is born as a Muslim, then this would mean that whoever dies as a child should go to heaven. But Muhammad said it may be in other ways because, "God created for heaven those who are fitted for it at the same time as they were yet in their father's loins and created for hell those who are to go to hell." So its destiny again and one more contradiction in Muhammad's words when he said

every Muslim is born as a Muslim, as in Sahih Muslim, Book 033, Hadith 6426:

> Messenger of Allah said: "No infant is born but by fitra (a Muslim). It is his parents who change him a Jew or a Christian or a Polytheist." A person said: "Allah's Messenger, what is your opinion if they were to die before that (before reaching the age of maturity) when they can differentiate between right and wrong?" He said: "Only Allah. Who apprehends what they would be doing?"

But wait, the boy who was killed in Qur'an 18:74-80 had parents who were good believing Muslims!

Qur'an 18:80:

> The boy, his parents were good Muslims, and "We were afraid that when he grew, he might be unjust and an infidel!"

So it's not parents anymore, as Muhammad said in Sahih Muslim, Book 33, Hadith 6426!

We continue with the topic of Destiny by turning to Fateh Al-Bari Fe Sharih, Sahih Al-Bukhari, Book of 'Qadar (Book of Destiny), Page 497, and Sahih Muslim, Bishare'h Al-Nawai, Page 155:

Allah wrote down the decrees of creation fifty thousand years before He created the heavens and the earth. Then Muhammad said in Bukhari:

فقه الدعوة في صحيح الإمام البخاري ـ القسم الأول الدراسة الدعوية للأحاديث الواردة في موضوع الدراسة ـ الفصل الثاني كتاب الجهاد والسير ـ باب لا يقول فلان شهيد ـ حديث إن الرجل ليعمل عمل أهل الجنة فيما يبدو للناس وهو من أهل النار

أولا : من موضوعات الدعوة : الإيمان بالقدر والعمل بأسباب النجاة : ظهر في هذا الحديث أهمية الإيمان بالقدر ؛ ؛
لأن النبي صلى الله عليه وسلم قال لرجل ظاهره الصلاح والشجاعة في الجهاد : " إنه من أهل النار " وقال :
البخاري الجهاد والسير (2742) ، مسلم الإيمان (112) ، أحمد (332/5). إن الرجل ليعمل عمل أهل الجنة فيما يبدو
للناس وهو من أهل النار ، وإن الرجل ليعمل عمل أهل النار فيما يبدو للناس وهو من أهل الجنة وهذا يدل على أن
الله عز وجل قد قدر المقادير ، فعن علي بن أبي طالب رضي الله عنه عن النبي صلى الله عليه وسلم أنه قال :
البخاري تفسير القرآن (4665) ، مسلم القدر (2647) ، الترمذي تفسير القرآن (3344) ، أبو داود السنة (4694) ،
ابن ماجه المقدمة (78) ، أحمد (129/1). ما منكم من أحد ، ما من نفس منفوسة إلا كتب مكانها من الجنة والنار ،
وإلا قد كتبت شقية أو سعيدة " فقال رجل ؛ يا رسول الله أفلا نتكل على كتابنا وندع العمل ؟ فمن كان منا من أهل
السعادة فسيصير إلى عمل أهل السعادة. وأما من كان منا من أهل الشقاوة فسيصير إلى عمل أهل الشقاوة ؟ قال : "
أما أهل السعادة فييسرون - ص 435 ـ لعمل السعادة ، وأما أهل الشقاوة فييسرون لعمل الشقاوة . ثم ق

In Musnad Ahmad (5/332) and book of Al Turmzi (Tafser Al Qur'an 3344), and book of abu Dawood Al Sunna 4649 and book of Musnad Ahmad 1/129, book of Ibn Maja (the interdiction 78) and in Al-Bukhari book of Jihad and Sair (2742) and Sahih Muslim 112, Muhammad said:

...the man will do the work of people of hell but he will go to heaven! And the man will do the work of heaven but he will go to hell! (Go back to in page 280-281; read Sahih Al-Bukhari, Book 55, Hadith 549)

...and these who do the work of happiness they been controlled (by Allah) to do so, and these who do the work of bad they are controlled (by Allah) to do bad.

This means that Muhammad admitted that work is not the reason for salvation. Is it luck? Maybe Christ!

This proves that all the duties Muhammad ordered Muslims to perform were useless, like:

- Five prayers;
- Fasting the month of Ramadan (28 days of fasting from sunrise to sunset);
- Hajj, or the pilgrimage to Mecca;
- Jihad;
- Praying during the night of power, equivalent of 83 years of prayers;
- Charity to Muslims, from the money they steal from Christians and Jews;
- Hating the infidels.

These are false duties Muhammad created just to keep the Muslims too busy to think about how legitimate Muhammad's teaching is. I can show you how

Muhammad worked out his plan to keep the poor Muslims spending their lives in fear:

⅄   There are 70 rules and prayers to say before they go into the bathroom, or Satan and his wife will play with the Muslim's ass! A Muslim should enter the bathroom with his left leg, and exit with his right leg, and during that he must be saying: "O, Allah I seek your forgiveness". If he does not, Satan will harm his ass. It's also forbidden to urinate while standing.

⅄   The fact that Muslims should not use just any toilet site is because Muhammad forbade them from using any hole. He said if a Muslim urinated or defecated, he would harm the jinn, who lived in the hole!

Sunan Abu Dawood, V1, Page 29, 1993 Printing, Egypt:

حدثنا عبيد الله بن عمر بن ميسرة حدثنا معاذ بن هشام حدثني أبي عن قتادة عن عبد الله بن سرجس أن رسول الله ـصلى الله عليه وسلم- نهى أن يبال في الجحر. قال قالوا لقتادة ما يكره من البول في الجحر قال كان يقال إنها مساكن الجن.
سنن أبي داود (1/29)

"Qatadah said: "The Messenger of Allah forbade us from urination into a hole." "What is disliked about urinating into a hole (asking the prophet)?" The Prophet said, "It is the residence of the jinn."

(The same story can be found in Sarih Al-Siu'ty Le-Sunan Al-Nisa'e, Book of Al-'Tahara, 1986 Printing, Page 34.)

⅄   Rules about how many times to wipe (wipe the ass three times).

⅄   Rules concerning how Muslims eat or enter their house: they have to say the name of Allah and say the prayer. If they don't, Satan will say to himself (Sahih Muslim, Book 023, Hadith 5006):

"Oh, I found a place to stay and eat in!"

⅄   Rules for having sex. They have to say specific words praying to Allah before they start having sex or Satan will wrap himself around the man's penis and will share the man's wife! Because of this, the woman might give birth to Satan's baby.

Sahih Al-Bukhari, Book 4, Hadith 143:

"Ibn 'Abbas reported from the prophet that he said: "When any one of you want to have intercourse with his women, he should say, 'Bismellaah, janibnaa Alshaytan wa janib Al-Shaetan ma raza'qtana (note you have to say it in Arabic or your prayer is not accepted and the protection will not work), by the name of Allah we pray to. Keep the Satan away from us and from what You will bestow upon us from our offspring Allah. After doing that and they had sex, they should have a child, the Satan will never be able to harm him."

⋏   Rules before entering the mosque (Sahih Abu Dawood, #458):

I seek refuge by the face of Allah from Satan...

To see more of these rules that make Muslims scared and worried about everything in their life, and which is going to freeze their brains, visit this Muslim site. You will see how Islam, or a big portion of Islam, is based on fairy tale stories:
http://islamicexorcism.wordpress.com/category/demons-possession-and-exorcism/

1. Muslims will do the work of the people of heaven, but they still end up in hell! This means works will never save the Muslim. It's Allah's established decision and that was made long before the individual is born into this life!

2. Whether I convert to Islam or not, nothing will change!

3. If I rape, kill, steal, lie, etc., it's still Allah's established decision as he wrote in his book in heaven. Possibly from the beginning of time!

4. This destroys Islam from the beginning to the end. There is no point in accepting Islam, or being good or bad.

5. Muslims believe in Islam to go to heaven, but still, doing and practicing Islam is not the way to go there! It's so clear that Muhammad made things up, contradicting himself and his god.

6. This explains why Muhammad said (Sahih Muslim, V4 Descriptions of Judgment Day and Heaven and Hell, Page 2170, Hadith 2816 {Arabic}):

صحيح مسلم » كتاب صفة القيامة والجنة والنار » باب لن يدخل أحد الجنة بعمله بل برحمة الله تعالى
الجزء الرابع 5038 [ص: 2170] 2816 حدثنا محمد بن المثنى حدثنا ابن أبي عدي عن ابن عون عن محمد
عن أبي هريرة قال قال النبي صلى الله عليه وسلم ليس منكم أحد ينجيه عمله قالوا ولا أنت يا رسول الله قال
ولا أنا إلا أن يتغمدني الله منه بمغفرة ورحمة وقال ابن عون بيده هكذا وأشار على رأسه ولا أنا إلا أن
يتغمدني الله منه بمغفرة ورحمة

NONE OF YOU WILL BE GRANTED SALVATION DUE TO HIS DEEDS

English text can be found at Sahih Muslim, Book 39, Hadith 6762;   Sahih Muslim, Book 39, Hadith 6761:

> He (Muhammad) said, "None of you will be granted salvation due to his deeds!" Muslims said to Muhammad, "And even you Prophet?" He said, "Not even I, unless Allah envelops me with His mercy!"

This opens Islam and the Qur'an to new contradictions.

Qur'an 28:54:

أُولَٰئِكَ يُؤْتَوْنَ أَجْرَهُم مَّرَّتَيْنِ بِمَا صَبَرُوا وَيَدْرَءُونَ بِالْحَسَنَةِ السَّيِّئَةَ وَمِمَّا رَزَقْنَاهُمْ يُنفِقُونَ (21)
(54 ,Al-Qasas , سورة القصص)

> Those (Muslims), twice more their reward Allah will give back to them, for that they have been patient, that they parry the wicked deeds with good deeds, since they spend for Islam from the wealth Allah gave them.

This verse is saying that when you do one good deed, Allah will take off two bad sins! This makes you earn your way to heaven, for sure. It's always easier to recover the bad you did. The scales always balance to the side of the Muslim. One good = two bad.

Muhammad said in the Hadith, that no one will earn his salvation by his good deeds! Was he making up a lie in this verse? As long as his bad deeds or good deeds won't make any difference at the end of the day, what will allow a Muslim to enter heaven? Then we see Muhammad making more mistakes, showing his hatred for Christians and Jews, when he said in Tafsir Ibn Kathir, Qur'an 23:10:

«يَجِيءُ يَوْمَ الْقِيَامَةِ نَاسٌ مِنَ الْمُسْلِمِينَ بِذُنُوبٍ أَمْثَالِ الْجِبَالِ،فَيَغْفِرُهَا اللهُ لَهُمْ وَيَضَعُهَا عَلَى الْيَهُودِ وَالنَّصَارَى

> On the Resurrection Day people from the Muslims will come (to Allah) with sins on the heights of mountains. However, afterwards, Allah will forgive them (the Muslims) and put their sin punishment over the sin on the Christians and Jews.

Also in Tafsir Ibn Kathir:

«إِذَا كَانَ يَوْمُ الْقِيَامَةِ دَفَعَ اللهُ لِكُلِّ مُسْلِمٍ يَهُودِيًّا أَوْ نَصْرَانِيًّا، فَيُقَالُ: هَذَا فِكَاكُكَ مِنَ النَّارِ»

Another reference for this is Sahih Muslim, Book of Al-Taubah, Hadith Number 4969 and 2767:

> On the Day of Resurrection, Allah will designate for each Muslim a Jewish fellow or Christian fellow, and it will be said to the Muslims {This is your ransom from the hell Fire}. (Meaning the Christian or the Jewish man will go to hell instead of you as payment (for his sins).)

As you see here, it does not matter what Muslims do. Allah will transfer their sin over to the Christians and Jews. We have to ask ourselves not only how fair Allah is, but won't this open the door for other contradictions in the Qur'an?

Let's look at Qur'an 6:164:

قُلْ أَغَيْرَ اللَّهِ أَبْغِي رَبًّا وَهُوَ رَبُّ كُلِّ شَيْءٍ ۚ وَلَا تَكْسِبُ كُلُّ نَفْسٍ إِلَّا عَلَيْهَا ۚ وَلَا تَزِرُ وَازِرَةٌ وِزْرَ أُخْرَىٰ ۚ ثُمَّ إِلَىٰ رَبِّكُم مَّرْجِعُكُمْ فَيُنَبِّئُكُم بِمَا كُنتُمْ فِيهِ تَخْتَلِفُونَ

(164 ,Al Anaam   سورة الأنعام)

Say (Muhammad): What! Shall I search for a God, another one than Allah? The one He is the Lord of the world; and no soul gains its sins but against itself, and no one will pay for the sin of another; then to your Lord is your return, so He will tell you what you disagreed about.

1. How can he say that every soul will pay for its own sin, not another soul, yet the Christians will pay for the sins of Muslims?
2. Maybe Islam does not count us as souls! How about humans?
3. He did say *every soul*!
4. It's so clear that Muhammad cannot be consistent with his own words.

As long as we have reached this point, let's take a look at the different perspectives on original sin between Christianity and Islam! The Muslims totally reject the doctrine of **original sin**. I will make a short study of this to see if Islam can be consistent in this claim.

First of all, original sin is simply based on the sin of Adam and Eve, which caused mankind to be expelled from paradise (which Christians understand to be the Garden of Eden) and face death and pain.

What about Islam? I mean what was the reason for Adam and Eve going out of paradise? Was it their sin or something else?

Qur'an 2:35-36:

وَقُلْنَا يَا آدَمُ اسْكُنْ أَنتَ وَزَوْجُكَ الْجَنَّةَ وَكُلَا مِنْهَا رَغَدًا حَيْثُ شِئْتُمَا وَلَا تَقْرَبَا هَٰذِهِ الشَّجَرَةَ فَتَكُونَا مِنَ الظَّالِمِينَ

فَأَزَلَّهُمَا الشَّيْطَانُ عَنْهَا فَأَخْرَجَهُمَا مِمَّا كَانَا فِيهِ ۖ وَقُلْنَا اهْبِطُوا بَعْضُكُمْ لِبَعْضٍ عَدُوٌّ ۖ وَلَكُمْ فِي الْأَرْضِ مُسْتَقَرٌّ 36 وَمَتَاعٌ إِلَىٰ حِينٍ

Qur'an Al-Baqara, 35, 36 ,سورة البقرة

35 We said: "Oh Adam! Live you and thy wife in the paradise; and eat of the enjoyable things therein as you wish; but approach not this tree, or ye will be from the unjust."

36 Then Satan made them humiliated going out of the paradise, from the happiness they had. We said: "Get ye down, all of you, with enmity between one to each other. On earth will be your home until later."

This means that, in a very clear way, the reason for Adam and Eve having to get out is:

1. Their sin.
2. Going out of paradise is a punishment.
3. I have to ask why Muslims and all mankind are not in paradise now if original sin is not the reason? Why are we all here?

4. Muslims will answer saying, "Well, we were born out of paradise, so we haven't been kicked out!"
5. The fact is, you do not deserve to be out of paradise for the sin you did not do. Allah made you to live in paradise, not out of it. To prove my point let's read this verse together:

Qur'an 20:117:

فَقُلْنَا يَا آدَمُ إِنَّ هَٰذَا عَدُوٌّ لَّكَ وَلِزَوْجِكَ فَلَا يُخْرِجَنَّكُمَا مِنَ الْجَنَّةِ فَتَشْقَىٰ

Then We (Allah) said: "You Adam! Definitely, this is an enemy to you and to your wife: so allow him not get you together out of the paradise, so you live in suffering."

-   This means the reason for the miserable life of Adam was Satan. Did this extend to us? Is Satan an enemy to Adam alone or all mankind? This is in the verse of Qur'an 2:36:

Then did Satan make them humiliated going out of the paradise, from the happiness they had. We said: "Get ye down, all of you, with enmity between one to each other. On earth will be your home until later."

This verse says to get down all of you and with enmity to each other until Allah sends his guidance and saves mankind again. It was a curse that came to us, or to Muslims, through Adam, for nothing the Muslims did wrong. It wasn't them who ate from the tree! This exactly represents the original sin.

The funny thing is, Allah forgave Adam, but still said that Satan will cause you to get out of paradise if you accept what he says. It is clearly a punishment, even after forgiveness! Read Qur'an 2:37:

فَتَلَقَّىٰ آدَمُ مِن رَّبِّهِ كَلِمَاتٍ فَتَابَ عَلَيْهِ ۚ إِنَّهُ هُوَ التَّوَّابُ الرَّحِيمُ

Then Adam received from his Lord words. And his Lord forgave him and accepted his repentance, for it's He who accepts who repent, he is the forgiven the Merciful.

This presents one more mistake in the Qur'an. When you forgive someone you do not go ahead and punish him, otherwise what's the forgiveness meant to be about!

Who Made Adam Commit Sin; It's His Destiny or It's Satan's

Qur'an 2:36:

Then Satan made them humiliated going out of the paradise, from the happiness they had. We said: "Get ye down, all of you, with enmity between one to each other. On earth will be your home until later.

Verse 2: 36 said "Satan made them!" This is a total contradiction to Sahih Al-Bukhari, Book 93, Hadith 606:

Reported Abu Huraira: Allah's Messenger said, that Adam and Moses argued with each other and Moses said, "Your offspring is out of heaven is because of You Adam." Adam answered, "You are Moses, whom Allah favored and selected for His Message and talked to you. One to one, even so, you blamed me about my wickedness, which had been determined for me even before my creation." Therefore, Adam overwhelmed Moses, with his reasoning.

Where is the Heaven of Allah; In the Sky or on the Earth?

Read with me Qur'an 2:36 again please:

> Then Satan made them humiliated going out of the paradise, from the happiness they had. We said: **"Get ye down,** all of you, with enmity between one to each other. On earth will be your home until later."

Allah forced Adam and Eve out of paradise, not by saying get out, but he said **"Get ye down." This** is clear evidence that paradise is up in the sky. Muhammad apparently confused the Garden of Eden with heaven and thought that Adam and Eve lived in heaven in the sky before they sinned and were cast out.

Following are some examples of the Garden of Eden being in the sky.

Muhammad Pickthal translation, Qur'an 16:31: "**Gardens of Eden which they enter**, underneath which rivers flow, wherein they have what they will. Thus Allah repayeth those who ward off (evil)."

Muhammad Pickthal, Qur'an 13:23: "**Gardens of Eden which they enter, along with all who do right of their fathers** and their helpmeets and their seed. The angels enter unto them from every gate."

These verses are about the coming heaven as you see, because they will be with their fathers.

Actually, Islam's afterlife is a concept that is simple to understand, and is known as Jannah. Loosely translated, Jannah means, "garden" hearkening back to the Hebrew concept of paradise with Eden, and the Christian concept of heaven.

However, in the Qur'an Muhammad seems to confuse the paradise of heaven with the Garden of Eden. In fact, a literal translation from the Qur'an would be Garden of Aden, as in the port city of Yemen by the same name. Would that then mean the Garden of Eden was in Yemen? Not in sky!

However, the Qur'an and Muhammad said many times that paradise is in the sky as we see in the Qur'an.

To make this clearer, read Qur'an 3:55:

> "Behold! Allah said: "Oh "'Isa! I will take thee and **raise thee to myself**....."

So now, Jesus is in the sky and specifically with Allah; **"raise thee to myself...."** But Muhammad himself went to seven heavens, which were up in sky too. When Jesus comes back, he will come down, therefore he is up and heaven is up in the sky, then why does the Qur'an in many chapters say they will enter the Garden of Eden?

In Sahih Bukhari, Book 34, Hadith 425, we read:

> Allah's Messenger said: "I pledge by Him in Whose hand is my life, the Son of Mary **will soon come down** among you as a just and ruler. He will tear crosses, slaughter the swine and abolish jizyah (penalty Christians have to pay, or they will be murdered) and the wealth will flow forth to such a measure that no one will halt to take it."

The answer to Muhammad's confusion can be found in the Bible as we read in Genesis 2:8 (New King James Version):

> Life in God's Garden

> 8 The LORD God planted a garden eastward in Eden, and there He put the man whom He had formed.

As Christians, we have been told in the Bible that Adam and Eve lived in the paradise which was on earth. Muhammad stole this from the Bible, but he forgot that Adam and Eve in his book had never been on earth until Allah forced them to get down as in Qur'an 2:36; **"Get ye down."** Just to let you know, this is a huge mistake in the Qur'an; the god who does not yet know where his paradise is located is a false god. Remember, as long as an earthly Eden was not the home of Adam and Eve, then where did Muhammad get this from? The answer is so clear that it is the Bible.

Garden of Eden appears in the Qur'an in:

Qur'an 9:72	Qur'an 18:31	Qur'an 35:33	Qur'an 61:12
Qur'an 13:23	Qur'an 19:61	Qur'an 38:50	Qur'an 98:8
Qur'an 16:31	Qur'an 20:76	Qur'an 40:8	

Good and Evil is From Allah

Qur'an 4:78 (Usama Dakdok Translation):

أَيْنَمَا تَكُونُوا يُدْرِككُمُ الْمَوْتُ وَلَوْ كُنتُمْ فِي بُرُوجٍ مُشَيَّدَةٍ وَإِن تُصِبْهُمْ حَسَنَةٌ يَقُولُوا هَذِهِ مِنْ عِندِ اللَّهِ وَإِن تُصِبْهُمْ سَيِّئَةٌ يَقُولُوا هَذِهِ مِنْ عِندِكَ قُلْ كُلٌّ مِّنْ عِندِ اللَّهِ فَمَالِ هَؤُلَاءِ الْقَوْمِ لَا يَكَادُونَ يَفْقَهُونَ حَدِيثًا
(An-Nis'a, 78 , سورة النساء)

Wherever you may be, death will overtake you even if you were in lofty buruj (towers). If good fortune befalls them, they say, "This is from Allah." And if misfortune befalls them, they say, "This is from you." Say, "All is from Allah." So what is the affair with those people? They are not near to understanding speech.

Only Good Comes from Allah

Qur'an 4:79 (Usama Dakdok translation):

مَّا أَصَابَكَ مِنْ حَسَنَةٍ فَمِنَ اللَّهِ وَمَا أَصَابَكَ مِن سَيِّئَةٍ فَمِن نَّفْسِكَ وَأَرْسَلْنَاكَ لِلنَّاسِ رَسُولًا وَكَفَىٰ بِاللَّهِ شَهِيدًا
(Al-Nis'a, 79 , سورة النساء)

Whatever good fortune befalls you is from Allah, and whatever misfortune befalls you is from your own self...

⚔ It's a clear contradiction. Allah is not sure where the bad deeds come from!

Can Any Muslim Change His Destiny?

Qur'an 3:145:

It's not capable of a soul to die other than by Allah's permission, it's [death] the period being arranged as by a time to come.

The verse is so clear that no one can change his fate. It is arranged as a time to come.

Although, in the coming hadith Muhammad's story does not fit with the Qur'an, Muslims all agree that no one can change his fate. But we will prove that destiny in Islam is nothing but a false claim, thus proving Islam wrong again.

Sahih Muslim, Book 30, Hadith 585:

صحيح مسلم ـ كِتَاب الْفَضَائِلِ ـ فلو كنت ثم لأريتكم قبره إلى جانب الطريق تحت الكثيب الأحمر

حَدَّثَنَا مُحَمَّدُ بْنُ رَافِعٍ حَدَّثَنَا عَبْدُ الرَّزَّاقِ حَدَّثَنَا مَعْمَرٌ عَنْ هَمَّامِ بْنِ مُنَبِّهٍ قَالَ هَذَا مَا حَدَّثَنَا أَبُو هُرَيْرَةَ 2372 4375
عَنْ رَسُولِ اللَّهِ صَلَّى اللَّهُ عَلَيْهِ وَسَلَّمَ فَذَكَرَ أَحَادِيثَ مِنْهَا وَقَالَ رَسُولُ اللَّهِ صَلَّى اللَّهُ عَلَيْهِ وَسَلَّمَ جَاءَ مَلَكُ الْمَوْتِ
إِلَى مُوسَى عَلَيْهِ السَّلَامِ فَقَالَ لَهُ أَجِبْ رَبَّكَ قَالَ فَلَطَمَ مُوسَى عَلَيْهِ السَّلَامِ عَيْنَ مَلَكِ الْمَوْتِ فَفَقَأَهَا قَالَ فَرَجَعَ الْمَلَكُ
إِلَى اللَّهِ تَعَالَى فَقَالَ إِنَّكَ أَرْسَلْتَنِي إِلَى عَبْدٍ لَكَ لَا يُرِيدُ الْمَوْتَ وَقَدْ فَقَأَ عَيْنِي قَالَ فَرَدَّ اللَّهُ إِلَيْهِ عَيْنَهُ وَقَالَ ارْجِعْ إِلَى
عَبْدِي فَقُلْ الْحَيَاةَ تُرِيدُ فَإِنْ كُنْتَ تُرِيدُ الْحَيَاةَ فَضَعْ يَدَكَ عَلَى مَتْنِ ثَوْرٍ فَمَا تَوَارَتْ يَدُكَ مِنْ شَعْرَةٍ فَإِنَّكَ تَعِيشُ بِهَا
سَنَةً قَالَ ثُمَّ مَهْ قَالَ ثُمَّ تَمُوتُ قَالَ فَالْآنَ مِنْ قَرِيبٍ رَبِّ أَمِتْنِي مِنْ الْأَرْضِ الْمُقَدَّسَةِ رَمْيَةً بِحَجَرٍ قَالَ رَسُولُ اللَّهِ
صَلَّى اللَّهُ عَلَيْهِ وَسَلَّمَ وَاللَّهِ لَوْ أَنِّي عِنْدَهُ لَأَرَيْتُكُمْ قَبْرَهُ إِلَى جَانِبِ الطَّرِيقِ عِنْدَ الْكَثِيبِ الْأَحْمَرِ قَالَ أَبُو إِسْحَقَ
حَدَّثَنَا مُحَمَّدُ بْنُ يَحْيَى حَدَّثَنَا عَبْدُ الرَّزَّاقِ أَخْبَرَنَا مَعْمَرٌ بِمِثْلِ هَذَا الْحَدِيثِ

Abu Huraira stated that the Angel of Death was sent to Moses to notify him, of his Lord's arraignment it's his time to die. When he came (the angel), Moses slapped him, and his eye was bumped out. The Angel of Death returned to the Lord and said: You dispatched me to a servant who did not desire to die. Allah replaced his eye to its suitable place and restored his eyesight, and afterwards Allah revealed: "Go back to him and tell him that if he wants life-span, he must position his hand on the rear of a bull, and he would be permitted as many years of life as the reckoning of hair hidden by his hand." Then Moses uttered, "My Lord. What would take place to me after that?" He answered, "Later you must strive for death." Moses answered: "Let it be now." And he asked Allah to escort him close to the holy land (Israel). Then Allah's Messenger (Muhammad) said: "If I were there, I would have shown you his burial place nearby to the road at the red hill."

1. Moses *changed* his destiny after Allah set his time to die.

2. Moses could stop the Angel of Death by a fight!

3. Allah obeyed the rejection of Moses, and gave him another date to be his day.

4. Allah does not act in accordance the Qur'an 2:117. Allah is the originator of the heavens and the earth; if he decides something he says, "Be, it will be."

5. He ordered the Angel to take the life of Moses, but apparently failed to use the word "be!"

6. Moses' reprieve from death is based on luck, not on Allah's account (reckoning of hair hidden by his hand).

7. Remember the hadith of Adam saying, "After that, Adam said, '**Did you find that written in my destiny before my creation?'** Moses said, 'Yes.' So Adam defeated Moses with this reasoning." (Sahih Al-Bukhari, Book 60, Hadith 260) (Sahih Muslim, Book 033, Hadith

6411).

8. Did Allah send the Angel of Death based on his destiny, which was written in the protected and unchangeable book before Moses' creation? Or did he have a book for emergency changeable things? See Qur'an 85:22 which says, "Engraved in a preserved tablet."

9. This, all together, proves that this is a fairy tale story. Nothing in it can be true. Since when does God send his angels to take a soul, and then and have it be rejected, or even that order to be overcome?

Allah Made Them Kill Their Children

Qur'an 6:137 (Usama Dakdok translation):

وَكَذَ لِكَ زَيَّنَ لِكَثِيرٍ مِّنَ الْمُشْرِكِينَ قَتْلَ أَوْلَادِهِمْ شُرَكَاؤُهُمْ لِيُرْدُوهُمْ وَلِيَلْبِسُوا عَلَيْهِمْ دِينَهُمْ ۚ وَلَوْ شَاءَ اللَّهُ مَا فَعَلُوهُ ۖ فَذَرْهُمْ وَمَا يَفْتَرُونَ
(سورة الأنعام , Al-Ana"am, Qur'an 6:137)

And likewise it was beautified to the many polytheists, the killing of their children for their partners, to make them turn a way, and they mix for them their religion. And if Allah willed, they would not have done it. So leave them and what they are forging.

Muslims explain this verse by saying that Satan is the one who is making the polytheists (non-Muslims) believe that killing their children is the right thing to do, and that Satan does this to deceive people away from the true religion, Islam (their religion). It makes sense to blame Satan for the evil act of killing one's own children, but let us examine what the Qur'an really says about the works of Satan.

In Qur'an 6:112, we saw that it was Allah himself who created Satan, and that it was by Allah's orders that Satan deceives the prophets. Since Satan is only following Allah's orders, then Allah is the real deceiver. By his commands, Satan is making people believe that killing their children is right. By Allah's commands, Satan is deceiving people away from Islam.

If that is not enough to convince you that Allah is a deceiver, and that he is behind the child killings, notice that Qur'an 6:112 and 6:137 contain the phrase, "if Allah willed, they would not have done it." In other words, it is by Allah's will that people are misguided into doing evil, because if he wanted to guide people away from evil, he could have easily done it. We know that he wants people to be misguided, because he specifically created and ordered Satan to misguide us. Deception starts and ends with Allah. Why is Allah deceiving us?

Qur'an 4:88 (Usama Dakdok translation):

> How is it that you divided into two parties concerning the hypocrites when Allah has cast them off because of what they have earned? Do you desire to guide those whom Allah has led astray? And whomever Allah leads astray, so you will not find for him a way.

The verse clearly tells us that Allah himself misguides people, and he wants them to stay misguided. He doesn't want them back. Allah is angry with Muhammad, because he tried to guide, or call back, the people that Allah cast away. Even Muhammad, Allah's prophet, has no authority to guide people back to the right path.

The fact is, Muhammad made up this verse before it was too late when he found out that it was time to kill the children. He did not want more and more people that might expose him as a fraud.

It's Destiny to Have and Obey a Bad King or Khalifa

These days we witness many Islamic countries seeking change and going against their leadership, but the fact is, all Muslims understand that this is against Islamic principles and teachings. The prophet of Islam made it clear that it's the wish of Allah; therefore it is not allowed for Muslims to go against Allah's wish, even if your king is a thief, and he beats your back and even does the will of the devil.

Qur'an 17:33 (Muhammad Shakir translation):

> And do not kill any one whom Allah has forbidden, except for a just cause, and whoever is slain unjustly, We have indeed given to his heir authority, so let him not exceed the just limits in slaying; surely he is aided.

It's forbidden to kill Muslims, but not the infidels, but this verse is quite clear that your ruler can even take your life, even when in the wrong, even as a Muslim, for he is authorized to do so.

Sahih Muslim, Book 020, Hadith 4554:

There will be rulers who will not rule by my teachings, and who will not follow my ways? Near by will be among them men who will have the hearts of Satan in the bodies of human beings. I said to the prophet: "What should I do. O Messenger of Allah, if I witness such a ruler?" He (Muhammad) responded, "You will listen to the Amir (The King) and Obey his orders; even if your back is flogged and your resources are stolen (by the king) you should listen and obey."

And as long as everything is from Allah, bad and good, it means if your ruler rapes your wife, it's Allah's will, if he kills you, it's Allah will, if he steals your money—It's Allah's will.
So is it the wickedness of a king or a wicked Allah?

The Bible order to obey rulers but not against God teaching or not the wickedness of men, as we read in the story of John the baptist the great man of God who paid his life for rejecting the wickedness of Herod, the ruler of Galilee read "Matthew 14".

Our Lord is the opposite of Allah as we read

Psalm 25

8
Because the Lord is righteous and good,
he teaches sinners the path they should follow.
9
He leads the humble in the right way
and teaches them his will.
10
With faithfulness and love he leads
all who keep his covenant and obey his commands.

Be sure to read Qur'an And Science in Depth

Due to the size of this book, I will continue with more priceless information and study in Qur'an And Science in Depth, answering the misleading claims of Muslims about their Qur'an's miracles, and at the same time showing that they're not only false claims, but they are scientifically in error.

To contact Christian Prince:

www.patreon.com/ChristianPrince

www.facebook.com/TheChristianprince

24021319R00165

Printed in Great Britain
by Amazon